MATTHEW
Evangelist and Teacher

Uniform with this volume:

MARK: EVANGELIST AND THEOLOGIAN
R. P. Martin

LUKE: HISTORIAN AND THEOLOGIAN
I. Howard Marshall

JOHN: EVANGELIST AND INTERPRETER
Stephen S. Smalley

MATTHEW

●Ⅱ●

Evangelist and Teacher

R.T. FRANCE

Wipf & Stock
PUBLISHERS
Eugene, Oregon

Wipf and Stock Publishers
199 W 8th Ave, Suite 3
Eugene, OR 97401

Matthew
Evangelist and Teacher
By France, R.T.
Copyright©1989 Patersnoster Press
ISBN: 1-59244-936-0
Publication date 10/8/2004
Previously published by Paternoster Press, 1989

To my colleagues and students at
LONDON BIBLE COLLEGE
1981–1988

CONTENTS

PREFACE

Someone who has recently published a commentary on Matthew's gospel needs an adequate excuse for adding further to the literature on Matthew. My reasons are two.

Firstly, the publishers have been importunate. Their three earlier publications on the other three gospels (I.H. Marshall, *Luke: Historian and Theologian*, 1970; R.P. Martin, *Mark: Evangelist and Theologian*, 1972; S.S. Smalley, *John: Evangelist and Interpreter*, 1978) have long demanded a companion to complete the series – and what student of Matthew could resist the call to bring to 'fulfilment' what has been so well begun? I have myself benefited greatly from those earlier volumes, and as a teacher I have been aware that they have filled an important place in the literature available for the study of the gospels. When students have asked me what book they should consult for a comparable study of Matthew, I have had no answer.

Secondly, to write a commentary, at least one designed for a non-specialist readership, is to realise how many issues there are underlying the text to which it is impossible to give adequate attention in the space available. Howard Marshall chose the better way, in writing his book about Luke *before* his commentary on the gospel, so that the latter could presuppose the former and thus dispense with a lengthy intro-duction. But that way was not open to me, so what I offer now is a sort of extended introduction to Matthew, as I might have written it had the scale of my commentary allowed it.

This book is not intended to be a guide to all that has been written in recent years about Matthew. An excellent guide covering the years up to 1980 has already been provided by G.N. Stanton, 'The Origin and Purpose of Matthew's Gospel: Matthean Scholarship from 1945 to 1980' (see bibliography for details of publication). The availability of his guide has left me free to concentrate on those areas which I find most interesting and important for the appreciation of a gospel which I have come to respect and value increasingly over the years. I think I have touched on most major areas of discussion in Matthean studies, but I have not attempted to respond to every article or even to provide a full bibliography of the steady flow of publications on a gospel which seems to be becoming a firm favourite among searchers for PhD topics!

In quoting from works in foreign languages, I have used published English translations where these were available; otherwise I have made my own translation.

DICK FRANCE
March, 1988

ABBREVIATIONS

ASTI	Annual of the Swedish Theological Institute
BZ	Biblische Zeitschrift
CBQ	Catholic Biblical Quarterly
EvTh	Evangelische Theologie
ExpT	Expository Times
Gospel Perspectives	R.T. France & D. Wenham (ed.), *Gospel Perspectives* vols 1-3 (Sheffield: JSOT Press, 1980-1983)
HTR	Harvard Theological Review
JBL	Journal of Biblical Literature
JETS	Journal of the Evangelical Theological Society
JOT	R.T. France, *Jesus and the Old Testament* (London: Tyndale Press, 1971)
JSJ	Journal for the Study of Judaism
JSNT	Journal for the Study of the New Testament
JTS	Journal of Theological Studies
NIDNTT	C. Brown (ed.), *The New International Dictionary of New Testament Theology* (Exeter: Paternoster, 1975-1978)
NovT	Novum Testamentum
NTS	New Testament Studies
RB	Revue Biblique
ST	Studia Theologica
TDNT	G. Kittel, G.Friedrich (ed.), *Theological Dictionary of the New Testament* (ET. Grand Rapids: Eerdmans, 1964-1974)
TS	Theological Studies
TynB	Tyndale Bulletin
ZNW	Zeitschrift für die neutestamentliche Wissenschaft

After the first reference, works are cited in the notes by an abbreviated title; full details of title and publication may be found in the bibliography.

⬛

THE FIRST GOSPEL

Matthew's place in the life of the church. Literary relationships and order of composition of the gospels.

A. MATTHEW'S PLACE IN THE LIFE OF THE CHURCH

THE ORDER OF THE GOSPELS

The traditional order of the gospels – Matthew, Mark, Luke, John – is probably found as early as the so-called Muratorian Canon, a document usually thought to have been written in Rome towards the end of the second century AD,[1] and is followed by such early Christian writers as Irenaeus and Origen. This is the order found in the earliest complete Greek manuscripts of the New Testament, Sinaiticus and Vaticanus, representing the convention in fourth-century Alexandria, and most of the early Greek and Syriac manuscripts have the same order. In the West there was at first an alternative convention, to put the two 'apostolic' gospels first, resulting in the order Matthew, John, Luke, Mark, which is found in the early Western manuscripts Bezae and Washingtonianus, and in some manuscripts of the Old Latin versions. Other orders for the four gospels were found from time to time until the traditional order finally became established.[2] But among all the variations, the one almost constant factor is that Matthew comes first.[3]

1. Luke and John are listed in the Muratorian Canon specifically as 'third' and 'fourth', but the account of the first and second gospels is lost. The concluding words of the lost paragraph say that the second evangelist 'was present however at some, and so recorded them', which is more likely to refer to Mark, the non-apostolic associate of the disciples in Jerusalem, than to the apostle Matthew.
2. For details of the order of the gospels in various ancient lists see E.J. Goodspeed, *The Formation of the New Testament* (University of Chicago Press, 1926) 187-203; B.M. Metzger, *The Canon of the New Testament* (Oxford: Clarendon, 1987) 296-297.
3. An exception appears in Tertullian, *Adv. Marcionem* IV 2: 'Of the apostles, therefore, John and Matthew first instil faith into us; whilst of apostolic men, Luke and Mark renew it afterwards.' There is a further reference to 'John and Matthew' in *Adv. Marcionem* IV 5, and the four gospels are mentioned in the same order in the 'Synopsis of the Old and New Testaments' attributed to John Chrysostom. F.C. Grant, *The Gospels, their Origin and their Growth* (New York: Harper, 1957) 65-67 suggests that the identification of the four evangelists with the four living creatures of Rev. 4:7 (which was already established when Irenaeus wrote his *Adv. Haer.* III 11.8) is to be explained on the basis

Matthew's place at the head of the list seems surprising to us, as we have been schooled to think of Mark as the earliest and most basic gospel, with Matthew and Luke as later expansions of it, and John as a subsequent and consciously alternative account. Some modern English versions of the New Testament have even gone so far as to 'restore' the 'true' order, putting Mark at the beginning of the New Testament.[4]

In early Christian texts the order of the gospels is generally taken for granted, and no explanation is offered. Irenaeus, however, writing near the end of the second century, says explicitly that the traditional order is that of composition,[5] and it is likely that this belief (which, as far as the relative order of Matthew and Mark was concerned, was unchallenged in the early church) was the main reason for the establishment of the traditional order of the gospels.[6] Indeed the alternative order established in the Western church, as mentioned above, had to be defended as a deliberate departure from the chronological order of composition for the sake of 'canonical arrangement'.[7]

I shall discuss later the validity of this judgement on the relative order of composition of the gospels. But whether or not it is chronologically correct, the traditional place of Matthew at the front of the list reflects accurately the value which early Christianity placed on it, at least as this is reflected in its use in the writings of the first Christian centuries. Whether its prominence was due to the belief that it was written first, and therefore had a special authority, or whether that belief itself arose from the fact that it had come in practice to be used in preference to the other gospels, the fact is that it was to Matthew's gospel that the Christians of the first two centuries automatically turned for the essential data for Christian teaching about Jesus.

---

of an accepted order Mark, Luke, Matthew, John (though Irenaeus in fact explains them in the order John, Luke, Matthew, Mark!), and the same order (or Mark, Matthew, Luke, John?) may be implied in the lay-out of a fifth century mosaic at Ravenna. Grant believes this may reflect a tradition as to the actual order of composition. It is remarkable, if such an order was traditional at any stage in the early church, that it left no trace in the writings of the Fathers or in the New Testament manuscripts (it first appears in a West Saxon manuscript of the gospels from the twelfth century! – see Metzger, *Canon*, 297).

4. E.g. E.S. Bates (ed.), *The Bible Designed to be Read as Literature* (London: Heinemann, n.d.); E.V. Rieu, *The Four Gospels* (London: Penguin, 1952); H.J. Schonfield, *The Authentic New Testament* (London: Dobson, 1955); W. Barclay, *The New Testament, a New Translation* (London: Collins, 1968).

5. Irenaeus, *Adv. Haer.* III 1.1.

6. Goodspeed, *Formation, 35-36* suggests, however, that this order 'began with the most Jewish of the gospels, and ended with the most Greek, being intended to be read through, from beginning to end, and to close with the new Greek recast of the Christian message', and was designed to win acceptance for the gospel of John which might otherwise be suspect in more conservative circles.

7. So the so-called Monarchian Prologue to John, a preface attached to some Latin versions from perhaps the third or fourth century: '(John), even though he is said to have written his gospel after all the others, is nonetheless placed after Matthew according to the arrangement of the established canon.'

MATTHEW IN THE POST-APOSTOLIC CHURCH

The subject has been studied exhaustively by E. Massaux,[8] and a brief summary of his findings may help us to appreciate the central place Matthew occupied in early Christian life and thought.

While the earliest attribution of a specific text to the Gospel of Matthew by name is not found until Apollinaris of Hierapolis (c. AD 175), the literary influence of this gospel is clear from the very earliest Christian writings outside the New Testament. Clement of Rome shows familiarity especially with the Sermon on the Mount (Massaux, pp. 7-17), but also with several other sayings of Jesus found in Matthew. The Epistle of Barnabas shows knowledge also of Matthew's passion narrative, and even quotes Matthew 22:14 with the formula 'as it is written'. For Barnabas Matthew is the only New Testament book from which 'an unambiguous literary influence' may be discerned (p. 93). The use of Matthew in the letters of Ignatius is such as to indicate that in the churches to which he wrote this gospel 'held pride of place' (p. 107). While Ignatius was strongly influenced by Paul, whom he took as his model, it was to Matthew that he habitually turned for 'the fundamental law of Christianity' (p. 133). So for these three earliest Apostolic Fathers Massaux concludes that when they referred to the teaching of Jesus, the form in which they presented it was almost exclusively derived from Matthew, even though their quotations were seldom verbatim (pp. 133-135).

In the succeeding period Massaux finds a similar pattern, but with a greater tendency to quote literally from Matthew, and more evident interest in the narrative parts of the gospel as well as the teaching of Jesus. Even for Polycarp, reputed to be a personal disciple of John, 'it seems clear that the gospel of Matthew is the one which is turned to as a matter of course for the sayings of the Lord', while there is no clear reference to the other gospels, even that of John! (p. 186).The Apocryphal Gospels which derive from this period are generally clearly based, at least in their narrative content, on the first-century gospels, and while others are brought into use (particularly Luke), it is Matthew who provides the basic text from which their versions are derived.[9] In the Gnostic works known to Massaux (he was writing before the publication of the Nag Hammadi literature) there is a clear attraction to the Gospel of John, which, particularly in its prologue, offered ideas

---

8. E. Massaux, *Influence de l'Evangile de saint Matthieu sur la littérature chrétienne avant saint Irénée* (Louvain/Gembloux: Publications Universitaires de Louvain/Duculot, 1950); reprinted with supplement covering bibliography to 1985, Leuven University Press, 1986.

9. An obvious exception to this is the Protevangelium of James, which uses the infancy narratives of both Matthew and Luke, but concentrates more on Luke since he offers a much fuller account of the period in which this work is interested.

and language much more congenial to Gnostic tastes. But even here, Massaux finds, the influence of Matthew is not to be denied. For instance, the commentary on John by the Gnostic Heracleon in fact discusses John *on the basis of its relationship to Matthew* 'as if Matthew was the norm to which one referred as a matter of course in his period' (p. 434). In the earlier part of the second century, then, Matthew's 'absolutely privileged position' (p. 452) in Christian thought and teaching is yet more strongly attested. Among all the New Testament writings, and especially among the gospels, 'Matthew seems to have been the only one to have had a normative role, and to have created the climate of Christianity at large' (p. 455).[10]

Among the Apologists, Justin stands out for his frequent direct use of the New Testament books. The same pattern is repeated and intensified. His presentation of the teaching of Jesus in *Apol. I* 15-17 is largely literarily dependent on Matthew (with a lesser use of Luke, sometimes in combination with Matthew), and in the *Dialogue* there are at least 42 passages which are clearly dependent on Matthew. In a number of these Matthew is cited under the formula 'it is written'. Finally Massaux considers the Didache, which he dates around the middle of the second century because he finds its use of the New Testament very similar to that of Justin. Its very title echoes Matthew 28:18-20, and large parts of the work are heavily dependent on Matthew, particularly the Sermon on the Mount (and, in the case of Didache 16, on Matthew 24). Sometimes the Didache seems like a tracing ('un décalque') of Matthew (p. 641). For its author τὸ εὐαγγέλιον effectively means only Matthew. Massaux's dating of the Didache is, of course, controversial; but if it is dated earlier the significance of its links with Matthew is increased (though if a date as early as AD 50-70 is accepted, as proposed by Audet and Robinson,[11] the question would need to be raised whether direct literary dependence on Matthew is the right explanation for these links).

There is much in the detail of Massaux's study which is open to question, particularly when he is dealing with free references to gospel sayings and narratives. To postulate a specific use of Matthew in such a case (unless of course the reference is to a passage peculiar to Matthew) can be hazardous, and the danger is increased by Massaux's unvarying

10. B.H. Streeter, *The Four Gospels* (London: Macmillan, 1924) 525-526, offers the suggestion that a formal council in Rome in AD 119 accepted the Gospel of Matthew as apostolic. The argument is taken much further by B.W. Bacon, *Studies in Matthew* (London: Constable, 1930) 50-59, who concludes that 'A Roman provincial synod was held under Sixtus I about 120 AD, whose verdict endorsed the title "According to Matthew" ' (p. 59), and that Rome, by means of this council *de recipiendis libris,* 'put the final stamp of its unparalleled authority upon the book as authentic and apostolic. Under this aegis its further triumph was assured' (p. 58).

11. J.-P. Audet, *La Didachè: Instructions des Apôtres* (Paris: Gabalda, 1958); J.A.T. Robinson, *Redating the New Testament* (London: SCM, 1976) 322-327.

method of dealing with each writing – he looks first for passages clearly
or possibly dependent on Matthew, and only then for *other* passages
which may depend on other New Testament books. Clearly this method
weights the scales in favour of discovering a Matthean reference in any
case where any of the other gospels might equally have been the source.
However carefully he tries, as he does, to establish specific verbal links
with Matthew's version in such a case, it is inevitable that where no
such specific links are discernible the benefit of the doubt will be given
to Matthew as the putative source. His method tends also to assume
that any link with the gospel tradition is to be understood in terms of
direct literary dependence on one written gospel, rather than familiarity
with a less clearly definable tradition of the teaching of Jesus.[12]

But when all such doubts have been given full weight, the study
remains an impressive demonstration that in the first century after the
writing of our New Testament gospels it was Matthew which quickly
established itself as *the* gospel par excellence, the natural place from
which to expect to derive the authoritative account of the words and
deeds of Jesus. By the middle of the second century the gospel of Luke
was being used more alongside Matthew, and in some circles John was
much appreciated. But neither of them ever seems to have rivalled
Matthew, in any part of the church for which we have documentation,
for the place of 'first gospel'. As for Mark, it is a constant refrain of
Massaux's work that it is totally eclipsed by Matthew. Hardly ever is
there a reference which is clearly to Mark rather than to Matthew; the
one case where Massaux is prepared to assert this positively[13] stands
out precisely as an exception to this general rule.

Massaux's study concludes before the end of the second century.
From that point on there was increasingly explicit recognition of the
four-fold character of the gospel canon, and consequently a greater
tendency to refer to more than one gospel (though even now the amount
of clear reference specifically to the gospel of Mark was minimal). But
there is no sign that Matthew lost its primacy among the four. When,
as often happened, copyists of New Testament manuscripts assimilated
'parallel' gospel texts to one another, it was generally Matthew's text
which prevailed. The version of the Lord's Prayer which passed into
general use was that of Matthew rather than that of Luke. In the church
lectionaries and in the passages of Scripture incorporated into the
liturgies Matthew was much more fully represented than the other

---

12. Massaux's findings were radically called in question by H. Köster, *Synoptische
Überlieferung bei den apostolischen Vätern* (Berlin, 1957), but subsequent discussion has
tended to support Massaux rather than Köster; see the introduction to the 1986 reprint
of Massaux's work by F. Neirynck.

13. Hermas, *Mandate* IV 1.6, where the teaching on remarriage after divorce does not
include the Matthean exceptive clause: Massaux, *Influence*, 284-285.

gospels. In other words, in most areas of the life of the church it was Matthew which, as in the first two centuries, continued to be *the* gospel.[14]

REASONS FOR MATTHEW'S PRE-EMINENCE

A number of factors probably combined to give Matthew this place of pre-eminence in early Christianity. One was no doubt the belief, however it may have originated, that Matthew's was the first gospel to be written, and therefore stood closest to source. Certainly as long as it was believed that Mark was, in Augustine's memorable phrase,[15] merely the *pedisequus et breviator* ('camp-follower and abbreviator') of Matthew, it was inevitable that the much fuller account of Matthew would leave Mark in the shade, and if Luke and John were also believed to be later, whether or not they were dependent on Matthew, it might be expected that, other things being equal, Matthew would be accorded the greater weight.

But the character of Matthew's gospel in itself probably added to its status. We have noted above that the earliest Christian use of the gospels focused on their function as a source for the *teaching* of Jesus rather than for his story, and for this purpose Matthew's gospel is immediately more attractive, both because it contains proportionately more ethical and pastoral teaching than the other gospels, and because it is set out in a more obviously systematic way. We shall be considering the structure of Matthew's gospel later, and we shall note that there is considerable disagreement over what is the primary rationale of its composition, but all are agreed that the author was careful to group his material in such a way that it is readily accessible for teaching purposes. Several large sections of the gospel (pre-eminently, of course, the Sermon on the Mount) are devoted to collections of the teaching of Jesus grouped around a common theme. Such sections would provide a suitable framework for teachers in the churches. And the character of much of the teaching in Matthew is such as to deal fairly directly with the concerns of a pastor or catechist. If C.F. Evans' description of Matthew as 'the gospel in the form of a catechetical manual, with all written out

14. Some indication of Matthew's continuing predominance may be gained from the listing of biblical references in patristic literature published by the Centre d'Analyse et de Documentation Patristiques under the title *Biblia Patristica* (Paris: Centre Nationale de la Recherche Scientifique, 1975ff). Volume One, covering the first two centuries, has the following number of pages of references to each gospel: Matthew 70, Mark 27, Luke 60, John 37; Volume Two (the third century except Origen) gives Matthew 64, Mark 5, Luke 18, John 31; Volume Three (Origen) gives Matthew 56, Mark 5, Luke 23, John 38. See also C.M. Tuckett, *Nag Hammadi and the Gospel Tradition* (Edinburgh: T. & T. Clark, 1986) 149-150 for a similar preference for Matthew in Gnostic literature (though his study does not include John).
15. Augustine, *De Consensu Evangelistarum* I 2.

plain and heavily underscored by scripture'[16] is something of an over-simplification, it does point to a real factor in the nature of the gospel which would naturally lead to its being given the first place, as 'a first text-book for congregational teachers'.[17]

Another feature of Matthew that strikes all readers is its sustained concern to present Jesus in the context of Judaism. We shall see that it is not easy to present a simple summary of Matthew's approach to the Jews and Judaism. There are apparently conflicting attitudes in what is often described as at the same time the most Jewish and the most anti-Jewish of the gospels. But these cross-currents reflect the tensions of a church struggling to come to terms with its real-life situation: on the one hand they saw themselves as the true fulfilment of all that God had done and promised for Israel, but on the other hand they had to recognise that, as the followers of a Messiah whom the majority of the Jews had failed to acknowledge, they were in fact a community already painfully distinct from the main stream of Judaism. We shall be considering later how these tensions are to be interpreted, and how far Matthew does in fact present a coherent understanding of the church vis-à-vis Judaism. But we may note here that this orientation would naturally lead to a fuller use of such a gospel in a church where the issue of the Jewish roots of Christianity was still a live one (and that was certainly the case at least into the latter part of the second century, if we may judge by Justin's *Dialogue with Trypho*.) Not only did they need apologetic material for their debate with Jews and to enable them to present Jesus to them in a relevant way, but they also needed guidance for their own living in relation to the Old Testament law. How was the 'fulfilment' aspect of following Jesus to be reflected in their attitude to the laws of the Old Testament and of later Jewish teaching? How radically 'new' was Christian discipleship intended to be? Such questions were inescapable for a church still close to its Jewish roots. Modern Christians who find Matthew's preoccupation with the subject tedious, and even distasteful, should realise that they live in a very different world from that of the early Christians, for whom the 'Jewishness' of Jesus and his church was not just a matter of historical interest but an existential concern crying out for answers, answers which Matthew's gospel offered to provide.

The predominant use of Matthew in the early church is, therefore, not hard to understand. It met more directly than the other gospels some of the deep-seated needs of the church; as a teaching document it provided, both in form and in content, what the church and its leaders

16. P.R. Ackroyd & C.F. Evans (ed.), *The Cambridge History of the Bible*, vol. 1 (Cambridge University Press, 1970) 272.
17. P.S. Minear, *Matthew: the Teacher's Gospel* (London: Darton, Longman & Todd, 1984) 3.

wanted. Thus C.F. Evans attributes the prominence of Matthew to the fact that 'it tallied most closely with what the church had come to wish its tradition to be'.[18] Massaux prefers to state the case the other way round; it was Matthew's gospel which 'created the climate of ordinary Christianity'.[19] It is not important to decide which was cause and which was effect. Either way, it is a fact that mainstream Christianity was, from the early second century on, to a great extent Matthean Christianity.

MATTHEW IN THE MODERN CHURCH

The situation which we have seen in the patristic period was not substantially changed until the eighteenth century. The belief that Matthew was the first gospel to be written went hand in hand with the tendency to use it as the primary source for an authoritative account of the words and deeds of Jesus. But the rise of critical study in the latter part of the eighteenth century began to raise some doubts as to whether Matthew really deserved this favoured position.

One emerging cause of concern was the assumption, firmly entrenched since the second century, that the original gospel of Matthew was written in Aramaic. If, then, our Greek Matthew is a translation, and not the apostolic original, is it to be trusted? J.D. Michaelis,[20] the first edition of whose *Einleitung in die göttlichen Schriften des Neuen Bundes* was published in 1750, based his concept of inspiration and canonical authority firmly on apostolic authorship (and therefore could find no good grounds for retaining Mark and Luke in the canon); the Greek Matthew therefore is not what the apostle wrote, and lacks verbal inspiration, so that it is possible that in places the translation mis-represents the original. A pupil of Michaelis, J.G. Eichhorn, writing in 1794, drove a firmer wedge between the Greek Matthew and its supposed Semitic original by adopting the suggestion of G.E. Lessing that behind all three Synoptic Gospels lay a lost 'Primal Gospel' written in Hebrew or Aramaic (this being the λόγια referred to by Papias), of which our Matthew, Mark and Luke are secondary developments, incorporating traditional embellishments of the gospel story, and so of dubious historical value. Eichhorn, like Michaelis, was concerned 'to reduce the Gospels to their apostolic content'.

Such ideas marked the beginning of a revolution in the respective valuation of the gospels. While as yet the chronological priority of

18. *Cambridge History of the Bible*, vol. 1, 271.
19. Massaux, *Influence*, 652.
20. For this and the subsequent paragraphs see further details and extensive quotations from the authors discussed in W.G. Kümmel, *The New Testament: the History of the Investigation of its Problems* (ET, London: SCM, 1973), pp. 69-71 (for Michaelis), 77-79 (for Eichhorn), 146-155 (for Lachmann, Wilke, Weisse and Holtzmann), 139ff (for Baur).

Matthew was virtually unchallenged,[21] the foundation for such a challenge was being laid as Mark's 'less developed' character was taken to suggest that it was closer to the supposed 'primal Gospel' than the more elaborate gospel of Matthew. It was not until 1835 that Karl Lachmann published his argument (based on the order in which the parallel material occurs in the Synoptic Gospels) that it is the gospel of Mark which offers the original narrative sequence. While Lachmann did not, as is generally assumed, argue directly for the literary dependence of Matthew and Luke on Mark,[22] he did have some hard words to offer about the Griesbach Hypothesis, and his work offered a foundation on which the theory of the literary priority of Mark could be built. This theory was first explicitly set out, independently of Lachmann, in the studies of C.G. Wilke and C.H. Weisse, both published in 1838. The theory received its most substantial presentation in 1863 from H.J. Holtzmann, and by the end of the nineteenth century, especially through the work of P. Wernle in 1899, was rapidly becoming the new critical orthodoxy in Germany and beyond. We shall be considering its subsequent fortunes shortly.

The most substantial resistance to the theory of Marcan priority came from F.C. Baur and his associates at Tübingen. Baur, while he was sceptical about much of the contents of all the gospels, regarded Matthew as the most primitive and reliable of them, in that here, especially in the teaching material, he expected to find some authentic evidence for Jesus among all the later and legendary additions. Baur reached this conclusion not on literary grounds, but on the basis of his historical reconstruction of the pattern of early Christianity; the 'Judaising' character of Matthew represents the original Palestinian Christianity as opposed to the 'Hellenising' gospel of Paul and the wider church. Baur's doctrinaire reconstruction would not be widely supported today, and his estimate of Matthew as a primitive, 'Judaising' document is strangely at variance with those modern scholars who see the same gospel as so out of touch with Judaism that it must come from an anti-Jewish Gentile environment! The priority of Matthew continued to be defended on such grounds by most of the members of the Tübingen School in the second half of the nineteenth century, but with the waning of the influence of that school the triumph of the theory of Marcan priority was assured, despite the continuing opposition of isolated scholars such as Theodor Zahn and Adolf Schlatter.

We shall return shortly to the arguments relating to the chronological order and literary relationships of Matthew and Mark. At this point

21. For two significant exceptions see G.C. Storr, *Über den Zweck der evangelischen Geschichte* (Tübingen, 1786), and the writings of J.G. Herder (for which see W.G. Kümmel, *The New Testament,* 79-83.
22. For this point see H.-H. Stoldt, *History and Criticism of the Marcan Hypothesis* (ET, Edinburgh: T. & T. Clark, 1980) 147-154.

the issue has been raised simply to supply the foundation for understanding the remarkable reversal in the fortunes of Matthew in Christian use which took place during the nineteenth century. On the one hand, it was being increasingly questioned whether the additional teaching material, which had been the basis of the higher valuation of Matthew in earlier centuries, did in fact give access to the teaching of *Jesus*, or whether it represented rather a developing church tradition. And on the other hand, the growing belief in the priority of Mark meant that for the first time the shortest gospel, so long over-shadowed, was coming to be seen as the one which was closest to source. From this time on it was to Mark rather than to Matthew that historians increasingly turned for the raw materials for rediscovering the life and teaching of Jesus.

The major new development in twentieth-century gospel criticism was the rise of form-criticism. This movement represented a shift away from looking to any one of the gospels as being in itself the source for historical information. Instead the aim became to penetrate behind the gospels to the earliest form of the tradition which can be reconstructed, and in this process any of the gospels may be expected to offer assistance. But form-criticism has operated exclusively on the basis of Marcan priority, with the result that wherever Matthew differs from Mark the presumption has been that the Marcan version is closer to the original tradition. One result of form-criticism has been, therefore, to put Matthew more deeply into the shadow. (One indication of this trend has been that, as compared with the other gospels, Matthew has suffered from a dearth of significant commentaries, at least in English; after McNeile's commentary in 1915, while commentary series continued to offer the obligatory treatment of Matthew, usually on a fairly small scale, it was not until the 1980s that the gap began to be filled, with the commentaries of Beare (1981), Gundry (1982) and Carson (1984).)

In reaction against the preoccupation of form-criticism with the hypothetical traditions underlying the gospels, at the expense of interest in the gospels themselves, it was inevitable that the tide should turn in due course. The form the change took was what has come to be known, rather unfortunately, as 'redaction-criticism'.[23] Its fore-runner, as far as Matthean scholarship was concerned, was G. Bornkamm's famous essay of 1948 on 'The Stilling of the Storm in Matthew', closely

23. It should, of course, be noted that this new direction of scholarship originating in the school of Bultmann in Germany did not represent the first attempt ever made to study 'the theology of the evangelists'! An interesting precursor, from a very different theological perspective, was the work of N.B. Stonehouse, whose *The Witness of Matthew and Mark to Christ* (London: Tyndale Press, 1944) in significant ways anticipated redaction-criticism. The relationship is interestingly explored in M. Silva, 'Ned B. Stonehouse and Redaction-Criticism', *Westminster Theological Journal* 40 (1977/8) 77-88, 281-303.

followed in 1956 by the same author's 'End-expectation and Church
in Matthew's Gospel'. These two essays were published together with
theses by two of Bornkamm's pupils, G. Barth and H.J. Held, in the
volume *Überlieferung und Auslegung im Matthäusevangelium* (1960)
which soon became recognised as the foundation volume of Matthean
redaction-criticism.[24] In these essays the focus shifted from the tradition
underlying the gospel to Matthew's own individuality as a writer with
his own distinctive theological and pastoral concerns. The method
employed was to a large extent the study of 'redaction', i.e. an analysis
of the way in which Matthew has used, and altered, the traditions from
which he is assumed to have worked in writing his gospel. But the focus
of interest was not the redactional method as such, but the theology
of the evangelist to which it points. Redaction-criticism, like its pre-
decessor form-criticism, has uniformly worked on the assumption of
Marcan priority, but for the purposes of the redaction-critic relative
chronological order does not determine the interest or significance of
a book.

Since the 1960s a flood of studies of Matthew from this 'redaction-
critical' perspective has continued unabated, and it will be a large part
of the aim of this book to analyse some of the more significant results
of this more recent approach to Matthew. So, while Matthew shows
no sign of regaining its place as *the* gospel par excellence in modern
thought (indeed such an evaluation of any one gospel would be quite
out of keeping with the current approach to the gospels in general),
recent years have seen something of a comeback after the period of
eclipse which resulted from the literary criticism of the nineteenth
century. Not that Matthew has necessarily regained any significant
ground as a primary source for historical reconstruction; rather the
spotlight has moved away from history to theology, and in the renewed
desire to rediscover the theological climate of the first-century church
Matthew has increasingly been recognised as both a sophisticated and
effective communicator and also a man with a clear grasp of the
significance of Jesus.[25] In so far as this theological perspective of Matthew
is distinctive from that of the other evangelists, and indeed of the other
New Testament writers, it is an important part of our data for understanding Christian origins – the more so because of the influence this

24. The English translation was G. Bornkamm, G. Barth & H.J. Held, *Tradition and
Interpretation in Matthew* (London: SCM, 1963). Bornkamm's essay on the stilling of
the storm first appeared in *Wort und Dienst* (1948) 49-54, and 'Enderwartung und Kirche
im Matthäusevangelium' in W.D. Davies & D. Daube (ed.), *The Background of the New
Testament and its Eschatology* (Cambridge University Press, 1954) 222- 260.
25. This new climate in Matthean studies is well summed up in the subtitle of Gundry's
recent major commentary: *Matthew: a Commentary on his Literary and Theological Art*
(Grand Rapids: Eerdmans, 1982).

particular viewpoint came to wield, as we have seen, in the post-apostolic church.

But Matthew did not write his book simply to expound his own views or to comment on the situation of the church of his time, but also, and primarily, to give an account of Jesus. It will therefore be our aim not only to learn about Matthew but to assess, in the light of modern study of his gospel, the nature and the importance of his portrait of Jesus for our understanding of how the Christian movement began.

But first we must return to the question, already raised, of the chronological order and literary relationships of the gospels. The belief of the early church that Matthew was the first to be written may have derived from the predominant role it had come to play in Christian thought and church life; or that role may itself have been due to an already established belief in its chronological priority. But, whichever way way it was, was there any historical basis for this belief? It is a question which cannot be answered today as briefly as it would have been answered twenty years ago.

B.   LITERARY RELATIONSHIPS AND ORDER OF COMPOSITION OF THE GOSPELS

Writing in 1930, B.W. Bacon could speak of 'the unanimous verdict of scholarship for the priority of Mark and S' (S being Bacon's own term for a lost source document used by both Matthew and Luke, which other scholars have called Q).[26] He went on in typically trenchant style: 'The verdict may justly be called unanimous, for even Zahn, greatest of the few surviving champions of the ancient doctrine of the priority of Mt, holds to it only in the roundabout form proposed by Grotius: a *lost* Hebrew Mt the common source of our Synoptic Gospels, the canonical Mt standing to this X in the relation of a translation whose language has been assimilated to Mk. This *lost* Mt naturally has all the qualities which pertained to the Princetonian *lost* inerrant Bible. It may not help the public, but it saves the face of mistaken apologists.'[27] Bacon does in fact recognise in the then recent work of Schlatter another 'belated attempt to rescue the Tübingen theory of the priority of this Gospel', but concludes that 'there can be no more forceful demonstration

26. Bacon in fact insists that 'Q is not S'; he uses Q to represent the actual shared material found in Matthew and Luke, a relatively definable entity, but distinguishes this from S as the lost source document from which the Q material was supposedly drawn, whose nature and extent can only be guessed but must not be assumed to be merely coextensive with the material which both Matthew and Luke agreed in drawing from it. Later scholars have been less careful in their terminology; it might have made for greater clarity if they had followed Bacon's suggestion.

27. Bacon, *Studies*, xiii.

of the priority of Mk than the pleas raised against it by its few surviving opponents'.[28]

Thirty years later a similar verdict would have seemed almost equally necessary. Mention would have had to be made of the attempts by the Catholic scholars J. Chapman and B.C. Butler to revive the so-called Augustinian view, but these had met with little favour, and the priority of Matthew could have been confidently dismissed as a lost cause.

Today the situation is very different. Not that the majority of New Testament specialists have changed sides; redaction-criticism continues to be practised on the confident assumption that it is right to treat Matthew's text as in some sense a revision of that of Mark. But this position can now be adopted only in the recognition that there is on the other side a strong body of scholarly opinion firmly convinced of the priority of Matthew, and a larger group who, while not prepared to declare their allegiance unequivocally for either side, regard the issue as more open than it has been since the nineteenth century. Perhaps more significantly still there are now a growing number of voices raised in opposition to *any* straightforward theory of literary priority and dependence, who believe it is more realistic to talk about shared traditions and a process of cross-fertilisation between the churches in which the gospels were produced than to envisage one evangelist simply 'using' the work of another.

Without attempting to 'solve' the whole Synoptic Problem in a few pages, I shall attempt here to chart in broad terms the course of these recent developments, and to offer some comments on the nature and weight of the various arguments on offer.

A 1700-YEAR CONSENSUS

The earliest preserved statements about the authorship and the circumstances of writing of the gospels are the quotations from Papias preserved in Eusebius, *H.E.* III 39. 14-16. Papias is usually dated about AD 140, though a substantially earlier date is defended by Gundry.[29] I shall discuss Papias' statement on Matthew (and the question of the date and reliability of Papias) when we come to the question of authorship,[30] but for our present purposes his comments on Matthew and Mark are disappointing, as he does not indicate the date of writing of either gospel, nor do we know from Eusebius' separate presentation of the two statements whether and in what way they were related to

28. *Ibid.* 496-504.
29. Gundry, *Matthew*, 610-611.
30. See below pp. 53-60.

each other in their original context.[31] One relevant detail might be the mention (however it is to be interpreted – on this too see later!)[32] that Matthew wrote 'in the Hebrew language'. *If* this refers to a Semitic original of the gospel of Matthew, and *if* Papias understood Mark's gospel to have been written in Greek, this *might* be taken to indicate that he believed Matthew to be the earlier gospel. But that would be a hazardous deduction, as we shall see. And it is counterbalanced by the possibility that Papias' verb in his account of Matthew, συνετάξατο, is to be translated 'set in order', in which case it *might* be intended to contrast his work with that of Mark, whose lack of order (τάξις) he has commented on; in that case it is possible that he understands the Aramaic Matthew to be a deliberate correction of an earlier work of Mark.[33] Altogether, Papias forms a flimsy basis for any conclusion on the question of priority.

The first clear statement about the order of writing which has survived is that of Irenaeus, *Adv. Haer.* III 1.1, that Matthew produced his gospel 'among the Hebrews, in their own language, while Peter and Paul were preaching and founding the church in Rome', but that it was 'after their departure' (ἔξοδος, usually interpreted as referring to their death in the persecution) that Mark produced his written account of what Peter had been preaching. Luke is mentioned next as having recorded the gospel as preached by Paul (without any specific chronological link to Matthew or Mark), and the list concludes with 'then John . . .'.[34] The priority of Matthew was, therefore the accepted belief in at least a part of the church before the end of the second century.

From that time on the tradition of the priority of Matthew seems to be unchallenged. It is explicit in Clement of Alexandria,[35] Origen, Eusebius, Jerome and Augustine, and is implied, as we have seen, in the order in which the gospels are listed in virtually all ancient references and manuscripts.

Equally firmly entrenched, however, is the tradition that Matthew wrote in 'Hebrew', which we shall consider when dealing with the Papias evidence in the next chapter. It may be that, since modern scholarship

31. C.M. Tuckett, *The Revival of the Griesbach Hypothesis* (Cambridge University Press, 1983), 57 tentatively suggests that the mere fact that Eusebius records Papias' words about Mark before those about Matthew, contrary to the traditional order which Eusebius himself held, 'may possibly indicate that this was Papias' belief about the order of composition'.
32. Below pp. 57, 62-66.
33. See below p. 57.
34. Text preserved in Eusebius, *H.E.* V 8.2-4.
35. Clement's account, as recorded by Eusebius, *H.E.* VI 14.5-7, is interesting, and characteristically original: the first gospels to be written were the two which include genealogies (Matthew and Luke); then came Mark, making a record of Peter's preaching while Peter was still around (in this Clement differs from Irenaeus and the more usual tradition, which has Mark writing after Peter's death); finally John, aware that the other evangelists had already presented the 'bodily' facts, added his more 'spiritual' gospel.

is unanimous that this latter tradition is mistaken (i.e. that the gospel of Matthew as we know it was written in Greek, and is not a translation of a Semitic original), the tradition that Matthew wrote first is also suspect by association with it! But, whatever its basis, the fact is that this is what Christians uniformly believed for at least 1700 years, until the early part of the nineteenth century.

A NEW CONSENSUS

In the nineteenth century everything changed. Already in the eighteenth century there had been doubts, as we have seen, about the relation of our Greek Matthew to the Semitic original which was still assumed to lie behind it. We have noted Eichhorn's suggestion that this Semitic gospel was not simply Matthew's gospel before its translation into Greek, but a more primitive account, not an earlier form of any one of our Synoptic Gospels, but the putative ultimate source of all of them. The erosion of the belief in a Semitic original of Matthew, which had been so central in patristic tradition about the gospel, did not necessarily carry with it the questioning of the other main factor in that tradition, the priority of Matthew, but it is perhaps not surprising that this soon followed.

I have sketched earlier the rise of the so-called 'Marcan Hypothesis' to become by the end of the nineteenth century the new consensus of scholarship concerning the relationships of the gospels. The whole process has been chronicled in detail in H.-H. Stoldt's study, *History and Criticism of the Marcan Hypothesis*.[36] Stoldt's book is not a dispassionate account, but a determined attempt by a convinced adherent of the opposing Griesbach Hypothesis to show that the theory of the priority of Mark arose more as the result of the ideological climate of the time than on the basis of objective research, and that in fact it lacked the essential foundation in detailed examination of the texts. (It should be noted that Stoldt's study is largely confined to German scholarship; attention to developments in Britain would have made the latter allegation much more difficult to sustain.)[37] Stoldt traces the appeal of the Marcan Hypothesis to the influence of David Friedrich Strauss, whose *Life of Jesus* (1835) was regarded by more orthodox

36. H.-H. Stoldt, *Geschichte und Kritik der Markushypothese* (Göttingen: Vandenhoeck und Ruprecht, 1977; ET, Edinburgh: T. & T. Clark, 1980).
37. See the account of developments in British scholarship before Streeter in W.R. Farmer, *The Synoptic Problem* (New York: Macmillan, 1964) 48-117. Farmer's concern is to show that the Griesbach Hypothesis did not receive a fair hearing; it is therefore the more impressive that his account does in fact indicate that there was on the part of such scholars as F.H. Woods, E.A. Abbott, V.H. Stanton and F.C. Burkitt a serious attempt to establish the theory of Marcan priority on textual rather than ideological grounds.

churchmen as an assault on the very foundations of the faith. Since Strauss had worked on the basis of the then dominant Griesbach Hypothesis, it was hoped that to destroy this hypothesis would discredit Strauss' work by undermining his source-critical presuppositions. The Marcan Hypothesis offered instead the possibility of defending the historicity of the gospel traditions by tracing their origin to two sources stemming from the apostolic circle, Mark as the first gospel carrying the authority of Peter, and the 'logia' (later to be dubbed Q) thought to derive from the apostle Matthew. The Marcan Hypothesis thus *grew out of theological commitment. It is a theologumenon.*[38]

Stoldt's account is hardly unbiased, and it is not likely that a movement of thought which developed over a broad scholarly front during more than half a century can be traced to a single ideological motivation in this way. Granted that the identification of Strauss with the Griesbach Hypothesis was noted and made the basis for attacking him by some scholars around the middle of the century, it is an over-simplification to see this as the only or even the main basis of the new consensus, particularly in view of the fact that in due course many whose historical scepticism was no less than that of Strauss were (and are) to be found among the advocates of Marcan priority.[39]

Whatever the reason, by the early part of the twentieth century it was clear that Marcan priority had won the day. True, Adolf Hilgenfeld, one of the last representatives of the older Tübingen School, continued to argue for the priority of Matthew (though not for the Griesbach Hypothesis as such) until his death in 1907, and, as we have noted, Zahn and Schlatter in their different ways, and from a different theological perspective, were advocates of the priority of Matthew until the 1930s. But with the dominance after the First World War of the form-critical school, with its firm conviction that Mark was the one responsible for first threading the individual pericopes of the oral tradition together into 'gospel' form, it seemed, as we have seen in the statements of Bacon, that nothing could ever again shake the theory of Marcan priority.

38. For this account of the ideological basis of the hypothesis see Stoldt, *Hypothesis*, 227-235. A similar account, though in less detail, had been offered earlier by Farmer, *Synoptic Problem*, esp. pp. 55-58. Farmer sees the same sort of motivation in William Sanday's sustained efforts to commend the emerging Two-Document Hypothesis to English scholarship, leading up ultimately to its crystallisation in the work of B.H. Streeter.

39. For a critique of Stoldt's work see C.M. Tuckett, *JSNT* 3 (1979) 29-60. Tuckett shows both that the 'anti-Strauss factor' was much less prominent in the rejection of the Griesbach Hypothesis than Stoldt alleges, and that, contrary to Stoldt's assertion, the Griesbach Hypothesis was not dismissed without specific argument, but rather was subjected to careful criticism by several of the leading advocates of Marcan priority.

THE TWENTIETH CENTURY CONSENSUS UNDER ATTACK

The first major attack on the new consensus came from Roman
Catholic scholarship, and more specifically from two successive Abbots
of Downside. Dom John Chapman's study *Matthew, Mark and Luke*,
was published posthumously in 1937.[40] It was a large and detailed
study, but was strangely ignored by the scholarly world. Even more
surprisingly, the much better-known work of his successor, Dom B.C.
Butler, on *The Originality of St. Matthew*,[41] while arguing for the same
basic position in the face of the virtual unanimity of the rest of the
scholarly world at that time, makes no mention of Chapman's work.
Butler's work in its turn, while noticed sufficiently to call forth several
hostile replies and to provoke a great deal of re-examination of
traditional views, has not won any significant following for the 'Augustinian' view which he and Chapman advanced (the order Matthew,
Mark, Luke, with Luke making use of both his predecessors' work,
and therefore no need for a Q to explain the material shared by
Matthew and Luke). But its sustained attack on the twin bases of the
Two-Document Hypothesis, Q and the priority of Mark, prepared for
further battles to come.

. What has been remembered from Butler's work is primarily one
phrase which he seems to have coined, and which has since become a
prominent factor in synoptic debate – 'The Lachmann Fallacy'. This,
the title of Butler's fifth chapter (the first four chapters are devoted to
an attempted demolition of the Q hypothesis, in favour of direct
dependence of Luke on Matthew), refers to the argument from the
order of material in the Synoptic Gospels, which has always held a
prominent place in the defence of the theory of Marcan priority, and
to which we shall return. There is, Butler suggests, 'a schoolboyish[42]
error of elementary reasoning at the very base of the Two-Document
hypothesis as commonly proposed for our acceptance,'[43] one of which
Lachmann himself may be fairly acquitted, but which others have
persisted in fathering on him. To observe, as Marcan priorists have
always done, that Mark is the 'middle term' between Matthew and
Luke (in that both in the order and the wording of the shared material
one or the other of them generally agrees with Mark but they do not,
except in very minor matters, agree with each other against Mark) does

---

40. J. Chapman, *Matthew, Mark and Luke: a Study in the Order and Interrelation of
the Synoptic Gospels* (London: Longmans, Green, 1937).
41. Cambridge University Press, 1951.
42. He adds in a note 'or schoolmasterish', and goes on (p. 66, n. 1) to make fun of
E.A. Abbott, himself a noted headmaster, for his attempt to portray the work of the
evangelists in terms of schoolboys copying from one another's work, and his failure to
recognise the alternative patterns of 'copying' which might lead to the same result!
43. *Originality*, 63.

not in itself entail that Mark came first. To assert that it does is to commit the 'Lachmann Fallacy'.

We shall meet this phrase again, as it has become one of the catchwords of the other and more successful modern challenger to the theory of Marcan priority. But Butler's book as a whole is of interest for our present purposes more as a sign that there were questions still to be answered by the twentieth-century consensus than because it had any lasting impact in itself.

With W.R. Farmer's *The Synoptic Problem* (1964) a new phase began, that of the revival of the Griesbach Hypothesis[44] (or, as the purists insist, the Owen-Griesbach Hypothesis).[45] This approach in its revived form[46] shares with Butler's 'Augustinian' view the elimination of Q and the rejection of the priority of Mark in favour of that of Matthew, but differs in seeing Luke as the second gospel, and Mark as a deliberate reworking of the material of Matthew and Luke into a shorter and 'mediating' gospel. Farmer supposes a church situation where both the gospels of Matthew and Luke had their advocates, and where to favour one at the expense of the other would be unpopular; so Mark has carefully made a selection of material from the works of his predecessors to form a fast-flowing narrative which would please both sides, and in so doing has scrupulously steered a middle course through the chronological discrepancies between Matthew and Luke. Thus the character of Mark as the 'middle term' is not a result of independent use of his gospel by Matthew and Luke (the 'Lachmann Fallacy'), but reflects his deliberately mediating policy as the last of the three synoptists.

While Farmer has been the most prominent representative of this new Griesbach movement, he has not remained, like Butler, a lone voice. There has now developed an articulate and self-confident 'New Griesbach School' in gospel criticism. Some (such as H.-H. Stoldt and J.B. Orchard) had already been working independently along similar lines, while others are more recent adherents. An impressive succession

---

44. James Moffatt would have found such a phrase highly disturbing: in 1911 he referred to Griesbach's *Commentatio* as 'the first vigorous appearance of this unlucky and prolific dandelion, which it has taken nearly a century of opposition . . . to eradicate' ! (*An Introduction to the Literature of the New Testament* (Edinburgh: T. & T. Clark, 1911) 177).

45. While the form in which this hypothesis had wielded such influence in nineteenth-century Germany was that set out by J.J. Griesbach in a succession of works culminating in his *Commentatio* of 1789, it had already been propounded by an Englishman, Henry Owen, in his *Observations on the Four Gospels*, published in London in 1764.

46. Farmer and the other proponents of this approach recognise that their theory has developed well beyond that of Griesbach, particularly in its attempt to account in detail for Mark's editorial aims and method; but the order of composition and the essential literary relationship postulated are those proposed by Griesbach. For a useful summary of the new movement, together with responses to some of the objections to it, see W.R. Farmer, 'Modern Developments of Griesbach's Hypothesis', *NTS* 23 (1976/7), 275-295.

of large-scale international scholarly conferences on the gospels have been devoted to the promotion of this view, and the volumes of papers which have come out of these conferences,[47] together with a steady stream of articles and monographs by individual scholars, have kept the new 'School' before the attention of the scholarly world.

By no means all those who have attended and read papers at the 'Griesbach Conferences' have been adherents of this school, and some have been openly hostile. A good number of established scholars, while prepared to listen to the arguments offered, have remained at most neutral. It would certainly be too much to claim at the present stage that there has been a revolution in scholarly thinking on the Synoptic Problem. But it is undoubtedly true that the question is now seen as more open than has been the case for many years. Most of those who have been used to operating on the Two-Document Hypothesis continue to do so (perhaps with rather more frequent recognition that theirs is not the only possible view than was formerly thought necessary!), and some have offered detailed arguments directed against the new Griesbach school.[48] The new school remains a minority, but a very aggressive one, clearly determined to maintain a high profile.

But it would be wrong to suggest that there is now a simple 'two-party' situation in Synoptic Studies, with a somewhat unequal campaign being waged between the Two-Document Hypothesis and the new Griesbach Hypothesis, and no other contender in sight. Ever since Austin Farrer's famous article 'On Dispensing with Q'[49] there have been some who, while maintaining Marcan priority, regard Q as an unnecessary hypothesis, and account for the 'Q material' by Luke's direct use of Matthew.[50] Others have concluded that the very impossibility, as it seems, of resolving the question of literary dependence with a simple order of

---

47. The first such conference (Pittsburgh 1970) resulted in the two volumes *Jesus and Man's Hope*, ed. D.G. Miller (Pittsburgh Theological Seminary, 1970-1971); the second (Münster, 1976) in *J.J. Griesbach: Synoptic and Text-Critical Studies 1776-1976*, ed. J.B. Orchard and T.R.W. Longstaff (Cambridge University Press, 1978); the third (San Antonio, Texas, 1977) in *The Relationships among the Gospels*, ed. W.O. Walker (San Antonio: Trinity University Press, 1978); and the fourth (Cambridge, 1979) in *New Synoptic Studies: the Cambridge Gospel Conference and Beyond*, ed. W.R. Farmer (Macon: Mercer University Press, 1983). A further conference in Jerusalem in 1984 had not produced a conference volume by the time of writing. Smaller local conferences resulting from the above have also been held, e.g. at Ampleforth in 1982 and 1983; some of the papers from these conferences are in C.M. Tuckett (ed.), *Synoptic Studies* (Sheffield: JSOT Press, 1984).

48. Notably C.M. Tuckett, *The Revival of the Griesbach Hypothesis* (1983). The instant, and rather defensive, response by W.R. Farmer in the introduction to *New Synoptic Studies* (1984) is perhaps an indication of the strength of Tuckett's case!

49. A.M. Farrer, 'On Dispensing with Q' in D.E. Nineham (ed.), *Studies in the Gospels* (Oxford: Blackwell, 1955) 55-88.

50. So M.D. Goulder in a series of contributions, especially *Midrash and Lection in Matthew* (London: SPCK, 1974) 452-471; 'On Putting Q to the Test', *NTS* 24 (1977/8) 218-234; 'The Order of a Crank' in C.M. Tuckett (ed.), *Synoptic Studies*, 111-130.

'copying' suggests that it may be time to try out a less 'tidy' solution. We shall return shortly to this apparently 'pessimistic' approach, and shall suggest that it may have a lot to be said for it in terms of historical probability, however dissatisfying it may be to those who like to have their literary sources neatly defined.

But first it may be worthwhile to assess in broad terms the nature and the value of some of the standard arguments used in efforts to resolve the question of literary priority. What sort of evidence might appropriately be used to prove either that Matthew 'used' Mark or that Mark 'used' Matthew? (We shall be concerned here with the relative order of Matthew and Mark, rather than with the Synoptic Problem as a whole.)

ARGUMENTS TO ESTABLISH PRIORITY – STREETER

Streeter hoped to establish the case for the priority of Mark 'beyond reasonable doubt' on the basis of five 'main facts and considerations'.[51] While these were not the only arguments used by Streeter and later defenders of Marcan priority, it will provide a suitable basis for our study to consider them and how they have fared in subsequent debate. Other considerations can be added as we proceed.

The first three of Streeter's arguments may be considered together, as all turn out to be in different ways demonstrations of the status of Mark as the 'middle term' between Matthew and Luke.[52]

The first relates to the proportions of Mark reproduced by Matthew (90% of Mark used) and Luke (55% of Mark used, and much of the rest paralleled by similar material from a different source), and the fact that in this shared material each of the other evangelists retains just over 50% of the actual words of Mark. (Note how Streeter's wording here, and throughout the discussion, presupposes his desired solution!) The second is an extension of the first, to note that where the three run parallel, most of Mark's words occur either in both the others or in either one of them where the other differs, whereas the wording of Matthew and Luke hardly ever agrees against Mark. The third argument is the observation that in the order in which pericopes are arranged once again Mark's order is followed either by both the others together, or by either one of them where the other differs (in Streeter's terms, 'where either of them deserts Mark, the other is usually found supporting

51. *Four Gospels*, 159-168, with a briefer summary 151-152.
52. It is so often taken for granted that the role of 'middle term' in this sense is one occupied by Mark alone that it is salutary to be reminded by E.P. Sanders, *NTS* 19 (1972/3) 459-464, that in some cases (explained by Streeter as 'Mark-Q overlaps') it is Matthew rather than Mark that is the 'middle term'. This fact already warns us against drawing firm synoptic conclusions from Mark's supposed 'middle' status.

him'), but that Matthew and Luke do not agree against Mark in the ordering of material in the triple tradition.

Streeter himself then combines these three observations as the basis for a single conclusion: 'This conjunction and alternation of Matthew and Luke in their agreement with Mark as regards (a) content, (b) wording, (c) order, is only explicable if they are incorporating a source identical, or all but identical, with Mark.'

Here is the 'Lachmann Fallacy' pure and simple! As Butler[53] observes, surely rightly, what has been offered is an 'accurate statement of highly important data', followed by 'an inference which is obviously false' (and for which no justification is in fact offered – it is assumed to be self-evident). Of course Streeter has set out his case in terms of Matthew and Luke 'reproducing', 'following', 'agreeing with', 'deserting' Mark, and if such terminology is correct, then the conclusion must follow. But in that case, of course, the conclusion is based not on the evidence but on an already presupposed solution. Here, as in so much of synoptic argument, what is obvious from one point of view is obviously wrong from another. To show that the data can be made to 'fit' with one hypothesis is not to prove that they cannot also fit another. It was the great merit of Butler's book that it forced scholars to recognise the circularity which had remained unnoticed in such arguments for so long as the ruling status of the Two-Document Hypothesis was un-disputed.

Nevertheless, arguments from the order of the material have continued to be freely used in more recent synoptic discussion.[54] To the surprise of some Marcan priorists, it is in this area that upholders of the Griesbach Hypothesis sometimes look for their strongest support. Thus Farmer[55] suggests that Mark's lack of any independent chronology (in that at all points his ordering is in agreement with either Matthew or Luke, if not both together) makes sense only if he was dependent on the other two gospels; any other view must suppose that Matthew and Luke 'would have had to conspire with one another or find some other way to contrive this chronological neutering of Mark, i.e. robbing his chronological independence'. Such arguments have gone to and fro, but in the end it seems essential to conclude, with C.M. Tuckett, that '*any* argument from order (including Griesbach's) is in itself, at the

53. *Originality*, 62.
54. See especially an important article by E.P. Sanders, 'The Argument from the Order and the Relationship between Matthew and Luke', *NTS* 15 (1968/9) 249-261, and a response to this and other studies of the subject by F. Neirynck, printed in his book *The Minor Agreements of Matthew and Luke against Mark* (Leuven University Press, 1974) 291-322. Sanders' article aims to show that the classical statement about order, that Matthew and Luke never agree against Mark, is based on an oversimplified approach to what constitutes 'order', and that there are in fact significant 'agreements against Mark' in the Marcan material, such as to suggest that Luke used Matthew.
55. W.R. Farmer, *NTS* 23 (1976/7) 293-295.

purely formal level, logically inconclusive. The facts of the case are undisputed – i.e. that there is a close similarity in order between all three gospels, as well as some disagreement, and that the Matthew-Luke agreements are almost always mediated through Mark. But these facts are open to a number of different interpretations.'[56]

We have noted Butler's observation that Streeter's first three arguments were not 'arguments for the priority of Mark' at all, but merely observations about synoptic relationships which in themselves do not require any particular solution. The same is true, as we shall see, of the fifth. But in Streeter's fourth argument (or rather cluster of arguments) Butler recognises 'an argument deserving serious attention' because it does offer the possibility of 'supporting the theory of Marcan priority to the exclusion of all other solutions.'[57]

This is the fact that Mark's gospel is perceived as in various ways more 'primitive', both in content and in presentation (style, grammar, preservation of Aramaic idiom). Thus Mark offers more vivid, expansive narratives in the style of folk-tradition; his Greek is less literary, marked by the breathless parataxis, historic presents, and the redundant phrases and digressions which characterise the impromptu preacher or story-teller, whereas 'Matthew and Luke use the more succinct and carefully chosen language of one who writes and then revises an article for publication'. (Indeed, where Matthew and Mark tell the same story, Augustine's description of Mark as Matthew's 'breviator' is diametrically wrong; Matthew reads more as a prosaic condensation of Mark's lively stories, sometimes to as little as one-third of their length.) And in the stories he tells there is more of a frankness, even occasionally irreverence, towards Jesus and the disciples, which is not found in parallel passages in Matthew and Luke; indeed it is possible to see in the detailed wording 'a constant tendency in Matthew and Luke . . . to improve upon and refine Mark's version'. Matthew and Luke, on the other hand, show a tendency to elevate the status of Jesus and the disciples, by a stronger emphasis on the miraculous and the use of more theologically weighted terms. In other words, between Mark and the other two synoptists can be seen the beginning of a process of hagiography which later Christianity was to take to extremes.

This is undoubtedly Streeter's strongest argument. To him it is conclusive. How anyone can work through all the details of synoptic parallels and still 'retain the slightest doubt of the original and primitive character of Mark I am unable to comprehend. . . . I can only suppose,

56. *JSNT* 3 (1979) 48. In his *Revival*, 6-7, Tuckett is rather more positive about the role of arguments from order in favour of the Two-Document Hypothesis; such an argument 'might not be logically probative, but it could still have value if supported by other considerations'.
57. Butler, *Originality*, 68.

either that they have not been at the pains to do this, or else that – like
some of the highly cultivated people who think Bacon wrote Shake-
speare, or that the British are the Lost Ten Tribes – they have eccentric
views of what constitutes evidence.'[58]

But again, what seems self-evident to one appears perverse to another.
That Mark does differ from Matthew and Luke along such lines as
listed above is agreed, but is Mark's 'primitivity' and a subsequent
'improvement' by Matthew and Luke the only, or the right, way to
explain these differences? Is it a necessary conclusion that what appears
to us more theologically or literarily sophisticated is therefore later?
As Butler wryly points out, 'The parish magazine is not necessarily of
earlier date than the *Summa Theologica* of St. Thomas.'[59] Literary and
theological character depend on the individual personality of the author,
the position of the church in which he is writing, the purpose of the
book, the special needs and interests of his readers, and many other
such factors, none of which requires an inexorable temporal evolution
from the more 'primitive' to the more 'advanced' – and all of which
depend ultimately on our assessment of the document itself, thus once
again introducing an element of circularity into the argument.

So Farmer[60] takes this apparently conclusive argument and goes
through ten of the most frequently cited examples of alleged 'improve-
ments' of Mark by Matthew and/or Luke to see whether the movement
is necessarily in that direction. Looking at them from the Griesbach
point of view he is able in each case to suggest an alternative scenario
which is at least plausible. How far any given reader will be persuaded
by Streeter or by Farmer is likely to be determined not by bare logic
but rather on the basis of the total understanding of the development
of early Christianity, and of the characters and aims of the evangelists,
which is brought to the reading.

Streeter's fifth argument again, in Butler's view, 'turns out to contain
no evidence in proof of Streeter's theory, but a series of deductions
from it'.[61] In it Streeter observes the way the Marcan material is combined
with non-Marcan material in each of the other gospels. Much of the
non-Marcan material, particularly that which Matthew and Luke share,
consists largely of sayings, with little internal indication of a narrative
context to which it belongs, and it is a remarkable fact that Matthew
and Luke never agree in inserting a given Q tradition into the same
Markan context. This Streeter explains by the different literary techniques of Matthew and Luke. Matthew, he suggests, has used Mark
as his framework, slotting in other material in places where it helps to

58. Streeter, *Four Gospels*, 164.
59. Butler, *Originality*, 171.
60. Farmer, *Synoptic Problem*, 159-169.
61. Butler, *Originality*, 67.

illuminate the narrative or teaching derived from Mark ('joining like to like'). This is particularly obvious in Matthew's five great discourses, in four of which a shorter Marcan nucleus has been expanded by material in a related subject-area, while the fifth (the Sermon on the Mount) forms an extended demonstration of Mark 1:22, with which it concludes. In Luke, on the other hand, 'Marcan and non-Marcan material alternates in great blocks', and in this case it is the non- Marcan material which seems to be the structural framework of the gospel, interspersed with virtually self-contained extracts from Mark. (It was this observation, of course, which formed the basis of Streeter's theory of Proto-Luke.)

All this makes sense, Streeter argues, if both Matthew and Luke had the same document to combine with other material, and each set about the task in his own distinctive way. And so it does, of course.[62] But that still leaves the question whether the same phenomena can be given an equally coherent explanation on any other hypothesis, and that Streeter did not consider. The attempt has been made particularly by J.B. Orchard,[63] working from the Griesbach perspective. Orchard explains how Luke has 'dismembered' and re-shaped the work of Matthew, and gives reasons for his doing so. Mark has then attempted to harmonise the two, though with a slightly greater leaning towards the order of Matthew. To read Orchard's account after being familiar with the Streeter approach is to realise how virtually every piece of data has a quite different meaning, depending on the framework within which you place it. Thus it is possible for Streeter to give a coherent account of the data within his theory, and for Orchard (after a sufficient mental revolution that he no longer thinks in an automatically Streeterian way!) to be equally satisfied of his totally different account. But for any one person to attempt *both* tasks adequately at the same time, and then to achieve an 'objective' evaluation of which better accounted for the evidence (on whose criteria?) would be an almost superhuman feat of mental gymnastics. Believe me, I have tried!

An analysis of Streeter's five arguments and of the responses to them has illustrated clearly the extreme difficulty of finding arguments in this area which can be made to stick. Some seem completely reversible,

62. It has often been remarked, however, that Matthew's procedure was less consistent than Streeter alleges, in that he follows the Marcan order very closely in the second half of his gospel, but restructures the material much more substantially in the first half, particularly in 4:23 – 11:1. This may be accounted for by assuming that Matthew has deliberately constructed a collection of miracles in chapters 8-9 to balance the collection of teaching in chapters 5-7, and that for this purpose he has drawn together material which is scattered over a wider section of Mark, though even so he has retained the Marcan order in some lesser sequences internal to his collection. For a full study of this alleged inconsistency of Matthew see F. Neirynck, in I. de la Potterie (ed.), *De Jésus aux Evangiles* (Gembloux: Duculot, 1967) 41-73.

63. J.B. Orchard, *Matthew, Luke and Mark* (Manchester: Koinonia Press, 1976).

particularly the classical argument from order. Some depend on assumptions concerning the 'evolution' of theological thought and of literary sophistication which are at least questionable. Most are to some degree circular, dependent on the solution to which they are supposed to lead. This is so not only in the formulation of the data, where we have seen that Streeter makes no attempt to present the evidence 'neutrally', but by terms like 'reproduces', 'follows' and 'deserts' inevitably weights the scales; few later writers, on whichever side of the debate, have been able to avoid similarly question-begging formulations. But this applies also to the forms of the arguments themselves, which typically consist of showing how the data fit the proposed scheme, rather than letting the scheme be suggested by the data. In such a complex area, with so many competing hypotheses, this is perhaps inevitable, but it is as well to be aware how little by way of 'firm' conclusions can be said to have emerged from Streeter's arguments.

A recognition of this fact helps to explain why many believe that the former 'consensus' can never be regained with the same confidence, in either direction. We are too much aware, now, how fragile were the foundations on which earlier consensuses were based, in the absence of positive arguments which would not cut the other way when wielded by another hand. The scholar who is convinced of his own hypothesis in this area, and for whom all the evidence points that way, is beginning to be more willing to recognise that those who see things oppositely are not simply perverse, and are not likely to be persuaded by such arguments as the above.

ARGUMENTS TO ESTABLISH PRIORITY – POST-STREETER

We cannot now go through all the arguments which have been pursued in this area since Streeter. Some have already been referred to in considering the responses to Streeter. The whole discussion is now much more complex than it seemed in his day. All I can offer is a purely personal selection of a few areas of discussion which seem to me to be particularly significant in today's debate.

One is a factor which figured largely in Streeter's discussion as 'the only valid objection to the theory that the document used by Matthew and Luke was our Mark', and which was generally regarded as settled by him for good, but which has now re-emerged as a favourite weapon of those who oppose Marcan priority, that is the *minor agreements of Matthew and Luke against Mark*. If Matthew and Luke both used Mark, while they are of course free to agree in their use of non-Marcan material from another source, it might be expected that in their versions of Marcan material they would either agree with Mark or alter him independently. The fact that there are within the triple tradition quite a considerable number of such 'minor agreements' against Mark has always been a problem for Marcan priorists. Streeter[64] explained some as the coincidences inevitable when two independent but cultured writers attempted the correction of Mark's style and content, some as belonging to traditions where Mark overlapped with Q,[65] but a large number of them as the result of textual corruption, so that an 'agreement against Mark' has been created where there was none in the original works. The last possibility was so real for Streeter that he was prepared to make it a principle of textual criticism that we should accept the reading which is compatible with the dependence of Matthew and Luke on Mark – i.e. that 'minor agreements' should on principle be ruled out as textual corruptions.

The lack of objectivity in this approach has been played on by opponents of Marcan priority, and these agreements against Mark have been declared 'the major stumbling block for adherents of the Marcan hypothesis'.[66] The discussion has become sufficiently central to justify a massive, book-length study,[67] in which the debate is charted and the relevant synoptic material set out with immense care in a designedly 'neutral' form. The use of this argument from the Griesbach camp has not remained uncontested. C.M. Tuckett has recently[68] attempted to turn it back by showing that several of the minor agreements are no easier for that hypothesis to account for, since they would require Mark deliberately to make minor alterations against the consensus of his two sources in ways which would be uncharacteristic of his style or interests elsewhere in the gospel.

But that was still an old argument from the Streeter era. Have no new arguments emerged? J.M. Robinson at the first Griesbach Conference in 1970 could still describe the period as 'a generation in which the Synoptic problem has been largely dormant' (would he have said the same today?), but went on to claim that 'the success of *Redaktionsgeschichte* in clarifying the theologies of Matthew and Luke on the assumption of dependence on Mark is perhaps the most important new argument for Marcan priority, just as perhaps the main ingredient lacking in William R. Farmer's argument for Marcan dependence on

---

64. *Four Gospels*, 295-331.
65. E.P. Sanders, *NTS* 19 (1972/3) 453-465, subjects the theory of 'Mark-Q overlaps' to searching criticisms.
66. Farmer, *Synoptic Problem*, 167, followed by many since. Farmer criticises Streeter's treatment of the minor agreements in detail, *ibid.* 118-152.
67. Neirynck, *Minor Agreements*.
68. Tuckett, *Revival*, 61-75. He goes on also (pp. 76-93) to argue that the theory of a Mark-Q overlap, often dismissed as a face-saving manoeuvre by Streeter in the face of an agreement against Mark, is in fact in many cases the most probable explanation, and that the Griesbach Hypothesis itself is forced at such times to postulate overlapping sources, together with a far less satisfactory editorial procedure on the part of Mark than its rivals propose for Matthew and Luke.

the other written Gospels is a convincing *Redaktionsgeschichte* of Mark based on that assumption'.[69] Both halves of that statement deserve to be noticed.

It is a fact that virtually all significant redaction-critical work has been based on Marcan priority, and a good measure of agreement has been achieved in some areas of Matthean and Lucan studies on the basis of this agreed assumption. Some of what has been agreed could, of course, have been discovered by a study of the text of the relevant gospel in itself, without specific consideration of literary relations and the use of sources. But in most cases the raw materials of redaction-critical study have been drawn from the 'changes' made by a later evangelist to what he is assumed to have found in Mark or Q, and any questioning of this literary dependence would necesssarily throw doubt on the conclusions. It can not be claimed, then, that redaction-critical agreement is in itself an argument for the correctness of the assumed source-hypothesis, so long as that hypothesis has not itself been called in question, and the results compared with those which might be reached on a different hypothesis.

That redaction-critics have shown no enthusiasm for such a 'control' study is hardly surprising. It would be a massive diversion from the whole enterprise, and one which would be very hard to control. It would raise again the exasperating difficulty mentioned above of how one can possibly hold in tension two completely different scenarios, in each of which the same pieces of evidence are likely to point in totally opposite directions. If a source-critically neutral redaction-criticism seems an uncomfortable and possibly unrewarding prospect, one which seriously attempts to do full justice to opposite source-theories at the same time seems an impossibility. Redaction-criticism continues therefore to operate within the assumption of Marcan priority, and, *given that assumption*, continues to have significant 'success in clarifying the theologies of Matthew and Luke'.

Redaction-criticism based on Matthean priority has, by contrast, not yet achieved significant visibility in the scholarly world. But the second part of Robinson's statement is important: does a theory of Marcan dependence on Matthew allow us to construct a satisfying picture of Mark's aims and methods as a redactor? A book on Matthew is not the place to attempt a proper answer to that question, but it may be worth recording that for me personally this is the single most telling argument in the whole debate on literary priority. I simply find it extremely hard to make sense of a Mark who, having the gospel of Matthew in front of him, could produce the sort of gospel he did.[70]

69. J.M. Robinson in *Jesus and Man's Hope*, vol. 1, 101-102.
70. Cf. J.M. Rist, *On the Independence of Matthew and Mark* (Cambridge University Press, 1978) 3-4 for the question of why Mark should be written in a community which already had Matthew.

Streeter's famous statement that 'only a lunatic would leave out
Matthew's account of the Infancy, the Sermon on the Mount, and
practically all the parables, in order to get room for purely verbal
expansion of what was retained',[71] while overstated, makes the point
well. When Mark felt able to tell most of the stories he took over from
Matthew at two or three times their original length (the additional
material being largely 'padding' to make the stories flow better and
more impressively), and at the same time felt no need to reproduce
teaching such as the Sermon on the Mount, what sort of book was he
writing?

A story-book, it might be suggested, and therefore he and his readers
had no need for or interest in teaching material. After all, whenever
Mark wrote, surely there was plenty more teaching material about than
he actually recorded. He must be allowed to follow his own interests,
and Jesus as teacher was not one of those. And this is in fact the way
people often write about Mark, as the activist Christian for whom the
cerebral was tedious and unnecessary. But I believe this is a fundamental
misunderstanding of Mark.

For one thing, a comparison of the use of 'teaching' terminology in
the Synoptic Gospels reveals that its incidence in Mark's editorial
comments is significantly higher than in those of Matthew and Luke.
If there is one synoptist rather than another who emphasises Jesus as
a teacher and depicts him as typically involved in teaching, it is Mark.
But secondly it is not true, as is often alleged, that Mark presents very
little of the teaching of Jesus. An analysis of the gospel shows that
roughly 50% of its verses are devoted to introducing or to presenting
the content of Jesus' teaching.[72] If you take Mark on his own terms,
not in comparison with Matthew and Luke, this is a significant presentation of Jesus' teaching, entirely in keeping with his editorial emphasis
on the subject.

But if Mark, with this expressed interest in the teaching of Jesus,
had Matthew in front of him, could he have simply ignored the Sermon
on the Mount and much of the rest of Matthew? It is one thing for
him not to include such material when writing from scratch (whether
because it was not available to him or for whatever other reason), but
quite another to take a deliberate decision to omit it when it stood in
the source text in front of him. I have not yet been able to make sense
of this procedure on the part of an author with Mark's expressed
interests.

Of course that is only one small sounding in a large area. But I
believe that further study of Mark on the assumption of his dependence

71. Streeter, *Four Gospels*, 158.
72. For both these points see my article 'Mark and the Teaching of Jesus' in *Gospel Perspectives* vol. 1, 101-136.

on Matthew is likely to throw up further unexplained factors in his editorial method. For all the efforts of the new Griesbach School to · reconstruct Mark's role as the conflator of Matthew and Luke, the portrait still seems to me to lack verisimilitude, particularly in view of the expansiveness of Mark's story-telling.[73]

Arguments for literary priority, then, have proved generally inconclusive or double-edged, and the debate remains open. For myself, the one relatively clear result is that I do not believe, for the reason just given, that Mark was literarily dependent on Matthew. Does this mean, then, that after all the protestations of preceding pages, I am thrown back to the twentieth-century consensus on the priority of Mark and the Two-Document Hypothesis? I am not so sure!

SIMPLE LITERARY DEPENDENCE QUESTIONED

While recent debate on the Synoptic Problem has been dominated by two main rival schools of literary dependence, the Two-Document and Griesbach schools, an undercurrent throughout the debate has been the presence of those who have begun to wonder whether the reason for lack of progress with such theories is that they are too simple and mechanical. Is it realistic, in the first century church, to talk as if gospels were 'published' at a given date, immediately distributed and available to Christians all over the Mediterranean world, and then 'copied', 'edited', 'reshaped' etc. by the next person to engage in gospel-writing, so that a straight line of dependence in only one direction can be established, whether Mark-Matthew-Luke, Matthew-Luke-Mark or whatever, with each writer directly (and on some views virtually exclusively) dependent on the work of his predecessor(s)?

In addition to the question whether this is how books were actually composed in the ancient world in general and the Christian church in particular, a further common feature of the sort of theories we have been discussing is their marked reluctance to envisage any sources other than our existing gospels, with the one conspicuous exception of Q (for those who still believe in it). And those who postulate a source Q have generally tended to see it as a single document (Bacon's S) from which all the non-Marcan material shared by Matthew and Luke must have come. Occam's famous principle that 'entities are not to be multiplied beyond necessity' is applied enthusiastically to hypothetical lost sources or earlier editions lying behind our existing gospels.

All this makes for much tidier source theories, and tidiness (or

---

73. Stoldt, *Hypothesis*, 260, speaks of 'the courage of the author in limiting his material quantitatively while qualitatively expanding the depiction of details'. For 'courage' I would prefer to read 'incomprehensibility'!

'simplicity') is often presented as a virtue in this area.[74] But simple explanations are helpful only in relation to simple facts, and the constant frustration of synoptic solutions as they have come up against an extremely complex web of factual data in the text of the gospels suggests that in this case there may be something to be said against simplicity. In particular, what is the logical basis for the assumption that first-century Christians made no written records of Jesus except those which have survived, and perhaps one other which those texts seem to demand? If, according to a statement far too little noted in modern discussion, Luke claimed to be writing after 'many' had already turned their hands to producing such a 'narrative' (διήγησις, Luke 1:1), why is it necessary to restrict those 'many' to simply Mark and Q, or simply Matthew, depending on your theory?[75] Is it not inherently likely that in the worship and teaching of the early churches there were indeed 'many' such records beginning to be compiled, quite apart from a rich fund of oral tradition on which a gospel-writer might draw?[76] It is this sort of reaction against 'simplicity' which characterises a number of quite different recent approaches to the Synoptic Problem.

E.P. Sanders concluded his dissertation on *The Tendencies of the Synoptic Tradition* with some observations on the then current state of the Synoptic Problem. Holding that neither the Two-Document Hypothesis nor any other solution on offer was firmly established, he appealed for 'a period of withholding judgements on the Synoptic problem while the evidence is resifted'. He looked forward to a new view which would be 'more flexible and complicated than the tidy two-document hypothesis. With all due respect for scientific preference for the simpler view, the evidence seems to require a more complicated one.'[77] But he did not at the time feel it right to offer such a solution.

One response has been to go for a theory which, while much less simple, is still in a sense 'tidy', in that in place of a clearly-defined relationship of a small number of documents is offered a no less clearly-defined web of relationships involving more documents, whether they be lost gospel sources or earlier editions of our gospels. This sort of solution has come especially from French scholars. Already in 1954

74. See e.g. Butler, *Originality*, 1, 158, appealing to C.H. Turner's dictum, 'I have an incurable preference for simple solutions to literary problems'.
75. Farmer, *Synoptic Problem*, 221-223 attempts to bring even Luke 1:1 into line with the Griesbach Hypothesis by the unusual suggestion that Luke is speaking of a *single* 'narrative', that of Matthew, resulting from the work of 'many' compilers.
76. Note the view of N.A. Dahl in an article on the Matthean passion narrative (in G.N. Stanton [ed.], *The Interpretation of Matthew* [London: SPCK, 1983] 48) that even in this section, where he believes 'the source critical question can be answered clearly and simply', the complexity of the question prevents our following a 'purely literary' approach', because in the church situation 'oral tradition was still living'.
77. E.P.Sanders, *The Tendencies of the Synoptic Tradition* (Cambridge University Press, 1969) 278-279.

L. Vaganay[78] had set out a theory based on an Aramaic Matthew (itself compiled from earlier 'essais évangéliques'), subsequently translated into Greek, to which was later added a second synoptic source, a Greek sayings source supplementary to the Aramaic Matthew. This whole group of lost documents then formed the basis for the canonical Mark, Matthew and Luke, in that order. Subsequently, A. Gaboury, in a complicated thesis,[79] has tried to reconstruct a basic 'gospel-structure' which all of them presuppose, and in the process has suggested multiple sources (he uses the symbols A1, A2, B, C, D, representing various more or less fixed sources or collections of material drawn on by the various evangelists). The second volume of a French synopsis[80] offers a study of the Synoptic Problem by M.-E. Boismard, who summarises his view in a diagram which has a first row consisting of four documents (A,B,C,Q), a second row containing intermediate editions of each of the four gospels, and a third row containing the final texts of the four gospels; lines of dependence criss-cross the chart in almost every conceivable direction, so that each gospel depends on two or more of the intermediate gospels, and each intermediate gospel on at least two of the postulated sources.[81]

I believe that the sort of complexity of source material and of contacts between developing gospel traditions which these more complicated solutions envisage is historically more realistic than the rather artificial simplicity of the classical hypotheses, which depend on the assumption of a literarily inactive church (and a relatively insignificant place for oral tradition) and of a method of gospel-composition by simple 'redaction' of one or at most two finished documents, in isolation from the currents of wider church life. Where I am much less convinced is in the ability of the modern scholar to work out the relationships and reconstruct the sources in such a way as to allow so neat a diagrammatic presentation. Is not this still to hanker for a 'tidiness' which history is not likely to allow us? Can we really expect to be able to identify, still less to reconstruct, the sources each writer used, particularly when there is the possibility that overlapping material may be due either to use of the same (or a similar) document or to oral tradition?

An even more radical approach to the question is promised by the title of J.M. Rist's monograph *On the Independence of Matthew and Mark*.[82] In view of the very considerable verbatim overlap between the

78. L. Vaganay, *Le Problème synoptique* (Tournai/Paris: Desclée, 1954).
79. A. Gaboury, *La Structure des Evangiles synoptiques* (Leiden: Brill, 1970). The theory is analysed and discussed by F. Neirynck in M. Didier (ed.) *L'Evangile selon Matthieu: Rédaction et Théologie* (Gembloux: Duculot, 1972) 37-69.
80. P. Benoit & M.-E. Boismard, *Synopse des quatres Evangiles en français* Tome II (Paris: le Cerf, 1972).
81. The chart is conveniently reproduced, and the theory discussed, in a review by H.F.D. Sparks in *JTS* 25 (1974) 485-486.
82. Cambridge University Press, 1978.

two gospels this seems a bold claim, and of course Rist is not claiming that each thought up the same material independently out of thin air. His claim is that in the first century church there was probably a lot wider currency of traditions, largely oral, than most recent scholarship allows, and that the independent quarrying of this rich deposit by the two evangelists (probably at about the same time, though he would not base his argument on an agreed date), sometimes drawing on verbally identical pericopes, sometimes on parallel but distinct versions, better accounts for the varying degrees of similarity which we actually find in their texts than any theory of direct literary dependence in either direction. His examination of the texts leads him to claim that there is no consistent indication of one of the evangelists being regularly dependent on the other. The common order of the two narratives (which he believes is less extensive that is generally claimed, particularly in the first half of the gospels) reflects a common tradition of the basic outline of the life of Jesus, many of the events having a natural sequence which requires no literary hypothesis to explain it. To observe the verbal variation in the presentation of the same traditions, even when these occur in the same sequence, is to cast doubt on a simple theory of literary dependence.

There is much in Rist's argument which I find very attractive, especially in his questioning of the rigid assumptions behind much traditional synoptic study.[83] But he dismisses too lightly the large amount of verbal agreement, and especially the close similarity of order in most of the parallel material, resulting in an overall 'shape' which Matthew and Mark share, which we shall be noticing when we consider the structure of Matthew. In his justifiable desire to avoid a theory of one-way dependence, he has gone too far to the opposite extreme of total literary independence, and has dismissed too quickly the possibility of mutual literary influence at some stage in the composition of the two gospels.[84]

A position somewhere between the elaborate reconstruction of the web of literary relationships by the French scholars and Rist's attempt to eliminate all direct relationship was suggested by Sanders' remarks at the end of his book *The Tendencies of the Synoptic Tradition*, and in a subsequent article,[85] where he calls for 'a theory which takes account of multiple and partially overlapping sources' to allow for the existence of overlaps which 'constitutes a difficulty for any rigid and simple solution of the Synoptic problem'. This proposal, together with the

83. For a much slighter protest along similar lines, arguing for oral tradition as the primary factor in synoptic relationships, see W.F. Albright and C.S. Mann, *Matthew* (Anchor Bible. New York: Doubleday, 1971) XXXVII- XLVIII.
84. Rist does notice this possibility, particularly as suggested by E.P. Sanders, on pp. 93-94, but dismisses it as requiring hypothetical earlier editions of both gospels, which he believes to be possible, but not necessary.
85. *NTS* 19 (1972/3) 464-465.

possibility that 'one or more gospels were produced after having been used by the other (or others)',[86] points towards the sort of approach adopted by J.A.T. Robinson.

In the course of his attempt to redate the whole New Testament to the period before AD 70, Robinson found it necessary to reconsider the nature of synoptic relationships. He proposed that 'the gospels as we have them are to be seen as parallel, though by no means isolated, developments of common material for different spheres of the Christian mission, rather than a series of documents standing in simple chronological sequence'. He goes on,

> We have been accustomed for so long to what might be called linear solutions to the synoptic problem, where one gospel simply 'used' another and must therefore be set later, that it is difficult to urge a more fluid and complex interrelation between them without being accused of introducing unnecessary hypotheses and modifications. But if we have learnt anything over the past fifty years it is surely that whereas epistles were written for specific occasions (though they might be added to or adapted later), gospels were essentially for continuous use in the preaching, teaching, apologetic and liturgical life of the Christian communities. They grew out of *and with* the needs. One can only put approximate dates to certain states or stages and set a certain *terminus ad quem* for them, according to what they do or do not reflect. And at any stage in this development one must be prepared to allow for cross-fertilization between the on-going traditions.[87]

Behind this continous 'gospel-writing' process, Robinson envisages both written and oral traditions, which might at different points be preserved in a more primitive form by any one of the synoptics, though he regards Mark as generally closer to source. He believes that each of the gospels went through several stages of composition ('editions'), and that Matthew in particular was subject to extensive 'accretions' (Harnack's term), making it 'in a real sense ... both the earliest and the latest of the synoptists'.[88] The process is summarised as follows:

1. Formation of stories- and sayings-collections ('P', 'Q', 'L', 'M'): 30s and 40s +
2. Formation of 'proto-gospels': 40s and 50s +
3. Formation of our synoptic gospels: 50-60 + [89]

86. From an article on 'Priorités et dépendances dans la tradition synoptique', *Recherches de Science Religieuse* 60 (1972) 519-540; quotation on p. 539.
87. Robinson, *Redating*, 94.
88. *Ibid.* 102.
89. *Ibid.* 107.

Robinson believes that at all stages of this process there was contact between the gospel traditions as they developed in the different churches, and Christians travelled from one centre to another. He does not attempt, however, like Boismard, to specify the various lines of contact or influence between these various documents or stages of tradition. Clearly he regards the whole process as too fluid and 'living' for such definition. Indeed his whole approach is a plea for recognition that such tidiness is in the nature of the case undesirable, and indeed impossible.

Robinson has not devoted to this subject the meticulous care in analysing each synoptic pericope which a purist would demand. Some of his argument is based on extrapolation from one sample study (of Mark 12:1-12 and parallels),[90] but much more on 'common sense', and a view of how things 'must have been' in the life of the early Christian communities. But in an area where detailed analyses continue to lead to such contradictory results, and where every 'tidy' solution finds itself obliged to find more or less plausible explanations for the facts which turn out not to fit the theory, I am attracted by Robinson's impressionistic approach, with its implicit rejection of the model of modern publishing and editorial procedures. If he is right, we are never likely to have, and might better stop looking for, a 'solution' of the Synoptic Problem, and the question of the relative priority of Matthew and Mark, from which this investigation began, turns out to be without significance, indeed to be, in the terms in which it is normally posed, an illegitimate question!

REDACTION-CRITICISM IN THE LIGHT OF SYNOPTIC UNCERTAINTY

If, as I believe, some such 'radical' perspective is the appropriate response to the current state of synoptic discussion, what effect is this likely to have on the whole redaction-critical enterprise, and the search for 'the theology of Matthew', since this has been, as we have noted, based generally on the assumption of Marcan priority and on the consequent study of 'how Matthew used Mark'? If, as I have suggested, it is at best simplistic to speak of Matthew 'using' Mark, does this leave the study of Matthew's methods and interests without any data on which to operate? Must we agree with G.N. Stanton that 'the attempt to make sense of the gospel as it stands without recourse to source critical hypotheses is rather like trying to play a violin or cello with

---

90. J.A.T. Robinson, 'The Parable of the Wicked Husbandmen: a Test of Synoptic Relationships', NTS 21 (1974/5) 443-461.

one's left hand tied behind one's back: rather limited results are still possible, but that is all that can be said!'[91]

That claim has been disputed by a number of recent Matthean scholars. W.G. Thompson's dissertation on Matthew 18[92] aimed to study 'Matthew's redactional techniques and distinctive viewpoint' without 'a prior and presupposed hypothesis about literary sources', expecting that 'the synoptic relations will thus emerge gradually from a careful study of the text itself'. His method was first to study 'Matthew in terms of Matthew' before goirg on to 'synoptic comparison' to enable him to determine the literary relationships. Similarly P.F. Ellis[93] has based a study of Matthew's theology on the explicit contention that 'the proper key to the theological purposes of any evangelist lies primarily in an analysis of his work as a whole and only secondarily in a comparison between his use of sources and that of another evangelist'. The latter approach has been important in synoptic studies, Ellis believes, only 'because the synoptic gospels were not in the past considered to be the proper literary works of individual authors'.

The issue has been interestingly focused in a recent exchange in the pages of the *Journal for the Study of the New Testament* between David Hill and Jack D. Kingsbury. In response to a study[94] in which Kingsbury moved from his previous redaction-critical approach into a reading of Matthew's gospel on its own and as a whole, Hill[95] objects that while some of Matthew's original readers must have had to read his gospel in the same way, without synoptic comparison, since we are aware of Matthew's literary relationships a consideration of Matthew's sources and redactional work is for us a necessary part of an adequate reading of the story. Kingsbury[96] responds with a defence of a literary-critical method which respects the 'wholeness' of the text, in contrast with a source- and redaction-critical study for which 'Not the wholeness of the text as such but the ability to disassemble it so as to lay bare whatever layers of tradition it contains is what counts most. The text in its totality constitutes the sum of layers of tradition.' 'Literary criticism', on the other hand, 'attends to the interplay of the constituent elements of Matthew's narrative, i.e. the elements that comprise its story and its discourse', and in so doing attempts to avoid 'the misguided

91. G.N. Stanton, 'The Origin and Purpose of Matthew's Gospel: Matthean Scholarship from 1945 to 1980', in W. Haase (ed.) *Aufstieg und Niedergang der römischen Welt*, 25/3 (Berlin: de Gruyter, 1985) 1896.

92. W.G.Thompson, *Matthew's Advice to a Divided Community* (Analecta Biblica 44. Rome: Biblical Institute Press, 1970). The methodological statement drawn on here is on pp. 5-7.

93. P.F. Ellis, *Matthew: his Mind and his Message* (Collegeville: Liturgical Press, 1974) 173-4.

94. 'The Figure of Jesus in Matthew's Story: a Literary-Critical Probe', *JSNT* 21 (1984) 3-36.

95. *JSNT* 21 (1984) 37-38.

96. *JSNT* 25 (1985) 61-62.

notion that traditional materials tell one little or nothing of the intention of the evangelist'.

Kingsbury's position in this exchange represents a growing tendency, especially among American scholars, to move away from the sort of redaction-criticism previously familiar especially in Germany, in favour of a literary criticism less focused on 'changes introduced into the tradition' by the evangelists and more concerned with what used sometimes to be distinguished as 'composition-criticism'. The desire to allow the text to speak for itself *as it is* rather than merely as a revised version of an earlier document or tradition, is surely to be welcomed. When Ellis[97] complains of 'the lack of intelligibility in many gospel commentaries' which results from 'the time when the evangelists were considered to be hardly more than inspired editors', it is easy to recognise the tendency he refers to, where every minute variation from the wording of the supposed source document was painstakingly analysed for clues to the evangelist's theology, while the impact of the narrative as a whole was scarcely noticed, or was attributed to 'the tradition' and therefore assumed to have no bearing on the evangelist's own concerns. On this understanding, whereas form-criticism had forgotten the evangelist in the search for the tradition, redaction-criticism had swung to the opposite extreme, and neither had been able to listen to the wholeness of the text as the evangelist intended it to be read.

If there is anything to be said for this emphasis, and I believe there is, then the loss of certainty about the nature and direction of literary dependence may not in fact be so disastrous for the study of the theology and purpose of the evangelists as Stanton's words quoted above might suggest. To approach Matthew without a firm conviction either of the priority of Mark or of that of Matthew does not prevent one from listening to his gospel as a whole, allowing it to make its own distinctive impact through its structure, its selection of themes, and its recurrent emphases. Nor does a suspension of judgement on the question of literary relationships prevent one from comparing Matthew fruitfully with each of the other gospels, not in terms of one of them 'using', 'following' or 'changing' another, but in order to see where the differences lie. To be unwilling to say that at this point Matthew has altered Mark's text (or vice versa) in a particular way does not disqualify one from noticing that they present the same story or the same teaching in different ways, and from drawing the appropriate conclusions as to their distinctive theological interests. That is what I shall be trying to do in much of this book!

Is this to 'play a violin with my left hand tied behind my back'? It is interesting that after making that comment Stanton goes on to

97. Ellis, *Matthew*, 174.

warn against the prevalent misuse of the traditional redaction-critical method.[98] He too appeals for attention to be given to the tradition Matthew retained as well as the changes he made; he points out the continuing areas of textual uncertainty, and the possibility of Matthew's Mark being different from the version that has come down to us; he suggests that Matthew's gospel may be 'the result of a much longer and a much more complex process than the "one-stage" redaction commonly envisaged' by redaction-critics. He also warns against the assumption that all alterations made by Matthew were made for specifically theological reasons, as well as the assumption that there must be a consistent pattern by which they can all be explained. 'Perhaps the evangelist was rather less consistent than some of his modern students.' These and other critical points add up to a substantial call for caution in drawing redaction-critical conclusions from the piecemeal study of 'changes' by the evangelist, and suggest a movement in the direct of a more 'holistic' appreciation of the evangelist's theology.

I believe, then, that an open verdict on the literary relationships of the synoptics is not a barrier to fruitful study of the distinctive methods and message of each of them. I hope that this book will give some indication of the appreciation of Matthew's theology which can be gained without assuming that Matthew was self-consciously writing a 'revised version of Mark'.

98. Stanton, 'Origin', 1896-1899.

❚❚

WHO WAS 'MATTHEW'?

The 'anonymity' of the gospels. Early church tradition on authorship.
Matthew the apostle. Individual authorship or a community product?
Authorship – can it be decided, and does it matter?

A. THE 'ANONYMITY' OF THE GOSPELS

It is conventionally stated that the four canonical gospels are anonymous. What is meant by this is that the author does not identify himself
by name in the course of the document, as for instance Paul does in
Romans 1:1 or 2 Corinthians 10:1, or John in Revelation 1:4,9. This
is a perfectly true observation (though the Fourth Gospel does include
an 'appendix' apparently identifying one of the characters in the narrative
as the author, without actually giving his name: John 21:24); but how
significant is it?

This sort of 'anonymity' is, after all, shared with the vast majority
of literary works. Except in the case of autobiographies or other works
concerned with events in which the author was himself involved, it is
not to the body of the work that we look for information on its
authorship, but to the title-page. The same is true of books in the
ancient world. Headings stating the authorship and circumstances of
composition are familiar from the books of the Old Testament, and
manuscripts written around the New Testament period also frequently
carry a heading (or a colophon at the end) identifying the work by
mentioning its (alleged) author.

The same is true of the gospels. In the earliest texts available in Greek
or in translation each of the gospels regularly carries a heading 'The
Gospel according to Matthew/Mark etc.'[1] There is no evidence for any
of the gospels ever existing without such a heading. Nor is there any
variation in the names of those to whom they are attributed.

New Testament scholarship has generally discounted these headings
for the purpose of determining the authorship of the gospels. They are

---

1. The form of the heading varies slightly, with the shorter form 'According to Matthew
(etc.)' occurring in the fourth century manuscripts Vaticanus and Sinaiticus, and longer
forms ('The Holy Gospel' etc.) in some later texts. But in all the early papyri which have
a title preserved, and in most of the subsequent manuscripts, the form is 'The Gospel
according to Matthew'.

assumed to be later additions, representing the belief of the church some time in the second century, and not to have any original connection with the gospels. The statement is frequently repeated, usually without discussion, that they came into use some time around AD 125.[2] While it may reasonably be suggested that titles added at that date would have been based on earlier traditions about authorship, the assumption seems to be generally made that before about 125 the gospels circulated anonymously.

The date AD 125 just mentioned is simply a scholarly guess, and is not meant to be more than an approximation.[3] It is early enough to allow for Papias' attribution of the first two gospels to Matthew and Mark around AD 140 (though the date would of course have to be brought forward if an earlier date for Papias is accepted, on which see later), and since there is no earlier external attribution to be accounted for there seems no reason to place the origin of the headings any earlier than 125. If, as is generally assumed, the attribution to Matthew is false, the longer the period between the original writing of the gospel and the addition of the superscriptions, the easier it becomes to explain the acceptance of a false attribution.[4]

But how likely is it (a) that gospels could have been in circulation for anything up to sixty years without a title, and (b) that titles could then have been attached uniformly to previously anonymous documents and so universally accepted that there is no trace of any rival attribution being even considered?

A recent carefully-documented attack on these scholarly assumptions has come from M. Hengel.[5] He considers the nature of references to the gospels in second-century Christian literature, and the general practice of book-distribution in the Greek world, where titles were necessary for identification of a work to which reference might be made. He recalls Tertullian's criticism of Marcion for publishing his 'Gospel' (his expurgated version of Luke) without the author's name, since no credence should be given to a book 'which does not hold its head up straight . . . and which makes no promise of reliability by the fulness of its title and the due acknowledgement of its author.'[6] He points out that when Christian writings began to be circulated, and especially to be used for reading in worship, titles with the name of the author would be needed to distinguish one from another as soon as a community

2. N.B. Stonehouse, *Origins of the Synoptic Gospels* (Grand Rapids: Eerdmans, 1963) 15-18 sums up the consensus for this date, and outlines some earlier discussions.
3. One scholar who attempts to be more specific is Bacon, *Studies*, 59, who traces the acceptance of this title to the council *de recipiendis libris* which he believes to have been held in Rome in AD 120; see above p. 16, n. 10.
4. See e.g. G.D. Kilpatrick, *The Origins of the Gospel according to St. Matthew* (Oxford: Clarendon, 1946) 4-6.
5. M. Hengel, *Studies in the Gospel of Mark* (ET, London: SCM, 1985) 64-84.
6. Tertullian, *Adv. Marcionem* IV 2.

possessed more than one such book ('as was certainly already the case round about 100');[7] indeed he argues that Christian 'community libraries' (for which presumably some handy method of identification of books would be essential) would already be in existence early in the second century. 'The titles were necessary for arranging the Gospels in community libraries and for liturgical reading. This is the only explanation for their great age and the complete unanimity in them towards the end of the second century.'[8]

It is this unanimity of attribution which leads Hengel to conclude that the titles cannot derive from 'some central redaction' in the second century, which could never have achieved such 'far-reaching success'. If the gospels had been originally anonymous there must inevitably have been some variation in the titles they eventually received (as did in fact happen with some second-century apocryphal gospels), but no such variation occurs. The titles must therefore 'go back to the time of the final redaction and first circulation of the Gospels themselves'.[9] They are, therefore, no more anonymous documents than any other book which names its author on the title page.

Even if Hengel is right about the date of origin of the gospel titles, of course, this does not in itself guarantee the truth of the attributions of authorship. Pseudonymity would still be a possibility to be reckoned with. But at least his argument would rule out the suggestion that the attributions were merely pious guesses at a time when the real origin of the gospels had long been forgotten.

Hengel's argument contains a number of statements as to what 'must have been' the case in the early Christian communities, and is open to challenge from those who propose another model. But his reconstruction is based on an extensive survey of the wider world of books and reading habits in the first century. If the theory of the anonymous circulation of gospels for a generation or two is to be established over against Hengel's model, it must be supported by an equally careful demonstration that such a procedure could 'make sense' in first-century Christianity. In recent scholarship no such demonstration seems to have been offered.

B. EARLY CHURCH TRADITION ON AUTHORSHIP

BEFORE PAPIAS

If Hengel's account of the gospel titles is correct, the discussion of this question usually begins in the wrong place. It is customary to start with Papias, as the first patristic writer whose explicit statements about the authorship of the first two gospels have been preserved. But if the

7. Hengel, *Studies*, 77.
8. *Ibid.* 81.
9. *Ibid.* 82

titles were already a part of the accepted text of the gospels from the earliest stage of their circulation, Papias represents only a relatively late reference to what was already common knowledge in all those churches to which the gospels had circulated. Far from being the originator of the tradition, on this view, Papias is the heir to a tradition already several generations old!

But that conclusion depends on the interpretation of κατὰ Ματθαῖον as an attribution of *authorship*, and that has been disputed. A typical account would be that of B.W. Bacon, who points out that in titles such as 'Gospel according to the Hebrews' or 'Gospel according to the Egyptians' the preposition obviously cannot indicate authorship. Rather he quotes Plummer for the view that it 'implies *conformity to a type*, and need not mean more than "drawn up according to the teaching of" ',[10] though both Bacon and Plummer accept that early Christian writers (especially Papias) did understand it as a statement of authorship. Hengel[11] agrees that κατά with the accusative is not in itself a simple statement of authorship, and indeed is rare in this sense in other Greek writings, but he draws attention to a parallel in the references of the Christian fathers to the alternative Greek versions of the Old Testament, where the *one* Old Testament is offered 'according to the Seventy', 'according to Aquila', 'according to Symmachus'; in such references κατά is to be understood as referring to the person (or group) responsible for producing the version concerned. Similarly in the case of the unique literary phenomenon whereby *one* 'gospel' is presented in four distinct versions, the unusual description of these as 'according to' those responsible for their production would be appropriate.

Undoubtedly κατά in itself *need not* be an attribution of authorship. But the fact that when used in relation to the four individuals after whom the versions of 'the gospel' are named it was apparently universally so understood in the early church from the time of Papias on surely places the burden of proof on those who suggest that it originally had a different meaning. And if that *is* what the phrase means, Hengel's argument would entail that the 'tradition' that Matthew was the author of the first gospel was already not only established but universally accepted long before Papias wrote his famous and ambiguous words on the subject.

THE SIGNIFICANCE OF PAPIAS

The earliest specific account of the authorship of the first two gospels is agreed to be that of Papias, a bishop of Hierapolis in Asia Minor.

10. Bacon, *Studies*, 28-29, quoting A. Plummer, *An Exegetical Commentary on the Gospel according to S. Matthew* (London: Robert Scott, 1909) vii.
11. *Studies*, 65-66.

None of Papias' writings has survived as such, but he was known to be the author of a treatise in five books entitled 'An Interpretation of the Oracles of the Lord' (*Λογίων κυριακῶν ἐξήγησις*), to which several later writers refer. It is from this work (the only work of Papias known to him) that Eusebius (*H.E.* III 39.14-16) quoted the two passages on the authorship of the gospels.

Eusebius himself had a very low view of Papias ('extremely weak in intelligence, as may be ascertained by his own words'!), but this seems to have been the result of his rejection of Papias' millenarian views as a literalistic misreading of the apostolic writings. More important, however, is the source of Papias' information.

Eusebius (*H.E.* III 39.1-7) first quotes Irenaeus to the effect that Papias was 'a hearer of John, an associate of Polycarp, an ancient man' ('ancient' represents *ἀρχαῖος*, presumably intended here to indicate one belonging to the immediately post-apostolic period, in contrast with Irenaeus himself, who claimed indirect contact with the apostolic generation through his early association with Polycarp). But Eusebius casts doubt on Papias' direct contact with the apostles (i.e. John), since he himself claimed only to have enquired from others what 'the elders' (he names Andrew, Peter, Philip, Thomas, James, John, Matthew and 'any other of the Lord's disciples') had taught (past tense) and what 'Aristion and the elder John, the Lord's disciples' were saying (present tense). From this Eusebius concludes (despite the statement of Irenaeus) that Papias was 'in no way a hearer or eyewitness of the holy apostles', and that the 'elder John' whom he had actually met and learned from (this is Eusebius' deduction – the words he quotes from Papias do not explicitly make this claim) was someone other than John the apostle. In this most modern scholarship has sided with Eusebius, placing Papias firmly in the generation subsequent to those who were personal followers of the apostles, and usually estimating his time of writing around AD 140 (thus making him a younger contemporary of Polycarp, who died about 155 at the age of eighty-six).

This now traditional dating of Papias is, however, only a guess based on the (not unbiased!) inferences of Eusebius. There is no independent evidence to corroborate this date, or Eusebius' view of Papias' place in the tradition, except perhaps a statement in Philip of Side, who wrote in the fifth century and probably depended on Eusebius, to the effect that Papias mentioned the beginning of the reign of Hadrian (AD 117). R.H. Gundry[12] points out an earlier passage in Eusebius (*H.E.* III 36.1-2) where Papias is associated with Ignatius (who died about 107), and argues that since Eusebius' discussion of Papias precedes his account of Trajan's persecution (about 110) he must in fact have understood him to have been writing before 110 (despite Philip of Side, whom

12. *Matthew*, 609-611.

Gundry believes to be inaccurate and confused). This would, of course, also fit Irenaeus' statement, which Eusebius quoted only to reject it.

But even if Papias' date should be placed as much as thirty years earlier than has become traditional, this does not in itself guarantee the validity of his information. He may still be, as Eusebius believed, and as he himself appears to indicate, quoting merely a second-hand report of the apostolic tradition, as received from the mysterious (but non-apostolic) 'elder John'. Here too, however, Gundry is not convinced.[13] He points out that Papias uses precisely the same terms ('elder' and 'disciples of the Lord') in referring to both the clearly apostolic group (Andrew, Peter, Philip, Thomas, James, John, Matthew) and to the John from whom his more recent information comes. (Aristion, on the other hand is, perhaps significantly, referred to as a 'disciple of the Lord' but not as an 'elder'.) The two groups (and the two 'Johns') are therefore not to be distinguished as representing different levels of tradition; rather the second reference to John is due to the fact that while the other apostles had died (or at least had not been known to Papias), Papias had heard John himself speaking in Asia Minor, so that the same 'elder John' who had been included in the first list as one of the apostolic group may be mentioned again as one who, together with Aristion, had continued to present the apostolic tradition within Papias' own circle. The 'elder John' is thus in fact no other than John the apostle.

In view of the major role which 'John the Elder' has come to play in modern discussion of the authorship of the Johannine writings of the New Testament, it may be worth while to point out that the *only* ground for believing in the existence of such a 'second John' at Ephesus is this passage of Eusebius, and that Eusebius' conclusion is an inference drawn entirely from the words of Papias and the fact that he knew of two 'tombs of John' in Ephesus.[14] It is therefore not as radical as it might at first seem to suggest that 'John the Elder' was a figment of Eusebius' imagination, particularly as he goes on to use this second John as a convenient candidate for authorship of the Book of Revelation, to avoid ascribing this rather embarrassing book to John the apostle!

So perhaps after all Irenaeus was right, and Papias *was* a 'hearer of John'. For what it is worth, there is further support of this tradition in the so-called 'Anti-Marcionite Prologue' to the gospel of John, which describes Papias as a 'beloved disciple of John', and as the amanuensis to whom John dictated his gospel. These prologues have

13. *Ibid.* 611-616.
14. Eusebius quotes a letter of Dionysius, bishop of Alexandria in the mid-third century, commenting on the two tombs supposedly of John, and suggesting that there may have been 'another John', though this is offered only as what he 'thinks', not as a tradition received.

been dated as early as the latter part of the second century (contemporary with Irenaeus), though others have placed them centuries later. Both their date and their origin are too uncertain to allow much weight to be placed on them.

On Gundry's view, then, what we have in the Papias quotations is, as Irenaeus' words would lead us to expect, the tradition as John the apostle himself passed it on in Ephesus. The introduction to Papias' account of Mark's gospel states explicitly that he is repeating what 'the Elder used to say', and that elder is the apostle John. While the account of Matthew carries no such introduction, it follows directly in Eusebius' text after that of Mark, and may therefore reasonably be assumed to derive from the same source. In that case what Papias offers us is an account of how one of the original apostolic group understood the first two gospels to have originated. And you cannot expect to get much closer to source than that![15]

There is room for considerable discussion of the details of Gundry's case, both with regard to the date of Papias and as to exactly what sort of relationship with John he claimed. But he has given good reason for questioning the traditional assumption that Papias' testimony represents a late and garbled version, based on a rather remote acquaintance with the beliefs of first-century Christians. Particularly when due allowance has been made for the bias of Eusebius against Papias, he may in fact be recognised as by far our best evidence for the earliest Christian understanding of the origin of the gospels.

PAPIAS AND THE ΛΟΓΙΑ

But to 'rehabilitate' Papias is not yet to answer the question of the authorship of the first gospel. The meagre fifteen words of his statement as quoted by Eusebius have been understood in many different ways, and on any interpretation they are hard to fit in with what we thought we knew from other sources. Something of their ambiguity may be gauged from the following (incomplete!) table of suggested meanings for the individual words he used.

Ματθαῖος	Matthew
μὲν οὖν	*(weak conjunction) – for his part *consequently (as a deliberate corrective to Mark's 'disorderly' account)
Ἑβραΐδι διαλέκτῳ	*in the Hebrew/Aramaic language *in a Semitic style

15. For a detailed argument reaching a similar conclusion see also C.S. Petrie, *NTS* 14 (1967/8) 15-27.

τὰ λόγια

*the oracles (meaning what?)
*the sayings (which?!)
*the gospel (not a normal meaning?)

συνετάξατο

*compiled/collected
*composed
*put in an orderly form (contrast Mark)

ἡρμήνευσεν δεαὐτα

*translated them
*interpreted them

ὡς ἦν δυνατὸ ς
εκαστο ς

everyone as best he could

Putting these various proposals for translating Papias' words together, we come up with several key questions as to his meaning:

1. Is this a detached statement about Matthew's work by itself, or is Papias explaining the nature of his work as a deliberate corrective to that of Mark, which is therefore assumed to have been written first? While Eusebius does not indicate the literary relation between the two passages of Papias which he quotes with reference to the work of Mark and Matthew respectively, it has been argued that he intended them to be seen as consecutive, and that the statement that Mark's gospel was written 'not in order' (τάξει) is intended to lead into the contrasting description of Matthew's gospel (συνετάξατο, 'put in order').[16] In that case there could be no doubt that Papias was talking about the gospel of Matthew as such, and he would have to be enrolled as an early (and totally isolated) witness to the priority of Mark.

2. Is Papias speaking of a document written in a Semitic language, which then had to be 'translated' into Greek by 'everyone as best he could'? Or is it possible to understand his words, as a few scholars have proposed, of a *Greek* document, written in a 'Semitic style', which then required careful 'interpretation'?[17] Most have concluded that, convenient as this understanding of Papias' words may be in order to avoid the awkward idea of an originally Semitic gospel, it is most unlikely that a Greek reader would naturally have understood the combination of Ἑβραΐδι διαλέκτῳ and ἑρμηνεύω of anything other than translation from one language to another.

3. What sort of literary activity is he describing, the compilation (as 'editor') of a collection of traditional material, or the composition (as 'author') of an original work? Perhaps in terms of the 'gospel-writing'

16. So e.g. Gundry, *Matthew*, 613-614.
17. So particularly J. Kürzinger in *BZ* 4 (1960) 19-38; *NTS* 10 (1963) 108-115, followed by Gundry, *Matthew*, 619-620.

activities of first-century Christians the difference is a matter of degree rather than of kind. The answer to this question in any case depends on the answer to the next and most difficult.

4. What is meant by τὰ λόγια? It seems clear that Eusebius understood him to be speaking of the gospel of Matthew, but is that what Papias in fact meant? Τὰ λόγια is not a normal way of referring to a 'gospel' – indeed as such it would be unique.[18] The evidence of the titles given to the gospels in early manuscripts indicates, as we have seen, that the normal descriptive term, already by the time of Papias, would have been τὸ εὐαγγέλιον. For this reason it is often suggested that Papias is referring to a Semitic collection of 'sayings of Jesus' (which is then sometimes identified as Q!), which may have been an important source of the Greek gospel of Matthew, but is not to be identified with it. Another suggestion, less frequently heard today, was that it referred to a collection of Old Testament testimonia in Hebrew which could then have formed the source for much of the scriptural material in the gospel of Matthew.

But it is not noted as often as it should be that Papias' use of τὰ λόγια with reference to the work of Matthew follows hard on a use of the same term with reference to Mark (at least in the sequence of Eusebius, whether or not this sequence represents the original pattern of Papias' work). Mark, he tells us, recorded from Peter's teaching 'the things either said or done by the Lord'; Peter's teaching, however, was given as need arose, 'not as if he were making an ordered collection (σύνταξις) of the Lord's oracles (τὰ κυριακὰ λόγια)', and that is why Mark's gospel lacked order (τάξις). There is no doubt that the reference here is to Mark's gospel as such, with its combination of 'things said and done by the Lord', and while the wording does not directly describe the gospel as τὰ λόγια, it is most naturally interpreted as describing Mark's work as a disorderly collection of τὰ κυριακὰ λόγια. If so, when we go on to read that Matthew by contrast τὰ λόγια συνετάξατο, 'put the λόγια in order', it is hard to avoid the conclusion that τὰ λόγια does mean the gospel of Matthew.

Λόγιον, usually translated 'oracle', is used of utterances of divine origin. In the Septuagint its use to denote 'words of the Lord' is not common, except in Psalm 119 where it is one of the regular synonyms for the 'word' or 'words' of God. In the New Testament the Old Testament is referred to as the λόγια of God (Rom. 3:2; cf. Acts 7:38, of the laws given at Sinai) but on two occasions the same phrase probably refers to Christian teaching understood as coming with divine authority (Heb. 5:12; 1 Pet. 4:11). In later Christian usage λόγιον continues to occur largely in the plural, in the majority of cases with

18. Lampe's *Patristic Greek Lexicon* offers as examples of the use of the phrase to refer to 'the gospels' only two phrases in the seventh century *Chronicon Paschale*.

reference to the Old Testament (in whole or in part),[19] but also in some cases apparently of the sayings of Jesus,[20] and in due course of the New Testament viewed as scripture together with the Old.[21] In the light of this usage it would seem that the phrase τὰ λόγια in itself should refer either to Old Testament prophecies or specifically to sayings of Jesus.[22] But, as we have seen, the phrase does not stand alone, and in the light of the use of the word in relation to Mark's account of the words *and deeds* of Jesus it is surely at least plausible that a reference in this way to the gospel of Matthew, already regarded as scripture, would be intelligible to his readers in the light of the wider context.

Another clue to the meaning of the term for Papias may be found in the title of the five-volume work from which the quotation comes, the Λογίων κυριακῶν ἐξήγησις.[23] As far as the actual words of the title are concerned, the linguistic evidence just considered suggests that it was most probably an exposition either of Old Testament proof-texts relating to Jesus or of recorded sayings of Jesus.[24] But the little we know of the contents of this work suggests that it may not have been so restricted in its scope. Eusebius tells us that Papias recorded from oral tradition such stories as a man raised from the dead and the harmless drinking of poison (both of these in the period of the post-Easter apostolic mission), together with 'some strange parables and teachings of the saviour, and other more mythical things', in particular his teaching of a millennial reign of Christ on this earth in bodily form; he also 'tells another story about a woman accused before the Lord of many sins, which the Gospel according to the Hebrews contains'.[25] Since Eusebius knew of no other work of Papias, these details are all presumably drawn from the Λογίων κυριακῶν ἐξήγησις. Philip of Side states that Papias talks of the martyrdoms of James and John in the second book of the same work, and mentions that Papias also records various miracles (apparently largely the same as those mentioned by Eusebius). Irenaeus[26] records from the fourth book Papias' teaching

19. The word occurs four times in 1 Clement, always of obedience to the λόγια of God, where the reference seems in all cases to be to Old Testament scripture.

20. The nearest parallel in time to Papias is in Polycarp's Epistle 7:1, but the λόγια τοῦ Κυρίου there referred to, which teach resurrection and judgement, could equally denote Christian teaching more generally rather than the sayings of Jesus as such. In 2 Clement 13:3-4 the λόγια τοῦ θεοῦ which Christians speak before the nations are illustrated by a loose quotation of the words of Jesus as recorded in Luke 6:32-35.

21. For full details see G.W.H. Lampe, *A Patristic Greek Lexicon* (Oxford: Clarendon, 1961) 805-806.

22. Lampe allows either of these meanings for the Papias text; he does not suggest that it could mean 'gospel' here.

23. Eusebius, *H.E.* III 39.1; the same title is recorded by Philip of Side, by Jerome in the Latin form *Explanatio sermonum Domini*, and by a number of later writers.

24. Jerome's translation of λόγια by *sermones* shows that he took it in the latter sense.

25. Eusebius, *H.E.* III 39.8-12,17.

26. *Adv. Haer.* V 33.3-4.

on the incredible fertility of the millennium, and his account of a
conversation between Jesus and Judas on the subject, while a fragment
of Apollinarius offers from Papias' fourth book a gruesome account
of the death of Judas.[27] The contents of Papias' work were therefore
quite varied, containing narrative as well as sayings material. While it
is possible that all these matters could have been included in an exposition
of the sayings of Jesus, it is perhaps more likely that Papias' own title
used λόγια in a broader sense, of the divinely inspired record of Jesus'
life and teaching (and even of subsequent events?). In that case, Eusebius
may not have been mistaken in assuming that when Papias spoke of
Matthew compiling the λόγια he was talking about a gospel record, not
just a collection of sayings.

The result of our consideration of these four questions, then, is the
belief that Eusebius correctly understood Papias to have taught (a) that
Matthew was responsible for the authorship of the first gospel (rather
than merely of a sayings-collection), and (b) that it was written in
Hebrew or Aramaic (for our purposes it does not matter which he
meant) and subsequently translated into Greek. And we have seen
reason to believe that Papias is a witness to be taken seriously.

And that means that Papias leaves us with a problem, to which we
shall have to return, in that modern scholarship is unanimous that the
gospel of Matthew as we know it is not a translation of a Semitic
document, but an original Greek work. But first we must see how both
parts of Papias' statement fared in subsequent patristic thought.

THE TRADITION AFTER PAPIAS

Both aspects of Papias' statement – authorship by Matthew and a
Semitic original – are regular features in subsequent patristic references
to the origin of the first gospel.

Irenaeus[28] is more explicit: 'Matthew produced a gospel in written
form (literally 'a writing, γραφή, of a gospel') among the Hebrews in
their own language (διάλεκτος again) at the time when Peter and Paul
were preaching the gospel and founding the church in Rome.' We shall
return later to the questions of the place of writing and the date, but
Irenaeus' view of the authorship and language are clearly the same as
those we found in Papias.

Tertullian, as we have noticed above,[29] while he gives no details of
the time or process of writing, affirms that among the gospel writers
two, John and Matthew, were apostles, the others 'apostolic men'.

27. All these texts are conveniently available in J.B. Lightfoot, *The Apostolic Fathers*
(London: Macmillan, 1891) 515-535.
28. *Adv. Haer.* III 1.1, quoted by Eusebius, *H.E.* V 8.2.
29. See above p. 13, n. 3.

Origen's commentaries on Matthew contained a brief account of the origins of all four gospels.[30] The account of the first gospel runs: 'The first to be written was that according to Matthew, once a tax-collector but later an apostle of Jesus Christ; he published it for those who had come to (Christian) faith from Judaism, and it was composed in Hebrew letters'. (The use of γράμματα, 'letters', would be unusual to denote a 'language', but presumably in the case of Hebrew, with its different script, this would be the meaning understood; I am not aware that it has been seriously suggested that he meant Greek transliterated into Hebrew characters!)[31] Here we have a more explicit identification of the author, together with an interesting suggestion as to the nature of the readership Matthew had in mind, to which we shall return.

The same interesting phrase 'in Hebrew letters' occurs in a report which Eusebius (*H.E.* V 10.3) quotes from Pantaenus, the Alexandrian church leader in the latter part of the second century, who travelled to India and found that he had been preceded there by the gospel of Matthew. Bartholomew the apostle had been and preached there, and had left for them 'the writing of Matthew in Hebrew letters'. Of what use such a document would have been to the Indians he does not explain!

Eusebius himself, besides quoting the accounts of others, sums up his own understanding of the matter in *H.E.* III 24.5-6: 'Among all those who were companions of the Lord only Matthew and John have left us their memoirs (ὑπομνήματα); and tradition has it that it was through force of circumstances that they turned to writing. For Matthew had preached at first to Hebrews, but when he was about to go off to others he handed on to them in writing the gospel according to his version, in his native language, and so by means of his writing made up for the lack of his own presence with those from whom he was being sent.'

With Jerome we come to a much fuller spelling out of the same traditions. 'Matthew, who is also called Levi, a former tax-collector then an apostle, first composed a gospel of Christ in Judaea, for the

---

30. Quoted by Eusebius, *H.E.* VI 25.3-6.
31. The phrase may perhaps be explained in the light of Jerome's account (*Contra Pelag.* III 2) of the Gospel according to the Hebrews, which he said was 'written in the Chaldaic and Syrian language, but in Hebrew letters' (and which was associated with Matthew). Aramaic (which is presumably what Jerome means by 'Chaldaic and Syrian') could be written in either the Syriac or the Hebrew alphabet, so that Origen's reference to 'Hebrew letters' may refer to an Aramaic gospel using the Hebrew alphabet. For the scripts in use in Aramaic of this period see J. Naveh, *Early History of the Alphabet* (Jerusalem: Magnes Press, 1982) esp. pp. 125-153; the range of scripts in use was in fact much wider than simply 'Syriac or Hebrew'! A suitable background for understanding Origen's comment may be provided by Naveh's statement that in the early Christian centuries under the influence of Edessa 'the Syriac script was also employed by the Palestinian Christians, although they spoke in a Western Aramaic dialect' (p. 147).

sake of those who had come to faith out of the circumcision, in Hebrew letters and words; who subsequently translated it into Greek is not known for sure. The Hebrew text itself is still preserved to this day in the library at Caesarea.'[32] He goes on to say that he has himself had access to it, and notes in particular the fact that in its Old Testament quotations it follows the Hebrew rather than the Septuagint.

In so far as the tradition can be traced up to the fourth century, then, it consistently ascribes the authorship of the first gospel to Matthew, who is generally identified as one of the apostles (and by Origen and Jerome as the former tax-collector) – and in the case of Papias and Irenaeus, who mention merely the name, it is reasonable to assume that it was this Matthew, the only one known to us in early church history, who was intended.

The other constantly recurring note is the belief that Matthew wrote in 'Hebrew' (or in 'Hebrew letters'). We must consider now how this tradition (and the actual Hebrew gospel of Matthew which Jerome saw) is to be reconciled with the general consensus that our gospel of Matthew was written in Greek, and is not a translation of a Semitic document.

'IN THE HEBREW LANGUAGE'?

It is of course not in itself improbable that Matthew (or any other of the early followers of Jesus for that matter) might have composed a gospel in Aramaic[33] (the language in which most of Jesus' ministry was probably conducted) for use in that part of the church which continued to speak Aramaic, and that it should subsequently be translated into Greek in order to gain a wider currency in the developing church. This is what the tradition we have been considering seems to have assumed, and it is an assumption which persisted, as we have seen,[34] at least until the end of the eighteenth century.

But, plausible as such a procedure may be, it does not seem to fit the facts. While even in this century a few have continued to argue for an Aramaic original for our present gospel of Matthew,[35] for most scholars it is now axiomatic that Matthew was written in Greek.

32. Jerome, *De Viris Illustribus* 3.

33. It is generally agreed that early Christian references to the 'Hebrew' language are likely to refer in at least some cases to Aramaic. While I have hitherto used the term 'Hebrew', because this is what the patristic writers actually said, from this point on I shall generally assume that what is in fact being talked about is Aramaic. Sometimes the term 'Semitic' will be used as a convenient umbrella term to cover both languages for our purpose.

34. See above p. 20.

35. C.F. Burney, *The Poetry of our Lord* (Oxford University Press, 1925); C.C. Torrey, *Our Translated Gospels* (London: Hodder & Stoughton, n.d.); P. Gaechter, *Die literarische Kunst im Matthäusevangelium* (Stuttgart: Katholisches Bibelwerk, 1966). This position was also held by A. Schlatter, and in a modified form by T. Zahn (see above pp. 23–24 for Bacon's comments). An unusual commentary on Matthew by G. Gander, *L'Evangile*

There are three main reasons for this conviction. The first is the assumed literary relationship with Mark. On the assumption that 'Matthew used Mark', the close verbal agreement virtually demands that Matthew was writing in Greek on the basis of a Greek Mark. Any other theory seems to require an unnecessarily complicated process whereby the translator of the Aramaic Matthew made constant reference to the Greek Mark. If on the other hand Mark was based on Matthew, it would be possible to argue that the verbal agreement is due to Mark's use of an already translated Matthew rather than the Aramaic original, and it is on this basis that Butler is favourably disposed to the tradition of an Aramaic Matthew.[36] If a less tidy and direct literary dependence is envisaged, as we have considered above, there is perhaps a little more room for manoeuvre, but the degree of Greek verbal similarity between the two gospels remains most easily explained by their both having originated in Greek.

Secondly, despite Jerome's comments on Matthew's use of the Hebrew rather than the Septuagint in his Old Testament quotations, it is in fact true that a large part of the Old Testament material in Matthew is Septuagintal. In a few cases it has been suggested that the argument depends on a distinctively Septuagintal text, though this argument is open to question when it is recognised that even in those passages where the Septuagint seems peculiarly appropriate to the application Matthew gives to the text the same point could have been made (with admittedly less sharpness) from the Hebrew or targumic text.[37] It is of course likely that a translator of an Aramaic Matthew into Greek would consciously conform all the Old Testament quotations to the Septuagint, as the version familiar in the church for which he was translating. But in that case we would expect a uniformly Septuagintal text-form, whereas what we in fact find in Matthew is a bewildering variety of text-forms, from the purely Septuagintal to the totally eccentric, and including some prominent quotations which, as Jerome noticed, seem closer to the Hebrew than to the Septuagint.[38] This mixed text-form, to which we shall return in a later chapter, is more plausible as the procedure of a writer in Greek who was familiar with Semitic forms of the text than as that of a translator.

de l'Eglise (Aix-en-Provence: Faculté Libre de Théologie Protestante, 1970) draws its material primarily from the Syriac versions rather than the Greek text, on the basis that 'Matthew's account, according to patristic writings, was first compiled in that language', an opinion which the author apparently accepts.
36. Butler, Originality, 164-166. He does not argue the case in detail.
37. I have argued this point at length with regard to the quotations attributed to Jesus in all the synoptic gospels in my Jesus and the Old Testament (London: Tyndale Press, 1971) chapter 2 and Appendix B, especially pp. 32-37, 247-258.
38. Jerome (De Viris Illustribus 3) singled out Mt. 2:15 and 2:23 for mention in this connection, though the latter in fact conforms to no known Old Testament text, Hebrew or Greek!

Thirdly there is the point that, while at certain points in the sayings of Jesus it is possible to reconstruct an Aramaic original with some conviction,[39] the gospel of Matthew as a whole does not read like translation Greek. The clearly Semitic turns of phrase and other features suggesting an Aramaic origin are largely confined to the sayings-material rather than to the narrative,[40] and even in the sayings-material it is seldom that one may appropriately speak of 'translation Greek', since 'the "translation" is not literal but literary'.[41] C.F.D. Moule's study of 'Translation Greek and Original Greek in Matthew'[42] notes the presence of clear 'Semitisms' in Matthew's editorial writing as well as in the sayings-material, but concludes that these are deliberately introduced for effect by a writer who is capable of writing good idiomatic Greek, and in fact does so elsewhere in the gospel.

In the light of these features, while it is highly likely that, at least in some of the sayings-material, Matthew was dependent on Aramaic sources, the conclusion that the gospel itself was originally written in Greek seems well founded. Even L. Vaganay, who believes in an original Aramaic 'proto-Matthew',[43] sees the canonical Matthew as a Greek work based on an earlier Greek translation of the Aramaic document. Others such as Black are content to talk of Aramaic sources rather than an Aramaic gospel. If Papias and those who followed him really did mean that the canonical gospel of Matthew was originally composed in Aramaic, modern scholarship, with very few exceptions, would agree that they were wrong.

If this tradition was mistaken, how could such a mistake have arisen?

It may have been a pure guess, based on the assumption that since Jesus and his apostles had spoken Aramaic rather than Greek as their native language, an account of Jesus and his teaching by one of those apostles must surely have been in Aramaic. Another basis for such a guess would be the clearly 'Jewish' character of the gospel of Matthew by comparison with the other gospels (a subject to which we shall return). Here is a gospel which devotes more space than the others to quotation of and meditation on the Old Testament, which is saturated with Old Testament language, which presents fuller accounts of Jesus' debates with the scribal and other Jewish authorities, and focuses more

39. Such 'back-translations' into Aramaic have been attempted by several twentieth-century scholars, notably C.F. Burney, *The Poetry of our Lord*; M. Black, *An Aramaic Approach to the Gospels and Acts* (Oxford: Clarendon, ³1967); J. Jeremias, *New Testament Theology 1: The Proclamation of Jesus* (ET, London: SCM, 1971) 1-37.
40. This is the conclusion of M. Black, *Approach*, 271-274, from which he concludes that all four gospels depended on an Aramaic sayings-source or sources, but not on Aramaic narrative-sources.
41. *Ibid.* 274-276.
42. C.F.D. Moule, *The Birth of the New Testament* (London: A. & C. Black, ³1981) 276-280. The discussion is undertaken in the light of the Papias tradition.
43. See above pp. 42-43.

on questions of Jewish legal observance and rabbinic discussion. Might it not be natural (particularly for those in Asia Minor and beyond, who may not have been aware of the extent to which Greek was spoken in Palestine) to assume that such a gospel originated in Aramaic (in the same way that the 'Jewish' features of the gospel have led some scholars to the conclusion that its author was a converted rabbi)? Once the idea was established (on the same basis?) that the gospel was written 'among the Hebrews' (i.e. in Palestine, presumably), this assumption would be the more easily made.[44]

So it may have been simply a guess. But it is possible that there was more to it than that. There is reason to believe that by the early second century there was at least one other 'gospel' in wide circulation which was in Aramaic or Hebrew, and which seems sometimes to have been associated with the apostle Matthew.

We have already noted the existence of a 'Gospel according to the Hebrews'. This is frequently referred to, and occasionally quoted, by patristic writers from at least as early as the late second century.[45] There are other references to a 'Gospel of the Nazaraeans' and a 'Gospel of the Ebionites' through the same period, and it is not easy to ascertain whether these were all separate documents, or whether two or more are alternative names for the same writing.[46] While many patristic writers refer to such a gospel, the most explicit accounts are in Epiphanius and Jerome. Epiphanius says that the Ebionites, whom he regards as heretical, based their teaching on a 'Gospel of Matthew' which they themselves called 'according to the Hebrews', which was in Hebrew, but which Epiphanius himself regards as 'falsified and mutilated': in particular he claims that it lacks the genealogy of Jesus, and in fact begins with John the Baptist. This account is supported by the fact that Irenaeus had earlier stated that the Ebionites used only the gospel of Matthew, but that they denied the virgin birth, so that presumably their 'Gospel of Matthew' lacked the first chapter at least. Jerome frequently refers to a 'Gospel according to the Hebrews' which he claims to have translated himself into both Greek and Latin. He associates it with the Nazaraeans, and it was the Nazaraeans who he claims gave him permission to copy the Hebrew original of the Gospel of Matthew. Yet the passages he quotes from the Gospel according to the Hebrews are clearly not from

44. There is an interesting example of such conclusions about original language being drawn from the tradition of place of writing in the Armenian version of Ephraem's commentary on Tatian's *Diatessaron* (as cited in Aland's *Synopsis*, 544), where it is stated that Matthew wrote in Hebrew, Mark (in Rome) in Latin, and Luke in Greek.
45. Such references are conveniently collected by W.C. Allen, *The Gospel according to S. Matthew* (ICC. Edinburgh: T. & T. Clark, ³1912) lxxxi-lxxxiii.
46. For a full discussion of the problems of identification, and of the relevant patristic references see P. Vielhauer, 'Jewish-Christian Gospels' in E. Hennecke (ed.), *New Testament Apocrypha*, vol. 1 (ET, London: Lutterworth, 1963) 118-139.

the canonical Matthew. Here, then, there is good reason to suspect a confusion between the assumed original Hebrew Matthew and a separate but related 'Gospel according to the Hebrews' which was in fact preserved in Hebrew/Aramaic.[47]

The situation is unclear in several ways, but there is enough common ground among the various patristic references to indicate the existence of at least one Semitic gospel in use among Jewish-Christian groups (Ebionites and Nazaraeans) which they associated with the name of Matthew, but which was in fact different from the canonical Gospel of Matthew. In that case it is at least possible that the tradition that the canonical Matthew was written in a Semitic language arose from a confusion such as we see in the case of Jerome.

Whatever the reason, it seems that the widespread tradition of the original language of Matthew was wrong. Does this then mean that the other main feature of that tradition, the apostolic authorship of the first gospel, is also not to be trusted? I suppose it is fair to claim that if they could be wrong on one score they could be wrong on another. But these two aspects of the tradition, while they regularly occur together, are not logically connected. Neither depends on the other (unless it is assumed that the apostle Matthew cannot have been fluent in Greek, an assumption which few would defend today in the light of the increasing evidence for at least a bilingual situation in first-century Palestine, particularly in Galilee). Each traditional claim must be examined on its own merits.

What then can be said for the claim that the apostle Matthew was the author of the first gospel? It is an early and unanimous tradition, but could it, like the notion of a Semitic original, be based on a misunderstanding?

C. MATTHEW THE APOSTLE

Matthew is not one of the better known of Jesus' first followers. In fact all that is known about him from the New Testament is that he was a tax-collector in Capernaum, that he was also called Levi, that he was one of the twelve, and (at least this seems a reasonable assumption!) that he was a Jew. All of these facts have featured in the discussion of his candidature for the authorship of the first gospel.

THE TAX-COLLECTOR OF CAPERNAUM

Assuming for the moment the identity of the Levi whom Jesus called from the tax-office in Mark 2:14 and Luke 5:27 with the Matthew who

---

47. For quotations and discussion of the relevant material from Epiphanius see Vielhauer, *ibid.* 123-126, and for Jerome, *ibid.* 126-136.

is described in the same words in Matthew 9:9, and with the 'Matthew the tax-collector' of Matthew 10:3, does Matthew's profession as a τελώνης, a minor local official responsible for the collection of customs dues on goods in transit,[48] have any bearing on the tradition of his authorship of the first gospel?

Firstly it has been claimed that certain features of the gospel of Matthew betray the specialist interest in matters of money and trade which might be expected of a customs official.[49] It is true that a number of passages peculiar to Matthew do involve financial transactions: Gundry mentions 17:24-27; 18:23-35; 20:1-16; 27:3-10; 28:11-15, to which we might add the 'thirty pieces of silver' in 26:15. But none of these betrays a specialist knowledge of the customs system, and it would be hazardous to suggest that one who records stories involving money is thereby revealing a professional interest.

Secondly a tax-collector must keep records and make up accounts, and so was necessarily literate and reasonably educated. In order to carry on this business in Capernaum, a border town between Antipas' Galilee and the territories of Philip to the north-east, he must be fluent in both Aramaic and Greek (as indeed was probably true of most of the population of Galilee at that time). These factors are at least consonant with the authorship of a Greek gospel which drew on Aramaic source-material.

But it has also been suggested that a tax-collector was peculiarly well-equipped for this role, since he was likely to be not only literate, but skilled in a sort of short-hand for the quick recording of transactions. A man with this skill would be ideally suited to the role of 'recorder' in the disciple group, and so it may be to the instant short-hand notes of Matthew the 'secretary' that we owe the gospel record of Jesus' teaching, subsequently written up by this same Matthew into the full gospel.[50] Goodspeed has assembled impressive evidence for the use of short-hand on quite a large scale in the Roman world of this period, but it can of course be only a matter of speculation whether a minor local customs official in Galilee could be expected to have this skill. The fact that no hint of such a role for Matthew occurs in the gospel records (or indeed in the subsequent church tradition which we have considered) must count against the suggestion.

48. Galilee under Antipas was not yet subject to direct Roman taxation. For a useful general account of customs and taxes in Palestine at this period see E. Schürer, *The History of the Jewish People in the Age of Jesus Christ*, vol. 1 (ET, new edition, Edinburgh: T. & T. Clark, 1973) 372-376.
49. So Gundry, *Matthew*, 620.
50. So E.J. Goodspeed, *Matthew, Apostle and Evangelist* (Philadelphia: J.C. Winston, 1959), followed by R.H. Gundry, *The Use of the Old Testament in St. Matthew's Gospel* (Leiden: Brill, 1967), 182-185. Gundry has not repeated this suggestion in the discussion of authorship in his subsequent commentary.

Another scholar who has drawn attention to the possibly 'secretarial' role of an ex-tax-collector is C.F.D. Moule,[51] though he would not wish to be associated with Goodspeed's theory as such. He suggests that the scribe (γραμματεύς) turned disciple pictured in 13:52 (often described as the author's self-portrait) should not be understood, as commentators regularly do, of a rabbinic scribe, but of a 'scribe in the secular sense', a well-educated writer. He goes on:

> The writer of the Gospel was himself a well-educated, literate scribe in this sense. But so must also have been that tax-collector who was called by Jesus to be a disciple. Is it not conceivable that the Lord really did say to that tax-collector Matthew: You have been a 'writer' (as the Navy would put it); you have had plenty to do with the commercial side of just the topics alluded to in the parables – farmer's stock, fields, treasure-trove, fishing revenues; now that you have become a disciple, you can bring all this out again – but with a difference.

Moule suggests that this 'scribe' Matthew (the apostle) was responsible for a collection of Aramaic traditions, which were subsequently worked over, with other material, by 'another scribe, a Greek writer' to form the present gospel of Matthew. Moule is not, therefore, arguing for apostolic authorship of the canonical Matthew, but for a major place for the former tax- collector in the formation of the gospel precisely because of his distinctive professional skills.

None of this adds up to any sort of proof of authorship, but at least we may suggest that the little we know about the individuals who made up the original apostolic group indicates that Matthew was better equipped than most by his previous profession for the role of gospel-writer.

However, there is another feature of the tax-collector's role which may seem to point the other way. By virtue of his involvement with the imperial system (even though, in Matthew's case, only indirectly through the régime of Antipas) a Jewish τελώνης was not accepted into orthodox Jewish society (in the case of Matthew this is made very clear in the story of the sequel to his call by Jesus, Mark 2:15-16).[52] He would seem to be as far removed as possible from the religious establishment, and therefore could hardly be expected to be well versed in rabbinic debate, as the author of Matthew is generally thought to have been. If the characteristics of the gospel could lead E. von Dobschütz

---

51. C.F.D. Moule, 'St. Matthew's Gospel: Some Neglected Features', *Studia Evangelica* II (TU 87. Berlin: Akademie-Verlag, 1964), 90-99; reprinted in Moule's *Essays in New Testament Interpretation* (Cambridge University Press, 1982) 67-74.
52. For the status of τελῶναι in society see Jeremias, *NT Theology*, 110-111.

to conclude that its author must have been a converted rabbi,[53] it can hardly be credible to propose that it was written by a tax-collector! This objection takes us to the heart of the paradox of Matthew, to which we shall return in the next chapter. The evident knowledge of and interest in matters of Jewish law and scripture is balanced by a clear dissociation from the religious establishment, and indeed in a way from Judaism as such. So marked is this feature that some scholars have swung to the opposite extreme from von Dobschütz in suggesting that the author was in fact an anti-Jewish Gentile. We shall consider this view in due course, but for the moment this polarisation of scholarly opinion serves to illustrate a tension within the gospel of Matthew which might be thought to fit rather well with the situation of a Jewish τελώνης, ostracised by the religious leadership of his own people, yet personally strongly conscious of his Jewishness.

MATTHEW AND LEVI

We have assumed so far that the name Levi which Mark and Luke use in their accounts of the call of the tax-collector disciple is an alternative name of Matthew, whom both of them include in their lists of the twelve (Mark 3:18; Luke 6:15; Acts 1:13) and whom Matthew in his version of that list identifies as the τελώνης (Matthew 10:3). Since no Levi occurs in the lists of Mark and Luke, and since the stories told of the calls of Levi and of Matthew are clearly the same, this seems the most economical explanation.[54]

Albright and Mann[55] have suggested that 'Matthew' and 'Levi' are not simply two alternative personal names of the same individual, but that 'Matthew' is his name and 'Levi' his tribe. He is 'Matthew the Levite'. As there were by this time more Levites than the conduct of temple worship required, some would need to seek a livelihood elsewhere. Matthew turned to tax-collecting, and in so doing forfeited the respect of his fellow-Levites, with their orthodox, Pharisaic background. This combination of an ecclesiastical education and interest with a personal estrangement from the religious establishment would fit the character of the gospel of Matthew admirably.

53. Von Dobschütz' famous essay appears in English in Stanton, *Interpretation*, 19-29.
54. For the possibility of two Semitic names being held by the same person, see Simon/Kepha (Peter), and for other examples drawn from inscriptions see W.L. Lane, *The Gospel according to Mark* (Grand Rapids: Eerdmans, 1974) 100-101, n. 29. This renders unnecessary the proposal of R. Pesch, *ZNW* 59 (1968) 40-56, adopted e.g. by F.W. Beare, *The Gospel according to Matthew* (Oxford: Blackwell, 1981) 224-225, that Levi is the true name, and that the first evangelist, wishing to identify this otherwise unknown 'disciple' as one of the twelve, substituted the name of a totally obscure member of the apostolic list, Matthew, whom he then dubbed τελώνης.
55. Albright & Mann, *Matthew*, CLXXVII- CLXXVIII, CLXXXIII-CLXXXIV.

This interesting theory depends on confusion at some stage in the tradition. Albright and Mann assume that, owing to 'the widespread disuse of the definite article in Aramaic in the NT period', a scribe or translator into Greek found himself confronted by 'Levi', meaning 'the Levite' and took it for a personal name. Some such explanation would be needed, since the Greek name 'Levi' is used always as a personal name (and not an uncommon one), not as an equivalent for 'Levite'. But even if this be granted, it is surely a problem for this theory that none of the New Testament texts offer the two 'names' together in a form which could have originated as 'Matthew the Levite'. We must assume on this theory that in the story as recorded by Mark and Luke the tax-collector was identified simply as 'the Levite' (or that another name was originally present and was dropped out after Levi was taken to be a personal name). There is also the question whether a Levite would at this period have sought or accepted employment as a tax-collector. Altogether, attractive as the theory is from the point of view of explaining the paradoxical character of Matthew, it remains at best speculative.

MATTHEW THE JEW

The local τελῶναι, as opposed to those responsible for tax collection for a whole province, were normally local people, familiar with the language and life-style of those with whom they had to deal. Matthew would therefore presumably be a Galilean Jew, as indeed were all Jesus' inner circle of twelve disciples, with the possible exception of Judas Iscariot. Both his names Matthew and Levi are Jewish names.

It has become a matter of lively debate whether the first gospel can be attributed to a Jewish Christian author. At the one extreme was the argument of von Dobschütz,[56] to which we have already referred, to the effect that such a gospel could have been written only by someone well versed by personal experience in the culture and concerns of rabbinic Judaism, whom von Dobschütz goes on to identify as a converted rabbi, and perhaps a former pupil of Johanan ben Zakkai. At the other extreme stands the quite substantial body of recent opinion which identifies the (final) author as a Gentile who had no personal sympathy with, or even close knowledge of, Judaism.[57] We shall return to this view in the next chapter and until we have discussed it there any conclusions reached here on the basis of the supposed nationality of the author must remain tentative.

56. E. von Dobschütz, 'Matthäus als Rabbi und Katechet', *ZNW* 28 (1927) 338-348; English translation in Stanton, *Interpretation*, 19-29.
57. So for instance K.W. Clark, P. Nepper-Christensen, G. Strecker, S. Van Tilborg. For details see below pp. 102-108.

This suggestion of a Gentile author appears surprising at first sight in view of the actual contents of the first gospel, which have led some to describe it as the most Jewish book of the New Testament. It can be held only by supposing a process of composition which began in a Jewish milieu, but then involved a later redactor with a very different background. Such a process of composition is felt to be necessary in order to account for the tensions which most interpreters find in Matthew between its evident 'Jewishness' and the extremely harsh and sometimes apparently gratuitous attacks on the Jewish leaders and even apparently on the Jewish race itself which have been introduced. A gospel which can depict Jesus at the same time as sent only to Israel (15:24) and as envisaging the coming of people from east and west into the Jewish messianic banquet (8:11-12); which in 10:5-6 can forbid the disciples to extend their mission beyond Israel and in 28:19 can send them to all nations; which can at the same time endorse the authority of the Jewish scribes (23:2-3) and denounce them in the rest of the chapter as hypocrites and rebels against God now ripe for final judgement – such a gospel, it is suggested, cannot have come from a single hand, but must represent different and indeed contradictory stages of Christian self-understanding vis-à-vis Judaism.

This is perhaps the central problem of Matthean studies. In the next chapter we shall be considering whether it is possible to envisage a life-setting in which these apparently incompatible elements could coexist, and shall be trying to account for the relation in which Matthew and his church stood to the Jewish faith and nation. In later chapters we shall be concerned more deeply with the theological basis of Matthew's understanding of Jesus and his church in relation to the Old Testament and to the continuing life of Israel. All this later discussion must be presupposed in a full answer to our present question about the authorship of the gospel. I shall be arguing that the paradoxes, even apparent contradictions, of Matthew are best accounted for not by successive editions of the gospel at the hands of redactors of conflicting sympathies, but by the painful tensions in the real-life situation of a Jewish Christian who at the same time sees in Jesus and his church the fulfilment of all that God has done and promised for Old Testament Israel and yet recognises that the Israel of his day has not, as a whole, responded to this final divine initiative, and indeed has met the Son of God with violent rejection and abuse. The mixture of 'Jewishness' and 'anti-Jewishness', I shall be suggesting, results not from literary incompetence, but from the existential situation of first-century Jewish Christianity.[58]

58. An interesting specific suggestion for the life-setting of the gospel was offered by E.P. Blair, *Jesus in the Gospel of Matthew* (Nashville: Abingdon, 1960), especially pp. 142-161, in his proposal that its outlook should be seen as one of 'a kind of reforming

For the moment all this must be taken on trust. But if the position I shall be offering has any validity, then to attribute the first gospel to a Galilean Jew who became a follower of Jesus is entirely plausible. Indeed the peculiar character of the gospel's attitude to Judaism seems to me virtually to *demand* some such person as author. If the understanding of Matthew's theology which I shall be presenting is anywhere near right, its very centre lies in the specific concerns of Israel as the people of God. A Gentile Christian writer might well develop an interest in such questions, as part of his attempt to understand the roots of his religion (as indeed Gentile Christians like you and me can do today); but I believe that the sense of personal involvement, one might almost say 'passion', with which these issues are handled in the first gospel goes too far beyond a mere academic curiosity to be attributed to a Gentile sympathiser.

I have specified that Matthew the tax-collector was a *Galilean* Jew. Is this distinction important? Is it possible to discern in the way the story is told, and in particular in the attitude to the Jewish leaders in Jerusalem, the special interests (prejudices?) of a Galilean, who has seen his Galilean master destroyed by the hostility of the Jerusalem establishment? There has been an increasing awareness in recent scholarship[59] of the distinctiveness of Galilee in the first century, and of the fact that to lump Galileans and Judaeans together as 'Jews' (even 'Palestinian Jews') may be no more culturally or politically correct than the tendency of North Americans to describe the Scots and the Welsh as 'English'! We shall note later the significance of Galilee for Matthew's theology;[60] the 'Galilean' features of the gospel which I shall suggest at that point may be a further reason for taking the tax-collector of Capernaum seriously as a candidate for the authorship of the gospel.

I believe, then, that the nature of the gospel points not only to a Jewish Christian tradition as the source of much of its material, but also to a Jewish Christian as the author in the fullest sense, as the one responsible for the final shape and 'tone' of the gospel. And in so far as it is possible to discern distinctively Galilean overtones in the work,

or nonconformist Judaism', parallel to that of the Hellenist group to which Stephen belonged, with its radical stance towards the temple, and comparable also with the similarly anti-establishment position of Qumran. He suggests that the author belonged to the 'Jewish-Christian "Hellenist" group of Jerusalem' associated with Stephen (a group to which he also traces the gospel of John). While Blair's specific identification of the Jewish group concerned has not been accepted, he has appropriately reminded us that the sort of love-hate relationship with official Judaism which we find in Matthew reflects a real current in what is known of first-century Judaism.

59. See esp. G Vermes, *Jesus the Jew* (London: Collins, 1973) chapter 2; E.M. Meyers & J.F. Strange, *Archaeology, the Rabbis and Early Christianity* (London: SCM, 1981) chapter 2; and especially the major study by S Freyne, *Galilee from Alexander the Great to Hadrian, 323 B.C.E. to 135 C.E.* (Wilmington: Michael Glazier, 1980).

60. See below pp. 138-139, 225.

the plausibility of the ascription to Matthew of Capernaum is strength-ened.

MATTHEW THE APOSTLE

The presence of Matthew in the list of the Twelve has been used as an argument against his authorship of the gospel.

On the assumption that the gospel was originally anonymous, it may be suggested that its association with Matthew was due merely to the desire to find an apostolic name to attach to it in order to enhance its authority in the church. Among the Twelve, Matthew would have no special claim to be so honoured, since he was almost as obscure as any of the others. But the fact that this gospel alone has an account of the call of Matthew under that name might be sufficient reason to posit him as its author. In other words, the association of the gospel with Matthew is due to his presence in the apostolic list rather than to any historical association he may have had with the book.

But we have seen above that the assumption of the anonymous circulation of gospels, after which names were attached to them purely by guesswork, is historically improbable. It is more plausible to suggest that it was pseudonymously attributed to Matthew by the original author, and that in the course of the church's use of this gospel as that of 'Matthew', what began as a literary fiction came to be accepted as fact. Certainly an apostle would be a suitable candidate for such pseudonymous attribution, though perhaps it might have been expected that one of the more prominent members of the group might be chosen. But this depends on whether there are good reasons to see the gospel as pseudonymous in the first place. The mere fact that it is attributed to an apostle does not carry this corollary by itself, unless it is accepted as an axiom of New Testament scholarship (and sometimes one almost gets the impression that it is) that no apostle can ever have turned his hand to writing!

Another argument against Matthew's authorship which is regularly offered is that it is inconceivable that an apostle could base his work on that of Mark, who was not an apostle. This argument has been repeated so often that it seems sometimes to be taken as self-evident. But really it is quite an extraordinary assertion. For one thing it depends entirely on the theory that Matthew was literarily dependent on Mark, and that, as we have seen, is a major question in itself. But even if that hypothesis be accepted, why should an apostle not make use of the work of someone else, provided of course that he accepted it as a correct and appropriate account from which to work? Modern ideals of literary originality and the stigma of 'plagiarism' are quite inappropriate to the first-century world, and the notion that an apostle would regard himself as somehow in a class apart from ordinary mortals shows just how far we have moved away from the value-scale which Jesus himself inculcated into Matthew and his colleagues!

Or is the argument based on the assumption that an apostle, having been personally present during Jesus'ministry, would not need to rely on *any* other source than his own memory? That will depend of course on the extent of the individual's involvement, and on the effectiveness of his memory; it is questionable whether apostleship may be assumed to have carried with it guaranteed powers of recall. But again it is in any case quite gratuitous to assume that one who was present for the events and teaching recorded would therefore not wish to avail himself of a ready-made framework which he could modify or expand on the basis of his own knowledge as appropriate.

A further factor is the tradition, again uniformly repeated from Papias onwards, that the source of Mark's record was the teaching of Peter. This is not the place to argue the case, but this tradition also is not inherently improbable, and if we were right to suggest that Papias' account of Matthew deserves greater credence than it is sometimes given, the same must apply to his account of Mark. In that case, Mark's gospel would have been recognised as apostolic in content, so that even if the odd idea that an apostle would have qualms about using a non-apostolic source were accepted, it would not be relevant to the case of Matthew and Mark. If Matthew recognised in Mark's gospel the reminiscences of the leader of the apostolic group, and one who on a number of occasions occupied a privileged place in relation to Jesus, it can hardly be supposed that he would regard this as an inappropriate basis for his own account.

We have now considered the meagre individual knowledge that we have of Matthew the apostle. It does not add up to an impressive body of evidence, and the arguments which have been built up around it have probably squeezed the last drop of significant data out of it – and a good deal more besides! But I have tried to show that, for what they are worth, these few facts about Matthew do not in any way rule out his candidature for the authorship of the first gospel, and in some ways suggest that he is better qualified for that role than most others known to us in the first-century church.

There is of course no compelling reason why the author of this document need be someone whose name is known to us from the New Testament record. But when the unanimous tradition of the post-apostolic church names Matthew as the author, and when we have reason to believe that that tradition can be traced back into the first century, common sense (even if not critical orthodoxy) might suggest that it could be right.

D. INDIVIDUAL AUTHORSHIP OR A COMMUNITY PRODUCT?

In this chapter so far I have assumed that it is appropriate to speak of the first gospel as the work of 'an author', and to discuss the possible identity of that author as an individual. This assumption has been shared by most recent writers on Matthew. Many have spoken of successive editions of the gospel, involving perhaps a final redactor whose outlook differed significantly from that of the work he was revising, and most have assumed tnat behind the gospel as we have it lie various sources, written or oral, most of which are no longer accessible to us. But it has been assumed that the final form of the work is the product of a single mind, and one which is sufficiently distinctive to allow us to analyse 'the theology of Matthew'.

But it has not always been so. G.D. Kilpatrick's important study of Matthew[61] concentrates on the role of the gospel in the life of the church out of which it came. It is a liturgical production, 'compiled out of materials which had already been read and expounded in the services of the church', and itself designed to fulfil the same role more fully. Three factors played a part in the creation of the gospel: firstly the source material which was already in use in the church, secondly 'the circumstances of its creation', and thirdly the contribution of the evangelist himself. The second of these factors is considered in a chapter devoted to discussing the nature of 'the community of the gospel', i.e. the church situation in which and for which it was designed. When Kilpatrick eventually comes to consider the evangelist himself,[62] while he recognises that 'circumstances and communities do not create books of themselves', and that the broad literary structure of the gospel in particular must be attributed to the individual design of the evangelist, he nonetheless finds it hard to 'disentangle' his specific contribution, since 'his outlook is very like that of the community for which he wrote'. He was a scribe working in and for the community, and it is likely that he did not write on his own initiative, but that it was an official task entrusted to him by the church leadership. The deliberately pseudonymous attribution to Matthew (on the basis of which the gospel carried the heading κατὰ Ματθαῖον from the beginning) was made with the church's authority, hence its wide acceptance. The result of this reconstruction is that the author has become a faceless church scribe, whose individuality is submerged in the distinctive outlook of the church which he represents.

An even more radical erosion of the individuality of the author was

---

61. G.D. Kilpatrick, *The Origins of the Gospel according to St. Matthew* (Oxford: Clarendon, 1946).
62. *Ibid.* 135-139.

proposed by K. Stendahl,[63] on the grounds that 'in the light of form-criticism, the conception of individual authorship, while it does not disappear, is felt to be an oversimplified approach to the gospels' (p. 11). Without wishing to deny 'the old concept of individual authorship' altogether, Stendahl's emphasis falls entirely on the origin of the gospel as 'a handbook issued by a school' (pp. 20-29). Its characteristics point not so much to a liturgical origin as to 'a milieu of study and instruction', which Stendahl finds paralleled most closely in the community life and scriptural study of the Qumran sect, out of which came works like the commentary on Habakkuk, whose approach to the Old Testament Stendahl finds closely parallel to that of Matthew. 'Thus the Matthaean school must be understood as a school for teachers and church leaders, and for this reason the literary work of that school assumes the form of a manual for teaching and administration within the church.' (p. 35) Matthew the author is himself therefore of no more individual importance than the unknown members of the Qumran community who produced that sect's uniformly anonymous writings.[64]

Neither Kilpatrick nor Stendahl wishes to deny that there was an individual who actually put the gospel together, but both regard his role and personal views as comparatively unimportant. On the other side, those who study the 'theology of Matthew' as an individual commonly acknowledge that it is unrealistic to imagine him working in isolation, and recognise that his contribution must be understood as made within the context of the life of the church to which he belonged, and that this context provided both the background and the occasion for his writing. (In a later chapter we shall be looking more fully at the way this gospel is directed towards the needs which arise in the life and teaching ministry of a real-life Christian congregation;[65] it is certainly not the academic product of a scholar's study.) There is not, therefore, a total separation between these approaches, and a good deal of what Kilpatrick and Stendahl concluded with regard to the views and concerns of Matthew's church or school has been adopted into subsequent studies of Matthew viewed as an individual theologian.

But as form-criticism, the explicit basis of Stendahl's playing down of individual authorship, has been succeeded by redaction-criticism with its focus on the author as such, so the 'old concept of individual

---

63. K. Stendahl, *The School of St. Matthew* (Uppsala, 1954; second ed., Philadelphia: Fortress, 1968).

64. The main focus of Stendahl's book is in fact not on its 'school' proposal, but on the analysis of the use of the Old Testament in Matthew, and we shall return to it in that connection. In the preface to the second edition, in which Stendahl responds to his critics, the focus is on the Old Testament material, and on the possible life-setting of the gospel in the development of the church out of Judaism, while the 'school' origin remains as a presupposition which is not discussed further as such.

65. See below chapter 7, especially pp. 251-260.

authorship' has been reasserted, and few scholars today would be happy to regard Matthew as merely the scribe or editor of the teaching of his community. In the following chapters we shall be confronted again and again with evidence both of a clear theological orientation and of a literary skill and sensitivity in the writing of the gospel which suggest that it came from the pen of a man with a mind of his own.

E. AUTHORSHIP – CAN IT BE DECIDED, AND DOES IT MATTER?

As far as I am aware, the apostle Matthew is the only specific name which has been seriously offered for the authorship of the first gospel. It is the name by which the gospel has always been known, probably from the time of its original circulation in the first century church. Those (and they are the vast majority of modern scholars) who feel unable to accept this attribution are therefore content to conclude that its author is unknown to us, even though a significant profile of the views, circumstances and personality of this unknown literary artist can be compiled from the work itself. They would find no problem in affirming of Matthew what Origen said about the Letter to the Hebrews: 'As to who in fact wrote it, only God knows the truth'!

Among the many reasons which are offered for not accepting the early church's view on the subject, two seem to be particularly important. One is the assumed date of the work; if it was not written until the last decade or so of the first century, this is getting very late for attribution to a man who was well launched into his professional career as a tax-collector by AD 30 at latest. The other is the complicated discussion, which we have already noted, about the nature of the church and the historical situation reflected in the work: is it the sort of book a Galilean apostle of Jesus might be expected to have produced, or does it reflect a situation remote from any he is likely to have experienced, and an outlook deriving from a different cultural background?

I have already commented on the second of these reasons, and we shall return to it in the next chapter. Personally I do not find it at all difficult to imagine a Galilean apostle displaying the sort of attitude to Judaism which we find in the gospel, nor do I find in it evidence of a church situation in which it is improbable that Matthew might have found himself. But what is plausible to me is out of the question to someone else, whose understanding of the nature and development of the early church in relation to Judaism is different from mine. There is, in other words, an inevitable element of subjectivity in such judgements. They are not taken in isolation, but form part of a total framework of historical reconstruction. There is an interconnected network of views on many aspects of the development of early Christianity, and a question such as the authorship of a gospel is likely to be decided not so much on the specific merits of the case, but as part of this larger whole. The arguments employed are therefore likely to possess a relative rather than an absolute force, and while they may seem self-evident to one who shares the same general outlook, they may seem to another to beg the whole question. This situation is not a cause for mutual accusations of obscurantism, so much as a call to recognise that such questions are not to be solved by a few slick arguments, and to be willing to reconsider some of the broader assumptions which divide the opposing views.

As for the question of date, we shall be looking at this in the next chapter, and a similar situation will emerge there, in that most of the arguments usually offered are themselves dependent on a wider range of assumptions. 'Hard data' are not easily found in this area, and it is more often the coherence of a given view with other aspects of a scheme of relative dating which determines the conclusion reached. On the other hand, a proposed date which threatens to upset the whole relative scheme which has been traditionally accepted is likely to meet with short shrift.

There is thus an apparently inevitable element of subjectivity, indeed of vested interest, involved in such a question as the authorship of the first gospel. When I record my own view that the tradition of the early church offers us an entirely appropriate candidate, and that I see no valid reason for doubting that Matthew could have been the author, nor for imagining that the attribution to him was either deliberately pseudonymous or a mere guess, I must recognise that what is plausible to me will remain impossible to others who do not share some of my wider framework of historical understanding.

This rather uncomfortable situation suggests that it is extremely unlikely that we shall arrive at an 'agreed solution' to the problem of authorship, and that anyone who suggests that there is such a solution is guilty of ignoring a large body of opinion which, on grounds no less historically arguable than his own, sees the whole question in a different total perspective as to the nature and development of first century Christianity and its literary activity. In other words, it looks as if we shall have to agree to differ on the specific questions such as the authorship of a gospel, at least for as long as we are unable to agree on the wider issues.

Ned B. Stonehouse, a staunch champion of conservative critical positions on the New Testament, committed himself just over twenty years ago to the remarkably bold statement: 'It is my considered opinion that the apostolic authorship of Matthew is as strongly attested as any fact of ancient church history.'[66] This could, however, be a double-edged way of phrasing his conclusion, for it raises the question, 'How well

66. Stonehouse, *Origins*, 46-47.

attested is *any* fact of early church history?' As far as the beliefs of the early Christians about the authorship of Matthew are concerned, I am sure Stonehouse is right that one could not ask for better attestation that it was universally regarded as the work of the apostle Matthew, even if they also mistakenly believed it to have been originally written in Aramaic. But the fact that this was the belief of Christians in the second (and even probably the late first) century does not suffice by itself to convince most scholars that the apostolic authorship is any more a 'fact' than the Aramaic origir.al. In other words, the 'attestation' which is required by most scholars is broader than merely the so-called 'external evidence', and as soon as we get into the subjective evaluation of the 'internal evidence' in the light of the wider context of early church history, the resultant relativity suggests that there will be few 'facts of ancient church history' which are not open to dispute. Experience confirms that this is so!

So while I believe that authorship of the first gospel by the tax-collector apostle Matthew is the most economical explanation of all the relevant factors, I would be reluctant to claim it as a 'fact' *tout simple*. It fits comfortably into my overall understanding of the development of gospel literature in the context of first-century church life, but it would not be responsible to claim objective certainty for my reconstruction any more than for those of other scholars.

Stonehouse goes on from the statement just quoted to draw a clear distinction between 'the witness of the Gospel itself' and 'the witness of tradition', and places the question of apostolic authorship firmly in the latter category, so that 'one should not elevate this testimony of tradition to the level of the Scripture and so regard it as a dogma of the Christian faith'. He concludes that 'the inspiration and authority of these anonymous writings ultimately do not depend upon the identification of their human authors but upon the activity of the Holy Spirit in the process of redemptive revelation'.[67] In other words, while it is, in his view, historically extremely probable that the gospel was written by the apostle Matthew, in the last resort it is not a matter of fundamental importance, for the theologically conservative any more than for any one else.

This is an important corrective to that sort of conservative apologetic which appears to hang the weight of its argument for the veracity of the gospels on the defence of their traditional authorship. Theologically, a belief in the divine inspiration of Scripture does not depend on our knowledge of the authors or the process of composition, helpful as this may be for the interpretation of the text. And historically there is no *a priori* reason why the apostle Matthew should be the only first century Christian in a position to provide a reliable record of the words and

67. *Ibid.* 47.

deeds of Jesus as they were remembered in the Christian community. A theological position which can accommodate the non-apostolic authors Mark and Luke as writers of inspired records of Jesus can hardly claim that the apostolic authorship of the first gospel is a *sine qua non* of the veracity of its record.

So I agree with Stonehouse that the apostolic authorship of Matthew should not be regarded as an article of faith; in that sense it does not really matter very much who wrote it. But I happen to believe that it fits the historical and literary data sufficiently comfortably to give us strong reason to accept that the early Christians who saw it as his work were not mistaken. In that sense it does matter, in that I want to understand the background and circumstances of the gospel well enough to be able to interpret it responsibly. It matters because in all areas of historical enquiry it is important that we should as far as possible get our facts right.

▯▯▯

THE SETTING OF THE GOSPEL

The date of the gospel. The place of origin. Relation to Judaism. Matthew's church. The purpose of the gospel.

IN THE PREVIOUS CHAPTER WE FOUND OURSELVES AT SOME POINTS ENGAGED in a process of argument which involved assuming the results of discussions still to come in later chapters. In this chapter the same procedure will be needed again. In order to determine the date, place, circumstances and purpose of the writing of the gospel, we must presuppose a certain understanding of its characteristic themes and emphases which will not be demonstrated until later chapters. Indeed while here, as in the case of authorship, there are certain traditions of the early church to offer us a starting-point for discussion, in this chapter even more than in the last we shall find that the decisive arguments are drawn from the internal characteristics of the gospel itself, and it is those characteristics which will be the focus of our study in the rest of the book.

It might seem, then, that it would be more sensible to work the other way round, to establish the characteristics of the book before going on to suggest, on the basis of those characteristics, when, where and why it came to be written. It is presumably for this reason that Gundry's commentary has abandoned the traditional format of an introduction considering the origin of the gospel before moving into the consideration of the text, and instead looks first at the text, and then, in the light of what has been discovered, draws 'Some Higher-Critical Conclusions' on date, provenance and authorship. There is a lot to be said for this method, but it too has its drawbacks in that decisions on the interpretation of the text will often depend on a prior understanding of its origin.

There is, then, an inevitable interdependence (circularity, if you like) between the two major aspects of a book such as this. Whichever aspect you begin with must be discussed in the light of the other, and that will mean taking on trust conclusions which cannot be justified until a later stage of the argument. In this situation there is clearly a danger of begging the question, of assuming what is yet to be proved, and then going on to 'prove' it on the basis of conclusions which themselves depended on that assumption. The strikingly different conclusions to which different scholars come on the basis of the same evidence suggest that this danger is not always avoided. At least it is important to be aware of the interrelated nature of the total argument of a book such as this, which makes it necessary to draw into the argument of this chapter (as of the last) aspects of the peculiar orientation of Matthew which must remain tentative until we are able to discuss them in subsequent chapters.

A. THE DATE OF THE GOSPEL

Discussion of the date of Matthew is a prime example of the relativity of much traditional argument. The arguments generally offered do not so much focus on specific features of the gospel which in themselves point to a certain date of composition, but rather consist of suggesting how Matthew may best fit into an overall scheme of dating for the New Testament documents and for the development of first-century Christian life and thought. Features of the gospel which seem to throw doubt on this relative dating scheme are seldom allowed to have independent weight.

The tradition of the early church points in a very different direction from the majority view among modern scholars. Matthew, as we have seen,[1] was universally believed (except perhaps by Papias?)[2] to have been the first gospel to be written. The one specific statement of the period of its origin is that of Irenaeus[3] that it was 'while Peter and Paul were preaching the gospel and founding the church in Rome'. This would place it in the early sixties at latest, and while no other such specific statement is made in the early references to the gospel which we considered in the last chapter, their understanding of the relation of Matthew to Mark shows that they would not have envisaged a date later than Irenaeus indicates.

Indeed, some would have dated it even earlier, for whereas Irenaeus dates the origin of the gospel of Mark shortly after the death of Peter (i.e. in the mid-sixties),[4] an alternative tradition, represented particularly by Clement of Alexandria, informs us that Mark wrote his gospel while Peter was still alive.[5] If this latter tradition is to be believed, and if

1. See above pp. 25-27.
2. See above p. 57.
3. *Adv. Haer.* III 1.1; see Eusebius, *H.E.* V 8.2.
4. *Adv. Haer.* III 1.1 (if the ἔξοδος of Peter and Paul is correctly understood as meaning their death). So also the Anti-Marcionite prologue (assuming the same meaning for *excessio*).
5. Two accounts by Clement which vary slightly, though they agree on the dating during Peter's lifetime, are quoted in Eusebius, *H.E.* II 15.1-2; VI 14.6-7. If the letter of Clement recently discovered by Morton Smith is genuine, this gives further evidence of Clement's view that the canonical gospel of Mark was written during Peter's lifetime.

Matthew wrote before Mark, this would put the origin of Matthew even earlier than Irenaeus' dating requires. Altogether, then, the patristic evidence seems unanimous that Matthew was written not later than the early sixties.

In contrast with this the majority view today is that Matthew was written after Mark, and since Irenaeus' dating of Mark is regularly followed rather than that of Clement of Alexandria, this puts Matthew certainly no earlier than AD 70. In fact a date around 80 or later is normally suggested.

ARGUMENTS FOR A DATE AROUND AD 80-90

1. The relationship with Mark just mentioned is clearly a central consideration. A date for Mark around AD 65 has been one of the 'fixed points' of much twentieth-century discussion of the dating of the gospels, though there have been many who put it rather later, perhaps around 70.[6] On a simple view of literary dependence of Matthew on Mark, this would seem to require a date for Matthew some time after 70, to allow time for Mark first to become known and available in another part of the empire.

The problems with this conclusion will be obvious by now. Firstly it assumes a date for Mark which is itself uncertain, and which, while supported by one strand of patristic evidence, conflicts with the equally widely supported tradition dating Mark during the lifetime of Peter. Secondly, it is entirely dependent on a particular approach to the Synoptic Problem which we have seen to be at least open to question. On a theory of Matthean priority this argument of course collapses altogether, but also on a theory of the parallel and mutually related growth of the gospel traditions such as I have proposed it loses its force. In other words, this argument assumes rather than demonstrates the relative dating of Matthew.

2. Jesus' predictions of the destruction of Jerusalem, while they occupy a significant place in each of the Synoptic Gospels, are more strikingly emphasised in Matthew (as we shall see in chapter 6), and this is regularly taken to be an indication that Matthew wrote his account after the events of AD 70. While Mark's relatively vague statements on the fate of Jerusalem might be seen as those of an alert observer who could see what was bound to come, Matthew's are said to display a

Clement's account is accepted by Jerome, *De Viris Illustribus* 8, and is probably supported by Origen's statement that Mark wrote in accordance with Peter's instructions (quoted by Eusebius, *H.E.* VI 25.5). For a full discussion of the patristic traditions about the date of Mark, favouring the Clement version, see Robinson, *Redating*, 107-115. For the opposite view see Hengel, *Studies*, 2-6.

6. For a recent discussion, opting for an unusually precise date in AD 69, see Hengel, *Studies*, 7-28.

circumstantial knowledge which must mark them as *vaticinia ex eventu*. In particular the incongruous statement in the parable of the Wedding Feast that the king 'sent his armies and destroyed those murderers and set their city on fire' (Mt. 22:7), which is peculiar to Matthew, is taken to be Matthew's reflection on an event which has now happened to fill out Jesus' threat of the rejection of Israel.[7]

Frequent repetition of this argument has invested it with an appearance of self-evidence, and yet what is there about 22:7 which is so obviously *ex eventu*? Its one unique feature among the gospel references to AD 70 is the firing of the city, which did in fact take place then,[8] but must one really have seen it happen to envisage such a climax? It was all too common in the punitive military campaigns of the ancient world. The language of this verse, as of other gospel predictions of the fall of Jerusalem, draws both on the regular features of Roman warfare and on the standard terminology of accounts of punitive expeditions in the Old Testament and Jewish world.[9] It is precisely the sort of language one might expect in a genuine prediction of political annihilation in the Jewish context, and does not depend on a specific knowledge of how things in fact turned out in AD 70.

The more fundamental question is, of course, whether such prediction could really have occurred. If this is ruled out *a priori*, then of course all the Synoptic Gospels must be dated after the event. This would be an argument on dogmatic rather than literary or historical grounds, and would therefore be limited in its appeal to those who share the same dogmatic viewpoint. On the other side it must be recognised firstly that even without supernatural knowledge any reasonably acute observer of first-century Palestine must have seen that Jewish revolt and Roman

7. The fact that this feature of the story is ludicrously out of place in an account of a wedding feast is not in itself an argument that it is a comment by Matthew slotted into an originally straightforward story. Parables are not accounts of real life, and incongruous features such as this occur in several of Jesus' parables, and indeed in other aspects of this one (especially vv 11-13). Their very incongruity jolts the hearer to attention and so serves to enforce their message. Of course if it is assumed that Jesus could have told a story like this on only one occasion, then either Luke has simplified it or Matthew has embellished it; but that assumption, though regularly made, is not self-evident; see the discussion by H. Palmer in *NovT* 18 (1976) 241-257, especially p. 255.

8. Robinson, *Redating*. 20-21, has argued that since 2 Baruch distinguishes between the throwing down of the wall and the burning of the *temple* specifically, a reference to the burning of the city as such is inaccurate, and therefore could only have been written by someone who did *not* know what actually happened. But Josephus, *B.J.* VI 353-355, 363-364, 406-408, makes it clear that large parts of the city were in fact burned.

9. This is demonstrated at length with specific reference to Mt. 22:6-7, with numerous examples from a wide range of literature from ancient Assyria to the rabbis, by K.H. Rengstorf in W. Eltester (ed.), *Judentum, Urchristentum, Kirche: Festschrift für J. Jeremias* (Berlin: Töpelmann, 1960) 106-129. He concludes that Mt. 22:6-7 cannot be used to determine the date of the gospel. The arguments of W. Trilling, *Das wahre Israel* (München: Kösel, ³1964) 85 against Rengstorf focus on the question of whether 22:7 represents Jesus' words or Matthew's embellishment, rather than whether it reflects knowledge of the fall of Jerusalem.

reprisals were at least a possibility, and that if this were to happen the destruction of Jerusalem, and especially of the temple, would be likely. . When to this is added the evidence for Jesus' supernatural knowledge, which is by no means confined to these few texts, it may be questioned whether the dogmatic rejection of prediction in such a case is justified. Bo Reicke characterises the argument for a post-70 dating of the Synoptic Gospels on the basis of their supposed *ex eventu* prophecies as 'an amazing example of uncritical dogmatism'.[10]

In fact Robinson, following Reicke, uses these predictions as the starting-point for his argument that all the Synoptic Gospels must have been written *before* AD70![11] If it had already happened, why all the need for warning; and why is there no hint anywhere that the prophecies have in fact been fulfilled?

3.   The occasional mention in the gospel that something referred to in the text has continued 'until today' (11:12; 27:8; 28:15) has been taken to suggest a long interval between the events recorded and the time of writing. But even if the gospel is dated in the early sixties, that still leaves an interval of thirty years, which is surely enough to explain such language. (An interesting feature of our modern study of first-century developments is an unconscious foreshortening of such intervals. Thirty years seems quite a negligible period at that distance, but it is not so for us in the twentieth century; the building of the Berlin Wall was less than thirty years ago, but it would not be regarded as inappropriate to state that it remains there 'to this day'!)

4.   More significant is the argument that the hostility towards official Judaism displayed in the gospel presupposes a period when the church no longer regarded itself as a reforming group within Judaism, but had become finally separated from its parent community. This is usually associated with the introduction into the Jewish synagogue liturgy of the so-called *Birkath ha-Minim*, a clause in the Eighteen Benedictions which were supposed to be recited three times a day by all Jews: 'Let Nazarenes (Christians) and *minim* (heretics) perish in a moment, let them be blotted out of the book of the living, and let them not be written with the righteous.'[12] Clearly from this point on no 'Nazarene'

10. B. Reicke, 'Synoptic Prophecies on the Destruction of Jerusalem' in D.E. Aune (ed.), *Studies in New Testament and Early Christian Literature: Essays in Honor of A.P. Wikgren* (Leiden: Brill, 1972) 121-134. On Mt. 22:7 Reicke argues that Matthew would hardly have interpreted the actions of the king in the parable, who represents God, in terms of the punishment of Jerusalem by pagan emperors. (Similarly Gundry, *Matthew*, . 599-600.) This is a questionable argument in the light of the willingness of Old Testament prophets to see the hand of God in the conquests of Israel by pagan empires, and the clear understanding of the destruction of Jerusalem as an act of divine judgement which we shall see in Matthew himself.

11. Robinson, *Redating*, chapter 2.

12. This is the version of the prayer found in the Cairo Geniza, and generally accepted as likely to be closest to what was in use at the end of the first century in Palestine; the Babylonian version (and that still in use in the synagogue today) is not specific as to

could continue to worship in the synagogue, and Christianity could no longer count itself as a movement within Judaism. The insertion of this clause is traditionally attributed to the Rabbis who met at Jamnia after AD 70; more specifically a date about AD 85 or 90 is generally agreed, though without firm evidence.[13] A date for Matthew around this period of final separation is therefore thought by many to be appropriate.

We shall be considering Matthew's attitude to Judaism in a later chapter, and later in this chapter we shall have to consider the likely situation of Matthew's church vis-à-vis Judaism. We shall see then that it is not by any means universally agreed that Matthew writes in a period when the break from the synagogue was final; I shall in fact be arguing that Matthew was himself still involved with non-Christian Jews, and that he shows the sort of love-hate relationship to Judaism which more appropriately fits a situation of continuing contact and even evangelistic possibility than one of total mutual rejection.

But I shall also be questioning how far it is realistic in any case to imagine that there was a straight line of development in Jewish/Christian relations, from a phase of continuing 'Jewishness' to one of mutual rejection, and that this development took place so evenly in the various areas of Christian involvement with official Judaism that it is possible to date a document by discerning its place along this line of development. Whatever may have happened at Jamnia towards the end of the century, and however widespread its eventual impact, is it not likely that at an earlier period there might be at the same time relatively friendly relations with non-Christian Judaism in one city and a total breakdown of relationship in another, and that even within a single community there would be some Christians who were more positive and accommodating towards their Jewish neighbours than others?

Here again, in other words, is an argument which depends on fitting Matthew within a relative scheme of the presumed development of early Christianity. I believe that that scheme is questionable both in terms of the dates it suggests for the supposed phases of development, and also in its assumption of a degree of uniformity in the situations of different Christian congregations which may not correspond to reality, and therefore that any dating of Matthew on such a basis lacks a firm foundation. But we shall return to this question later.

5.   This leads us to what is not so much a single argument as a whole complex of issues which are frequently raised in this connection. Matthew is said to represent a relatively late stage in the development of Christian life and thought. It presupposes a well-developed concept of the church,

which 'doers of wickedness' are in mind. For the various versions of the prayer and their development see Schürer, *History*, vol. 2 (1979) 455- 463.

13. In the Talmud (*Berakoth* 28b) it is attributed to Samuel the Small, and dated to the time of Gamaliel II, who was head of the academy at Jamnia about AD 90-110.

and a structure of church leaders and organisation which would not be found in the more spontaneous atmosphere of earliest Christianity. It displays a high level of christological sophistication, using titles like 'Son of God' freely, and even placing 'the Son' alongside the Father and the Holy Spirit in what looks like a stereotyped baptismal formula (28:19). The reverence shown towards Jesus and the disciples by avoiding the more 'human' traits visible in Mark is part of a steady movement away from historical reality towards pious hagiography. The supernatural dimension is more prominent in the appearance of angels and the more spectacular events surrounding the death and resurrection of Jesus in this gospel. So one could go on. The same features of the gospel which suggest to many that it must be a deliberate 'improvement' on that of Mark are taken as evidence that it must come from a period towards the end of the first century.

On some of these points there is room for debate as to how 'developed' Matthew's thought and situation really are, particularly with regard to the 'ecclesiastical' character of the gospel; we shall return to this in chapter 7, where I shall suggest that the discovery in Matthew of a more formalised church structure is to a large extent the result of reading later meanings into his language.

But the basic question here is how far it is possible to plot the development of theological sophistication in strictly chronological terms. Is it possible to establish dates before which, say, the term ἐκκλησία could not have been used as Matthew uses it? Must all Christian writers before AD 70 be relatively 'primitive'? Is it not possible for both 'primitive' and 'sophisticated' theology to be expressed at the same period, determined not so much by the date as by the personal interests and capacity of the writer concerned?

What is at stake here is the overall view of the growth of early Christianity which is presupposed. A doctrinal development which seems to one scholar to require two generations or more may be seen by another as a much less protracted process. Who is to say that a given development need have taken fifty rather than thirty years? We noticed earlier the tendency for time-scales to be foreshortened when we look back over several centuries. Thirty years in the life of a new religious community is a very long time. After all it took a lot less than that to produce Paul's letter to the Romans (and its author was not himself one of the original members of the group, but a more recent convert). When I read that Matthew's theology demands a period in the last decade or two of the first century, I wonder how it is that the great Pauline letters could have been written, as is universally agreed, well before even the earliest date commonly suggested for any of the gospels. On the basis of this sort of argument, should not Paul be dated after the Book of Revelation?!

So arguments for a date for Matthew around 80-90 turn out to be dependent either on a relative dating scheme which lacks a clearly fixed point or on subjective impressions as to the situation and stage of development reflected in the gospel. What is noticeably lacking is any feature of the gospel which in itself unambiguously points to an origin in this period. Are there, then, any features which point to an earlier date?

INDICATIONS OF A DATE BEFORE AD 70

1. There is first, of course, the patristic tradition, which we have already noted. In the absence of clear arguments to the contrary, it would seem reasonable to take seriously Irenaeus' specific dating in the early sixties, which the rest of the patristic evidence indirectly supports.
2. With relation to the events of AD 70, we noted above Robinson's argument that the entirely forward-looking nature of all the references to the destruction of Jerusalem should, other things being equal, point rather to a date before the event than after it.

But it is also worth noting that not all references to the temple in the gospel focus on its destruction. Matthew records Jesus' instructions to his disciples on the right attitude in which to present an offering in the temple (5:23-24) and on oaths focusing on the temple and its ritual (23:16-22). At the time when Jesus taught this was of course entirely appropriate, and it is quite possible that Matthew has simply recorded Jesus' teaching for its own sake, leaving it to his readers to draw from it principles which they could use in a situation where the teaching no longer had a literal application. But at least it may be claimed that to include such sayings in Matthew's presumably selective account would make more immediately relevant sense in the period when the temple was still standing.

The inclusion of the story about the temple tax (17:24-27) points more strongly in the same direction, since it implicitly approves the payment of this tax. Before AD 70 this would have been a meaningful gesture of solidarity with Israel, but after AD 70 it would carry a quite different connotation, for the tax was not abolished when the temple was destroyed, but rather diverted to the temple of Jupiter in Rome.[14] All Jews were obliged to continue to pay it, but whereas it had previously been an offering for the worship of the true God, it was now resented

14. Josephus, *B.J.* VII 218. Cf. Dio Cassius LXV 7.2. Thompson, *Advice* 67-68, suggests that the 'true successor to the defunct half-shekel tax' was a tax imposed at a later date for the support of the rabbinic establishment at Jamnia. This conflicts, however, with the clear view of Josephus that the new Roman tax was perceived as the direct successor to the tax for the temple in Jerusalem. It began to be paid to Rome immediately after the fall of Jerusalem (see for full details E.M. Smallwood, *The Jews under Roman Rule* [Leiden: Brill, 1976] 371-376), whereas the tax for Jamnia was not levied until some time later.

as a contribution to idolatry. It is hard to see how Matthew, for all his desire to preserve stories of Jesus for their own sake, could have allowed this implication to stand without comment if he were writing after 70.
3. A similar point can be made with reference to the gospel's attitude to Judaism. 23:2-3 and 23:23 are regularly noted as betraying a surprisingly positive attitude to the Jewish scribes in view of the generally hostile tone of the rest of the gospel. We shall be looking later at the question of how these differing perspectives within the one book are to be reconciled. Here again it is possible that Matthew has simply preserved these sayings because Jesus said them, however uncomfortably they fit with his own life-setting. But it is undoubtedly easier to envisage his retention of such sayings in a situation before the break with the Jewish establishment was total. Similarly the fact that Matthew, unlike Mark, feels no need to explain for his readers the nature of the Jewish purification rituals referred to in 15:2 (contrast Mark 7:2-4) suggests a readership which has not yet severed its links with Judaism to the extent of forgetting its roots. The same inference may be drawn from the 'Jewishness' of the gospel as a whole, to which we shall return.

In this and the previous point we have taken up two of the issues already raised in favour of a later date (the gospel's relation to the events of AD 70 and to continuing Judaism), and by looking at other aspects of the evidence have drawn an opposite conclusion. It is a matter of judgement whether one or the other argument carries more weight, or whether the fact of their opposite force simply serves to throw doubt on the validity of either!
4. In arguing for a date for Matthew not later than AD 90, Kilpatrick[15] points out that whereas the Apostolic Fathers frequently betray knowledge of the Pauline epistles, in Matthew 'there is no sign that the Epistles were known', not only because Matthew's terminology and theological emphases are different from those of Paul, but also because some passages (e.g. Matthew 28, with its lack of awareness of the list of resurrection appearances in 1 Corinthians 15) could hardly have been written as they are by someone who knew Paul's letters. For Kilpatrick a church 'as yet unaffected by Paulinism and unacquainted with the Pauline Epistles' cannot be envisaged later than 90, but it may well be asked how easily any significant Christian group could remain unaware of Paul for even as long as thirty years after the writing of the main Pauline letters. The earlier the gospel is dated, the more easily this 'isolation' may be understood.
5. In response to the usual arguments that the life and thought reflected in the gospel are those of the post-70 period, Gundry[16] has brought

15. Kilpatrick, *Origins*, 129-130.
16. Gundry, *Matthew*, especially 602-606. The whole discussion of the date of the gospel (599-609) is an instructive example of how the accepted reasoning of traditional scholarship may be challenged by a fresh approach to the data.

together an impressive collection both of specific passages and of general aspects of the gospel which seem to him to point decisively to the period before the Jewish War. They are of varied character, some more convincing than others. It would be inappropriate to list them all here, the more so since many are dependent on the detailed exegesis which Gundry has set out in the preceding commentary. But the reader who has gained the impression from more traditional commentaries that all the distinctive emphases of Matthew mark him out as a relatively late contributor to the synoptic tradition would be well advised to work through Gundry's material. Here again, then, a line of argument which is traditionally used to support a later date has been turned round by drawing from a different set of passages (and sometimes in fact from the same ones!) an opposite conclusion as to where the gospel best fits into the first century Jewish and Christian scene.[17]

It may be readily conceded that none of these arguments for a pre-70 date for Matthew is conclusive. What I have been concerned to show is that a plausible case can be made out for this view, as much as for the later date. Sometimes it has been a matter of selecting different aspects of the gospel as the focus of attention, to show that it does not all point the same way; in some cases, however, the same evidence can be seen as pointing in a different direction, depending on the overall framework of historical reconstruction with which you come to it. In all the arguments, on both sides, the most impressive fact is the lack of any firm data which are not dependent on some other (equally questionable) theory of first century developments.

It is easy to dismiss Robinson's plea for *Redating the New Testament* as an eccentric scholar's game (which was in fact how it began, according to his own account, p. 10!), and therefore his placing of Matthew in the sixties as required by the theory rather than by the evidence. That is the sort of response most of New Testament scholarship has accorded to his book.[18] But the theory is in fact backed up by careful argument, and at least as far as the case for Matthew is concerned Robinson does not stand alone. The essence of his book is its questioning of the whole relative dating scheme which recent scholarship has taken for granted, and his discovery that once any part of this scheme is disturbed the whole structure is found to rest on few if any fixed points. A similar conclusion is reached by J.M. Rist,[19] who argues that the only significant

17. For an earlier example of a similar challenge to the accepted approach to dating see Allen, Matthew, 325-330, taking up some aspects of Harnack's work on the dating of the gospels, and arguing from the church situation implied for 'a date nearer 50 than 70 A.D.'.
18. There is what appears to be a wry comment on his own experience in this connection in Robinson's posthumous work, *The Priority of John* (London: SCM, 1985) 10: 'One must always beware of the tendency of the critical establishment to close ranks against anything that disturbs its fundamental presuppositions.'
19. Rist, *Independence*, 5-7.

reason for dating Matthew after 70 is the assumption that it depends on Mark. And even that assumption apparently does not necessarily entail a late date, for Gundry, who accepts Matthew's use of Mark, is still able to date Matthew some time before AD 63 (which is the date he assigns to Luke, whom he takes to be dependent on Matthew). Even so cautious a scholar as C.F.D. Moule regards the apostolic period, and specifically before AD 70, as 'the most plausible dating' for Matthew.[20]

It seems then that the ripples which began when Harnack threw his *Date of Acts and the Synoptic Gospels* into the pool of New Testament scholarship have not died away, and while the majority continue to uphold the standard dating scheme, with minor variations, a solid case can be made for reopening some of its fundamental assumptions. Once that is done, there seems no good reason for disputing the unanimous tradition of the church from the second century on that Matthew's gospel belongs to the apostolic period, and more specifically that it was written before the Roman persecution of the mid-sixties.

B. THE PLACE OF ORIGIN

We have seen that patristic tradition regarded Matthew's gospel as written for Jews in their own language. It is therefore hardly surprising that it was also generally believed that the gospel was written where most Jews were to be found, in Palestine. This is probably the meaning of the statement of Irenaeus, *Adv. Haer.* III 1.1, that the gospel was written 'among the Hebrews' (though of course there were plenty of 'Hebrews' living in other parts of the empire), and Eusebius' account of Matthew's writing the gospel when he was obliged to go away from 'Hebrews' to work among others suggests the same idea. In the Anti-Marcionite Prologue (to Luke) and in Jerome the location is quite explicit: the gospel was written 'in Judaea'.[21] There are no circumstantial details suggesting a particular city, nor does there seem any reason to see this patristic location as any more than a rather obvious guess, since Palestine (not necessarily restricted to 'Judaea' proper) is where an apostle might be expected to be and where a ministry to Jews, and a book written in 'Hebrew', would be most likely.

A Palestinian origin would apparently fit the Jewish character of much of the contents of the gospel, particularly its concern with the teaching of the Pharisees, its inclusion of Aramaic words and Jewish customs without explanation, and the apparently deliberately Semitic

---

20. Moule, *Birth*, 242; on pp. 173-174 Moule expresses his agreement with this aspect of Robinson's *Redating*, and points out that he had himself anticipated its thesis in the first edition of *Birth*.
21. For the relevant texts see above pp. 60-62.

character of the Greek in some of the editorial material.[22] It has also been suggested that the bilingual character of the Old Testament material in the gospel would fit most comfortably with an origin in Palestine in the pre-70 period.[23]

On the other hand, as far as our knowledge of the nature of Jewish communities in other parts of the Eastern Mediterranean goes, none of these characteristics would be inappropriate for a city outside Palestine where substantial numbers of Jews had settled (and there were many such). It has been suggested too that the occasional references to those among whom Jesus travelled and taught as 'they' and to the scene of his ministry as 'that region' (7:29; 9:26; 9:31; 11:1; 13:54 etc.) indicate a viewpoint outside the country; such phrases are quite satisfactorily understood, however, in the narrative context as references to specific groups or areas within Palestine (i.e. the people in the story, rather than Palestinians in general).

The majority of scholars today tend to opt cautiously for the origin of the gospel being somewhere in Syria. This consensus can be traced to the influence of Streeter's classic presentation of the case for an origin in Antioch.[24] Antioch is in general terms a suitable candidate, with its large Jewish community and flourishing Christian church, in which the claims both of Jewish-Christian conservatism and of the Gentile mission were strongly represented; such a cosmopolitan centre, and yet not too far from Palestine, would be likely to exhibit the sort of linguistic and cultural mixture which we find in the gospel. But these are characteristics which Antioch would have shared with other Jewish centres where the church was established.

Two of Streeter's arguments, however, may be thought to point specifically to Antioch. One was the observation that Matthew was the version of 'the gospel' most used in the letters of Ignatius, Bishop of Antioch, and in the Didache, which Streeter believed to be of Syrian origin.[25] As we saw in chapter 1, the same could be said of most second century Christian writers, whatever their geographical location, but the fact that these two very early writers, one certainly and the other arguably associated with Antioch, gave such prominence to Matthew may be significant. The other 'infinitesimal point' offered by Streeter is that Matthew 17:24-27 assumes that a stater is the equivalent of two didrachmae, and only in Antioch and Damascus was this exactly so.[26]

22. On this last point see Moule, *Birth*, 276-280.
23. So Gundry, *Use*, 174-179. In his commentary, however, Gundry has changed his mind on this point, and opts for an origin in Antioch, *Matthew*, 609.
24. Streeter, *Four Gospels*, 500-527.
25. *Ibid.* 504-511. For Streeter a location for the origin of Matthew in 'Syria' must in fact mean Antioch, because of his conviction that each of the gospels came out of one of the 'great churches'.
26. *Ibid.* 504.

This bare statement is in fact very questionable,[27] and is certainly not sufficient basis for such a conclusion.

But if Streeter's arguments for Antioch specifically are not compelling, the general suitability of a church centre in Syria may be granted. Kilpatrick[28] in fact argued that a location in southern Syria would be more suitable than Antioch, perhaps Tyre or one of the neighbouring Phoenician cities, which would be closer to Palestine and therefore would allow the 'close contact with the Judaism of Jamnia' which he discerned in Matthew. Goulder follows Kilpatrick, though without wishing to specify a particular city.[29] Most remain content to speak simply of 'Syria'.

But of course there were Jews in other parts of the empire as well. One particularly prominent Jewish community was that at Alexandria, and Matthew has been located there too. S.G.F. Brandon[30] saw Matthew as the expression of the peculiar situation of the Jewish-Christian community in Alexandria as the natural successors to the original Jerusalem church after AD 70. He found in the gospel 'an attempt to confine the new wine of Christianity in the old wine-skins of Judaism', and in particular an attack on the increasing influence of Pauline teaching. The same location has been proposed by S. Van Tilborg,[31] but it is interesting to see that his reasons are almost exactly the opposite of Brandon's. Whereas for Brandon Matthew represented the vain attempt of conservative Jewish-Christianity to stem the tide of Pauline universalism, for Van Tilborg Matthew writes (as a Gentile) 'in a world in which Judaism was no longer a serious competitor', and as spokesman of a community which, 'broadminded though it was, could give Israel no place in its thinking'. The fact that such opposite reconstructions of the milieu of the gospel have led to the same suggested location must give one pause!

---

27. Streeter offers this information as what 'the commentators say', with no documentation, and since then the same information is generally offered with Streeter as the authority! The subject is in fact very complex, and only a skilled numismatist is likely to give an adequate account. According to J.D.M. Derrett, *Law in the New Testament* (London: Darton, Longman & Todd, 1970) 248-250 (cf. also N.J. McEleney, *CBQ* 38 [1976] 179, n. 2), the shekel (stater) of Tyre would be the normal coin in which to pay the temple tax for two people, and the Antiochene stater was in fact significantly heavier than that of Tyre; in that case 17:27 would constitute an 'infinitesimal' argument *against* Antioch as the place of origin! But in any case, there was apparently no more fixed scale of equivalence among local currencies then than there is in international exchange today, and even the individual coins of a single city could vary in weight. The only way in which 17:27 could be used properly in this connection would be if it could be shown that the term στατήρ as a Greek equivalent for 'shekel' was peculiar to Antioch; in fact it seems to have been in more general usage.

28. Kilpatrick, *Origins*, 131-134.

29. Goulder, *Midrash*, 149-150.

30. S.G.F. Brandon, *The Fall of Jerusalem and the Christian Church* (London: SPCK, 1951) 217-243.

31. S. Van Tilborg, *The Jewish Leaders in Matthew* (Leiden: Brill, 1972) 171-172. He is apparently unaware of Brandon's argument.

Other suggestions for the place of origin of the gospel have been made, but let us return to Palestine (which it will be remembered was where patristic writers located it). Few recent scholars have been prepared to argue with any conviction for this view, but there is an impressive exception in an article by B.T. Viviano.[32] Viviano's specific proposal is Caesarea (where Jerome claimed to have seen the Hebrew original of the gospel preserved in the library),[33] which he defends by a somewhat contrived argument from a few patristic statements. What is more significant is the first part of his article in which he shows the lack of evidence supporting the post-Streeter consensus for Syria, and argues in favour of Palestine as the more appropriate general location. I suspect there is some truth in his allegation that this position has been set aside simply because it has in the past been defended by more conservative scholars, who associated with it 'other, less acceptable, assumptions such as the priority and apostolic authorship of the gospel in its present form, and an early date'.

Another recent article suggests an origin not strictly in Palestine, but in Transjordan. H.D. Slingerland[34] notices that in Matthew 19:1 and 4:15 areas to the west of the Jordan are described as 'beyond the Jordan'. He suggests that these texts, the former of which in particular has long puzzled commentators (the latter being in an Old Testament quotation, and not therefore necessarily representing Matthew's geographical standpoint), indicate the geographical perspective of the writer, somewhere in the Decapolis. He tentatively suggests Pella as the specific location. G.N. Stanton[35] finds Slingerland's argument 'particularly perceptive, but I am not persuaded that we need look no further than Pella'.

The only conclusion one can draw from this variety of opinions is that in relation to the place of origin of the gospel, as for the date, we are not likely to find a solid basis for a scholarly consensus. While we may come to some general agreement about the characteristics of the gospel (though even that may well be limited, as we shall see) the variety of geographical situations in the first century Christian world which might 'fit' is considerable, and there is again a lack of hard evidence for any one place, or even general area, over against another. Again the patristic tradition, while it may well have no firmer basis than modern scholars' conjectures, offers us a general locality, Palestine, which seems at least as possible as others on offer.

But perhaps agreement here is not terribly important. Of all the traditional introductory questions, the geographical location in which

32. B.T. Viviano, *CBQ* 41 (1979) 533-546.
33. See above pp. 61-62.
34. H.D. Slingerland, *JSNT* 3 (1979) 18-28.
35. Stanton, 'Origin', 1942.

the gospel originated is probably the least significant for a sound understanding of the text.

C. THE RELATION TO JUDAISM

Perhaps the central problem in the study of Matthew's gospel is how to make sense of the apparently inconsistent attitude towards Judaism which the gospel displays. The question has already occurred a number of times in our discussion, and it will keep on recurring. Words like 'paradox', 'tension' and even 'contradiction' regularly appear in discussions of the subject.

As in many other areas of biblical studies, a popular option is to find the answer in a process of composition whereby incompatible strands of tradition and of editorial bias became woven together into the final document, so that it is pointless to look for a consistent viewpoint in the latter. In the particular case of Matthew a common approach is to assume that a relatively conservative Jewish-Christian body of tradition (or even an earlier document from such a background) has been worked over by a subsequent writer (or writers) who was no longer in close touch with official Judaism, perhaps indeed himself a Gentile. So the religious conservatism of the original tradition has been mixed with the final editor's outright hostility to non-Christian Judaism to produce a gospel which is at the same time one of the most Jewish and one of the most anti-Jewish documents in the New Testament.

While this is, of course, an entirely plausible scenario, it must assume that the final editor either did not notice or did not care about the incompatibility of the material he left side by side in his work. In view of the literary and theological sophistication which we shall find as we study Matthew's gospel, this is an uncomfortable conclusion – he does not seem generally to be so insensitive to the implications of what he writes. This raises the question, then, whether the paradox of the gospel is necessarily the result of two or more different life-settings, or whether it is possible to envisage a situation in which the whole range of attitudes to Judaism reflected in the gospel might have coexisted.

In later chapters we shall be considering the gospel's theology of fulfilment and of the relation of Jesus and his church to Israel. That discussion is obviously essential for a full answer to our present question of the relations between Matthew's church and official Judaism, and where the gospel fits best within the complex history of Jewish- Christian relations in the first century. But no discussion of the setting of the gospel can omit this question. At this point we may, then, at least survey some of the views to which scholars have come on the issue, and offer some preliminary suggestions on the sort of life-setting which might produce such a paradoxical document, leaving it to the discussion in later chapters to fill out what must for now be tentative suggestions.

MATTHEW AND JEWISH CHRISTIANITY

Particularly since Jean Daniélou's classic study of *The Theology of Jewish Christianity* [36] the definition of the term 'Jewish-Christian' has been controversial. Daniélou's book was in fact about 'a type of Christian thought expressing itself in forms borrowed from Judaism', whatever the ethnic or sociological situation of the writer; as such 'Jewish-Christianity' forms the first stage of Christian theological development, to be succeeded eventually by the Hellenistic and Latin forms. This definition focuses not on a sociological category (what group within early Christianity a person belonged to) but on a theological tendency.[37]

Since the translation into English of Daniélou's book, some writers in English have suggested that, while 'Judaeo-Christian' may appropriately be used for the sort of theological orientation Daniélou described, the term 'Jewish Christian' should be restricted rather to the sociological or ethnic sense of Christians of Jewish origin.[38] The resultant discussion has sometimes been over-subtle, but what has emerged is the importance of recognising that in first-century (and later) Christianity there was no necessary relation between a Christian's ethnic or cultural origin and his theological position. Some Christians of Jewish origin (such as the Ebionites) remained apparently more Jewish than Christian; others, following Paul, scandalised their more conservative brothers by their emancipation from the law, while some Gentile Christians could become more 'Jewish' than Paul. A wide range of theological views and of approaches to unconverted Judaism occurred within different 'Jewish Christian' circles. In what follows I shall therefore adopt the convention of using 'Jewish Christian' as a sociological term, to denote a Christian who was of Jewish origin and belonged to a church made up primarily of such people, without prejudice as to what particular theological position he (or they) may have held.

The traditional belief that Matthew belongs in a Jewish Christian context (cf. Origen's statement that it was written 'for those who had

36. J. Daniélou, *Théologie du Judéo-Christianisme* (Paris: Desclée, 1958). English version published as volume 1 of *A History of Early Christian Doctrine* (London: Darton, Longman & Todd, 1964).

37. Daniélou's definition and general approach are usefully discussed by R.A. Kraft in *Judéo-Christianisme: Recherches historiques et théologiques oflertes en hommage au Cardinal Jean Daniélou* (Paris: Recherches de Science Religieuse, 1972) 81-92. See also M. Simon, 'Réflexions sur le Judéo-Christianisme' in J.Neusner (ed.), *Christianity, Judaism and other Greco-Roman Cults. Vol. 2, Early Christianity* (Leiden: Brill, 1975) 53-76; Simon laments the inability of French to reproduce the German distinction between *Judenchristentum* (Christians of Jewish origin) and *Judaismus* (Christianity, whether Jewish or Gentile, which interprets the faith in terms of conformity to Jewish law). It is this same distinction which is attempted in English in the next paragraph.

38. This convention was proposed by R. Murray, *Heythrop Journal* 15 (1974) 303ff. For subsequent discussion of terminology see especially A.F.J. Klijn, *NTS* 20 (1974) 419-431; B.J. Malina, *JSJ* 7 (1976) 46-57; S.K. Riegel, *NTS* 24 (1978) 410-415; R. Murray, *NovT* 24 (1982) 194-208; R.E. Brown, *CBQ* 45 (1983) 74-79.

come to faith from Judaism') has generally been supported by noting some of its distinctive linguistic and cultural features, and special emphases. A gospel which without explanation includes transliterated Aramaic words (ῥακά, 5:22; μαμωνᾶς, 6:24; κορβανᾶς, 27:6) and references to details of Jewish custom (handwashing at meals, 15:2; phylacteries and tassels, 23:5; burial customs, 23:27; sabbath travel problems, 24:20), which displays an almost obsessive interest in and subtlety in the use of the Old Testament, which includes a genealogy of Jesus beginning with Abraham and focusing around David and the monarchy of Judah, and which introduces 'Son of David' as a title of Jesus on several occasions when the others do not, which restricts the mission of both Jesus and his disciples to 'the lost sheep of the house of Israel' (10:5-6; 15:24; cf. also 10:23; 19:28), and which unlike Luke mentions Samaritans only to exclude them from the mission, which can apparently countenance the continuing validity of Jewish scribal teaching (23:2-3; 23:23), and finds it necessary to insist on Jesus' respect for the Jewish law (5:17ff), which includes teaching and narrative focusing on such Jewish concerns as fasting, sabbath observance, temple offerings, the payment of temple tax, etc. – it is hardly surprising that such a gospel has always been recognised as distinctively 'Jewish Christian'.[39]

It is not just a matter of a few incidental details, but of the whole tone of the gospel, which seems calculated to present Jesus in terms which a Jew would understand, however radical and objectionable he might have found some aspects of its teaching. The scriptural colouring of so much of the narrative (of which the formal quotations are only an occasional more prominent outcrop) seems calculated to delight the Jewish mind which is skilled in midrashic interpretation of scripture, and the apocalyptic flavour and terminology of many passages (primarily but not only chapters 24-25) seems to presuppose the sort of reader who will immediately recognise what is meant by terms like 'abomination of desolation', and who would not miss the rich associations with biblical and later apocalyptic thought in a passage like 25:31-46. As for chapter 23, with its constant references to details of scribal teaching and practice, and its concluding comments on the culmination of Israel's rebellion against God, would a non-Jewish reader then have found it any less puzzling and unattractive than many do today?

A Gentile writer, or a Jewish Christian writing primarily for Gentiles, might well have incorporated a great deal of very 'Jewish' traditional material in his gospel, as is clear from the case of Luke. All the gospels are clearly 'Jewish' in the orientation of a large part of the material they contain (and this is hardly surprising since they tell the story of

39. Cf. Allen, *Matthew*, lxxvi-lxxix for other indications of 'Jewish Christian character', including a list of distinctively 'Jewish phraseology' in the sayings material. Kilpatrick, *Origins*, chapter VI contains much other support for this conclusion.

a Jewish teacher who hardly ever moved outside Palestine!). But is it adequate in the case of Matthew to understand this characteristic of the work as reflecting only the nature of the tradition and not also the stance of the final author? The fact that most of the characteristics mentioned above are peculiar to Matthew, and that they represent pervasive traits of the gospel as a whole rather than occasional intrusions, suggests otherwise. As we study the special characteristics of this gospel in later chapters, it will, I believe, become increasingly difficult to see the author as one who had no personal stake in the question of Jesus and Israel, or who wrote for a church which could view the issue with no more than a detached interest.[40]

We shall see shortly that this is not a universal view, that some have argued that the final author of the gospel was himself a Gentile, and that he and his community had no existential involvement with Judaism. But such a position is supported not so much by positive evidence of Gentile background or by a clear cultural distance between the author and Judaism, but rather by the undoubted fact of Matthew's hostility towards non-Christian Judaism as he knows it, together with his approval of the Gentile mission. The question we shall need to keep in mind is whether such an attitude is not equally, or even more, understandable on the part of a Jewish Christian who finds himself and his community increasingly cut off from their cultural roots, and recognises that the purpose of God is now being worked out on an international scale.

WAS MATTHEW'S CHURCH 'INSIDE' OR 'OUTSIDE' JUDAISM?

Even if the Jewish Christian character of Matthew's church is granted, however, much discussion has centred on the question of whether this community regards itself as still a part of Judaism, conducting a debate with fellow-Jews on the significance of Jesus to Israel, and still hopeful of winning other Jews to follow him, or whether the breach between the church and non-Christian Judaism is already so complete that the two communities must now be left to go their own separate ways in an attitude of mutual hostility and rejection. The relevance of this question to the date of the gospel is obvious; it is often assumed that the transition between these two phases must be linked with the

40. Goulder, *Midrash*, 5, takes up von Dobschütz' view that Matthew was a converted rabbi, and modifies it to make him rather a converted scribe, 'a provincial schoolmaster'. He goes on (pp. 9-27) to present a detailed case for the scribal training and sympathies of the author, while his book as a whole is devoted to locating Matthew's method within that of Jewish midrash. While I shall be registering my disagreement with much of Goulder's thesis (see below pp. 116-117, 201-205), his demonstration of Matthew's 'Jewishness' is impressive.

introduction of the *Birkath ha-Minim*, estimated to have been around AD 85,[41] so that the gospel tends to be placed before or after that date depending on which phase it is thought to reflect.

G.N. Stanton has provided a careful analysis of the views of recent writers on Matthew as to whether the debate with Judaism was being conducted *intra muros* or *extra muros*.[42] He mentions Kilpatrick's view that 'the Gospel clearly reflects the conditions that led to the breach' – i.e. it was imminent, but not yet final (even though Kilpatrick in fact dated the gospel after the *Birkath ha-Minim*). G. Bornkamm in 1956 followed Kilpatrick, insisting more firmly that the struggle was still an internal one, though Stanton believes that Bornkamm has 'modified his position' when in 1970 he speaks more in terms of a community already cut off from Judaism. He cites as other exponents of the *intra muros* view R. Hummel, W.D. Davies, M.D. Goulder and S. Brown. On the other side Stanton cites as representatives K. Stendahl, C.F.D. Moule and E. Schweizer, and in fact the list could have been extended at some length, since in so far as recent scholars have expressed themselves directly on this issue the majority have tended to see Matthew as launching his attacks on official Judaism from the outside.

But while this sort of 'inside/outside' language has come to be widely used in recent discussion, a reading of Stanton's survey may well provoke doubts as to whether this is the right way to set up the question, particularly if it linked with a dating of the gospel in relation to a specific transition point from 'inside' to 'outside'.

It is interesting, for instance, to see Moule listed (quite correctly) as supporting the 'outside' view, in the sense that he pictures Matthew as belonging to 'a Christian group who lived . . . close to antagonistic Judaism', 'constantly "up against" opposition from non-Christian Jews living very close to them'.[43] Yet Moule is one of the few modern scholars who dates the gospel not only before the *Birkath ha-Minim*, but also before the fall of Jerusalem![44] For Moule clearly such communal antagonism can be envisaged long before the supposed break in AD 85. D.R.A. Hare, who expresses hiself as strongly as anyone for the *extra muros* position ('The First Gospel . . . assumes the abandonment of the mission to Israel. The synagogues of Jewry . . . have become hostile institutions. . . . For Israel the future holds only Judgment.'), and believes that 'Matthew and his friends have left both the synagogue and the Jewish quarter', nevertheless dates the gospel just *before* the *Birkath ha-Minim*, 'when in some areas at least the separation had

---

41. See above pp. 85-86.
42. Stanton, 'Origin', 1911-1916. Cf. a similar survey of the 'opposite camps' by J.P. Meier, *Law and History in Matthew's Gospel* (Rome: Biblical Institute Press, 1976) 9-13.
43. Moule, *Essays in New Testament Interpretation*, 69, 72.
44. Moule, *Birth*, 173-174, 242.

already been completed'.[45] On the other hand, we have noticed that
Kilpatrick, who sees in the gospel 'an opposition within Judaism',[46]
nonetheless dates it after the *Birkath ha-Minim*.

In view of such divergence, it is reasonable to ask whether the dating
of the beginning of Jewish/Christian antagonism specifically to AD 85
or thereabouts is not a drastic oversimplification. Do things happen as
neatly as that in real life? Is it not possible to envisage a growing
separation, even in the period before AD 70, so that hostility with 'the
synagogue across the street' might develop and express itself in the
language of mutual rejection long before the Christian group found it
necessary to cease thinking of itself as a part of Judaism, indeed as the
true expression of Judaism? Need we see the transition to 'outside' as
being a once-for-all development involving the whole Jewish-Christian
movement at once?[47] Might the situation not develop at a different rate
in different areas, so that one part of the church might produce fiercely
anti-Jewish writing while another part was still engaged in relatively
friendly dialogue? Indeed may we not imagine the same variety of
approach between individuals within the same community?

In this connection it is worth questioning whether Bornkamm really
did 'modify his position' between 1956 and 1970. When he states that
Matthew's church 'knows itself to be cut off from the Jewish community',
he betrays no awareness of having changed his ground, and indeed a
few pages later says that 'Matthew and his congregation presuppose
Hellenistic Christianity which had already outgrown its Jewish origin,
but they oppose the enthusiasm that wants to cut itself off completely
from Judaism'.[48] Is it perhaps only when seen within the artificial
framework of the 'inside/outside' debate that such language is seen as
inconsistent with his earlier views?[49]

When Stanton quotes Stendahl in favour of the *extra muros* position,
he is right in terms of Stendahl's statement that Matthew's community
'existed in sharp contrast to the Jewish community in town', but at the
same time it should be noted that Stendahl sees the blending of Jewish
and Hellenistic elements in the gospel as evidence of 'a church which
had learned to make the transition to an increasing gentile constituency

45. D.R.A. Hare, *The Theme of Jewish Persecution of Christians in the Gospel according
to St. Matthew* (Cambridge University Press, 1967) 105 n. 3, 127, 147-149.
46. Kilpatrick, *Origins*, 122.
47. Cf. Kilpatrick's view (*Origins*, 123) that the 'transitional period for Christianity,
from a Jewish sect to a religion with a life and structure of its own' lasted roughly from
AD 70 to 130.
48. G. Bornkamm, 'The Authority to "Bind" and "Loose" in the Church in Matthew's
Gospel', in *Jesus and Man's Hope*, vol. 1, pp. 41, 48 (= Stanton, *Interpretation*, 88, 95).
49. See further the account of Bornkamm's views in J.P. Meier, *Law*, 9-11. His use
of the 'early' and 'late' Bornkamm to represent the two poles of opinion on the relation
of Matthew's community to the synagogue is hardly fair when Bornkamm himself
recognises no such radical volte-face.

without suffering much tension or problem in that process'. Matthew's gospel is, for Stendahl, 'a witness to a far smoother transition from Judaism to Christianity than we usually suppose. Luke is irenic by effort, as his Acts show. Matthew is comprehensive by circumstance, and that makes it a rich and wise book.'[50] Such language suggests caution in attributing to Stendahl a specific placing of Matthew in relation to any sudden change in Jewish-Christian relations.

I believe then that the whole 'inside/outside' debate is an artificial one, based on an unrealistic understanding of the way Jewish/Christian relations are likely to have developed in the first century. Like many such debates it can generate much passion, and has great power of self-propagation. But it assumes wrongly, in my view, firstly that the *Birkath ha-Minim* (even if its introduction could be reliably dated) represented the beginning of a totally new situation, before which relations between Christians and Jews were relatively untroubled, and after which no meaningful contact was possible.[51] And secondly it assumes that it is impossible at the same time to be both 'inside' (in the sense of seeing yourself as a Jew among Jews) and 'outside' (in the sense of a fierce repudiation of official non-Christian Judaism). I believe on the contrary that such an uncomfortable tension was inevitable for the Jew who followed Jesus, and that it could have led at any time during the century to the sort of 'paradox' which we find in Matthew's attitude towards what Hummel suggestively terms his 'hostile brothers' (*feindliche Brüder*).[52] R. Mohrlang speaks appropriately of Matthew's 'dual citizenship', as a Jew and as a Christian; 'Matthew belongs simultaneously to two different communities and traditions (Jewish and Christian), the relation between which is only very imperfectly worked out in his thinking. . . . Matthew and his community seem to be still struggling to find their way; they are a community in transition.'[53]

In relation to the date of the gospel, this means that its special blend of Jewishness and anti-Jewishness might comfortably fit into almost any part of the first century, and certainly is not in itself determinative of a date after AD 85, or even after AD 70.[54] And in relation to our present question, Matthew may appropriately be described as repre-

50. Stendahl, *School*, second edition, xiii-xiv.
51. Against this assumption see especially R. Kimelman, '*Birkat Ha-Minim* and the Lack of Evidence for an Anti-Christian Jewish Prayer in Late Antiquity', in E.P. Sanders, A.I. Baumgarten & A. Mendelson (ed.), *Jewish and Christian Self-Definition*, vol. 2 (London: SCM, 1981) 226-244.
52. R. Hummel, *Die Auseinandersetzung zwischen Kirche und Judentum im Matthäusevangelium* (München: Kaiser, ²1966) 55.
53. R. Mohrlang, *Matthew and Paul: a Comparison of Ethical Perspectives* (Cambridge University Press, 1984) 22, 130-131.
54. See Gundry, *Matthew*, 600-601, 605 for an effective argument that 'conflict between Pharisaism and Christianity need not point to a post-Jamnian date' and that 'by the time Jerusalem was destroyed, the church had long since become a counterpart to the synagogue'.

senting 'Jewish Christianity' without this requiring us to declare for or against an *intra muros* situation. What it does mean in terms of Matthew's view of the present and future status of Judaism, and of the Jews as the people of God, we shall see more fully in chapter 6.

THE 'GENTILE BIAS' OF MATTHEW

The 'anti-Jewishness' of Matthew's gospel has been noticed by all interpreters, in that it displays remarkable hostility to the Jewish establishment, particularly in the onslaught on the 'scribes and Pharisees' in chapter 23, focuses more strongly than the other Synoptic Gospels on the coming destruction of Jerusalem, which it apparently interprets in terms of God's rejection of his people in order to replace them by 'another nation' (21:43), and consequently welcomes and encourages the admission of Gentiles to the Christian community. But it is only relatively recently that there has been a significant movement towards the view that this clear orientation means that the final author of the gospel could not himself have been a Jew, or writing for Jews, even though much of the material he included in his gospel still bears the marks of its Jewish-Christian origins.

This was proposed by K.W. Clark in an influential short article entitled 'The Gentile Bias in Matthew',[55] in which he argued that no Jew could have been responsible for such a uniformly negative view of the future of Israel. A full-scale book pointing in the same direction came soon after from P. Nepper-Christensen,[56] who denied that the gospel was specifically directed to the concerns of a Jewish-Christian readership, and argued in the light of its championing of the Gentile mission that it 'was written with a view to the Gentiles'; he confines his discussion to the readership rather than the authorship of the gospel, and so does not pronounce directly, as Clark does, for a Gentile author.

G. Strecker's important study of Matthew's theology begins with a detailed argument that the 'redactor' was not a Jewish Christian.[57] His argument is based partly on the gospel's attitude to Jews and Gentiles in relation to God's purpose for his people, but also on details of the

---

55. *JBL* 66 (1947) 165-172. Others who have followed Clark's approach include, in addition to those mentioned in following paragraphs, R. Walker, *Die Heilsgeschichte im ersten Evangelium* (Göttingen: Vandenhoeck & Ruprecht, 1967); W. Pesch, in P. Hoffmann (ed.), *Orientierung an Jesus: zur Theologie der Synoptiker. Für J. Schmid* (Freiburg: Herder, 1973) 286-299; L. Gaston, *Interpretation* 29 (1975) 24-40. Trilling, *Israel*, 215 n.10, mentions some German scholars in the nineteenth and early twentieth centuries who had already proposed that Matthew was a Gentile Christian revision of a Jewish-Christian original.
56. P. Nepper-Christensen, *Das Matthäusevangelium: ein juden-christliches Evangelium?* (Aarhus: Universitetsforlaget, 1958).
57. G. Strecker, *Der Weg der Gerechtigkeit* (Göttingen: Vandenhoeck & Ruprecht, ³1971; first edition 1962) 15-35.

text which he believes indicate an author who is unfamiliar with Judaism in detail (aspects of Jewish law or Hebrew style allegedly misunderstood, a generally less Semitic style of Greek than Mark, familiarity with the Hebrew text of the Old Testament only at the preredactional stage).[58] He concludes not only that 'Matthew' was a Gentile, but that he belonged to a church which was rapidly leaving behind its Jewish-Christian traditions. 'A new Gentile-Christian generation is taking over from Jewish-Christianity. To be sure, Jewish thought-patterns will also retain some influence in the future, but only in so far as they can be integrated into the Gentile-Christian context. The independence of the Gentile-Christian element marks the beginning of the road to early Catholicism. Matthew, as an exponent of this movement, plays a not insignificant role in its development.'

W. Trilling[59] also finds a clearly Gentile-Christian orientation in the final edition of Matthew, but is less clear as to whether the author or his community is in fact non-Jewish. His focus is on the self-understanding of Matthew's church as the true Israel, taking the place of unbelieving Judaism, and in this true Israel Gentiles have a prominent place; but this 'Gentile-Christian, universal' perspective of the final editor is one which in principle a Jewish Christian could also hold, and Trilling stops short of identifying the editor as a Gentile.[60] Indeed he characterises the church he writes for as one of mixed race, in which 'the differences between Gentile- and Jewish-Christians did not play, or at any rate no longer played, a significant role', but which 'seems indeed to have been a milieu of a predominantly Jewish-Christian character.' It is at least doubtful, therefore, whether Trilling can properly be enrolled as an advocate of a Gentile setting for the final edition of Matthew.

We have already noted the thesis of S. Van Tilborg that Matthew's gospel originated in Alexandria, in a community which 'could give Israel no place in its thinking', the final editor being himself a Gentile.[61] This proposal is offered in only the last page of a dissertation which is devoted to 'the situating of the Mt gospel by a study of those texts dealing with the Jewish leaders'.[62] The study of the texts has no difficulty in showing 'the anti-Israel thinking of Mt', but the step from this

58. For a response to these points see Goulder, *Midrash*, 21-24, and for the question of the Old Testament text-form, chapter 5 below.
59. Trilling, *Israel*, chapter 11; quotations from pp. 215, 223-224.
60. No such circumspection is seen in the argument of E.L. Abel (*NTS* 17 [1970/1] 138-152, esp. pp. 148-151) that two 'Matthews' can be distinguished; 'Matthew (1)' was a Jew, 'Matthew (2)', the final editor, a Gentile. The argument is based largely on the 'anti-Jewish' material, which is assumed to demand a non-Jewish editor, but Abel also offers the remarkable argument that a Jew would not have used Χριστός 'as a surname for Jesus' or used the phrase 'son of God'; was Paul then a Gentile?
61. Van Tilborg, *Leaders*, 171-172.
62. *Ibid.* 1.

unquestionable observation to the assumption that such a violent repudiation of the Jewish leadership in favour of the disciples of Jesus (with a benevolent attitude towards the 'crowds') could be exhibited only by a Gentile 'in a world in which Judaism was no longer a serious competitor' seems to be made without the need being felt for any further demonstration. The possibility that just such an attitude might have been characteristic of a Jewish Christian confronted by the unbelief of official Judaism is not even considered.

The assumption that hostility towards 'Judaism' and a favourable attitude to the Gentile mission indicate at least a final editor who was not himself a Jewish Christian lies behind most of the recent suggestions of a Gentile origin for the gospel. It should be noted therefore that other scholars who are no less sensitive to these characteristics of the gospel have found no difficulty in postulating a Jewish Christian milieu in which such an attitude might be expected. D.R.A. Hare, for instance, presents a stark picture of the 'anti-Jewishness' of Matthew as a gospel in which 'there is almost no continuity between Israel, the People of God in the old dispensation, and the Church, the new People of God', for which 'the invitation which Israel has refused so rudely is now to be offered exclusively to the Gentiles', and which 'assumes the abandonment of the mission to Israel';[63] yet he rejects the idea of Gentile authorship, and depicts Matthew as a Jewish Christian looking back on the failure of the mission to Israel in which he has been principally engaged.[64] A theology of the rejection of unbelieving Israel and of the mission to Gentiles is not, for Hare, in itself an indication of a Gentile author.

G.N. Stanton has offered a suggestive parallel, where the same 'Matthean paradox' is exhibited (and indeed may be traced to the influence of the gospel of Matthew) in an undeniably Jewish-Christian milieu. In a study of '5 Ezra and Matthean Christianity in the Second Century'[65] he finds in this short document (which appears as chapters 1-2 of '2 Esdras' in the Apocrypha) a second-century Jewish-Christian tract which takes up and develops from Matthew the theme of the rejection of Israel, to be replaced by 'a people soon to come'. But this 'coming people' is in continuity with the Israel of the Old Testament; in them Israel's destiny is completed. Thus '5 Ezra is at the opposite end of the theological spectrum from Marcion'. The 'Matthean paradox' is here writ large: 'Discontinuity could hardly be sharper, for Israel is totally and finally rejected. Continuity could hardly be stronger ...' For our present purposes the implication of this parallel is clear. If an

63. Hare, *Persecution*, 157, 171, 147-148. Similarly radical statements appear throughout the book.
64. *Ibid.* 164-166.
65. *JTS* 28 (1977) 67-83.

admittedly Jewish-Christian document of the second century could exhibit these same characteristics, in an exaggerated form, surely it is not only unnecessary but also improbable that the first century gospel on which they are based should come from a Gentile pen. We may well dismiss, then, the suggestion that Matthew's 'anti-Jewish' tone could only have come from a Gentile author or final editor. We noticed, however, that Strecker offers more specific arguments for a non-Jewish origin, and these have been repeated and extended by others. A useful summary of some of the issues raised in this connection is offered by J. P. Meier.[66] One line of argument, little emphasised by Meier, is from Matthew's linguistic usage, which is said to be less 'Semitic' than is generally thought to be the case. This is a questionable argument; while it is true that Matthew generally displays 'more acceptable Greek usage' than Mark, this in itself does not point to a Gentile author – many Jews could write good Greek! In fact the combination of good Greek with apparently deliberate Semitism which Moule has demonstrated[67] points rather to a Jew with a good knowledge of Greek writing in a milieu where 'Semitisms' would be appreciated. More significant is Meier's other main line of argument, from Matthew's alleged mistakes about 'matters which an intelligent, well-educated, highly articulate and artistic Jew should have known'.

Meier gives just two examples of such mistakes. One is Matthew's introduction of a second animal into the entry to Jerusalem, resulting, so Meier believes, in Jesus riding two animals at once, and all on the basis of a misunderstanding of the Hebrew parallelism of Zechariah 9:9. This hoary argument has been discussed so often that little more need be said. The supposition that anyone, Jewish or Gentile, could solemnly have pictured Jesus sitting on two animals at the same time is surely no less 'ludicrous' than the various alternative explanations to which Meier gives this epithet. Is it probable that Matthew, whose literary and narrative skills are increasingly recognised, could have perpetrated such an absurdity with the text of Mark in front of him (as Meier assumes to be the case) simply because he misunderstood Zechariah? Such a wooden argument seems to me less plausible than the rather obvious possibility that Matthew records the memory that there was a second animal there in addition to the *one* Jesus rode on, and that in this insignificant detail (not surprisingly ignored by the other evangelists) his midrashic imagination noticed a point of contact with the form of the text in Zechariah which in no way requires that he was unaware of its primary semantic force. Such imaginative exploit-

---

66. Meier, *Law*, 16-20. In a later book, *The Vision of Matthew* (New York: Paulist Press, 1979) 19- 23, Meier gives a similar account, but expresses himself more firmly in favour of the hypothesis of Gentile authorship.
67. Moule, *Birth*, 276-280.

ation of details of the Old Testament text is typical of rabbinic Judaism; it is an argument for the Jewish origin of the gospel rather than against it.

Meier's other argument is more serious: Matthew is wrong about the Sadducees. Two of the three passages in which Matthew mentions Sadducees are cited in support of this assertion. In 22:23 Meier argues that Matthew's different wording from the other synoptists indicates that whereas they were aware that denial of the resurrection was basic to the Sadducean position, Matthew presents this as merely their ploy on this one occasion. This conclusion is reached solely on the ground that Matthew has λέγοντες for Mark's οἵτινες λέγουσιν and Luke's οἱ ἀντιλέγοντες; a minor stylistic change which is easily explained on other grounds.[68] Even if it were true that Matthew's participle is intended to denote the Sadducees' approach on a single occasion rather than their general theological position, it is quite gratuitous to assume that he was therefore unaware that this was their characteristic doctrine; surely one would assume, unless there is some indication otherwise, that they formulated their challenge in accordance with their beliefs rather than against them!

But if 22:23 does little to advance Meier's case, 16:1-12 looks more like the ignorance of a Gentile, for here Matthew associates the Pharisees and the Sadducees together as if they and their teaching were practically the same, whereas everyone knows that they were opposing parties both in theology and in politics. In 16:1 where Mark mentions Pharisees and Luke merely 'others', Matthew depicts the interrogating party as 'Pharisees and Sadducees'; in 16:5 Mark mentions the 'leaven of the Pharisees and of Herod', Luke merely 'of the Pharisees', but Matthew 'the leaven of the Pharisees and Sadducees', a phrase which he repeats in a conclusion in verses 16:11-12 which is peculiar to him, in which also he defines this 'leaven' as 'the teaching of the Pharisees and Sadducees'. Is this then an uncritical equation of two groups which every Jew must have known to be very different? This depends on whether 'the leaven/teaching of' followed by two nouns necessarily implies that the two are identical. In Mark's parallel passage the reference is to 'the leaven of the Pharisees and the leaven of Herod', surely an even more unlikely combination, which can hardly be taken to imply that Mark thought Herod was a Pharisee! To mention together two groups who for different reasons were opposed to Jesus, and to warn collectively against their 'teaching', does not necessarily imply unawareness of their differences on essential points of theology. The Matthew who included an account of the distinctively Sadducean approach to Jesus on the resurrection, and who avoids other opportunities to

68. See Gundry, *Matthew*, 444.

associate Sadducees with Pharisees and scribes as the target of Jesus' accusations, does not seem to have been so naive. Why then the repeated association of the two groups in 16:1-12? It originates in 16:1, where the two form an apparently official 'commission of enquiry'. This is closely parallel to the only other place where Matthew mentions Sadducees, where again a group of 'Pharisees and Sadducees' came to investigate the mission of John the Baptist. Since these two opposing groups together made up the bulk of the Sanhedrin (see Acts 23:6) is it too simplistic to see here a sort of 'two-party' delegation of the Sanhedrin to investigate a new religious teacher? If that is the reason for the association of the two groups also in 16:1, then the repetition of the same pairing in the remainder of the same pericope would follow naturally, and need imply no unawareness of the difference between the two groups.[69]

Other arguments for a non-Jewish origin for Matthew have focused on the apparent distance between the author and Jewish culture expressed in the phrases 'their synagogues' (4:23; 9:35; 10:17; 12:9; 13:54; cf. 23:34 'your synagogues') and 'their scribes' (7:29). Kilpatrick[70] argued that the repeated addition of αὐτῶν could not be accounted for merely by reference to a clear antecedent in the context, and marked a deliberate dissociation between the author and these institutions (though this did not lead him to see the gospel as of Gentile origin, but merely as reflecting a breach between two groups of Jews, Christian and non-Christian). In most of these cases, however, the context supplies, if not always a strict grammatical antecedent, at least a clear reference for the αὐτῶν as referring to a particular group rather than to Jews as a whole. In 4:23, 9:35, 12:9 and 13:54 it refers to the particular geographical area of the next phase of ministry, in 10:17 and 23:34 specifically to those who oppose the Christian movement, and in 7:29 to the crowds just mentioned. In none of these cases is there any need to understand the author as dissociating himself from synagogues and scribes in general. There is also in the gospel a single case of 'Ιουδαῖοι as a general ethnic or at least regional description (28:15) such as a Gentile might use, but the frequent use of οἱ 'Ιουδαῖοι in a much more clearly hostile sense in the gospel of John, whose 'Jewishness' is increasingly recognised, suggests caution in building an argument on this one isolated use. It is after all among 'Jews' that one would expect a story issued by the Jerusalem priests to circulate, and an author aware of the need to counter this official Jewish propaganda (for which see also Justin, *Dial.* 108 – it was still put forward by 'Jews' in the second century) might well express himself in this way even if himself a Jew.[71]

Among the various arguments which have been offered for a Gentile authorship for Matthew, the presence of the Sadducees in 16:1-12 is probably the strongest, though we have seen that it is far from conclusive. When this argument is set over against the extensive evidence of Jewish background and interests which we have noted, and which will emerge more fully in succeeding chapters, it seems unlikely that this viewpoint, despite its recent vogue, will achieve lasting success. When the fullest account has been taken of the paradox of Matthew's 'Jewish' and 'anti-Jewish' characteristics, the most plausible explanation remains that the author was writing in the painful situation of a Jew who, by following Jesus, had begun to find himself increasingly at odds with official Judaism, and to recognise that the purpose of God in fulfilment of his Old Testament promises was now to be discerned on a wider front than merely that of ethnic Israel. Subsequent chapters will allow us to fill out this picture, and to assess more fully Matthew's attitude to Israel and to the Christian mission both to Jews and to Gentiles.

D. MATTHEW'S CHURCH

Our discussion so far suggests that the setting of the gospel may be seen as that of early Jewish-Christianity, late enough for there to be a clear distinction and indeed hostility between the Jewish Christian community and unbelieving Judaism, but early enough for the relation between the two communities to be still a live issue, and for the members of Matthew's church to see themselves more as the true fulfilment of the Old Testament people of God than as some sort of 'third race', They were by no means a purely Jewish group, in that they expected and welcomed converts from all nations, and saw the purpose of God as now reaching its fulfilment outside the structure of the Jewish nation. They may well have included a good proportion of Gentile believers among them, but still thought primarily in Jewish categories. The following chapters will fill out this picture.

But can we be more specific about the particular circumstances of the church in and for which Matthew was writing? How far does his gospel enable us to reconstruct its particular needs and tensions, and its place within the spectrum of first-century Christianity? Modern New Testament scholarship has focused a great deal on trying to discern behind the various writings the circumstances to which they relate, and

71. See also the arguments of M. Lowe, *NovT* 18 (1976) 101-130 (cf. E. Schillebeeckx, *Christ* [ET, London: SCM, 1980] 872-873, n.36) that οἱ Ἰουδαῖοι in John should be understood as a more narrowly geographical term, 'Judaeans'; if that usage is allowed, Matthew's reference here would be to a story particularly circulated in the area around Jerusalem.

in particular the opponents, or at least unacceptable tendencies, which the author is attacking. Sometimes this search has been taken to the extreme of postulating an identifiable heretical group to account for almost every theme which the author wishes to emphasise, assuming a polemical intention even where he is apparently making positive statements with no ulterior motive! But it is generally true that the New Testament documents are occasional writings, so that it should in principle be possible to reconstruct something of the situation which caused the author to put pen to paper. Such reconstruction is clearly easier in the case of the letters of Paul, which often deal directly with questions and problems raised in the church, and where these issues apparently constitute the main reason for writing. But even in the case of a gospel, whose framework is provided not by a particular set of problems, but by the life and teaching of Jesus, it may be possible with caution to suggest that an evangelist angles his presentation in a particular way because of certain tendencies in the church for which he is writing. Few authors write *purely* from an abstract love of their subject.

In recent discussion of the circumstances of Matthew's church a few issues have been prominent, though there has perhaps been more agreement on the issues for debate than on the conclusions reached!

ATTITUDES TO THE LAW

As we shall see in chapter 5, the role of the law (both that of the Old Testament and the subsequent expansion of Jewish scribal teaching based on it) in relation to Jesus and his teaching is a prominent theme in Matthew. It is the subject of a full-scale discussion in 5:17-48, and many other pericopes revert to the theme as it relates to various specific legal issues. Bornkamm[72] noted that the discussion in chapter 5 is specifically addressed to those who might 'think that I have come to abolish the law and the prophets', and his pupil G. Barth developed the view, based primarily on 5:17ff, 7:15ff and 24:11ff, that a main aim of the gospel was to combat antinomianism in Matthew's church.[73] In view of the strong emphasis in Paul's letters on the Christian's emancipation from bondage to the law, it is likely that some Christians would tend towards the radical view that the law has no longer any validity for the church. But Barth believes that those against whom Matthew directed his attack had gone further than Paul or any other Jewish Christian could have gone, and must represent a Hellenistic

72. Bornkamm, Barth & Held, *Tradition*, 24.
73. *Ibid.* especially 159-164.

element in the church, whom Barth describes as 'libertines', for whom 'Christ has abolished the law'.[74] While Barth is reluctant to identify this supposed group more specifically, subsequent discussion has tended to regard even this cautious statement as too specific. It is possible to envisage irresponsible tendencies in Matthew's church which would adequately explain the polemic of passages like 7:15ff without going so far as to reconstruct a doctrinaire Hellenistic antinomianism. As Mohrlang rightly points out, the charge of ἀνομία leveled apparently against members of the disciple community in 7:23; 13:41; 24:11f 'is probably best taken in a broader moral sense, as the antithesis of Matthew's δικαιοσύνη, and not identified with the concept of antinomianism (in the narrow, more literal sense) against which he battles in 5.17-19'.[75] No doubt there were then, as there always have been, Christians whose life did not match up to the expectations of a conscientious pastor, but one does not have to be a 'theological antinomian' to indulge in behaviour incompatible with Christian discipleship! And the apparently apologetic tone of 5:17-19 is as easily explained in the light of non-Christian Jewish suspicions about Jesus' radicalism[76] as by postulating a deliberately antinomian movement within the church.

RELATION TO PAULINE CHRISTIANITY

In view of the prominence of Paul and the breadth of his influence in the church around and after the middle of the first century, it is hardly surprising that the relation of Matthew's church to Pauline Christianity has been debated.[77] A lengthy discussion by W.D. Davies,[78] while it focuses on the Sermon on the Mount, takes in the wider perspective of Matthew's theology. Davies recognises in Matthew significant differences from Paul's presentation of the gospel, and from the sort of Christianity which may be assumed to have arisen on the basis of Paul's teaching. But difference is not opposition, and Davies concludes, in contrast with many earlier writers, that Matthew does not display a deliberate polemic against either Paul or Paulinism. Indeed,

---

74. J. Zumstein, *La Condition du Croyant dans l'Evangile selon Matthieu* (Fribourg: Editions Universitaires/Göttingen: Vandenhoeck & Ruprecht, 1977) 171- 200 similarly sets out to examine the divisions within the Matthean community. Focusing on the pejorative terms of the gospel, ἀνομία, πλανάω, σκάνδαλον/-ίζω and ψευδοπροφήτης, he discerns 'a serious confessional conflict', focused on the question of the validity of the law. See especially pp. 172-173, 198-200.
75. Mohrlang, *Matthew and Paul*, 16.
76. For this view, with a mention of some of its proponents, see *ibid*. 16-17.
77. For a brief survey of such discussion see Mohrlang, *ibid*. 5-6.
78. W.D. Davies, *The Setting of the Sermon on the Mount* (Cambridge University Press, 1963) 316-366.

he goes further and argues that Paul, in his dependence on the words of Jesus, was not as far from Matthew as is often suggested. 'He shared with Matthew a common understanding of Christ and his words.' This line of approach has been taken substantially further by M.D. Goulder, who takes the relation between Matthew and Paul to the point of suggesting that 'time and again we find Paul's teaching reappearing, if not actually echoed, in Matthew'.[79] At some points in Matthew Goulder finds direct literary dependence on the letters of Paul. Not that he regards Matthew as 'a Pauline Christian': Matthew is far more conservative than Paul. But he is well acquainted with and strongly influenced by Paul's thought, which is a natural starting-point for his own distinctive theology and ethics.

There is room for debate as to how much 'Paulinism' it is appropriate to see in Matthew, but the studies of Davies and Goulder do at least indicate that the older tendency to see Matthew as engaged in a polemic *against* Paulinism (whether that of Paul himself or of his more extreme followers) is to go too far in exaggerating the difference between the two writers. That such a difference exists, both in their usage of key terms such as $\pi i\sigma\tau\iota\varsigma$ and $\delta\iota\kappa\alpha\iota o\sigma\upsilon\nu\eta$ and in the focus of their understanding of the nature of salvation and of discipleship, is undeniable. In the area of ethics this difference of perspective has recently been effectively demonstrated by Mohrlang, but with the conclusion that 'the emphases of the two are complementary' rather than in opposition to one another.[80]

It is, then, likely that Matthew's church was aware of and influenced by the teaching of Paul, but most unlikely that Matthew was unhappy with the degree of this influence, or designed his gospel to counter it.

TEACHING IN THE CHURCH

P.S. Minear has labeled Matthew 'The Teacher's Gospel', by which he means both that Matthew was himself a skilled teacher (a Christian 'scribe') and also that he wrote for teachers, 'men and women who, like many of us, were charged with basic educational work among adult believers in Jesus Christ.'[81] He sees the immediately intended readership as professional Christian scribes, for whom Matthew prepared this collection of traditions about Jesus for use in their work of oral teaching in the churches. Kilpatrick similarly draws attention to the mention by Matthew (only) of Christian 'prophets and wise men and scribes' (23:34), and concludes from a few other Matthean uses of these or similar terms that Matthew's church had 'a ministry of prophets and teachers', who

79. Goulder, *Midrash*, 156. The question is discussed *ibid.* 153-170, and is further developed in his *The Evangelists' Calendar* (London: SPCK, 1978) 223-240.
80. Mohrlang, *Matthew and Paul*, especially pp. 126-132.
81. Minear, *Matthew*, xii.

played a role in the worship of the church, but were particularly important in guiding and supporting the church in the face of 'moral laxity, the peril of false doctrine, and persecution from Jew and Gentile'.[82]

It is certainly true, as we shall see in chapter 7, that there is much in this gospel which would be relevant for dealing with such problems in the church. It would have been then, as it has proved ever since, a valuable resource book for teachers (and equally for ordinary church members) in facing up to many of the practical and intellectual problems of Christian discipleship. It is less certain, however, that it is appropriate to see it as angled specifically to the needs of the church leader or teacher. That there were such leaders in the congregation is likely enough, but they do not seem to be specifically addressed in Matthew's gospel (except perhaps in 23:8-10 ?). Even 18:15-17, which is often cited as a clear example of instruction for church leaders on disciplinary procedure, is not in fact addressed to a leadership group, but to the individual church member. To describe the gospel (or even any part of it) as primarily a manual for church leaders or teachers seems far too restrictive, however appropriate some of its contents might be for their needs. G. Bornkamm, for instance, has been particularly associated with the description of Matthew 18 as a 'Rule for the Congregation' (*Gemeindeordnung*), though he recognises that only vv. 15-18 appear on the surface to be so intended, and that Matthew is conspicuously lacking in the rules and regulations for officials of the congregation which one finds in the Pastoral Epistles or the Didache.[83] W. G. Thompson argues to the contrary that the contents of chapter 18 'are better classified as wisdom sayings or advice rather than as regulations or prescriptions for a "community-order" (*Gemeindeordnung*)'.[84]

It has sometimes been suggested that Matthew's gospel might better be described as a manual not so much for the leader as for the ordinary church member, perhaps for use in connection with a course of catechesis.[85] A section such as the Sermon on the Mount would obviously lend itself to such use. But again the question arises whether a use for which the gospel might be appropriate need be seen as its primary *raison d'être*, or indeed whether it is realistic to define *one* single purpose for which the gospel was written. We shall return to this question.

As far as the nature of Matthew's church is concerned, then, it is to be assumed in any case that a first-century church would contain teachers and taught, leaders and catechumens. We may reasonably

---

82. Kilpatrick, *Origins*, 126-127.
83. See especially his article, 'The Authority to "Bind" and "Loose" in the Church in Matthew's Gospel'.
84. Thompson, *Advice*, 266. The whole dissertation tends to question an understanding of Matthew 18 which relates it specifically to the role of official leaders in the church.
85. Kilpatrick, *Origins*, 78-80, assumed that the main rival to his view of a liturgical purpose for the gospel would be that it was written as a catechetical manual.

suppose that the special emphases of the gospel reflect some of the topics of current concern within the community, and that the gospel would have a natural role in guiding both the leader and the ordinary church member on these issues. But beyond these very general and obvious points, it is hard to draw any more specific conclusions from the gospel with regard to the nature of the teaching office within this particular church.

'THE SCHOOL OF SAINT MATTHEW'

A more specific delineation of the nature of the teaching group which lay behind the gospel was attempted by K. Stendahl in his significant monograph of the above title, to which I have already referred.[86] While the main concern of the book was with the detailed analysis and discussion of the formal quotations from the Old Testament in the gospel, this study led him to the conclusion that so distinctive an approach to the understanding and use of the Old Testament must have come out of an equally distinctive life-setting. Writing in the days when the Qumran discoveries were beginning to become available to New Testament scholarship, and when there was a consequent tendency to view most aspects of New Testament studies in their light,[87] Stendahl found his model for the origin of Matthew in the Qumran community. Their no less distinctive scriptural exegesis derived, he believed, from a scholarly circle perhaps rather like the monks who worked in the library of a medieval monastery. Matthew's community too had such a 'school' of skilled exegetes, who worked together to produce a document which may be compared in its form and function with the 'Manual of Discipline' of Qumran (1QS) or the Didache, with its mixture of instruction for the individual disciple and directions for the church leadership. To describe its purpose as 'catechetical' is too limited; it belongs rather to 'a milieu of study and instruction', a 'school for teachers and church leaders'.

As we noted in discussing Stendahl's book earlier, the advent of redaction-criticism has produced a new climate in gospel studies which is less favourable to ideas of corporate authorship. Few would now argue for the production of the gospel by a 'school' just as Stendahl pictured it.[88] But it is certainly true, as we shall see in chapter 5, that some very sophisticated exegetical and theological thought lies behind and finds expression in some of the peculiarly Matthean uses of the Old Testament. Even if these are to be credited more to the individual

86. See above pp. 75-76.
87. Stendahl himself was aware of the danger; see *School*, 31, 'the temptation to over-stress the relevance of the Qumran Scrolls just now when they are so new to us'.
88. See the critical assessment of Stendahl's view by Gundry, *Use*, 155-159.

genius of the author than to the working of a scholarly 'cooperative', they require for their *Sitz im Leben* a church where such sophisticated discussion might be expected to meet with a sympathetic response on the part of at least some of the members. I have argued in an article devoted to the four formula-quotations of chapter 2 that Matthew may have been deliberately catering for different levels of erudition and sophistication among his readership, from those who were virtually scripturally illiterate to those who had the expertise and the midrashic subtlety to appreciate his more abstruse allusions and typological connections.[89] In that case we are to envisage a church which, while it may not have included so defined a 'school' as Stendahl proposed, had within it some (who are likely to have been leaders, perhaps preachers) who were at home in sophisticated scriptural exegesis. Perhaps the gospel itself may be seen not so much as a manual of instruction but rather as exhibiting, in its presentation of the stories and the teaching of Jesus, the sort of preaching which would have been heard by a visitor to Matthew's church.

THE GOSPEL IN THE CHURCH'S WORSHIP

It was not long before Matthew's gospel, in common with the other gospels, came to be read consecutively in the worship of the church, just as it still is in many Christian circles today. Most of the early manuscripts of the gospels contain some sort of divisions or paragraph markers, and it may be suggested that these were introduced to indicate the accepted divisions of the text for such lectionary purposes (though it is more commonly assumed that these division markers, like those worked out by Eusebius in the fourth century, were put in to facilitate the comparison of synoptic parallels).[90] To observe this is not necessarily to discover anything about the church in which the gospel originated, but only about the later use of the gospel. But it has been suggested that the gospel was designed specifically for such use; if this were true, it would give us some insight into the worshipping life of Matthew's church.

Modern discussion of this possibility was launched by Kilpatrick, though it should perhaps be mentioned that P. Carrington's studies of Mark as a lectionary document included, apparently independently of Kilpatrick, the assumption that Matthew too was written for the same

---

89. 'The Formula-Quotations of Matthew 2 and the Problem of Communication', *NTS* 27 (1980/1) 233-251. See further below pp. 183-184.
90. For a basic account of such markers and their function see B.M. Metzger, *The Text of the New Testament* (Oxford University Press, ²1968), 21-25, 30-31. Metzger mentions specifically lectionary markers only in 'the later uncial manuscripts'.

purpose.[91] Kilpatrick observes that Matthew's gospel bears less indication of being intended for 'missionary propaganda' than that of Luke, and concludes that it was designed for use within the Christian church. And since there was, he assumes, no class of private readers sufficient to justify the production of a book specifically for their needs, it must have been for public use. He reconstructs the nature of that use from the practice of the synagogue, where the public reading of the Law and the Prophets followed by exposition was a regular feature of worship. Once Christians began to meet on their own, they would tend to follow this same pattern, but with the use of their own specifically Christian books along with those of the Old Testament. Kilpatrick sees this as the genesis of 'such documents as Mark, Q, and M'. As these documents were repeatedly read and commented on 'there was bound to develop a fixed element in exposition', leading to the recasting of the gospel materials, and out of this process Matthew's gospel emerged, itself intended for regular reading in worship.

Kilpatrick presents this hypothesis as a reconstruction of what is likely to have been the case, rather than as a necessary conclusion from the evidence.[92] The hypothesis is then tested in a long chapter[93] examining various indications of 'the liturgical character of the gospel', in the course of which Kilpatrick also argues against a catechetical purpose, which he takes to be the only serious alternative proposal for the setting of the gospel in the public life of the church. Both in Matthew's abbreviations of Marcan stories and in his additions to the tradition Kilpatrick finds evidence of a liturgical purpose. The clear structure and use of repeated formulae are taken to point the same way, as is the 'improvement' of some rougher features of Mark, and the 'smoother' style in some Q material. And the fact that Matthew's gospel was the most quoted in the early church is taken to point to its success as a liturgical production.

While it may be admitted that these and the other features listed by Kilpatrick would be appropriate to a book designed for liturgical reading, it is hard to see why any of them, or even all of them collectively, may not equally well be explained by some other purpose which required a clear, concise, well-structured text. Kilpatrick rightly points out that the focus of interest in the gospel is wider than merely the instruction of new converts,[94] but the obvious conclusion from this fact is surely not that a liturgical purpose is left as the only conceivable setting, but

91. P. Carrington, *The Primitive Christian Calendar*, vol. 1 (Cambridge University Press, 1952) 27-28, 60-62 makes this assumption, without detailed argument; the focus of the book is on Mark, not Matthew. No reference is made to Kilpatrick's work, published six years earlier.
92. It is set out in *Origins*, 59-71.
93. *Ibid.* 72-100.
94. *Ibid.* 78-79.

rather that it is not realistic to restrict the author's aim to a single function within the life of the church. We shall take up this point later. When Kilpatrick goes on to argue at length 'that much of the material in the Gospel shows signs of previous homiletic use', this may tell us a lot about the nature of the traditions available to the evangelist, and indeed about Matthew's own role as a preacher, but it hardly demands that the book was composed specifically for liturgical reading, however appropriate it may in fact have proved to be for that purpose in due course.

While Kilpatrick's thesis has not been widely supported, it has found an enthusiastic and industrious champion in M.D. Goulder, whose *Midrash and Lection in Matthew* is largely devoted to developing this thesis, and who has subsequently extended his studies to the Gospel of Luke, which he believes to be designed, on the basis of Matthew, also to fit into the church's lectionary.[95] Whereas Kilpatrick had argued merely on the grounds of the general suitability of the form and features of Matthew for liturgical use, Goulder has attempted to reconstruct the actual cycle of Old Testament readings into which Matthew was designed to fit, and to demonstrate how each pericope of the gospel fits in with the Old Testament lection to which it thus belongs. Indeed he goes further, and suggests that most of the non-Marcan contents of the gospel derive not from tradition but from Matthew's own 'midrashic' imagination brought to bear on the Old Testament lections.

Leaving aside for the moment the question of Matthew's use of traditions other than Mark, Goulder's lectionary theory is a bold attempt to provide a comprehensive account of the origin of Matthew in the context of the church's worship. His own summary is worth quoting:

> The theory that I wish to propose is a lectionary theory: that is, that the Gospel was developed liturgically, and was intended to be used liturgically; and that its order is liturgically significant, in that it follows the lections of the Jewish Year. Matthew, I believe, wrote his Gospel to be read in church round the year; he took the Jewish Festal Year, and the pattern of lections prescribed therefor, as his base; and it is possible for us to descry from Ms. evidence for which feast, and for which Sabbath/Sunday, and even on occasion for which service, any particular verses were intended. Such claims do not err on the side of modesty . . .[96]

It should be noted that Goulder does not wish to present Matthew as an innovator in this regard, but suggests that many parts of the Old Testament were similarly designed for regular reading, and attempts

95. Goulder, *The Evangelists' Calendar.*
96. *Midrash,* 172.

to demonstrate this in the case of Chronicles, which he sees as the most significant parallel to the sort of 'midrashic' work he finds in Matthew.[97]

Any attempt to reconstruct the likely pattern of readings in synagogue worship in the first century AD is full of problems, requiring complex argument from very inadequate evidence. It is an area where the non-specialist must tread with caution, aware that several conflicting, indeed mutually exclusive, reconstructions have been attempted both by Jewish and Christian scholars.[98] To move from Jewish practice to Christian is to compound the uncertainty.[99] Goulder proposes to avoid some of the uncertainties by focusing initially on the Festal cycle rather than a sabbath cycle, which is where most of the disagreement about synagogue practice has centred (though he subsequently postulates Matthew's familiarity with a one-year sabbath cycle as well). But the 'Christian version of the Jewish Festal Year' which he sets out is based not so much on actual evidence of how the first Christians organised their worship as on statements of what is 'likely' or 'would be' the case.[100] It is based, moreover, on only one of a number of competing systems of division of the text found in the early manuscripts, that of Codex Alexandrinus and related manuscripts.

It is *possible* that Scripture was read in the way Goulder suggests, both in the synagogue and in the church, and it is *possible* (with some ingenuity!) to fit the Alexandrinus divisions of Matthew to the appropriate dates; once one has started down Goulder's lectionary road, this may be a plausible way to reconstruct the situation. But what is lacking is any clear reason to wish to start along this road in the first place, and the sequence of tenuous links in the argument which it necessitates suggests that the enterprise may have been from the start an unnecessary and unprofitable labour.[101]

There is no doubt that Matthew's gospel eventually proved well suited to provide regular lectionary readings in Christian worship, and it is possible that some at least of the division markers in early manuscripts derive from this use. But this fact does not require us to believe that the gospel was composed for this purpose, or that the church within which it was written had as yet developed the habit of regular reading of Christian writings alongside the Old Testament.

97. *Ibid.* 202-224.
98. Goulder's own account of previous discussion is sufficient to suggest caution: see *ibid.* 173 (especially n. 9), 182-183; also *The Evangelists' Calendar* 101-102. See further L. Morris in *Gospel Perspectives*, vol. 3, 134-139, questioning whether there was any settled lectionary in Jewish use in the first century AD, let alone whether we can now reconstruct it.
99. See L. Morris, *ibid.* 139-143.
100. *Ibid.* 183-192.
101. For a trenchant methodological critique of Goulder's theory, focusing on his tendency to present as fact what is mere speculation, see L. Morris, *art. cit*, 143-149. More gently, but no less decisively, see Stanton, 'Origin', 1938-1939.

A PORTRAIT OF MATTHEW'S CHURCH

One of the most interesting attempts to provide an overview of the Christian community which is reflected in the gospel of Matthew is that of E. Schweizer.[102] In this conservative Syrian congregation, for whom questions about the law are still vital, even though 'the group of Jesus' disciples has long since separated from "their" (i.e. the Jewish) synagogues', Schweizer notes certain recurrent characters. Of particular importance are the prophets. Matthew's polemic against *false* prophets indicates the beginning of a problem which continued to vex the church, as reflected in the Didache and Hermas; but it also presupposes that prophets as such were an important and acceptable part of the community. Charismatic activity is welcomed, even though it can be abused (7:15-23). The itinerant, miracle-working and teaching activity of Jesus himself, the 'charismatic prophet and healer', which is drawn out particularly in the Matthean formula-quotations, is 'a model for the disciple whose obedience in following Jesus is understood quite literally'.

Then there are wise men and scribes, with authority to 'bind' and 'loose', to interpret the will of God. But they do not appear as a distinct group; and while the role of the twelve is emphasised, and particularly that of Peter, their special position is a matter of their historical role rather than a difference in principle; 'everything that is said to them applies in principle to every disciple of Jesus'. And together with the prophets in 10:41-42 appear 'the righteous', and 'these little ones', (cf. the 'least' of 25:40,45, again described as 'righteous') which again are not terms for special sub-groups, but general designations for all disciples.

In practice not all were prophets, and not all had the special expertise to 'bind' and 'loose', but Matthew's concern is to prevent the development of a distinct 'ministry'. Especially in chapter 18, it is to every disciple that the commission is given to care for each 'little one'. 'It is thus a community which seems to know neither elders nor bishops nor deacons.' It is open to charismatic gifts, but above all committed to simple obedience to the teaching of Jesus.

This attractively simple and uncluttered form of early Christian piety had its subsequent development, Schweizer believes, in the radical unworldliness of the monastic movement. This development in Syria can be traced through the Didache, the Gospel of Thomas and other Christian apocrypha, but finds its clearest echo in the Apocalypse of Peter from Nag Hammadi, in which the 'little ones' refuse to be called

102. E. Schweizer, 'Matthew's Church', in Stanton, *Interpretation*, 129-155, translated from Schweizer's collection of essays, *Matthäus und seine Gemeinde* (Stuttgart: Katholisches Bibelwerk, 1974) 138-170. This article develops further the lines of thought suggested in Schweizer's article, 'Observance of the Law and Charismatic Activity in Matthew', *NTS* 16 (1969/70) 213-230.

bishops and deacons, and display a charismatic and ascetic quality which owes a lot to Matthew.[103].

J.D. Kingsbury[104] has questioned some aspects of Schweizer's portrait. In particular he argues firstly that when the whole contents of the gospel are taken into account it cannot be claimed that the majority of Matthew's church were wandering charismatics who had given up home and possessions, and secondly that the gospel does not indicate that the disciples were primarily healers and miracle-workers, but rather that teaching and preaching constituted their primary calling. Thus the life-style of Jesus and of his entourage during his ministry offered for Matthew's church not a literal blueprint for imitation by all disciples, but rather 'served a paradigmatic function, setting forth the nature, not necessarily the specifics, of discipleship'.

Perhaps Schweizer's portrait was too starkly drawn, and imposed an unrealistic uniformity on Matthew's church. No doubt it, like most churches, had its 'bourgeois' element, who had learned to adapt the radical ideals which they applauded to the realities of living in society, and whose 'light shone among men' more by a transformed scale of values than by a radically alternative life-style. Certainly if Schweizer intended to suggest that Matthew's church had devalued the ministry of teaching and preaching he was wide of the mark. But what is important in his portrait is its implied protest against the tendency of many interpreters to see Matthew as 'the ecclesiastical gospel', reflecting a developed institutional church and a hierarchical system of church government. The unstructured, almost egalitarian, nature of the church of the 'little ones' which he describes does far more justice to the atmosphere of chapter 18. No doubt the church had its teachers and its taught, and no doubt in practice the responsibility for 'binding' and 'loosing' tended to fall frequently on the same shoulders, but for all that it was (or at least it wanted to be) a church of servants, a church in which titles like 'rabbi', 'father' and 'leader' (23:8-10) had no place, a church of 'little ones'.

E. THE PURPOSE OF THE GOSPEL

The various attempts noted in the last section to define the special characteristics of Matthew's church or its life-setting have generally been linked with the search for the purpose for which the gospel was composed.

103. See G.N. Stanton in *JTS* 28 (1977) 80-83 for further analysis of the links of the Matthean community with the Apocalypse of Peter. Stanton finds the same strands picked up in 5 Ezra.
104. J.D. Kingsbury, *JBL* 97 (1978) 62-73.

Thus it may be suggested that Matthew wrote to convert non-Christian Jews, or to defend the gospel against Jewish hostility and misunderstanding. Or perhaps he wrote to help Christians develop their arguments against Pharisaic Judaism, and to help them to understand and to present the nature of the relationship between the Old Testament and its fulfilment in Jesus and the church.

Or was he gunning for a particular group within the church, those whose sense of emancipation from the law had led them into throwing off all restraint? Was he writing to correct certain emphases of Pauline Christianity – or conversely to reinforce them? Or was his gospel a protest against the increasing institutionalisation of what had begun as a spontaneous charismatic movement?

Did he have a particular segment of the church in mind: the leaders, in their pastoral and teaching responsibilities, or the new converts undergoing catechesis? Was his gospel then some sort of manual, for 'classroom' use? Did it derive from the discussions of a 'school' devoted to erudite scriptural exegesis, or was it meant to encapsulate the preaching ministry in which Matthew and his associates were engaged?

Or did the gospel arise out of the liturgical reading of earlier Christian documents, itself designed to take their place in the regular worship of the church? Was this, rather than a projected use as an instruction manual, the reason for its clarity of structure, its use of balancing sections and memorable formulae, and its conciseness in narration?

All these aims, and no doubt many more, have been offered in the search for 'the purpose of Matthew'. Many of them, if not all, may well reflect real-life uses to which the gospel was in fact put, and may indeed have been intended to fulfil. But I must confess that the eager search for 'the purpose of' each New Testament book seems to me often to lose touch with reality. How many books are ever written with just one purpose in mind? How many authors are able, or would wish, so to discipline their writing that the whole document is single- mindedly directed to one specific goal? How many books are written in a situation which allows one to predict that they will fall only into the hands of a clearly-defined target audience, so that no-one else need be considered by the author? I know that I have never yet written such a book, nor do I expect to! Was Matthew's situation, or his psychological make-up, necessarily different? I am well aware that the nature and purpose of book-production in first-century society is likely to have been very different from what it is today, but I wonder whether we have any reason to suppose that an author then would be more likely to operate under the constraint of a single all-determining purpose than we are today. Is not our ignorance of the real-life situation of such an author and his potential readers such that we should be very cautious in trying to reconstruct such a dominant aim?

With some books of the New Testament it may be more plausible to suggest what is *the* purpose in writing. Paul's letters are typically occasional documents written in response to a particular situation. But even here scholars have not found it easy in most cases to agree on what was the primary aim, or even to define the target audience with any precision. And few if any of Paul's letters could be regarded as *solely* directed to that one aim, whatever it may be. He is rich in what seem to us digressions and asides, in subsidiary themes and passing applications to different groups among his audience. All the diversity of the pastor's concerns and the breadth of the pastor's sympathies finds its way into his writings.

This is surely true also of Matthew, but with the important difference that in his case there is not on the surface a particular occasion which caused him to take up his pen. Rather his work is to be seen as falling within the continuing life and multiple concerns of the church to which he belonged. Discussion of how, if at all, the *genre* 'gospel' is to be defined continues vigorously, and is so far from reaching any clear consensus that it is tempting to conclude that the most that can be said is that a 'gospel' is a book about Jesus!

Granted, of course, that Matthew had a number of very clear 'bees in his bonnet', themes which would be bound to emerge in anything which he wrote, and that several of the specific targets suggested above do seem to be clearly indicated in the way the book is written. But to pick out any one (or more) of these themes or targets as *the* purpose of the book seems quite unrealistic, and the variety of answers which have been given to the question underlines its futility. Matthew's 'book about Jesus' was written to say the things about Jesus which Matthew believed to be important and was 'angled' at various points towards particular views or situations to which he felt he had something to say. But is there any reason to doubt that he designed it, in so far as his own horizons allowed, to communicate to *anyone*, Christian or non-Christian, who might wish to know more about Jesus, and into whose hands it might fall, or who might be present to hear it read in a gathering of the church?

In this chapter, then, I have attempted to analyse not so much the *purpose* of Matthew, as the setting in which and for which the gospel came to be written. At many points the reconstruction is uncertain, controversial, even to the point where virtually opposite theories are equally strongly advanced by different scholars. Our ignorance of the life and concerns of the first-century Christian community to which Matthew belonged is far greater than our knowledge. But while the enterprise has not led to agreed results, the discussion has alerted us to many features of the gospel which will be important in trying to understand its message. If we are not in a position to put ourselves confidently into the skins of Matthew's first readers, we have, I trust, become more sensitive to some of the issues with which they were confronted, and to which Matthew addressed himself in the distinctive form in which he chose to tell the story of Jesus.

IV

LITERARY CHARACTER OF THE GOSPEL

'Gospel' as a literary genre. The style of Matthew's writing. The structure of Matthew's gospel. Matthew's presentation of Jesus' teaching.

A. 'GOSPEL' AS A LITERARY GENRE

In the first chapter of his book on the gospel of Mark (in the same series as the present work),[1] Ralph Martin surveyed the discussion up to 1972 on the question 'What kind of a book is a gospel?'[2] This was the title of an interesting presentation of the question by C.F. Evans[3] in which he pictured the dilemma of a librarian at Alexandria wishing to classify a copy of Mark. The issue has been discussed primarily along the lines of whether or not a gospel is a 'biography', but there has not been agreement on what exactly constitutes a biography. Since Martin wrote, this question has been more vigorously pursued, particularly in American scholarship.

Until recently the New Testament gospels have been widely regarded as representing a unique literary phenomenon, with Mark as the 'creator' of this new genre. Their mixture of narrative form and kerygmatic aim, their remarkable concentration on the last few days of the life of their subject, while ignoring those aspects of his life and character on which a modern biographer might be expected to focus, their implicit (and sometimes explicit) presentation of Jesus not so much as an admirable teacher and example of the past but rather as a living object of faith in the present, and their clearly 'propagandist' aim, all these have been thought to mark the canonical gospels out as *sui generis*. But this view has recently been strongly challenged.

David Dungan and David Cartlidge compiled in 1971 a *Source-Book of Texts for the Comparative Study of the Gospels*, which has since gone through a number of editions.[4] Their aim is to set the gospels alongside

---

1. R.P. Martin, *Mark, Evangelist and Theologian* (Exeter: Paternoster, 1972) 17ff.
2. For a rather more wide-ranging survey covering the same period see R.H. Gundry, 'Recent Investigations into the Literary Genre "Gospel" ', in R.N. Longenecker & M.C. Tenney, ed., *New Dimensions in New Testament Study* (Grand Rapids: Zondervan, 1974) 97-114.
3. C.F. Evans *et al*, *The New Testament Gospels* (London: BBC, 1965) 7ff.
4. First published by the Society of Biblical Literature in 1971; revised and augmented third edition in 1973; completely revised again and published under the title *Documents for the Study of the Gospels* (London: Collins, 1980).

comparable literature of their period, generally treated as 'background' to the study of the canonical gospels; the result, they believe, should be to demonstrate that the four canonical gospels are not so totally distinct from their literary environment as has generally been supposed, and that there are significant similarities both in form and content. The range of material is wide, including both pagan and Jewish stories of remarkable men, and also later Christian 'gospel' material which is traditionally separated off as 'apocryphal' and thus inappropriately, they believe, placed in a different category. Most interestingly for our purpose, the comparison takes in not only specific accounts of events comparable with those in the gospels, but also whole works which in their literary character are regarded as similar to the gospels. The non-Christian works which they suggest as the closest parallels to the gospel genre are Philostratus' *Life of Apollonius of Tyana* (third century AD) and Philo's *Life of Moses* (first century AD).

The work of Dungan and Cartlidge at least rules out the simplistic notion that Jesus appeared as a sort of alien being in a world which had no ready-made categories against which to interpret him. But does it also indicate that the gospels would have been recognised by a non-Christian reader as a relatively familiar type of literature, which Dungan and Cartlidge describe as 'sacred biography'?[5] The term 'aretalogy' has also become familiar in New Testament scholarship to describe such accounts of extraordinary men, particularly as a result of the work of M. Hadas and M. Smith, *Heroes and Gods*.[6] The subtitle of that work, 'Spiritual Biographies in Antiquity', similarly emphasises the 'supernatural' flavour of such accounts. It may be questioned, however, whether the 'sacred' element is in itself a necessary ingredient in defining the genre; even in a world in which the distinction between 'sacred' and 'secular' was less clearly drawn than it is for us, some of the accounts of great men deriving from the Graeco-Roman culture of the time are not outstandingly 'sacred' in presentation, but it may be doubted whether that fact in itself puts them into a different literary category.[7]

A wide-ranging analysis of Graeco-Roman 'biographical' writing, to serve as a model for defining the genre of the gospels, has been attempted by C.H. Talbert.[8] In opposition to Bultmann's dictum that 'the gospels are not biographies', Talbert illustrates the range and character of writings in the Mediterranean world of the first century which might be described as βίοι, and shows how many of their characteristics are

5. Dungan and Cartlidge, *Documents*, 203.
6. New York: Harper & Row, 1965.
7. For a cautious assessment of the relevance of 'aretalogy' as a model for the study of the gospels, see P.L. Shuler, *A Genre for the Gospels: the Biographical Character of Matthew* (Philadelphia: Fortress, 1982) 15-20.
8. C.H. Talbert, *What is a Gospel? The Genre of the Canonical Gospels* (Philadelphia: Fortress, 1977).

found also in the canonical gospels. He proposes to group ancient biographies into five categories indicating the function which they were designed to fulfil: A, to provide a pattern to copy; B, to dispel a false image of the subject and substitute a true model; C, to discredit the subject by exposé; D, to show where the true tradition arising out of the subject's teaching is to be found; E, to provide a hermeneutical key to the subject's teaching.[9] All the gospels, he believes, fit into category B, and as such exhibit a central characteristic of ancient biographical writing. But whereas in the case of Mark and John the type B classification is straightforward, with Luke an element of type D is added by the extension into Acts, and Matthew is essentially of type E (while retaining B characteristics).

This final classification is made rather hastily in the conclusion of the book, and is in need at least of considerable refinement. But this is not the main point of Talbert's work. For his central thesis of the similarity in terms of literary genre between the gospels and ancient Graeco-Roman biographies, he has made a plausible case in broad terms, however much his treatment may require modification in detail.[10] Perhaps the Alexandrian librarian imagined by C.F. Evans would have been so completely baffled by their classification as has traditionally been thought.

It is of course true that the gospels were not written in a primarily Graeco-Roman context, and Talbert's concentration on Graeco-Roman rather than Jewish literature means that his work can be seen only as an exercise in comparison across cultural frontiers. It may help us to understand how the gospels may have been received by readers outside the Jewish milieu from which they came, but it cannot tell us anything about how the writers themselves understood their task unless it can be shown that they, like Philo, were writing with an eye to a primarily non-Jewish readership. This drawback of Talbert's approach applies also to many of the other recent discussions of gospel genre, which tend to assume that the Alexandrian librarian represents the readership which the authors had in view. For Matthew at least that is, as we have seen, a most unlikely assumption.

Talbert's attempt to locate the gospels within the milieu of Graeco-Roman biography has been taken further, and applied specifically to Matthew, by P.L. Shuler.[11] Noting that the gospels focus on a single person whom they aim to praise and commend, Shuler proposes to include them in the genre of laudatory biography, or, as it came to be

---

9. *Ibid.* 92-98.
10. For a lengthy and devastating critical review see D.E. Aune, in *Gospel Perspectives*, vol. 2 (1981) 9-60.
11. Shuler, *Genre*. The bulk of the book is on the question of biographical genre in general. Only pp. 92-109 focus specifically on Matthew.

called by the rhetoricians, *encomium* (such as the Lives written by
Cornelius Nepos and Plutarch). His study of this genre in Greek and
Latin literature covers many of the same works mentioned by Talbert,
and again it is note-worthy that the cultural context is throughout that
of the Graeco-Roman world, rather than the Jewish milieu to which
the gospels more directly belong. Two works by Jewish authors are
included (Philo's *Life of Moses* and Josephus' 'autobiography'), but it
is questionable how far either belongs to the cultural world of Matthew.
Shuler believes, however, that 'the gospels belong to the milieu of the
Greco-Roman world', and that, even if their authors were 'less educated
as authors, and their work less self-conscious', their writing nonetheless
displays a pattern 'similar in many ways to the ubiquitous pattern
found in laudatory biography of antiquity'.[12]

In applying this theory specifically to Matthew Shuler looks for τόποι,
literary techniques and indications of the author's purpose which correspond to those of Graeco-Roman *encomia*. Plausible points of comparison can be discovered in all these areas, though it is remarkable
that the search for τόποι (stock topics) is confined to chapters 1-4 and
26-28, which suggests that the bulk of Matthew's work offers little
ground for comparison in this area. As for Matthew's purpose, only
two points are made: that Matthew wishes to state Jesus' identity as
Messiah and Son of God, and that he wishes to move his readers to a
response of imitation and faith, both of which Shuler regards as locating
Matthew's work within the genre of *encomium* biography. It is certainly
true that at certain points there are similarities, particularly in the area
of literary techniques, between Matthew's work and various of the
Graeco-Roman laudatory biographies Shuler has studied, but they are
generally at the level of broad stylistic traits, and the failure to adduce
any examples of the τόποι characteristic of such works from the core
of Matthew's work (chapters 5-25) suggests that the differences may
be more significant than the similarities.

The question arises whether the whole attempt to define a genre and
to fit Matthew into it is not artificial. It may be true that Graeco-Roman
rhetoricians self-consciously discussed such genres, and the literary
techniques and emphases appropriate to them, and even that some
writers did consciously design their works so as to be recognised as
belonging to a particular genre (though I suspect that the extent to
which this was a controlling factor in ancient writing is easily exaggerated). But it is another matter to discern certain similarities to such
patterns in a work which derives from a different cultural milieu and
to conclude from these that the author was self-consciously conforming
to such a pattern, even though he gives no specific indication that this
was his intention. When the similarities are found to be as limited as

12. *Ibid.* 92.

those adduced by Shuler, it needs to be questioned how useful the comparison is for our understanding either of Matthew's own purpose or of the likely reception of his work by its intended readers.

Did Matthew or his readers, I wonder, *need* to have a genre classification in mind? Evans' Alexandrian librarian may have had a professional need for such a decision, and he may have found, like Shuler, sufficient similarity of approach to be happy to put Matthew into his 'biography' section (or even into his *encomium* biography' section, if he had one!). But this does not mean that a browser in his library who picked Matthew off the shelf along with Cornelius Nepos and Plutarch would have recognised the three as soul-mates. Indeed I suspect that he would soon have found himself thinking, 'This is an odd sort of biography', and that Matthew would not have been surprised or displeased by that reaction (if indeed he knew anything of Nepos – Plutarch had not yet written!). As for the readers Matthew had in mind when he wrote (whom I do not believe to have been dispassionate browsers in the library of Alexandria), I doubt whether they had, or needed, any such ready-made category into which to put Matthew's 'book about Jesus'. If they already knew one or more of the other gospels (or of the 'many' other narratives, διηγήσεις, to which Luke 1:1 refers), this would be a much more obvious category, not only in terms of subject-matter but also of literary form, and they would no doubt have recognised that Matthew was engaged on a similar enterprise.

Shuler makes the important point that genre 'is a dynamic, not a static, concept'.[13] Authors may and do display creativity as well as conformity. They may reshape existing genres to meet their particular aims. New genres emerge, perhaps by the combination of existing ones, perhaps because no existing model is appropriate to the task in hand. They do not emerge in a literary vacuum, and total innovation would be likely to result in complete incomprehensibility for any reader who was not specifically trained to the new model. But no writer worth his salt is bound to a rigid literary form. A comparison of Matthew's gospel with other 'biographical' writing of his day will not show him to be operating in a literary world of his own, but it will show that he and the other gospel writers have produced something which has in significant ways broken new ground in terms of literary genre. R.H. Gundry may be right in suggesting that it is inappropriate to 'speak of a genre known as "gospel" ',[14] but it may be still more misleading to attempt to fit the gospels simply into some other existing genre.[15]

13. *Ibid.* 25-28. Cf. D.E. Aune, *Gospel Perspectives* vol. 2, 46.
14. R.H. Gundry, 'Recent Investigations', 114.
15. Cf. on the whole question of the gospels in relation to ancient biographical writing the careful assessment by G.N. Stanton, *Jesus of Nazareth in New Testament Preaching* (Cambridge University Press, 1974) 117-136.

B. THE STYLE OF MATTHEW'S WRITING

'BIBLICAL' GREEK?

In discussing the authorship of the gospel we have noted that while the author clearly was capable of writing in good, idiomatic Greek, he also felt it appropriate on occasion to give a 'Semitic flavour' to his work.[16] Quite apart from the occasional use of transliterated Aramaic words (ῥακά, 5:22; μαμωνᾶς, 6:24; κορβανᾶς, 27:6), there are turns of phrase which would strike the Greek reader as rather 'quaint', perhaps in much the same way that phrases of Authorised Version English might alert a modern reader that the author wished to evoke a 'biblical' atmosphere in his writing.

Such turns of phrase include the frequent καὶ ἰδού ('and behold'); the awkward ἐχάρησαν χαρὰν μεγάλην σφόδρα ('they rejoiced a great joy, exceedingly') in 2:10; the redundant ἐκτείνας τὴν χεῖρα ('he stretched out his hand and') in 26:51 and other similarly 'redundant' participles (especially the frequent ἀποκριθείς before a verb of speaking); and the strikingly Semitic formula καὶ ἐγένετο ὅτε ἐτέλεσεν ὁ 'Ιησοῦς . . . (7.28; 11:1; 13:53; 19:1; 26:1), whose special literary function we shall notice shortly. Many other such apparently deliberately 'Semitic' features could be listed.[17] Whether by nature or by design, Matthew's book strikes the reader as distinctively 'biblical' in its style.

THE MARKS OF THE PREACHER

One of the reasons which E. von Dobschütz gave for his belief that Matthew was a converted rabbi was the observation of his fondness for repetition; 'when Matthew has once found a formula he sticks to it as much as possible and uses it repeatedly'.[18] The observation, if not also the deduction of a rabbinic background, is valid.

We shall be discussing the structure of the gospel shortly, and we shall note then the presence of such repeated formulae which may function as structural markers. We shall be noticing also in the next chapter the repetition ten times over of the formula 'This was to fulfil what was spoken by the prophet saying . . .', or very similar words to introduce a formal Old Testament quotation. But the phenomenon of repetition is much more widespread than that.

Sometimes whole stories seem to appear in duplicate in different

16. See above p. 64; cf. also 96-97.
17. See Moule, *Birth*, 276-280; Butler, *Originality*, 147-156. Moule offers a further interesting discussion of passages where Matthew may have deliberately exploited variant versions of an Aramaic word or phrase in his *Essays in New Testament Interpretation*, 70-72.
18. E. von Dobschütz, in Stanton, *Interpretation*, 19-29.

parts of the gospel: two very similar stories of the healing of two blind men appear in 9:27-31 and 20:29-34 (where Mark and Luke have only one parallel story, of a single blind man),[19] and two healings of a dumb demoniac followed by a Pharisaic accusation of collusion with Satan in 9:32-34 and 12:22-24. The editorial summary of Jesus' ministry in 4:23 reappears in almost identical form in 9:35. Sayings of Jesus are sometimes reintroduced in a closely similar form (e.g. 5:29-30 and 18:8-9; 7:16-20 and 12:33; 10:38-39 and 16:24-25; 12:38-39 and 16:1-2,4; 13:12 and 25:29; 19:30 and 20:16), and the description of the fate of the wicked as 'weeping and gnashing of teeth' occurs no less than six times. The list could be extended.[20] Matthew seems more like the preacher, whose favourite phrases and illustrations recur without embarrassment, and who regards repetition as a valuable teaching aid, rather than the literary purist who regards repetition as a stylistic *faux pas*.

Such repetitions sometimes serve to alert the reader to points of comparison between different characters in the story. For example, Matthew establishes by means of verbal echoes a closer link between John the Baptist and Jesus than is found in the other gospels. The summary of Jesus' preaching in 4:17 is an exact repetition of that of John's message in 3:2; John's trenchant epithet for the Pharisees and Sadducees, 'brood of vipers' (3:7), is used also by Jesus for the Pharisees in 12:34 and for the scribes and Pharisees in 23:33; John's 'fruit' metaphor

19. These stories are also examples of the curious Matthean phenomenon that in a number of cases where the other gospels mention a single actor in a story, Matthew mentions two. Apart from the stories of the blind man (men), there are the cases of the Gadarene demoniac(s) in Matthew 8:28, and of the two animals at the entry to Jerusalem (21:2,7). A further case where Matthew alone specifies 'two' is in the account of the trial in 26:60, but in that case his mention of two false witnesses stands for an unspecified (plural) number in Mark, not just one. In the last case it is likely that Matthew specifies two in order to achieve the minimum legal number for valid testimony, as laid down in Nu. 35:30; Dt. 17:6; 19:15, and it has been suggested that the same motive may lie behind his 'doubling' of the blind men and the demoniacs, all of whom function after their healing as 'witnesses' to who Jesus is; NB especially the use of 'Son of God' in 8:29 and of 'Son of David' in both 9:27 and 20:30f. (So J.M. Gibbs, *NTS* 10 (1963/4) 456-457.) A less plausible explanation is that Matthew has in this way compensated for the omission of other stories of healings of the same type (the exorcism of Mark 1:23ff and the blind man of Mark 8:22ff), thus retaining the same total number healed while reducing the number of stories. This not only seems a remarkably unsubtle and mechanical approach to the composition of the gospel by a man who elsewhere shows himself nothing if not subtle; but it also fails to take account of the repetition of the story of the blind man, which results in four blind men healed in all, not two! As for the two animals, the factor of the parallelism in the text of Zc. 9:9 which is quoted at that point clearly places this in a different category; see above pp. 105-106 for the reasons why I do not believe that Matthew simply invented a second animal because he mistakenly thought the text required it (again, could *Matthew* of all people be guilty of such literary insensitivity with regard to the Old Testament?). No single explanation is going to cover these very different cases of 'doubling' by Matthew, and perhaps they do not constitute a sufficiently consistent phenomenon to deserve mention as a Matthean stylistic trait.
20. See e.g. von Dobschütz, in Stanton, *Interpretation*, 20-23.

(3:8,10) is repeated several times by Jesus (7:16-20; 12:33; 21:41,43),
with an exact verbal repetition of 3:10 in 7:19; John's attack on the
complacency of the 'children of Abraham'(3:9) is taken up by Jesus in
8:11-12; John's metaphor of the gathering of the grain into the barn
to represent the ultimate salvation of the true people of God (3:12) is
used also by Jesus in 13:30. Verbal echoes are used also to establish a
similar continuity between Jesus and his disciples, whose preaching is
also described in 10:7 in the same words as 3:2 and 4:17, and whose
mission 'to heal every disease and every sickness' (10:1) exactly echoes
that of Jesus in 4:23 and 9:35, while the list of their healing activities
in 10:8 closely follows the pattern of Jesus' ministry as described in
chapters 8-9. Their mission, like that of Jesus, is restricted to 'the lost
sheep of the house of Israel' (10:6; 15:24).

It is not only in the echoes of earlier wording, but also in the form
of the individual sayings themselves that the skill of the teacher or
preacher may be discerned. A fascinating chapter in Goulder's *Midrash
and Lection in Matthew*[21] analyses 'Matthew's poetry'. Without attempting, as Burney and Jeremias have done, to produce a back-translation
of the Greek sayings into Aramaic, Goulder shows that Matthew has
many more 'poetic' sayings than do Mark and Luke. By 'poetic' he
means those which display a balanced structure, such as 'Many are
called but few are chosen', or 'Be wise as serpents and harmless as
doves'; in fact Goulder separates out (under his own rather quaint
designations) eleven different types of 'rhythm' or parallelism. Such
sayings are instantly memorable, and would be of obvious use to the
teacher or preacher who wanted his message to be retained. One might
question whether 'poetry' is always the right term (at least in our own
literary context – Hebrew poetry was of course very different from
ours); many of these sayings are more of the nature of epigrams or
proverbs. But there is no doubt that the presence of so many such
sayings in Matthew's gospel goes a long way to account for its popularity
in early Christian teaching. A study of Goulder's chapter will leave the
reader profoundly impressed by the literary and communicative skill
of the mind which lies behind such teaching, both that of the teacher
from whom the sayings originally derive and also that of the evangelist
who appreciated and shared his master's expertise as a teacher.

Another feature of Matthew's style which reminds one of the preacher
or teacher is the way so much of the material, particularly the teaching
material, is grouped in symmetrical structures, often marked out by
repeated words or phrases. The effect is to make this gospel a suitable
quarry for blocks of material for easy memorisation. Obvious examples
are the eight 'beatitudes' with which the Sermon on the Mount opens

21. Chapter 4, pp. 70-94.

(with the first and last sharing the same second clause, and the first four all beginning in Greek with the letter π); the six 'antitheses' which take up the second half of chapter 5, all introduced by variants of the formula, 'You have heard that it was said . . ., but I say to you . . .'; the three-fold exposure of religious showmanship in 6:1-6, 16-18, where each of the three cameos is framed in identical language; the unforgettable exhortation to persistent prayer, again in balancing three-fold form, in 7:7-8.

Those examples are taken only from the Sermon on the Mount, and do not exhaust the evidence for this trait even in that section of the gospel alone. In the gospel as a whole there are many more, and in particular a fondness for groups of three (a number hallowed by long experience of preachers as the optimum structure for retention by the congregation!). There are the three groups of fourteen generations which make up the genealogy (a point which Matthew specifically draws to his readers' attention, 1:17), three temptations with their three quotations from Deuteronomy in reply, three parables directed against the religious authorities in 21:28–22:14, seven 'woes' on the scribes and Pharisees in 23:13-36 (with repeated formula, 'woe to you, scribes and Pharisees, hypocrites, because . . .'), three prayers of Jesus in Gethsemane and three returns to the sleeping disciples, three challenges to Peter met by three denials.[22]

Not all of these groupings are peculiar to Matthew, but most of them are, and the cumulative effect is to suggest an author who was used to preaching and teaching his material, and who expected it to be so used in its written form. No doubt this was a skill he had learned from his own Teacher, and several of the examples we have noticed seem to be inherent in the form of the teaching of Jesus as Matthew would have received it; but it was a habit of presentation which Matthew the disciple copied and developed with enthusiasm.

Some parts of the gospel show signs of more large-scale structuring (i.e. sections of a chapter or more where some sort of symmetry is apparent which is additional to the overall structural patterns of the whole gospel) in a way which was apparently meant to be noticed and remembered. A remarkable example is the collection of parables and teaching about parables which makes up the bulk of chapter 13, the structure of which may be set out as shown on p. 132.

The chapter on parables is one of the five great discourses marked out by the use of the formula καὶ ἐγένετο ὅτε ἐτέλεσεν ὁ Ἰησοῦς . . ., to which we shall return shortly. It is generally agreed that these discourses owe their structure to Matthew's editorial work, though

22. A considerably longer list, not all items in which are equally impressive, is offered by Allen, *Matthew*, lxv.

Introductory parable: the sower (1-9)

Interlude: the purpose of parables (10-17)
explanation of the sower (18-23)

Three parables of growth: the weeds (24-30)
the mustard seed (31-32)
the yeast (33)

Interlude: the purpose of parables (34-35)
explanation of the weeds (36-43)

Three further parables: the treasure (44)
the pearl (45-46)
the net (47-50)

Concluding parable: the householder (51-53).

none of the others displays so obvious a structural pattern for the whole discourse as does chapter 13. The collection of Jesus' teaching on discipleship which makes up the Sermon on the Mount finds its coherence more in its theme than in its structure, though it contains within it a number of carefully structured units, as we have seen. But it may reasonably be suggested that the Sermon on the Mount itself forms part of a larger section consisting of chapters 5-9, which sets out first the activity of the Messiah in teaching (chapters 5-7), then in healing and other miraculous activity (chapters 8-9) – thus illustrating the ministry of 'teaching, preaching and healing' which was introduced in 4:23 (a summary repeated at the end of the section in 9:35).

And the second part of this dual presentation of the Messiah's ministry itself displays a structural form not unlike that of chapter 13. Chapters 8-9, like the preceding Sermon on the Mount, are something of an anthology of material (in this case stories) which is scattered in different parts of the other Synoptic Gospels. They contain ten specific miracles, but as two of them are interwoven in a single story (9:18-26), there are nine narrative units of Jesus' miraculous activity. These may be seen as arranged in three groups of three (8:1-15; 8:23 - 9:8; 9:18-34), which are separated as in chapter 13 by 'interludes', the first presenting Jesus' healing ministry in general as the fulfilment of Scripture (8:16-17) together with examples of what it means to follow him (8:18-22), the second offering in the call of Matthew and the succeeding discussion a further insight into the nature of discipleship (9:9-17). Attempts to identify common features in each of the three groups of miracles have not been widely accepted, and the structure is less precise and symmetrical than that of chapter 13, but it is perhaps sufficiently clear to indicate the same organising mind at work.

The perception of such structural patterns is a notoriously subjective business, and I am generally sceptical of those who claim to find symmetrical patterns in sections of biblical books where they have not generally been perceived by ordinary readers, particularly when they dignify their discoveries with the magic name 'chiasmus'. Occasionally an otherwise unexplained lack of continuity may suggest a deliberate arrangement of this type, as when the story of the guard achieves surprising prominence in the final section of the gospel by being told in two episodes, which suggests the possibility that Matthew intended the following pattern to be noticed:

> Jesus dead and buried (27:57-61)
> Setting of the guard (27:62-66)
> The empty tomb and the risen Lord (28:1-10)
> Report of the guard (28:11-15)
> Jesus alive and sovereign (28:16-20).

That one happens to appeal to me, but I must recognise that not everyone would see it as self-evident, and in general I do not favour the search for such patterns which have hitherto escaped detection.

But even with this caution in mind, there is enough clear structuring of sections within the gospel of Matthew, quite apart from the question of its overall framework, to indicate a writer who was used to having his material well-organised, and who expected his readers to notice and take advantage of this organisation. Is it not reasonable to see in these features the mark of the preacher?

MATTHEW AS STORY-TELLER

One of the most marked features of Matthew's gospel as compared with Mark's is his tendency to condense the narrative. Augustine could hardly have been more wrong when he described Mark as Matthew's *breviator*; in the narratives where they run parallel the situation is precisely the opposite.

A striking example of this may be seen by comparing Mark chapter 5 with the parallel sections of Matthew, 8:28-34 and 9:18-26. Mark contains in this section no additional story, and yet what occupies 43 verses in Mark (and 31 in Luke) takes up only 16 in Matthew. The difference is accounted for primarily by Mark's expansive style of story-telling, where Matthew is compact and 'businesslike', getting to the essentials of the narrative with as little distraction as possible.

Thus in the story of the Gadarene demoniac(s) Mark's vivid account of the attempts to tame the wild man are represented in Matthew by only two words, χαλεποὶ λίαν, 'very difficult'! Mark's account of his behaviour, and of the discussion with Jesus over his name ('Legion'),

has no parallel in Matthew. The graphic account of the reaction of the
locals appears in Matthew merely as 'they begged him to leave their
region', and the response of the demoniac himself, his desire to follow
Jesus and Jesus' refusal, is simply not mentioned. Attention is thus
focused on the fate of the pigs, as a remarkable instance of the power
of Jesus and the sensation which it caused, rather than on the deliverance
of the (two) possessed men. As this story features as part of the collection
of miracles displaying the authority of Jesus the Messiah in action
(chapters 8-9 of Matthew), it seems clear that Matthew has pruned the
narrative to what was essential to convey this message. Here, and
generally, he has an eye not so much to the intrinsic interest of the
story, but rather to its function in his total presentation of Jesus.

Similarly, the healing of the woman with a haemorrhage, which is
told in 154 words in Mark 5:25-34 (and 114 in Luke), takes up a mere
48 words in Matthew 9:20-22. Gone are the accounts of her long,
expensive, and useless involvement with the medical profession, of Jesus'
discussion with his disciples about who touched him, and of the woman's
fear of discovery. Yet Matthew's bare account contains all the essential
elements: the length of her illness, her conviction that a mere touch of
his garment would suffice, Jesus' declaration, 'Take heart, daughter,
your faith has made you well', and the fact of her instant healing. It
is so stark that the reader cannot miss the point of the nature and
crucial importance of the woman's faith, as a recognition of the
miraculous authority of the Messiah.

Many other examples of Matthew's tendency to 'condense' narrative
could be cited, such as the death of John the Baptist (Mark 249 words,
Matthew 136) or the 'epileptic' boy (Mark 272 words, Matthew 131).
These are clearly the sort of stories which give rich scope to a vivid
story-teller, and Mark takes full advantage of the opportunity, whereas
Matthew gives little more than the bare essentials required to draw out
the significance of the event.

In drawing out the significance, however, Matthew makes sure that
the important pronouncements of Jesus are not obscured, and are even
enhanced. In the story of the 'epileptic' boy the mere observation that
Matthew's account is less than half the length of Mark's does not take
account of the fact that in the concluding verses of the story, where
Jesus discusses with the disciples what the event has to teach about
effective prayer, Matthew is actually longer than Mark (47 words as
against 32), because he includes an extra saying about faith, and identifies
the disciples' problem as ὀλιγοπιστία, 'little faith', a frequent Matthean
theme. It is on the 'scenery' that Matthew economises, not on those
aspects of the story, and especially the key pronouncements of Jesus,
in which the moral is drawn out. As a result some stories are actually
longer in Matthew than in Mark. That of the Canaanite woman in

Matthew 15:21-28, for instance, includes the crucial saying of 15:24, limiting the scope of Jesus' primary mission, and by involving the disciples in the debate as to how Jesus should respond to an appeal from a non-Israelite turns what might have been seen as a simple exorcism story into a thought-provoking, even disturbing, analysis of the effect of the Jew/Gentile divide on the mission of Israel's Messiah.

In Matthew's treatment of the narrative tradition, then, we see the single-minded focus of the teacher rather than the indulgence of the raconteur. This tendency of Matthew undeniably makes his gospel less 'fun' to read than that of Mark. By comparison it seems almost austere. Matthew is more interested in getting across his message than he is in entertainment. As a master of compression and concentration, he makes greater demands on his reader.

But it would be a mistake to conclude from this feature of Matthew's work that he is lacking in literary sensitivity. The subtitle of Gundry's recent commentary, *Matthew: a Commentary on his Literary and Theological Art*, picks out an aspect of the gospel of Matthew which has been an increasing focus of interest in recent years. Both on a small scale, in his crafting of individual stories and units of teaching, and on the large scale of the total structure and movement of the story, Matthew proves himself well able to carry his reader with him into an informed perception of the meaning of the life and ministry of Jesus as Matthew understands it. Most of the rest of this book will testify to the validity of this observation in one way or another, as we look at the way the book as a whole has been designed, and at the various themes around which Matthew focuses his account. We shall see his skill in drawing attention at many levels to the way in which Old Testament Scripture has reached its culmination in Jesus. We shall look at the sensitive way in which Matthew analyses and illustrates the tension between the traditional role of Israel as the people of God and the new situation which Jesus has brought. We shall see how key words and phrases are dropped into the account from time to time to help the reader to follow the development of christological understanding, while frequent hints remind the reader that the story is not presented simply as interesting information about the past, but as a guide to what discipleship must mean for him as well.

All this will come later, but at this point we may illustrate briefly the narrative skill which puts Matthew well in contention with some of the world's greatest novelists and dramatists.

DRAMATIC DEVELOPMENT

Take, for instance, what is perhaps at first sight a rather formless section of the gospel, between the sending out of the disciples in chapter

10 and what is generally recognised as the turning-point of the whole narrative in chapter 16 with Peter's declaration at Caesarea Philippi and the subsequent revelation of the true nature of the Messiah's mission, with its focus on the rejection, suffering and death which will form the culmination of the story in chapters 26-27. Before chapter 10 we had an introductory account of who Jesus is and how his mission began (chapters 1-4), followed by a presentation of his messianic ministry in word (chapters 5-7) and deed (chapters 8-9). The extension of Jesus' mission to his disciples in chapter 10 then introduces what seems like a rather random collection of episodes in Jesus' northern ministry leading up to Caesarea Philippi, after which the public ministry in the north is largely concluded, and the journey to Jerusalem will begin. If Matthew had other stories to tell, which had no clearly appropriate specific 'slot' in the narrative, this seems the place in which to insert them. And to some extent that is probably what Matthew has done. But while not every section forms part of a clearly purposeful sequence, there is a continuity of presentation throughout this section which carries the reader persuasively towards the resolution of the key question, 'Who is Jesus?'.

The overriding impression left by this section of the gospel is of the diversity of response to Jesus. Already in 7:13-27 Jesus has warned of the division between true and false discipleship, between 'insiders' and 'outsiders', which results from his teaching, and in chapters 8-9 this division has begun to be illustrated in the Gentile centurion's faith which points up the lack of faith in Israel (8:10-12), the differing responses to the call of discipleship in 8:18-22, the passage about fasting and feasting, the old and the new, in 9:14-17, and the division between the reactions of the crowd and the Pharisees in 9:33-34. That last episode presages the outright opposition of the religious authorities to Jesus which will become an increasing feature as the narrative progresses. Accordingly chapter 10 has warned of differing response to the disciples' preaching (10:11-15), and the rest of the chapter has envisaged a situation of persecution, characterised by the deep divisions foreseen by Micah 7:6 (10:21,35-36). Jesus' mission brings not peace, but a sword, but while some will persecute them to the point of martyrdom, others will welcome their mission because they represent Jesus (10:40-42).

Chapter 11 then begins to call witnesses to Jesus, some favourable, some hostile, some uncertain. John the Baptist's question allows Jesus to point out the true nature of his mission (11:2-6), and the resultant discussion of John illustrates the perversity of popular response to the man of God (11:7-19). The pride which rejects Jesus outright (11:20-24) is balanced by the superior spiritual awareness of the 'babes' who discover the relief Jesus came to bring (11:25-30). In chapter 12 the lines of official opposition are more clearly drawn, first over the sabbath question, which leads up to a formulated desire to get rid of Jesus (12:1-14), while Jesus' non-violent response to such opposition is seen as fulfilling the scriptural pattern (12:15-21). The accusation that Jesus is in collusion with Satan is the cue for Jesus to spell out the irrevocable consequences of taking the wrong side (12:22-32), and the subsequent demand for a sign to authenticate his claims leads into a scathing attack on the failure of *this generation* (which will become a key phrase in Matthew's account) to respond to God's messenger, and a warning of the consequences of such unbelief '12:38-45). This last section brings to a head the argument begun in 12:5-8 that in Jesus 'something greater' is present, in which the patterns of God's approaches to his people in the past have now come to their culmination. Chapter 12 then closes by contrasting even Jesus' natural family, whose attitude to his mission is at least ambivalent, with the true 'family' of his disciples, who do the will of his Father (12:46-50).

The collection of parables and of teaching on parables now follows not as a *non sequitur* but in order to explain the situation which is developing. Division is a constant theme of the chapter, both in the content of the parables (different soils producing different yields when the good seed is sown; wheat and weeds growing together; good and bad fish in the same net),and in the teaching which intersperses them, in which a clear demarcation is made between 'you' to whom the secrets are revealed and 'them', from whom the truth is hidden (13:11-17). Parables thus serve to underline, and to explain, the division which Jesus' mission has created among those who hear him. All the parables of chapter 13 are about the 'kingdom of heaven', and all in different ways explain what happens when that 'kingship' makes its way into human society, as we have seen it doing in chapters 11-12.

In chapters 14-15 the scenario is extended. We meet Herod Antipas, whose absurd ideas of Jesus serve to reinforce the link between his mission and that of John the Baptist (14:1-12); the crowds whose enthusiastic following of Jesus lead to the need for miracles of feeding (14:13-21; 15:32-38) and of healing (14:14,34-36; 15:29-31); the disciples whose experiences on the lake lead them to confess Jesus in a moment of wonder as 'Son of God' (14:22-33); the Canaanite woman whose faith outweighs her status as a Gentile (15:21-28). All in their different ways testify to a growing awareness that in Jesus God is now acting in a unique way. But alongside these witnesses stands the menacing appearance on the scene of 'Pharisees and scribes from Jerusalem', which leads to a full-scale confrontation in 15:1-20, followed by another challenge to produce a sign (16:1-4), which leads into Jesus' explicit repudiation of their authority in 16:5-12.

Thus when we come to Caesarea Philippi, and to the question, 'Who are people saying that the Son of Man is?', the scene has been well and truly set, and the reader has no difficulty in appreciating both the importance of Peter's statement and the significance of the confrontation with Jewish officialdom which will increasingly dominate the story as it moves inexorably towards its climax in Jerusalem.

I am not arguing for any tight structuring of these chapters; indeed at times the arrangement of the individual pericopes seems almost random. But in the overall progression of the narrative, and in the selection of material for insertion in this part of the gospel it seems clear to me that Matthew is operating with a clear sense of dramatic progression, which enables the reader, perhaps unconsciously, to move with the author as the plot unfolds. Thus in this section of the gospel, which I deliberately selected as one whose structure and coherence is not as obvious on the surface as in other parts, we see Matthew skilfully preparing the reader both for the immediate climax at Caesarea Philippi and also for the increasing conflict with official Judaism which will dominate subsequent chapters, and will bring the whole story to its powerful climax in the events of passion week.

One device which plays an important role in highlighting the nature of the drama is the contrast between Galilee and Jerusalem. The whole shape of the story emphasises this contrast, with the bulk of the ministry being among enthusiastic crowds in Galilee, but with periodical reminders after Caesarea Philippi that the climax of the mission must be in Jerusalem, where Jesus will meet with rejection and death (16:21; 20:17-19). When, for the first and only time in this gospel, the prophet of Galilee comes to Jerusalem in chapter 21, it is in a dramatic gesture, as Israel's king coming to his capital, a gesture which inevitably provokes the authorities to challenge his assumed authority, and leads into a period of increasingly bitter confrontation which will culminate in his death outside the walls of the 'holy city'. But before that death Jesus himself will point forward to a restoration in Galilee (26:32), and in the messages at the empty tomb this same perspective is reinforced (28:7,10).

All this is, of course, not peculiar to Matthew. The same shape is seen in all the synoptic narratives (in contrast with that of John), and it has long been noted that in Mark's gospel this same Galilee/Jerusalem motif is a significant emphasis.[23] But if it is not peculiar to Matthew, it is certainly a theme which he exploits effectively by his own contri-

23. The classic presentation is by E. Lohmeyer, *Galiläa und Jerusalem* (Göttingen: Vandenhoeck & Ruprecht, 1936). The same theme was developed by, among others, R.H. Lightfoot, *Locality and Doctrine in the Gospels* (London: Hodder & Stoughton, 1938), and more recently W. Marxsen, in Study Two of *Mark the Evangelist* (ET, Nashville: Abingdon, 1969). Even if there is reason to question the tendency of these authors to read off from this geographical focus certain conclusions about the circumstances of writing of the gospel of Mark, the observation of a deliberate contrast between Galilee and Jerusalem is in itself valid and important.

butions to the story. As early as 2:3 we find 'all Jerusalem' perturbed
at the prospect of the birth of the new 'King of the Jews', and in 2:22-23
Matthew emphasises the divine guidance which took the young king
from his Judaean birthplace to his home in Galilee. His withdrawal
from the Jordan area back to Galilee for the beginning of his mission
is marked by one of Matthew's emphatic formula-quotations, identifying
Galilee as the place where light is to shine into the darkness (4:12-16).
When Jesus does eventually come to Jerusalem, Matthew draws a clear
distinction between the messianic enthusiasm of his Galilean followers
and the commotion which his arrival caused in 'the city', provoking
the question 'Who is this?' – to which the Galilean crowd had their
patriotic answer ready! (21:10-11) (This distinction is important for our
understanding of the identity of the crowd in Jerusalem who shouted
for Jesus' crucifixion, and calls in question the common assumption
that these were the same people who welcomed him with hosannas a
few days earlier.) Thereafter the mutual rejection of Jesus and the
Jerusalem authorities is greatly intensified, especially in chapter 23. And
then at the end of the gospel Matthew's double pointer towards Galilee
at the empty tomb (28:7,10; cf Mark 16:7) prepares the way for their
magnificent fulfilment, when 'the city' is left behind in its sordid intrigue
to cover up the fact of resurrection (28:11), and it is from Galilee that
the risen Lord sends his disciples out in their mission to bring all nations
under his kingship. The cumulative effect of these Matthean comments
and additional features is to underline more heavily the Marcan
opposition between the two areas. To this must be added also the
repeated emphasis in Matthew on the coming destruction of Jerusalem,
and especially of its temple, which we shall examine in chapter 6, behind
which lies the conviction that Jerusalem has become the centre of
resistance to the ongoing purpose of God. Geographical locations are
thus pressed into service in order to highlight the conflict between the
message of Jesus and the established régime at the heart of the existing
Israel.

It is, of course, from chapter 21 onwards that this conflict is most
fully seen. Here Matthew's dramatic skill is still more effectively deployed. After the repeated pointers to confrontation in Jerusalem, the
king comes to his capital, and in a series of dramatic gestures (the royal
ride on the donkey, the expulsion of traders from the temple, and the
symbolic cursing of the fig-tree) declares both his own messianic
authority and his repudiation of the existing régime. To this challenge
the authorities respond by demanding his authority for such high-handed
action (21:23-27). Jesus replies by linking his authority with that of
John the Baptist, whose mission they had similarly repudiated, and
goes on in a sequence of three polemical parables to challenge the right
of the official leadership of Israel to their assumed status: they are to

be supplanted by those they most despise (21:28-32); they are to lose their tenancy of the Lord's vineyard (21:33-43); and their place at the wedding feast is to be taken by those who were not invited (22:1-14). Throughout these parables the emphasis is on the contrast between profession and performance: the true people of God are those who produce the fruits (21:43). The authorities understand the direction of the polemic (21:45-46), and the confrontation is intensified (22:15-46).

Most of this, except the devastating sequence of parables, is shared with Mark, but then Matthew goes on to develop the theme in his own distinctive way. The authorities are silenced (22:46), and Jesus launches into a monologue against them, appealing over their heads to the crowds (23:1-12). Then in a sequence of seven 'woes' he exposes the nature of their failure as the leaders of the people of God (23:13-36), culminating in a stinging indictment of 'this generation', whose rejection of God's messengers represents the final culmination of the sins of their fathers. Judgement can no longer be delayed (23:36), and so Jesus laments the coming destruction of Jerusalem and its 'house'(23:37-39). All this has taken place in the temple, but now Jesus leaves the temple (24:1), and goes on to predict its total destruction (24:2). This then leads into a long discourse on judgement, where the fate of the temple, and its culmination in 'this generation' (24:34), leads into a longer perspective of the future parousia of the Son of Man in glory and judgement. The total mutual repudiation of Jesus and the Jerusalem authorities thus set out lays the necessary foundation for the narrative of chapters 26-27, when the plots against Jesus appear to achieve final success, and of chapter 28, where the situation is dramatically reversed, and the authority of the Son of Man is triumphantly reasserted, as he himself had predicted in 26:64.

That is only the barest outline of the terrific dénouement to which the plot of the gospel leads in these final chapters. Many details in these narratives and in the great discourse on judgement further contribute to the impact. The whole forms an impressive climax, which owes not a little to the subtle interweaving of themes which Matthew has achieved in order to underline the theological understanding of the significance of these events which he wants to convey. We shall be looking more closely at his theology of Jesus and Israel in chapter 6, but my intention here was rather to illustrate the assessment of Matthew as no mean dramatist. The selection of the material, the handling of the details, and the structuring of the whole all combine to produce a work of literary power, taut and carefully controlled, but perhaps for that reason no less compelling than Mark's more immediately attractive style.

The preceding paragraphs have offered a few illustrations of Matthew's literary skill in terms of the broad structures and sequence of his story. But in the presentation of an individual narrative too the same skill may often be seen. An impressive instance has been carefully analysed in an article by B. Gerhardsson on the twin narratives of the trial of Jesus and the denial by Peter.[24] The article is entitled 'Confession and Denial before Men', and Gerhardsson shows how carefully the two contrasting examples of Jesus and of Peter are related to each other in Matthew's narrative. The whole section, he argues, is so constructed as to offer two case-studies of opposite responses to persecution, or the threat of it, 'in the light of the Jewish and early Christian theme "confess-deny" '. Each of the examples is constructed, he believes, in a deliberate three-fold form which invites comparison of one with the other; and in each story there is an escalation through the three episodes both in the severity of the challenge and in the explicitness of the response, whether of confession (Jesus) or of denial (Peter). While the basic form of the story is shared with Mark, Gerhardsson finds from his detailed study of the text numerous indications of Matthew's careful manipulation of the literary shape of the tradition in order to emphasise this contrast. Here, then, is another example of the literary skill of Matthew brought into play in order to communicate more effectively the significance of the traditional stories for contemporary discipleship.

Whether on the small or on the large scale, then, there is plenty of evidence that Matthew, far from throwing his material together in a random manner, has carefully planned the shape of the different parts of his story. The result is both a coherent narrative, with an impressive dramatic power, and also a teaching document which effectively guides the reader into Matthew's own perception of the meaning of the traditions he has recorded.

If Matthew has been so careful in his structuring of the parts of his gospel, it is reasonable to expect that he has been equally concerned over the structure of the whole. And indeed discussion of the intended structure of his gospel has proved a prolific area of discussion, to which we now turn.

C. THE STRUCTURE OF MATTHEW'S GOSPEL

We have already noted that there is a planned development of the story throughout Matthew's gospel, with a good deal of narrative skill devoted to interweaving the various elements into a coherent and purposeful plot. But a well-coordinated plot is not necessarily the same thing as a literary structure. Are there, then, in this gospel any markers of a more formal structure for the work as a whole?

24. B. Gerhardsson, *JSNT* 13 (1981) 46-66.

'THE FIVE BOOKS OF MATTHEW'?

One repeated form of words which seems to fulfil such a function is the formula which concludes five lengthy sections of the teaching of Jesus: καὶ ἐγένετο ὅτε ἐτέλεσεν ὁ Ἰησοῦς ... ('and it happened when Jesus had finished ...') followed by 'these words' or a similar indication that it is a section of teaching which has just been concluded (7:28; 11:1; 13:53; 19:1; 26:1). After this in each case comes an indication of the beginning of a new phase in the story, generally by means of a move to a new geographical area. The formula itself is noticeable for its unusual language; only in one other place (9:10) does Matthew introduce a new paragraph with the Semitic construction καὶ ἐγένετο (representing the Old Testament wayehi, traditionally translated 'And it came to pass'), and the verb τελέω (in the sense 'finish') occurs in only one other place in his gospel (10:23), not in connection with completing a speech. And the position of the formula at the end of the five most prominent concentrated collections of teaching in the gospel is clearly deliberate. We shall be looking further at the nature of these five collections shortly, but that Matthew intended to mark them out by this concluding formula seems indisputable.

An attempt has recently been made to suggest that the beginnings of these five discourses are similarly marked by a stereotyped introduction. T.J. Keegan[25] notices certain repeated forms of words or motifs in the introductory passages 4:25-5:2; 9:36-37; 13:1-3; 18:1-3; 24:3-4. In three of them Jesus is presented as *seated* (as a teacher must be); indeed in 13:1-2 he apparently sits twice! Moreover in the first and last cases he sits on a *mountain*. In 5:1; 18:1; 24:1,3 we are told that *the disciples came to Jesus* (in 24:1,3 this phrase is used twice), and in 13:2 the crowds gathered to him, while the disciples came to him for private instruction in 13:10 and 13:36. At the beginning of each of the first three discourses there is also a mention of the gathering of *great crowds* as the context in which the teaching occurs (4:25; 5:1; 9:36; 13:2). Thus at the beginning of each of the discourses one or more of these narrative motifs occurs, and these features Keegan sees as Matthew's way of providing us, 'by means of precise and distinctive terminology, with a clear indication of where he intends each of the five major discourses to begin'.

Compared with the concluding formula, Keegan's 'precise and distinctive' opening formulae are hardly impressive. The form is very variable, and the elements he mentions variously distributed, so that the only 'formula' to be seen in 18:1 is the disciples coming to Jesus with a question, and in 9:36-37 Jesus' 'seeing the crowds' and speaking to his disciples (and that some six verses before the connected discourse

25. *CBQ* 44 (1982) 415-430.

begins). Moreover, all these motifs occur also in other parts of the gospel, so that they do not stand out as specifically designed to introduce discourses. The most that can be said is that when Matthew is about to introduce a significant collection of teaching, he tends to use one of a number of readily recognisable narrative motifs to alert the reader to what is going on, but these motifs do not constitute the sort of stereotyped formula which concludes the discourses. They are not so much structural markers, indicating a definable group of passages unlike anything else in the gospel, but rather hints to the reader that what follows is to be understood within the context of the ministry of Jesus the teacher who offered special instruction to his disciples, away from the crowd.

Be that as it may, it is certainly true that the five sections of the gospel which conclude with the formula 'and it happened when Jesus had finished . . .' constitute a striking group of 'discourses', or collections of Jesus' teaching. We shall be looking in section D of this chapter at the nature and method of composition of these five discourses, which are so obvious a characteristic of this gospel. The question before us now is whether they may properly be taken as the key to the structure of the gospel as a whole.

It was B.W. Bacon who gave the classical presentation of the theory that the five-fold formula concluding the discourses marked the conclusion also of major sections of the work, so that the whole gospel constituted 'The Five Books of Matthew Against the Jews'.[26] The proposal was not by any means new – indeed Bacon claimed to be able to trace the idea of 'Five Books of Matthew' as far back as the second century, and in more recent scholarship it was already a widely accepted view. On this theory the number five was no accident, but was a deliberate counterpart to the Five Books of Moses.[27] The five major discourses, on this theory, form the concluding sections of five 'books', each of which has an overriding coherence of theme running through both narrative and discourse. The fact that the last of the five formulae occurs a full three chapters before the end of the gospel means that the whole of the passion narrative must fall outside the five-book scheme, and is thus labelled the 'epilogue'. This is then balanced by separating off chapters 1-2 from the narrative of the 'First Book' (chapters 3-4), and calling them the 'preamble'.

26. This was the title of an article in *The Expositor* 15 (1918) 56-66, in which Bacon set out his view of the book's structure. It is presupposed, and more fully developed, throughout his *Studies in Matthew* (1930).

27. Advocates of a 'pentateuchal' structure in Matthew point out the existence of other Jewish and Christian works in five books or sections, such as the five books of the Psalms, the Book of Lamentations, the five Megilloth, the history of Jason of Cyrene (2 Macc. 2:19), the five books which comprise 1 Enoch, the five chapters of *Pirke Aboth* (subsequently expanded to six!), the five books of Papias' Λογίων κυριακῶν ἐξήγησις or of Irenaeus' *Adversus Haereses*. See further Davies, *Setting*, 15-16.

The total structure of the book, using Bacon's headings, thus appears as follows:

This outline, though not necessarily with Bacon's headings, has been repeated many times, and is taken for granted in many commentaries and studies of Matthew.[28] It has, however, also been widely called in question. W.D. Davies[29] offers a characteristically cautious literary critique of Bacon's theory. He finds it 'questionable', but regards the arguments as from a purely literary point of view 'inconclusive'. He therefore adds a lengthy discussion of whether Matthew betrays a special interest in a New Exodus or New Moses typology, and concludes that these motifs 'are not sufficiently dominant to add any significant support to Bacon's pentateuchal hypothesis, which must, therefore, still remain questionable, though possible'.[30] A further study of how Mosaic

28. For a listing of those who up to 1972 have, to varying degrees, followed Bacon's scheme see J.D. Kingsbury, *Matthew: Structure, Christology, Kingdom* (Philadelphia: Fortress, 1975) 3, n. 13. More recently one might mention a strongly 'Baconian' discussion of the structure of Matthew, though one which dissents from Bacon's specific divisions and headings at several points, by Minear, *Matthew*, 12-23. Most recent writers, even if they have argued for the structural importance of the five discourses, have been much more cautious about adopting Bacon's 'Five Books' approach as a whole.
29. Davies, *Setting*, 14-25.
30. *Ibid.* 93, summing up the discussion which takes up pages 25-93.

categories are transcended in Matthew leads ultimately, however, to the conclusion that the five-fold structure 'does not necessarily point to a deliberate interpretation of the Gospel in terms of a new pentateuch as, in its totality, a counterpart to the five books of Moses. At this point, though certainly not at others, it might prove profitable to exorcize the awe-inspiring ghost of Bacon from Matthaean studies.'[31] Other discussions critical of Bacon's view are summarised by Kingsbury.[32] Some have pointed out that significant parts of the gospel are not adequately accounted for on Bacon's scheme; there are, for instance, other 'discourse' sections, such as much of chapter 11, and particularly chapter 23, which is formally distinct from chapters 24-25.[33] Further, many have objected to the relegation of chapters 1-2 and 26-28 to the status of 'preamble' and 'epilogue' – the latter is in fact the dramatic climax of the whole work! Others have noted how Bacon's scheme requires the artificial placing under a single heading of quite disparate groups of material, both within some of the narrative sections ('Division A') and in the combination of narrative and discourse into a single 'book' under one all-embracing title; the homogeneity of the material in, e.g., 'Book Fourth: Church Administration' seems to be required by the theory rather than obvious from the contents!

Nor does the five-fold formula in itself suggest that it is intended to close a 'book'. Its explicit reference is to preceding discourse only, not to narrative. It functions, as Bacon himself noted, and many others have repeated since, not so much as a conclusion, but rather as a 'transition formula' to a new phase of the story. It serves, therefore, both to mark a discourse as completed and to move the story along (in most cases by leading to a new geographical location for the subsequent events).

SOME OTHER SUGGESTIONS OF STRUCTURAL PATTERNS

This last point has been developed by D.W. Gooding,[34] who notes that each 'concluding refrain' forms part of a paragraph introducing the next phase of the narrative. There is a similar introductory paragraph in 4:23 – 5:1, which necessarily lacks the 'concluding refrain', since no discourse has yet been recorded, but still performs the same introductory function. This enables Gooding to bring both the opening and the

31. *Ibid.* 107.
32. Kingsbury, *Matthew: Structure,* 4-5.
33. On this basis H.B. Green, *Studia Evangelica* IV (TU 102. Berlin: Akademie-Verlag, 1968) 47-59, proposed that the gospel was deliberately structured around seven discourses, not five.
34. D.W. Gooding, 'Structure Littéraire de Matthieu, XIII, 53 à XVIII, 35', *RB* 85 (1978) 227-252. The discussion of the overall structure of the gospel occupies pp. 227-238. The article develops proposals made by C.H. Lohr in *CBQ* 23 (1961) 427-430.

closing chapters of the gospel into his overall scheme, which thus consists
of seven main sections, as follows:

  I Birth, baptism, temptation, beginning of ministry (1:1–4:22).
      Introductory paragraph.
  II Healing and teaching in Galilee (4:23–7:27).
      Concluding refrain and introductory paragraph.
  III The authority of Christ and of his disciples (7:28–10:42).
      Concluding refrain and introductory paragraph.
  IV Tactics for establishing the kingdom (11:1–13:52).
      Concluding refrain and introductory paragraph.
  V The divinity of Christ and the authority of his church
      (13:53–18:35).
      Concluding refrain and introductory paragraph.
  VI Healing and teaching in Jerusalem (19:1–25:46).
      Concluding refrain and introductory paragraph
  VII Arrest, crucifixion, burial, resurrection (26:1–28:20).

Gooding's proposal is attractive in that it takes seriously the prominence of the discourse formula, while avoiding some of the more obvious
problems of Bacon's scheme. It does, of course, dispense entirely with
a 'pentateuchal' structure as such, even though his sections 3-6 correspond closely to Bacon's Books 2-5. The question still remains, however,
whether the contents of each of these 'sections' are sufficiently homogeneous to be regarded as deliberately collected to present the theme
suggested by the section headings.

Gooding goes on to propose that the seven sections are to be seen
as 'concentrically' arranged, so that I corresponds to VII, II to VI, and
III to V, leaving section IV, with its great 'mysteries of the kingdom',
as the central point of the gospel. The headings given above indicate
some of the suggested areas of correspondence, and Gooding offers a
few other similarities which may point in the same direction, but the
theory is not worked out in sufficient detail to carry conviction as it
stands. That there are many repeated themes and phrases throughout
Matthew's gospel is obvious, but that they are intentionally structured
around such a concentric pattern needs to be argued on the basis of a
much more careful analysis.

More elaborate structural analyses have been offered recently by
scholars working within the context of modern linguistics and discourse
theory. D.J. Clark and J. de Waard[35] offer a reading of the gospel as a
connected drama, which they admit is 'to some extent impressionistic
and intuitive'. The whole narrative is seen as a drama in three 'acts',

35. D.J. Clark & J. de Waard, 'Discourse Structure in Matthew's Gospel', *Scriptura*,
special issue 1 (Stellenbosch, 1982).

chapters 1-9, 11-17 and 19-26. In the course of the narrative five 'discourse blocks' (those recognised by Bacon) are inserted, though their subject matter is found not to relate closely to the unfolding of the story. They form a symmetrical pattern:

Act 1   Narrative–discourse–narrative
Act 2   Discourse–narrative–discourse–narrative–discourse
Act 3   Narrative–discourse–narrative

The discourses in Acts 1 and 3 are each long (three chapters), while in Act 2 the discourse material is divided into three shorter blocks, giving a more elaborate central section.

Structural patterns in the narrative of each act are then analysed in detail, each providing a number of separate 'scenes', themselves subdivided into 'episodes'. The discourse blocks are similarly searched for structural patterns. Many emerge quite obviously, as we would expect on the basis of our previous observations of Matthew's fondness for carefully structured sections of teaching. Others need rather more special pleading!

In a final section of the study the authors discuss Matthew's frequent use of apparently duplicate themes or stories, which we have noted above; several of these duplications are found just before and just after one of the discourse blocks, thus forming a sort of framework around the discourse, while the motif of John the Baptist 'interweaves and interpenetrates this whole pattern'. These observations form the basis of an impressive-looking structural chart on p. 78, though it is left unclear how this new framework relates to the structure of acts and scenes earlier set out. It is described as 'under-the-surface patterning'. One is left wondering how far such an 'invisible' structural pattern, which had to be teased out by careful literary analysis, could be expected to be noticed by any of the original readers (still less the hearers) of the gospel.

Some of the structural patterns observed by Clark and de Waard in smaller sections of the gospel have long been noted by readers and commentators – indeed it would be hard to miss the balanced structure of the eight Beatitudes, for example. Everyone too must acknowledge the clear markers provided by the repeated discourse formula. But when it comes to overall structural patterns what seems plausible to one student of the text may be completely opaque to another. Where Clark and de Waard discern one structural principle, other readers may (and do) discern another which apparently cuts across it. Perhaps both are really present, and it is not impossible that both were intended by Matthew. But in that case it is hazardous to elevate one such observation into *the* basic structural principle of the gospel as a whole. The more competing structural theories are proposed, the more one wonders whether Matthew did in fact set out on his work with any one of them as his guiding principle.

A different structural theory is proposed by H.J.B. Combrink.[36] He too aims to find a structural pattern which will do justice to the development of the story. He takes as his starting-point the assumption that the 'five discourses' are our clue to a symmetrical structure in the gospel, with the parable discourse of chapter 13 as the focal point. His structure largely separates narrative from discourse, and is thus more elaborate than that proposed by Gooding as noted above, but it follows a broadly similar line in the correspondences proposed. It is set out as follows:[37]

A. 1:1–4:17 **Narrative**: The birth and preparation of Jesus.
  B. 4:18–7:29 Introductory material, *First Speech*: Jesus teaches with authority.
    C. 8:1–9:35 **Narrative**: Jesus acts with authority – ten miracles.
      D. 9:36–11:1 *Second Discourse*: The Twelve commissioned with authority.
        E. 11:2–12:50 **Narrative**: The invitation of jesus rejected by 'this generation'.
          F. 13:1-53 *Third Discourse*: The parables of the kingdom.
        E'. 13:54–16:20 **Narrative**: Jesus opposed and confessed, acts in compassion to Jews and Gentiles.
      D'. 16:21–20:34 *Fourth Discourse* within **Narrative**: the impending passion of Jesus, lack of understanding of the disciples.
    C'. 21:1–22:46 **Narrative**: Jesus' authority questioned in Jerusalem.
  B'. 23:1–25:46 *Fifth Discourse*: Judgement on Israel and false prophets. the coming of the kingdom.
A'. 26:1–28:20 **Narrative**: The passion, death and resurrection of Jesus.

Combrink distinguishes, however, between the *means* of the narration (i.e. the author's presentation of the story through structural patterns, markers and editorial comment), and the *message*, or the plot, the actual development of the story itself. Here he divides the gospel into three main sections:

1. The setting (1:1–4:17).
2. The complication (4:18–25:46).
3. The resolution (26:1–28:20).

Thus the sections marked A and A' above convey the introductory and concluding sections of the narrative plot, while sections B–B' (the bulk of the gospel) set out the 'complication', the development of the

36. H.J.B. Combrink, 'The Structure of the Gospel of Matthew as Narrative', *TynB* 34 (1983) 61-90.
37. Cf. a similar structure set out by Ellis, *Matthew*, 10-13, also finding the centre of the pattern in chapter 13, and based, like Gooding's proposal, on the work of Lohr.

story in such a way as to lead inevitably into the climax of the 'resolution'. This central section contains all five discourses, the first and last of which form its outer limits. The structural pattern (the 'means') thus subserves the effective telling of the story (the 'message').

Just as we noted that the scheme proposed by Clark and de Waard was inevitably subjective, we might make a similar comment on Combrink's symmetrical scheme for the total structure of the gospel. While it is on solid ground with the observation of the five discourse formulae, the symmetry of the pattern which is discerned around these five elements is less clearly shown to be Matthew's deliberate design. It is quite possible for a modern reader to 'discover' such a neat all-embracing scheme by noting some of the recurrent themes of the gospel and plotting their incidence in the presumed 'sections' suggested by the placing of the discourses, but it is much less easy to show that Matthew either intended or would have recognised such a symmetry.

But in making a distinction between the structure and the plot, the 'means' and the 'message', Combrink has introduced an important element into the discussion. Is it possible that the obsession of Matthean scholars with the discovery of literary structure has obscured what Matthew is really trying to get across, a powerful *story*, with its own internal development, which gives the gospel a coherence and a *movement* which no mere symmetry of structure could produce? If we look at the book not so much as a neatly-constructed pattern of literary elements but rather as a compelling drama which moves inexorably to its climax in Jerusalem, are we not likely to be nearer to the 'structure' of the gospel as Matthew himself envisaged it? This is not to belittle Matthew's quite evident concern for comprehensible organisation of his material, particularly of the recorded teaching of Jesus, but rather to question the elevation of any such scheme into an overarching 'structure' for the whole work.

THE GOSPEL AS A DRAMA

In our earlier discussion of 'dramatic development' in Matthew we have seen reason to believe that Matthew has a clear sense of direction in the way various parts of the gospel are designed to build up towards the dramatic climax of the confrontation of Jesus with the authorities in Jerusalem. It is therefore reasonable to expect that the main principle for the structure of the gospel as a whole is not so much a symmetrical pattern of balancing sections, but rather the effective presentation of this dramatic movement.

We noted in particular that Matthew shares with Mark an emphasis on the contrast between Jesus' ministry in Galilee and that in Jerusalem, and has in a number of ways heightened the contrast. All three synoptic evangelists share the same pattern of a ministry exclusively in Galilee and the north up to the time of the one and only recorded visit of Jesus to Jerusalem – to die! Analyses of the structure of Mark's gospel have generally taken this crucial geographical movement as their starting-point, and have therefore focused on geographical locations as indicating stages of development in the story. The resultant analyses have typically looked something like this, by Vincent Taylor:

  I   Introduction (1:1-13).
 II   The Galilean ministry (1:14–3:6).
III   The height of the Galilean ministry (3:7–6:13).
 IV   The ministry beyond Galilee (6:14–8:26).
  V   Caesarea Philippi: The journey to Jerusalem (8:27–10:52).
 VI   The ministry in Jerusalem (11:1–13:37).
VII   The passion and resurrection narrative (14:1–16:8).

Only two of the transition points in this outline do not derive from a change of geographical location (those at 3:6 and 13:37). Even the 'Introduction' is separated off from what follows by its repeated references to 'the wilderness', after which the story proper begins with Jesus' deliberate move to Galilee.

But Mark's interest is not in geography for its own sake. The geographical movement reflects the development of Jesus' ministry and of people's reaction to it. The open preaching and healing ministry of the early chapters, when Jesus meets with widespread enthusiasm and 'success', leads to increasing tension with regard to who Jesus is. Particularly after the death of John the Baptist and the feeding of the five thousand in chapter 6 Jesus moves about less openly, and after the declaration of the nature of his mission at Caesarea Philippi he concentrates more on the private teaching of his disciples, in preparation for the climactic events in Jerusalem which increasingly dominate the gospel from the end of chapter 8, long before the narrative actually reaches Judaea. Thus when Jesus arrives in Jerusalem a sense of expectation has been created, and the developing confrontation of chapters 11-13 leaves no doubt of the inevitability of what must follow. So geography serves to highlight the dramatic development of the story.

All that has been said of Mark's structure applies equally to that of Matthew; indeed, as we have seen, he has further emphasised the significance of geographical location, as well as sharpening up at several points the dramatic force of the conflict between Jesus and official Judaism. In particular, his addition of a triumphant climax in Galilee following the fatal conflict in Jerusalem has heightened the dramatic focus on the significance of the two geographical areas. One little feature of Matthew's vocabulary serves to underline this approach, his distinctive use of the verb ἀναχωρέω ('withdraw') to describe Jesus' changes of location, usually clearly attributable to circumstances which necessitated a change in his style of ministry (4:12; 12:15; 14:13; 15:21; cf. also its use in 2:12,14,22). References to Jesus' geographical movements punctuate Matthew's narrative even more clearly than Mark's: see e.g. 3:13; 4:12-16; 4:23-25; 9:35; 11:1; 14:13; 15:21; 15:29; 15:39; 16:13; 16:21; 17:22; 19:1; 20:17-18; 20:29; 21:1, etc. There are many other references to more localised movements particularly in and around Galilee.

Those who believe that Matthew based his work directly on that of Mark may therefore fairly claim that he has not only perceived but also made his own the dramatic structure established by Mark and the geographical framework in which it is focused. Those who are less certain of the nature of the literary relation between the two evangelists may nonetheless speak of a shared perception of the dramatic shape of Jesus' ministry. Whether one of them derived it from the other, or both received it as part of the traditional understanding and presentation of the story of Jesus, it seems clear that the 'Marcan outline' forms the basic structure of the story told by Matthew. Indications of the structure should therefore be sought not so much in aesthetically satisfying literary patterns, but rather in pointers to the forward movement of the story.

It is for this reason that I have postponed until this point another approach to the structure of Matthew which has been widely discussed recently, that associated particularly with the name of J.D. Kingsbury. It focuses, like that of Bacon, on a repeated formula, though this one occurs only twice: in 4:17 and 16:21 we read Ἀπὸ τότε ἤρξατο ὁ Ἰησοῦς ... ('From this time on Jesus began ...') after which a new phase of ministry is introduced. In 4:17 the reference is to the beginning of public preaching in Galilee; in 16:21 it is to Jesus' preparation of his disciples for his rejection and death in Jerusalem. The possibility that this formula was a clue to the intended structure of the gospel was noted by N.B. Stonehouse,[38] and developed in a short article by E. Krentz.[39] J.D. Kingsbury has taken up this proposal and in a series of publications has enthusiastically promoted it.[40] On the basis of this formula,

38. Stonehouse, *Witness*, 129-131.

39. E. Krentz, 'The Extent of Matthew's Prologue', *JBL* 83 (1964) 409-414. Krentz notes that E. Lohmeyer had already pointed in this direction. Cf. also McNeile's comments on 4:17 and 16:21, which he sees as 'dividing into two main parts the teaching of Jesus'.

40. Kingsbury set out the theory in an article in *CBQ* 35 (1973) 451-474, and more briefly in *Interpretation* 29 (1975) 13-23, before incorporating these studies into a fuller statement in his book *Matthew: Structure, Christology, Kingdom* (1975) 1-37. More recently he has engaged in a debate with D. Hill (who follows Bacon's structural theory), which included a discussion of the structure of the gospel among other contentious issues; Kingsbury's article in *JSNT* 21 (1984) 3-36 received a reply from Hill, *ibid.* 37-52, to which Kingsbury further replied in *JSNT* 25 (1985) 61-81. In Kinsgbury's subsequent work, *Matthew as Story* (Philadelphia: Fortress, 1986), the same structural scheme is taken for granted, though the discussion has moved on to a more full-blown 'narrative-critical' approach to the gospel, in which the focus is more on 'plot' than on 'structure'.

Kingsbury proposes to divide the gospel into three major parts, as follows:

I 1:1–4:16   The Person of Jesus Messiah
II 4:17–16:20   The Proclamation of Jesus Messiah
III 16:21–28:20 The Suffering, Death and Resurrection of Jesus
                Messiah.

I have introduced this three-part structural theory at this point because it will be obvious that the two turning-points marked by this formula correspond closely with two of the major geographical and dramatic turning-points of the 'Marcan outline', the beginning of public preaching in Galilee, and the introduction of the theme of messianic suffering which leads directly towards the climax in Jerusalem. Both the geographical location and the style of Jesus' ministry change radically at each of these points, and there seems no good reason to doubt that Matthew intended this form of words to mark the fact.

But, as with the five-fold formula which concludes the discourses, it needs to be asked whether a form of words which clearly moves the story on to a new phase is therefore to be treated as marking off separate sections of the book which may be seen as to some extent self-contained units. This question is particularly acute in the case of the formula at 16:21, which falls in the middle of the account of the Caesarea Philippi episode. The new emphasis introduced by these words is the direct response of Jesus to what Peter has just said about his role as Messiah, and the welcome which Jesus has given to Peter's declaration in 16:17-19 is poignantly balanced by the rebuke of Peter's false perspective in 16:22-23. A division of the gospel which does not allow these sections to be read in direct sequence is surely not going to do justice to Matthew's dramatic purpose. In other words, while 16:21 marks the beginning of a new emphasis in Jesus' ministry, it does not mark the end even of the episode which immediately precedes it, let alone the end of a whole major section of the gospel.

It seems better, then, to treat this formula, like that which concludes the discourses, not as marking out a self- conscious literary division of the work, but rather as simply a deliberate and important notification by the author that a new phase of the story is here being introduced, a new phase which does not interrupt the flow of the narrative, but rather weaves a further strand into the 'complication' which will lead in the end to the 'resolution' in Jerusalem and its final triumphant outcome in Galilee. (Cf. 26:16, where ἀπὸ τότε occurs again, though without the remainder of the 'formula', in order to introduce another new strand into the plot, the involvement of Judas on the side of the opposition.)

PLOT AND STRUCTURE

In the search for the structure of Matthew various competing patterns of composition have been proposed, and none have been able to impose themselves as being clearly the principle which Matthew self-consciously adopted for the organisation of his material. The more elaborate and the more symmetrical the structure proposed, the more difficult it has proved to account for the presence of all the material which in fact occurs within each of the sections required by the theory. The structural patterns suggested seem mostly to be too subtle to be noticed by anyone at first reading or hearing of the story, and depend on a careful study of the text not for its message but for its shape, a study which it may be questioned whether Matthew ever intended or would have encouraged. We have seen plenty of evidence that he so constructed sections of Jesus' teaching and of the narrative tradition that a reader would more easily assimilate and remember the content, and be able to appreciate its homiletical significance. But these carefully constructed sections seem to indicate more the communicative skill of the teacher and preacher than a delight in literary or stylistic form for its own sake. Clear evidence of an overall concern for pattern or symmetry in the shape of the work as a whole seems to be lacking.

But what does seem to be unquestionable is the dramatic flow of the narrative, as each new element finds its place within the developing plot. For the work as a whole, therefore, it seems more plausible to suggest that the plot *is* the structure, that the principle on which Matthew has collected his material is the desire to carry the reader as cogently as possible through the story of Jesus so that by the time it reaches its end the reader will be able to say, 'Yes, of course, that was how it had to be'.

The development of the story is signalled by a number of literary devices, including the two 'formulae' noted above which have been seen as structural markers, 'From that time on Jesus began . . .', and 'And it happened after Jesus had finished . . .'. Each serves not so much to mark out a 'section', as to move the story on to the next phase of its development. Notes of geographical movements also serve a similar purpose, and since geographical movement is clearly one of the major factors in the shaping of the plot, it is hardly surprising that such notices sometimes coincide with one or other of the 'formulae' (e.g. 4:12–17; 19:1). But to single out any one of these narrative techniques as in itself an adequate pointer to the total intended structure of the book is to miss the crucial fact that Matthew's account of Jesus is not a static and symmetrical structure, but a powerful drama with a dynamic force of its own.[41]

41. The term 'plot' has become a new focus for some further studies of Matthew from the point of view of contemporary literary criticism. F.J. Matera, 'The Plot of Matthew's

D. MATTHEW'S PRESENTATION OF JESUS' TEACHING

THE PLACE OF THE DISCOURSES IN THE STORY

The account I have just given of the dramatic force of Matthew's gospel may seem hard to square with the fact (duly signalled by the five-fold concluding formula) that considerable sections of the book are in fact devoted to collections of Jesus' *teaching*. For sometimes as long as three chapters at a time the 'action' is suspended while Jesus delivers a lengthy monologue. Indeed the first and longest of these (chapters 5-7) is inserted when the story proper has barely begun, and the escalating tension of chapters 21-22 is not allowed to reach its natural conclusion in the passion narrative until Jesus has first delivered a lengthy diatribe against the scribes and Pharisees, followed by an even longer wide-ranging discourse about future events.

Yet even these long sections of teaching have their part to play in the dramatic structure. None of them are mere interludes, marking time until the story can resume, but all are integrated into the onward movement of the story. This is, after all, no more than one would expect from any competent dramatist.

Gospel', *CBQ* 49 (1987) 233-253 claims to know of only two published discussions of Matthew's 'plot' before his own, those of R.A. Edwards, *Matthew's Story of Jesus* (Philadelphia: Fortress, 1985) and of J.D. Kingsbury in *JSNT* 21 (1984) 3-36. He presumably wrote his article before the publication of Kingsbury's *Matthew as Story*. Each of these writers aims to discern the structure of Matthew's account from the perspective of narrative development, but each of their proposed analyses is different. Matera proposes that Matthew's story focuses on six 'major events, kernels, cruxes in the narrative on which other events depend' (p. 243):

The birth of Jesus (2:1a)
The beginning of Jesus' ministry (4:12-17)
The question of John the Baptist (11:2-6)
The Caesarea Philippi conversation (16:13-28)
The cleansing of the temple (21:1-17)
The Great Commission (28:16-20).

The resultant analysis is in terms of six 'narrative blocks': 1:1 - 4:11; 4:12 - 11:1; 11:2 - 16:12; 16:13 - 20:34; 21:1 - 28:15; 28:16-20. Edwards also discerns six parts, which he describes as 'basic segments or moments in the continuing narration':

1:1 - 4:22   Establishing the framework of the story
4:23 - 7:29   The demands of the kingdom
8:1 - 11:1   The power of the kingdom
11:2 - 18:35 The response to the coming of the kingdom
19:1 - 25:46 The message of the kingdom presented in Judea
26:1 - 28-20 The conflict takes place.

The fact that these two attempts to outline the 'plot' turn out so differently is surely due to the inevitably subjective decision as to what constitute 'kernels' or 'basic segments' in a continuous narrative. (It should be noted, however, that four of Edwards' 'segments' do in fact conclude with the discourse formula which formed the basis of Bacon's analysis.) Kingsbury's analysis, which is again quite different from either of these, did at least take as its starting-point a recurrent 'formula' in the text, though if it invested this 'formula' with too much significance as a deliberate structural marker on Matthew's part. All three of these analyses of Matthew's 'plot' do in fact discern real stages in the development of the narrative, but it is doubtful whether Matthew would have recognised in any of them a total structural pattern which he consciously designed.

It is here that the formula 'And it happened when Jesus had finished
. . .' plays an important role in alerting us to Matthew's method. While
the various sections of teaching concluded by these words are not
uniform in their style and composition, each is a careful compilation
of teaching focused around a central theme; and each of these themes
serves both to develop the reader's understanding of what has been
happening in the story so far, and also to prepare for the development
of the plot in the narrative which follows.

The theme of chapters 5-7 is discipleship, the nature and demands
of the distinctive way of life of the kingdom of heaven. This follows
appropriately on 4:18-25, where we have read of the calling of the first
disciples, and of the large crowds among whom, and in distinction from
whom, their new role is to be worked out (a distinction which 5:1
appropriately points out in introducing the discourse). Following
chapters will illustrate in many ways the nature and demands of
discipleship (see esp. 8:18-22; 9:9-17; 9:35-10:4). A further function
of these chapters, as we have noted earlier, is to serve as the counterpart
to the collection of miracles in chapters 8-9, so that we see the authority
of Jesus displayed at the outset of his ministry both in word and in
deed. The effect of his teaching is to raise the question, 'Who is this,
who teaches with such authority?', a question which is central to the
developing presentation of people's varying responses to Jesus which
will occupy succeeding chapters.

The call to discipleship is further developed in the second discourse
(chapter 10), with its presentation of the disciples' mission as parallel
to that of Jesus himself. But a theme already briefly introduced in the
first discourse (5:10-12) now comes to the fore, the inevitability of
persecution for the messengers of the kingdom of heaven, since men
will be deeply divided in their response to God's call. This becomes the
major theme of chapter 10, and so prepares the way for the analysis
of differing reactions to Jesus which, as we have seen, will be the
connecting thread through the following chapters. The increasingly
clear division between 'insiders' and 'outsiders' which runs through
chapters 11-12 and climaxes in 12:46-50 then leads directly into the
third discourse (chapter 13), which both explains the nature of the
coming of the kingdom of heaven (already announced in 12:28) and
sets out clearly the resultant division among mankind as a result of
their response. Here then is a theological background against which
the reader may interpret the paradoxical effects of Jesus' ministry as
the narrative is increasingly revealing them.

In the following chapters, and particularly in and after the episode
at Caesarea Philippi, the focus moves increasingly from the crowds to
the disciples, and we are given clearer glimpses of the emergence of the
community of those who by their response to Jesus have become a new

group, 'my ἐκκλησία' (16:18), distinguished from the rest of the world in the way 5:13-16 had already outlined. But such a group will have its own inner tensions, with possibilities both for mutual damage and for mutual concern and help. The fourth discourse (chapter 18) focuses therefore on relationships within the disciple community, and subsequent events will show how necessary this will prove for their life together (20:20-28). By the time the narrative brings Jesus to Jerusalem, therefore, the reader is already aware of the existence in embryo of a new 'people of God' resulting from his ministry, so that he may interpret the confrontation with the official leaders of the 'people of God' in Jerusalem in the light of the newly constituted alternative. This confrontation will then reach its climax in the diatribe of chapter 23, which builds up in 23:29-39 to an explicit declaration of the parting of the ways and the resultant judgement facing Jesus' opponents and their régime. The reader is thus prepared for the discourse on judgement (chapters 24-25), which develops a broader eschatological context in which to understand the coming destruction of Jerusalem as the necessary sequel to what will be narrated in chapters 26-27, the repudiation of Israel's Messiah.

This sketch of the place of the discourses in the development of the plot is not intended to explain their contents in detail. We shall return to the discourses particularly in chapter 7, when we shall consider the relevance of the teaching selected not only to the dramatic flow of the story but also to the pastoral concerns of the church in which Matthew wrote. I hope, however, that it is sufficient to show that the presence of long and carefully constructed sections of teaching in Matthew's gospel does not detract from its dramatic effectiveness, but rather enables the reader to follow the story with greater appreciation of the deeper issues involved.

It remains now to examine how Matthew has gone about the task of compiling these discourses, which are so prominent a feature of his book, and to which he clearly intends to draw attention by the set formula with which they are concluded.

THE COMPILATION OF THE DISCOURSES

In most cases the introduction to the discourse indicates a specific occasion for its delivery (18:1 is the least specific), and the concluding formula seems to suggest the end of a single connected discourse. Were these then records of actual 'sermons' delivered by Jesus each on a single occasion (though presumably considerably condensed – the discourses of chapters 10, 13 and 18 would each take less than five minutes to deliver as they stand!)? They have traditionally been so interpreted, particularly the Sermon on the Mount, to which we shall return in the next section.[42]

But not all of them read as connected discourses. In chapter 18 there is a question by Peter in verse 21, after which Jesus resumes in verse 22. This in itself is no problem for the 'single sermon' theory, since we can hardly imagine Jesus as the sort of teacher who does not welcome and make use of audience participation. In chapter 13, however, the situation is more complicated. What begins as a public address from a boat (verse 2) is interrupted by a private response to a question from the disciples, in response to which Jesus talks about the wider crowd as 'they' (verses 10-17). The next three parables are all introduced by 'Another parable he put before them, saying . . .' (verses 24, 31, 33), and verse 34 explains that the 'them' concerned was again the crowds, a point which Matthew proceeds to comment on from the Old Testament (verse 35) before the 'discourse' is resumed. It is resumed, however, again in private with the disciples, the crowds being explicitly left behind (verse 36), and from then on the remainder of the parables flow on without interruption (and therefore presumably to the same audience) until the concluding question and answer (again presumably with the disciples) in verses 51-52. This is hardly a 'single sermon', and it seems that the larger part of it is not addressed to the audience stated in verse 2 at all.

The other discourses are not broken by such narrative insertions (assuming that chapter 23 is not to be construed as part of the same discourse as chapters 24-25)[43] and may more plausibly be seen as unbroken monologues delivered on a single occasion. But a consideration of their contents may suggest otherwise. Within them are many shorter sections which could as well have stood on their own, not because their theme is out of keeping with the context in which they now appear, but because they do not relate explicitly with what precedes and follows them. For instance, the two parables and the vision of the last judgement which make up chapter 25 could each have stood alone. Each is appropriate to the wider context of chapters 24-25, and each contributes important elements to the total impact of these chapters, but each is in itself a self-contained literary unit. The same could be

42. For a recent defence of this position see D.A. Carson, *Matthew*, (in F.E. Gaebelein [ed.] *The Expositor's Bible Commmentary* vol. 8 [Grand Rapids: Zondervan, 1984]) 123-125.

43. It was so construed, of course, by Bacon, who has been followed in this by many commentators. See D.E. Garland, *The Intention of Matthew 23* (Leiden: Brill, 1979) 26-30 for a cautious defence of this view. It is certainly possible to discern a continuity of theme in the motif of 'judgement', but the total change of location and of audience in 24:1-4 is more marked than any of the audience changes in chapter 13. There is, of course, an important theological continuity between the public denunciation of the scribes and Pharisees in chapter 23 and the private teaching to the disciples on judgement to come in chapters 24-25, but formally speaking they are not the same discourse.

said of many of the sections which make up the Sermon on the Mount; indeed, while the principle of arrangement of most of the 'Sermon' is quite intelligible, the reader has some difficulty in seeing any clear sequence of thought between the four smaller sections which make up 7:1-12. Those verses, delivered in sequence as part of a longer sermon, would be likely to leave the audience rather bewildered! Similar observations could be made on the different sections which make up each of the discourses.

The principal argument against the 'single sermon' interpretation of the five discourses, however, is derived not from their contents viewed solely in their Matthean construction, but from a consideration of how the material in these sections of Matthew relates to parallel passages in Mark and Luke. Each of the discourses does in fact have a 'parallel' in one of the other gospels, but the relevant sections of Mark or Luke are very much shorter, accounting in most cases for well under half of the Matthean discourse concerned. The following 'parallels' are suggested:

Matthew 5-7 (107 verses)	Luke 6:20-49 (30 verses)
Matthew 10 (38 verses)	Mark 6:7-13 (7 verses)
Matthew 13 (50 verses)	Mark 4:3-34 (32 verses)
Matthew 18 (33 verses)	Mark 9:35-48 (14 verses)
Matthew 24-25 (94 verses)	Mark 13:5-37 (33 verses).

In the cases of the first, third and fifth discourses these parallels are clear enough to be regarded as representing the same basic discourse. In the second and fourth the 'parallel' suggested is simply a passage in Mark where there is material comparable to the opening verses of the Matthean discourse (though in the case of Mark 9:35-48 the differences are more striking than the similarities), while the remainder of Matthew's discourse moves into new areas. In all cases except chapter 13 the bulk of the Matthean discourse is not found in the synoptic 'parallel', and even in the parable discourse, where Mark offers three parables and the 'parabolic sayings' of 4:21-25, Matthew gives eight parables, only two of which are the same as those in Mark.

To observe that Matthew's accounts of these 'sermons' are longer than those of Luke and Mark need mean no more, of course, than that Matthew has preserved a fuller account of what was in fact said on that one occasion. But this explanation suffers from the further observation that a good part of the additional material in Matthew does in fact have synoptic parallels, located not in the 'parallel' passages listed above, but in other places in Mark or Luke. The most striking example of this phenomenon is the Sermon on the Mount, which we shall consider in the next section. But take for example also the second discourse. The parallels may be set out roughly as follows:

Matthew	Mark	Luke
10:5-6		
10:7-8		9:2
10:9-11	6:8-10	9:3-4
10:12-13		10:5-6
10:14	6:11	9:5
10:15		10:12
10:16		10:3
10:17-18	13:9	21:12-13
10:19-20	13:11	12:11-12
10:21-22	13:12-13	21:16-17
10:23		
10:24-25		6:40
10:26-33		12:2-9
10:34-36		12:51-53
10:37-38		14:26-27
10:39	8:35	17:33
10:40		10:16
10:41		
10:42	9:41	

Complicated as it appears, the above chart is in fact a considerable over-simplification of a very complex web of literary relationships; defining 'parallels' is a rather subjective matter, when there are sometimes verbal echoes, sometimes similarities of thought, sometimes themes which recur in varying forms in different places in each of the gospels. But it is sufficient to show that this discourse is not simply a matter of a fuller account of what is briefly recorded in Mark 6:7-13 and Luke 9:1-6 (or 10:1-12, or both!), but rather a compilation of traditional sayings of Jesus which appear in recognisably similar forms at many other points in Mark and (particularly) Luke.

Similar charts could be made up for the third, fourth and fifth discourses. They would not be quite so complex, as in the third and fifth discourses the area of overlap with the basic 'parallel' in Mark is much greater, and in all three discourses there is a larger proportion of material which has no parallel in either Mark or Luke. But in each case the same phenomenon would emerge, of an apparent weaving around a Marcan framework of other sayings material which is either separately recorded by the other evangelists or found in Matthew alone.

It is on the basis of such observations that most students of Matthew have concluded, rightly in my view, that Matthew's discourses are not single sermons delivered all together on one occasion, but careful compilations of sayings of Jesus which Matthew has brought together into 'anthologies' to illustrate Jesus' teaching on particular themes. In each case there is a starting-point in a larger or smaller unit of teaching preserved by the other evangelists, but beyond that the principle of coherence of the discourse is the relevance of the subject-matter of the individual sayings or sections of teaching to the theme Matthew is presenting, rather than their origin in a single sermon. In other words, the teaching is that of Jesus, but the arrangement is that of Matthew.

THE SERMON ON THE MOUNT

The longest of Matthew's discourses is a particularly clear example of the style of compilation we have been considering, and raises in an interesting way the question of the relation of the discourse as it appears in Matthew to the underlying sermon structure on which it is based. Again it will help to set out the 'parallels' in a chart (on the next page). This chart shows a complexity of literary relationships similar to that in chapter 10, except that in this case the parallels with Mark are very few and incidental. The parallel material is again found scattered in many parts of Luke, even though there is a broad correspondence with the pattern of Luke 6:20-49 for some parts of chapters 5 and 7 of Matthew. Even these parallels, however, are not as close as might appear from the chart, for in a number of cases, while the content is clearly parallel, the wording is as different as could be achieved while still conveying the same message. A striking example of this is Matthew 5:39-42 / Luke 6:29-30, where Matthew's 49 words parallel 34 in Luke, and only 17 of these are the same. As for the 'beatitudes' with which each discourse opens, not only does Matthew have eight against Luke's four, but even for those four the similarity does not extend much beyond the beatitude form itself (indeed even that differs in that Matthew has them in the third person, Luke in the second); even where there are verbal parallels ('poor', 'hungry'), these are qualified in Matthew as 'spiritual' ('poor in spirit', 'hungry for righteousness') while in Luke there is no hint of anything other than a material sense, and this is further confirmed by Luke's balancing set of woes against the rich and well fed, to which Matthew has no parallel.

It should be noted too that while there is a broadly similar order in the sections which are paralleled in Matthew 5-7 and Luke 6, this sometimes breaks down: see the order of clauses in Matthew 5:39-48 (and 7:12) as compared with that in Luke 6:29-36. And while most of the content of Luke 6:20-49 finds a parallel in the Sermon on the Mount, some parts of it appear instead in other places in Matthew (for Luke 6:39 see Mt. 15:14; for Luke 6:40 see Mt. 10:24-25; for Luke 6:45 see Mt. 12:35).

SYNOPTIC PARALLELS TO THE SERMON ON THE MOUNT

Sections found only in Matthew are given in bold type; sections found in the basic 'parallel' passage in Luke 6:20-49 are underlined. Brackets in the right-hand column indicate a 'parallel' which is significantly different in content from the Matthew text.

Matthew	Mark	Luke
5:1-2	(3:13)	(6:17,20)
5:3-6		(6:20-21)
5:7-10		
5:11-12		6:22-23
5:13		14:34-35
5:14		
5:15	4:21	8:16; 11:33
5:16		
5:17		
5:18		16:17
5:19-20		
5:21-24		
5:25-26		12:58-59
5:29-30	9:43-48	
5:31		
5:32		16:18
5:33-37		
5:38		
5:39-42		6:29-30
5:43		
5:44		6:27-28
5:45-48		6:32-36
6:1-8		
6:9-13		11:2-4
6:14-15	11:25	
6:16-18		
6:19-21		12:33-34
6:22-23		11:34-35
6:24		16:13
6:25-33		12:22-31
6:34		
7:1-5	(4:24)	6:37-38, 41-42
7:6		
7:7-11		11:9-13
7:12		6:31
7:13-14		(13:24)
7:15		
7:16-20		6:43-44
7:21		6:46
7:22-23		(13:25-27)
7:24-27		6:47-49
7:28-29	1:22	(7:1)

All of this suggests that a view of Matthew 5-7 and Luke 6:20-49 as variant accounts of a single sermon is a good deal too simple. But what is the alternative?

The logically opposite position is to say that the two discourses are literarily entirely independent, each based on a separate strand of oral tradition. This view has been argued by H.-T. Wrege.[44] It is attractive in that it accounts fully for the remarkably different form and even content of some of the 'parallel' passages in the two discourses (particularly of the beatitudes). But it is hard to believe that it does justice to the basically similar framework of the two sermons, each of which begins with beatitudes and ends with the parable of the two houses, while containing a great deal of common material in roughly the same order in between. It is possible, of course, that this was a sermon outline used by Jesus on a number of occasions, two of which were separately remembered and transmitted to Matthew and Luke respectively. But in view of the way Matthew's other discourses seem in each case to be compiled around an existing 'core' preserved elsewhere in the synoptics, this seems an unnecessarily complicated proposal.

More likely, then, both Matthew and Luke had access to the outline of a sermon preached by Jesus (whether preserved in 'Q' or in oral tradition). That still leaves us with two possibilities: either Luke drastically abbreviated and slightly rearranged a sermon which Matthew has recorded in something like its original form, and then proceeded to scatter many of the sections he had removed from the original sermon in many other parts of his gospel, or Matthew has taken the basic core more or less as preserved by Luke and has expanded it to nearly four times its Lukan length by adding other traditional teaching material which he felt to be appropriate to its theme.

It is hard to explain why Luke should undertake such a drastic demolition job on an existing sermon, but very easy to see why Matthew should expand it in this way, for this is clearly in line with what we have seen to be his typical procedure in the other discourses. His respect for the basic outline which he received has caused him to begin with a set of beatitudes, but they are a very different set from those recorded by Luke. Similarly while he has included passages on turning the other cheek and on the two house-builders, his wording of these sections suggests that he was more concerned to preserve the outline of the

---

44. H.-T. Wrege, *Die Überlieferungsgeschichte der Bergpredigt* (Tübingen: Mohr, 1968). Wrege doubts the theory of a Q-source underlying the two discourses primarily because this would make Matthew himself responsible for the construction of the antitheses of 5:21-47. But since these antitheses on his view effectively annul the provisions of the Old Testament they can hardly be the work of the Matthew who understood the ministry of Jesus as above all one of fulfilment of the Old Testament. The antitheses must therefore derive from pre-Matthean tradition, which is clearly different from the tradition preserved in Luke 6.

content of the sermon than to adhere strictly to a set form of words. While therefore it is right to describe the contents of Matthew 5-7 as the teaching of Jesus, there is an important sense in which these chapters must be described as *Matthew's* 'sermon on the mount'. It is to Matthew's organising genius that we owe the compilation as we now find it, and a study of its structure and contents will tell us much about Matthew's own understanding of what discipleship means.

What has just been said assumes, of course, that the compilation was the work of Matthew himself rather than of some other handler of the Jesus tradition from whom Matthew received it ready-made. This has recently been disputed by H.D. Betz.[45] Betz sees the sermon as an epitome of the teaching of Jesus compiled by Jewish Christians in Jerusalem around the middle of the first century, for whom Jesus was no more than an authoritative teacher of the Torah; the kerygma of saving death and resurrection was no part of their religion, and they rejected Gentile Christianity. Matthew, himself a champion of Gentile Christianity, has taken over this carefully composed document and incorporated it in his work despite the fact that it differs significantly from his own viewpoint.[46] This position depends on discerning a polarisation between the viewpoint of the Sermon and that of the rest of the gospel which seems to be required by the theory rather than clear from the text. To take a small instance, the anti-Gentile stance of the sermon is concluded from the disparaging references to Gentiles in 5:47; 6:7; 6:32, without also noting the presence of no less 'anti-Gentile' language in 10:5; 18:17; 20:25, not to mention the almost offensively 'Jewish chauvinist' tone of 15:21-28. The view of the sermon as lacking a christology beyond that of Jesus as a revered interpreter of the Torah is also strangely at odds with most modern interpretation, as we shall see shortly. But our concern here is with the literary origins of the sermon. Until Betz has published his arguments for its coming intact to Matthew from an alien source, it is hard to give credence to a theory which postulates so different an editorial procedure for the first of Matthew's discourses from what we see in the other four, particularly when the phenomena of its literary relations with synoptic parallels present so similar a picture to what we find for the other discourses.

45. H.D. Betz, *Essays on the Sermon on the Mount* (Philadelphia: Fortress, 1985). The theory is set out particularly on pp. 17-22 and 90-93, but is presupposed throughout the volume. Betz refers to his forthcoming major commentary on the Sermon on the Mount (Hermeneia series) for fuller substantiation of the theory. Brief responses to Betz' proposals are offered by G.N. Stanton in G.F. Hawthorne & O. Betz (ed.), *Tradition and Interpretation in the New Testament: Essays in honor of E.E. Ellis* (Grand Rapids: Eerdmans, 1987) 181-192, and by C.E. Carlston, *CBQ* 50 (1988) 47-57.

46. Betz claims (p. 18, n. 3) that this theory had already been put forward by Kilpatrick, *Origins*, 14-25 (*sic*). In fact Kilpatrick concludes his discussion on pp. 24-26 with the view that it was Matthew who composed the Sermon by 'conflation of two written sources', Q and M – a very traditional view quite unlike that of Betz!

If Matthew compiled the sermon as we have it, what was his purpose in so doing? I have already suggested that its focal theme is that of discipleship. It follows the narrative of the call of the first disciples, and is specifically addressed to them in distinction from the larger crowds who also follow Jesus (5:1-2). It assumes throughout a distinction between 'you' (or, in the beatitudes, those to whom the kingdom of heaven belongs) and 'men' in general, and requires the disciples to be visibly distinct from the rest of society. Their life, unlike that of others, is governed by their special relationship to 'your Father in heaven' (a phrase which occurs ten times throughout the sermon, with 'your Father' a further seven times). A series of cameos in 7:13-27 makes it clear that while the border-line between true and false discipleship is not always easy to discern, the divide is total and of vital importance. The Sermon on the Mount is presented then not as a general treatise on ethics but as a prescription for the distinctive life of those who are under the rule of God ('the kingdom of heaven').

It has not always been so understood. H.K. McArthur gives an interesting survey of twelve different ways in which ethical conclusions have been drawn from the sermon.[47] They range from Tolstoy's 'absolutist' interpretation of the contents of the sermon as literal and universally applicable rules of life to the modern Dispensationalist belief that its provisions belong to a still future period ('the kingdom of heaven') so that it has no direct application to living in the present age, whether for disciples or for the rest of the world. Most interpreters have, of course, fallen somewhere between these extremes, and many, while taking the sermon as a universal ethical guide, have used various arguments to modify the absoluteness of its demands.

To treat it as a universal code of ethics, however, not only fails to recognise the clear sense of separation between 'you' and 'them' which runs through its text, and the 'family' relationship with God which it presupposes in its audience, but also involves ignoring the literary context in which it is set. This is true both of the immediate context of the gathering of the disciples around Jesus, and of the wider context of Matthew's total presentation of Jesus and his message. We have already noted that one of the most prominent themes running through the gospel, and especially through the sequence of the five discourses, is the separation between the true 'people of God' who respond to Jesus' message and the society around, who are increasingly seen as in opposition to the 'kingdom of heaven', and the resultant growth of an 'alternative society'. It is the values and ethics of this new society which the Sermon on the Mount sets out. It is a manifesto of life in the kingdom of heaven, of the difference it makes when you put God first.

47. H.K. McArthur, *Understanding the Sermon on the Mount* (London: Epworth, 1961) chapter 4.

But even when the sermon is recognised as a discourse on discipleship rather than on general ethics, there still remains a further important aspect of its role in Matthew's total presentation. Recent commentators have increasingly emphasised (*pace* Betz!) its *christological* implications.[48] As W.D. Davies puts it, 'The Sermon on the Mount compels us, in the first place, to ask who he is who utters these words: they are themselves kerygmatic'.[49] As throughout Matthew's gospel, it is those who respond *to Jesus* who come under the rule of God. It is for his sake that they are persecuted (5:11), it is in their relationship to him (7:21-23) and their obedience to his words (7:24-27) that their ultimate security rests. Their attitude to the law must derive from how the law relates to him (5:17-20), and his sovereign pronouncement 'But I say to you' overrides all previous interpretations (5:21 etc.). As R.J. Banks puts it, 'It is not so much *Jesus'* stance towards the Law that he [Matthew] is concerned to depict: it is how the *Law* stands with regard to him, as the one who brings it to fulfilment and to whom all attention must now be directed'.[50] So we are not surprised to read at the end of the sermon that it was the *authority* of Jesus which impressed the bystanders (7:28-29). When the following narrative of chapters 8-9 goes on to set out the authority of Jesus displayed in miraculous activity, this is a natural sequel to the christological impact already made by the authoritative teaching recorded in chapters 5-7. The Sermon on the Mount thus takes its due place in the development of Matthew's plot, the revelation of Jesus as Messiah and the consequences of men's response to his message. Far from being an independent document from a group out of sympathy with Matthew's theology, it forms the essential foundation for Matthew's reader to appreciate all that will follow.

The Sermon on the Mount thus illustrates what we have found to be true of the gospel as a whole, that Matthew was not a haphazard compiler of unrelated bits of tradition, but a careful and skilful composer of an integrated story, in which discourse and narrative combine powerfully to lead the reader into a deeper appreciation of who Jesus was and of the meaning of his life and teaching. It is a story which from the outset shows Jesus' contemporaries as confronted with a fundamental choice in their response to him, and which will not allow the reader to regard that choice as merely a matter of historical interest.

48. For a useful recent summary of this aspect of the sermon see R.A. Guelich, *The Sermon on the Mount: A Foundation for Understanding* (Waco: Word Books, 1982) 27-33, summarising what is demonstrated in detail in the commentary that follows.

49. Davies, *Setting*, 435.

50. R.J. Banks, *Jesus and the Law in the Synoptic Tradition* (Cambridge University Press, 1974) 226.

'FULFILMENT'

Matthew's preoccupation? 'That it might be fulfilled . . .'. 'Typology'.
Jesus and the law. Fulfilment and history.

A. MATTHEW'S PREOCCUPATION?

In the remainder of this book we shall be considering Matthew's
special emphases and interests. In this chapter I aim to highlight what
I believe to be the central focus of his theology, a theme which will
underlie the more specific areas of interest to be examined in the
following chapters. I am aware of the danger of imposing an artificial
unity on the diverse interests which are likely to come to light in any
individual's work. The search for 'the central theme' in Old Testament
theology which occupied the energies of many writers of the 'Biblical
Theology' school a few decades ago resulted in a variety of conflicting
'central themes', and there is a danger that even in the study of a single
book to propose one theme as the dominant emphasis will either lead
to distortion of the writer's thought or result in a proposition which is
so vague and all-embracing that it serves no useful purpose. I remain
convinced, however, that in the case of Matthew the theme I propose
is one he himself would have accepted as summarising his message,
and one which has a clear content which is decisive for the whole
orientation of Matthew's work.

The theme I propose is that of 'fulfilment'. I realise, of course, that
any Christian writer of the first century is likely to focus, at least to
some degree, on the idea of Jesus as the fulfilment of the hopes of Israel
and of the writings of the Old Testament. All the gospel writers
necessarily draw attention to this theme. It was what the Christian
gospel was all about, at least for any one who remained to any significant
degree in touch with the Jewish roots of Christianity. It was both the
enthusiastic assertion of early Christian preaching and also the bone
of contention between the growing church and Judaism. But in
Matthew's gospel this theme assumes a more dominant role. It is a
preoccupation of the author, one which leads him to explore aspects
of the significance of Jesus which others might regard as less essential.
Where others might be content to quote a few rather obvious texts as
'fulfilled' in Jesus, Matthew explores the nature of fulfilment with

remarkable ingenuity, and with a systematic attention to the place of
Jesus' ministry within the unfolding purpose of God which affects and
controls his presentation of all aspects of the story and the teaching of
Jesus.

This proposal is not new, of course – indeed it may seem hackneyed
and obvious. But I am not sure that its implications have always been
as fully appreciated as they should. In this chapter we shall consider
the theme of fulfilment in general, and particularly in relation to
Matthew's direct use of the Old Testament; in the following chapters
we shall consider Matthew's view of Israel, of the church, and of Jesus
himself, all of which derive from Matthew's understanding of the nature
of fulfilment in Jesus.

One recent writer who has particularly emphasised this theme is H.
Frankemölle. He writes of the word πληροῦν ('fulfil'), 'This verb indicates
in the briefest and most pregnant way Matthew's fundamental theological idea.'[1] Matthew 'works over the tradition he has received on
the basis of the Old Testament, and he does so in all the key areas (his
christology, his ecclesiology, questions about the law, his theology of
history . . .). Thus as far as christology is concerned, Jesus is for Matthew
not only the fulfiller of the promise of a Son of David, he is not only
the Son of Abraham, the incarnation of Wisdom, the Son of God, but
also the fulfiller of prophecies about Bethlehem, Galilee, etc., about
the Messiah, the King of Israel or rather the King of the Jews, about
the gentle King, the suffering Servant of God, and also about the Son
of Man. . . . All these aspects appear to be focused in the field of
meaning of the verb πληροῦν, which was indeed already available to
Matthew as a motif found in the Old Testament, but which is the special
trademark of his "gospel".'[2] I believe that the following chapters will
show the truth of this assessment.

Perhaps I should point out that my concern is much wider than
merely the incidence of the verb πληρόω in Matthew, prominent as it is.
This verb, and the formulae in which it is incorporated, are only the
most visible signs of a whole orientation of thought which comes to
expression in many other ways.[3]

1. H. Frankemölle, *Jahwe-Bund und Kirche Christi: Studien zur Form- und
Traditionsgeschichte des "Evangeliums" nach Matthäus* (Münster: Aschendorff, ²1984)
388.
2. *Ibid.* 169-170. Cf also T.L. Donaldson, *Jesus on the Mountain: a Study in Matthean
Theology* (Sheffield: JSOT Press, 1985) 204-205.
3. This point is brought out especially in C.F.D. Moule's important article, 'Fulfilment-
words in the New Testament: Use and Abuse', *NTS* 14 (1967/8) 293-320, reprinted in
Moule's *Essays in New Testament Interpretation* (Cambridge University Press, 1982) 3-36.
Moule argues that while many of Matthew's uses of the verb πληρόω are in the context
of what he calls 'mere prediction-fulfilment', of a superficial and theologically barren
type, his use of the word may be derived from Jesus' own usage, where its content was
much more theologically significant, carrying the concept of a *Heilsgeschichte* which

MATTHEW'S PROLOGUE AS A MANIFESTO ON 'FULFILMENT'

This orientation of Matthew's gospel is made clear right from the beginning. The first 17 verses are devoted to a genealogy, which has as its primary purpose to link Jesus as closely as possible with the developing purpose of God as revealed in Old Testament history. The echo of Genesis in the first two words, βίβλος γενέσεως, the evocative title Χριστός which follows immediately, the repeated names of Abraham and David, the way the subsequent list follows the royal line of Judah, and is structured around the key turning-points of the beginning and end of the actual monarchy of Judah (a point drawn out rather pedantically in v. 17 for the sake of any who may have missed it!), all these make Matthew's purpose plain, and the neat (if artificial) symmetry drawn out in v. 17 conveys the impression that all that has gone before adds up to a rounded era of history, to which Jesus comes as the due culmination.

The remainder of the 'prologue', from 1:18 to 2:23, generally described rather inadequately as 'infancy narratives', consists in fact of a series of five brief sketches, each of which focuses on an Old Testament quotation which is said to be 'fulfilled' in that particular aspect of Jesus' birth and childhood travels.[4] It is the quotations rather than the narrative which introduces them which are apparently the structural principle of the whole section. The whole of chapters 1-2 could, in other words, appropriately be entitled 'A presentation of Jesus as the fulfilment of the Old Testament'. Nor is this presentation restricted to those appeals to Old Testament precedent which stand out on the surface. The narratives which surround and lead up to the prominent quotations are themselves steeped in echoes of Old Testament stories, particularly those of the birth and preservation of Moses and of the wicked king whose slaughter of the children failed to eliminate Israel's deliverer. Other echoes of the Old Testament fill the story of the visit of the wise men to Jerusalem bringing gifts to the king, son of David, as the Queen of Sheba did long ago, while the gifts themselves recall passages which took that incident as a foretaste of further homage to come (Ps.

reaches its climax in the ministry of Jesus, a concept which Matthew also shared and expressed in other ways. While I would wish, as will soon be clear, to defend Matthew's usage of πληρόω as being less theologically neutral than Moule suggests (see my remarks in *NTS* 27 [1980/1] 250-251, in response to Moule's further comments on this subject in his *The Origin of Christology* [Cambridge University Press, 1977], ch. 5), I agree strongly that there is much more to Matthew's idea of 'fulfilment' than merely his use of this verb.

4. For a stimulating account of the purpose of chapters 1-2, with special attention to the significance of the geographical locations of Jesus' childhood, as these are drawn out in the formal quotations, see K. Stendahl, 'Quis et Unde? An Analysis of Mt 1-2' in W. Eltester (ed.), *Judentum, Urchristentum, Kirche* (Berlin: Töpelmann, 1960) 94-105; reprinted in Stanton, *Interpretation*, 54-66.

72:10-11,15; Is. 60:4-6). And 1:18-25, usually inadequately headed 'the birth of Jesus', is in fact an account of how a child who was not the natural son of Joseph 'son of David' (v 20) was brought under divine direction into the family of David so that his legal claim to the role of Χριστός might be established.

The last paragraphs barely scratch the surface of the rich scriptural meditation which runs through these two chapters in a profusion of quotations, echoes and themes from the Old Testament which all add up to an exuberant claim that in Jesus the time of fulfilment has arrived. We shall return later in this chapter to some of these themes, and we shall see that from the point of view of strictly formal interpretation they do not all fit comfortably together – Jesus corresponds both to the Israel which was rescued (2:15) and to the leader through whom that rescue was achieved. But in Matthew's hand the various threads are woven into a tapestry whose overall effect is striking. My point here is not to analyse these chapters in detail, but to argue that a man who begins his book about Jesus with a prologue like this can surely justly be said to be preoccupied with the theme of 'fulfilment'.[5]

MATTHEW'S PREOCCUPATION WITH THE OLD TESTAMENT: AN EXAMPLE

As the gospel proceeds the Old Testament is employed in various ways, not all of which are directly related to the theme of fulfilment, as indeed one might expect of a Jewish writer who was brought up to refer every sort of question to the bar of what is 'written'.[6] But, even where an ethical or legal issue is under discussion, one is never far away from the question of the status of Jesus himself in relation to the Old Testament.[7]

In 12:1-8, for example, a discussion of sabbath law turns into a christological manifesto, and in the process the Old Testament is appealed to in characteristic ways. The passage has parallels in Mark and Luke, and a comparison with their versions is instructive. The basic argument leading up to the pronouncement 'The Son of Man is lord of the sabbath' is the same in all three versions: David's act

5. I have devoted a number of articles to analysing some of the themes worked out in these chapters. See 'Herod and the Children of Bethlehem', *NovT* 21 1979) 98-120, especially pp. 105-111; 'The Formula-Quotations of Matthew 2 and the Problem of Communication', *NTS* 27 (1980/81) 233-251; 'Scripture, Tradition and History in the Infancy Narratives of Matthew' in *Gospel Perspectives*, vol. 2 (1981) 239-266.

6. An interesting study of this variety in the use of Scripture, both in first century Judaism in general and in Matthew in particular is offered by L. Hartman, 'Scriptural Exegesis in the Gospel of St. Matthew and the Problem of Communication', in Didier, *Matthieu*, 131-152.

7. See esp. below section D of this chapter, for the christological and 'fulfilment' implications of the way Matthew presents Jesus in relation to the Old Testament law.

of 'sacrilege' in taking the holy bread is taken as justification for Jesus' high-handed attitude in allowing his disciples to infringe current Pharisaic understanding of the requirements of sabbath law. In Luke the logic of this argument is not explicit (one can only assume that it involves some rather·more compelling point than that if the law has been broken once it can be broken again!). In Mark the inclusion of 2:27 between the David story and Jesus' conclusion perhaps suggests that the argument is seen as hinging on the priority of human need over rules and regulations. But in Matthew it is clear that the argument turns on the relationship between the great David and the greater Jesus, and therefore establishes Jesus' authority on an *a fortiori* basis. If David, because of who he was, was entitled to do what no other layman might dare, so too Jesus, because of who he is, has no less an authority.

It is perhaps in order to establish this direct comparison between the two men that Matthew includes the word ἐπείνασαν in v. 1, to be echoed in the ἐπείνασεν of v. 3; in both cases it was hunger which led to the unorthodox action. But what makes Matthew's logic clear is the addition of vv. 5-6, in which a parallel argument is offered, this time in connection with the 'violation' of the sabbath law by the priests in the temple (with reference perhaps to their duty to offer sacrifice and carry out other regular ritual acts, or perhaps more appropriately to the reaping of the offering of the first sheaves, which the Pharisees regarded as permissible on the sabbath while the Sadducees disagreed).[8] Here there is no question of emergency or human need; it is simply a question of the supersession of the sabbath law by a higher authority, that of the temple. And the logic of its relevance to Jesus is spelled out in v. 6: 'Something greater than the temple is here'. The same might have been said with regard to the preceding argument, 'Something greater than David is here'. The same formula recurs twice later in the same chapter: 'Something greater than Jonah is here'; 'Something greater than Solomon is here' (vv. 41,42). Thus Jesus is placed alongside some of the greatest 'authorities' of the Old Testament era (the kings David and Solomon, the temple and its priests, the prophet Jonah), and declared 'greater' than all. This is the basis of his unique authority, and it is on this basis that 'The Son of Man is lord of the sabbath'.

Matthew's scriptural reinforcement of the argument does not end there. He also includes here in v. 7 (as also in 9:13, where again it is absent from the other synoptists) a quotation from Hosea 6:6. Here the intention is not directly to prove Jesus' authority from Scripture, but to provide a scriptural basis for the bold attitude to law in which that authority has just been displayed. The basic orientation of Jesus' attitude to the sabbath regulations is that which Hosea too required. Yet this verse is only one among many from the Old Testament which

---

8. Mishnah, *Menahoth* 10:3,9; cf. E. Levine, *NTS* 22 (1975/6) 480-483.

ye shall keep my ordinances

might have been applied to the same question, and a very different orientation might have been achieved by appealing instead to Lev. 18:4-5 or Dt. 27:26. Matthew's Jesus is one who claims the right to declare the priority of Hosea's principle over the strict legal observance which was a hall-mark of Pharisaism. So the conclusion that 'The Son of Man is lord of the sabbath' flows no less from the quotation of Hosea 6:6 than from the more elaborate *a fortiori* argument of the preceding verses.

We have seen then in Matthew 12:1-8 just one example of the way Matthew's preoccupation with the question of Jesus' relation to the Old Testament comes to expression in the differences between his gospel and the parallel passages in the other gospels. We shall see many more such examples as we go through this chapter and those that follow.

B. 'THAT IT MIGHT BE FULFILLED...'

Even more prominent in Matthew's gospel than the formula 'And it happened when Jesus had finished...', considered in the last chapter, is the clause 'to fulfil (or 'then was fulfilled') what had been spoken by the prophet, saying...'. The formula varies slightly, sometimes including the name of the prophet, once referring to 'prophets' in the plural and omitting 'saying',[9] twice specifying that it was 'the Lord' who had spoken through the prophet. Ten references to the Old Testament are introduced in this rather ponderous way (1:22-23; 2:15; 2:17-18; 2:23; 4:14-16; 8:17; 12:17-21; 13:35; 21:4-5; 27:9-10). Somewhat similar formulae also involving the verb πληρόω occur elsewhere (13:14; 26:54, 56), but this group of ten passages (together with 2:5-6, where the formula is reduced to exclude the verb πληρόω but which for other reasons is generally seen as part of the same group) has come to be distinguished as Matthew's 'formula-quotations', and has been the object of extensive study.[10]

---

9. This is 2:23, the formula introducing a 'quotation' which notoriously is not recognisable as any specific Old Testament passage. The change of formula in this case may therefore be deliberate, in order to indicate a reference to a general prophetic theme rather than to a single text; see my discussion in *NTS* 27 (1980/81) 246-249.

10. Important studies include particularly Stendahl, *School*, 97-127, 183-206; Strecker, *Weg*, 49-85; Gundry, *Use*, 89-127; R.S. McConnell, *Law and Prophecy in Matthew's Gospel* (Basel: Reinhardt, 1969) 101-141; W. Rothfuchs, *Die Erfüllungszitate des Matthäus-Evangeliums* (Stuttgart: Kohlhammer, 1969); F. Van Segbroeck, 'Les citations d'accomplissement dans l'Evangile selon saint Matthieu', in Didier, *Matthieu*, 107-130; G.M. Soares Prabhu, *The Formula Quotations in the Infancy Narrative of Matthew* (Rome: Biblical Institute Press, 1976), of which pp. 18-161 discuss the formula-quotations in general, before focusing on chapters 1-2. Since Soares Prabhu's monograph the flow of studies seems to have eased. There is a useful summary of where the debate had reached by 1977 in R.E. Brown, *The Birth of the Messiah* (London: Chapman, 1977) 96-104.

The introductory formula itself, for all the minor variations in wording, is clearly distinctive.[11] Similar formulae are surprisingly absent from other Jewish and Christian literature of the period, the only significant parallel being John's use of the formula 'that the scripture might be fulfilled' or the like on six occasions with reference to Old Testament predictions (Jn. 12:38; 13:18; 15:25; 17:12; 19:24, 36; he also uses a similar formula twice for the fulfilment of predictions made by Jesus himself, Jn. 18:9,32). A few Old Testament passages supply a possible model on which such a formula might have been based (1 Ki. 2:27; 2 Ch. 36:21-22 = Ezra 1:1), and the wording has a rather formal, even archaic, sound which evokes in the reader a sense of awe at the outworking of the agelong purposes of God revealed long ago by divine declaration. Apart from the sense of purpose conveyed by Matthew's key word πληρόω, there is also the participle ῥηθέν, which is not used at all in the New Testament outside Matthew, while he uses it only in these ten formulae and in three other passages which equally direct the reader's attention to prophetic predictions or a divine declaration in the Old Testament (3:3; 22:31; 24:15).[12] Then there is the regular mention of a 'prophet' as the medium of revelation, even in 13:35 where the quotation is in fact from a psalm! The formula as a whole, then, is designed to prepare the reader for a solemn declaration of how God's previously announced purpose has reached its due conclusion in Jesus.

THE TEXT-FORM OF THE FORMULA-QUOTATIONS

Direct quotations from the Old Testament in Matthew's gospel, where he is passing on material shared with the other synoptic gospels, are usually given in the LXX version, which became the standard Greek version of the Old Testament in use by the early church. This in itself is not surprising. A translator of a work which regularly quotes from the Bible naturally presents those quotations in the form in which they appear in the current translation of the Bible in the language into which

11. See the detailed examination of the formula and its background in Soares Prabhu, *Formula Quotations*, 46-63.

12. We might note in passing that the same formal and archaic connotation seems to attach to the other passive forms of the verb ἐρῶ, which supplies some of the forms for λέγω, 'to say'. While the future and perfect active ἐρῶ, and εἴρηκα, are used freely in normal narrative contexts, the passive forms are used in the New Testament only of divine pronouncements (including scriptural quotations): Luke uses the perfect passive to appeal to Old Testament texts (Lk. 2:24; 4:12; Acts 2:16; 13:40; cf. also Rom. 4:18, the only NT use outside Luke), while the aorist passive ἐρρέθη (from which comes Matthew's distinctive participle ῥηθέν) is used only for divine pronouncements, whether in scripture or subsequently (Rom. 9:12,26; Gal. 3:16; Rev. 6:11; 9:4). It is this same archaic form ἐρρέθη which Matthew chooses to introduce his six quotations of what 'was said to the men of old' in 5:21,27,31,33,38,43. In the light of this usage of the passive, it seems clear that the participle ῥηθέν has the same sort of connotations as a deliberate archaism in English like 'Thus saith the Lord'.

he is translating, unless there is something about that translation which makes its version inappropriate to what his text is trying to convey by means of the quotation. In most cases this is the procedure which the gospel writers adopted in conveying quotations originally made by Jesus presumably in Aramaic. And where they are themselves referring directly to the Old Testament they, and the rest of the New Testament writers, generally use the familiar LXX version. This is only to be expected.[13]

It is, then, striking to discover that among the eleven formula-quotations of Matthew the only one to offer a text which is the same as the LXX is 1:23 (except for the alteration of 'you will call' to 'they will call', which is required to make sense when it is quoted out of context). In all the others, however short (2:15 quotes only six words!), the text differs substantially from the LXX. In some cases the LXX of the passage concerned was a free and possibly misleading translation, and Matthew's version offers a more direct translation of the Hebrew (this is true particularly of 2:15 and 8:17). In 2:18, while the LXX would apparently have served as well, Matthew has given an independent and slightly abbreviated (but equally 'correct') rendering of the Hebrew. But in most of them Matthew offers a text which departs not only from the LXX but also from any other known version of the relevant passage (and in 2:23 it is not even clear what passage he intends to quote, if any single one is in mind!).

In some cases the divergence is due to the incorporation into the basic text of words and phrases drawn from one or more other Old Testament passages which relate to the same theme; thus 2:6 begins in Micah 5:2, but concludes with 2 Sam. 5:2; 21:5 introduces the quotation of Zech. 9:9 with some words from Is. 62:11; and 27:9-10, while its basis is clearly Zech. 11:12-13, is introduced as a quotation from Jeremiah[14] and includes echoes of Jeremiah 19:1-13 (and/or other Jeremiah texts?) not only in the surrounding narrative but perhaps also in the wording of the quotation.[15] In most cases, however, Matthew's version seems to be simply an independent[16] and 'free' rendering of the passage concerned, sometimes apparently adapting the text to allow the reader

13. Cf my discussion of this issue in my *JOT*, 25-26.
14. For a similar attribution of a composite quotation to only one of the prophets concerned see Mark 1:2-3. The Jeremiah attribution is usefully discussed by D.P. Senior, *The Passion Narrative according to Matthew* (Leuven University Press, 1975) 366-369.
15. On the scriptural background of this passage see D.J. Moo, *The Old Testament in the Gospel Passion Narratives* (Sheffield: Almond, 1983) 191-198; also in *Gospel Perspectives*, vol. 3 (1983) 157-161.
16. Sometimes there are echoes of other ancient versions, as in the long quotation of Is. 42:1-4 in 12:18-21, where some phrases correspond to the LXX, some look like literal rendering of the Hebrew, but others echo phrases of the Greek version of Theodotion, the Syriac Peshitta, or the Aramaic Targum Jonathan (for details see Stendahl, *School*, 107-115); the quotation as a whole, however, does not correspond to the text lying behind any of these versions.

to see more clearly how it has found its fulfilment in Jesus. Thus in 2:6 where Micah described Bethlehem as 'little' among the clans of Judah, Matthew has 'by no means the least'; it was, of course, Bethlehem's future greatness in contrast with its present 'littleness' which was the point of Micah's description, but Matthew, in view of the prophecy's fulfilment already in Jesus, can indicate in his version that Bethlehem is no longer so 'little'.[17] The most elaborate example of this creative handling of the actual 'text' quoted is, of course, the 'Jeremiah' quotation in 27:9-10, where an interaction of the quotation with its introductory narrative and with a number of other Old Testament passages has resulted in something very different from Zech. 11:12-13 as we know it elsewhere. We shall look further at the question of the mutual influence of text and narrative in the next section.

Stendahl concludes from the very distinctive text-form of these eleven quotations that they represent the results of the work of Matthew's 'school' of scriptural interpretation, which he envisages as similar in its approach to those who wrote the *pesharim* ('commentaries') of Qumran, particularly that on Habakkuk. While Matthew's quotations which he shares with the other synoptists retain the LXX text-form, this group, which appear in Matthew alone, owe their distinctive form to their origin in the 'School'.[18]

We shall return to the question of the 'School' in the next section.[19] But at this point we should note that the comparison with the Habakkuk commentary is not in fact so close as Stendahl suggests, and indicates an intriguing difference of approach. Both Matthew and the Qumran commentator take 'liberties' with the text, but while the latter does not alter more than a suffix or a couple of letters in order to achieve his desired interpretation, Matthew is much more radical in his textual surgery; on the other hand, however, whereas for the Qumran writer the meaning of the text in its original context is of little interest, so that he can freely allegorise details and apply the whole text to situations which have no recognisable relation to the original setting, in Matthew's case the original meaning of the text is the necessary starting-point of his interpretation, however boldly he may locate its fulfilment in a new situation.[20] One reason for this difference is of course that whereas the Qumran commentator was confronted with an existing text, for which he then had to find contemporary applications as best he could, Matthew's texts are chosen specifically because they already have a perceived relevance to the story being told. The enterprises in which the two 'commentators' are engaged are therefore fundamentally differ-

---

17. For this and other textual changes in 2:6 see my comments in *NTS* 27 (1980/1) 241-243.
18. Stendahl, *School*, esp. 126-127, 194-206.
19. See also above pp. 113-114.
20. See further my *JOT*, 206-207.

ent. But even if the comparison with Qumran is overdrawn, Stendahl's emphasis on the distinctive nature (and therefore different origin?) of the text of this group of quotations is significant.

A strong challenge to this view comes from R.H. Gundry, who points out that Stendahl's study focused only on the formal quotations in Matthew, and ignored the much larger body of allusive references to the Old Testament. By taking these into account, Gundry believes, it can be shown that the text-form of the formula-quotations is not distinctive from other uses of the Old Testament by Matthew, but only from the formal quotations which Matthew derived from Mark.[21] In other words, it is Mark's adherence to the LXX, not Matthew's more free text-form, which constitutes the distinctive approach. This argument must be advanced with caution, because it is not easy to establish the text-form on which an allusive reference is based, but Gundry's point is well taken that Stendahl has set up an artificial distinction. He rightly points out that the purely Matthean quotations in the Sermon on the Mount, which are not classed among the formula-quotations and are passed over very briefly in Stendahl's discussion, are in fact far from purely Septuagintal, and in some cases treat the Old Testament text as freely as some of the formula-quotations. It was, Gundry argues, 'Matthew the targumist' himself, not a school, who characteristically offered his own free rendering of the text, of which the formula-quotations are only the most prominent examples. Similarly Soares Prabhu[22] concludes a rapid survey of the text-form of all Matthew's quotations outside the formula-quotations with the verdict that 'the LXX is not "Matthew's Bible" ' and that there is no reason to doubt therefore that Matthew himself was responsible also for the text-form of the formula-quotations.

Gundry's phrase 'Matthew the targumist'[23] probably points us in the right direction. Our modern preoccupation with 'accuracy' in quotation finds little echo in the world of the New Testament. Most ancient versions of the Old Testament, including many parts of the LXX as we know it, were not very literal (the second-century AD version of Aquila was remarkable precisely because its painful literalism was unusual), and the Aramaic targums that have survived bear witness to a living tradition of biblical translation/interpretation from the world of Christian origins in which there was no rigid separation between text and interpretation, so that extensive paraphrase, or even interpolation, in order to bring out the perceived meaning of the original

21. Gundry, *Use*, 2-5, 155-159. Unfortunately Gundry's thesis, though completed in 1961, appeared in print too late to receive a response in the preface to Stendahl's second edition (1968).
22. *Formula Quotations*, 83-84.
23. This is the title of a useful section of Gundry, *Use*, 172-174; it is taken up and used as a section heading also by Soares Prabhu, *Formula Quotations*, 73-77.

was normal and acceptable. In this milieu it requires no 'school' to explain Matthew's 'freedom' in the handling of quotations which he is keen to display to the reader as 'fulfilled' in the events of Jesus' life.

The mention of targums does, however, raise the possibility that to speak of 'the Hebrew' and 'the LXX' as the main or only textual resources available to Matthew is at least an oversimplification. While the Old Testament Hebrew texts found at Qumran have strongly confirmed that the Hebrew text which has come down to us is not markedly different from that known to Jews in Palestine at the time of Jesus, the presence of minor variants in those texts indicates that what we regard as 'the Hebrew text' of a given passage may at least in its details be only one among a number of versions which might have been known to Matthew. The same is even more clearly true of the Old Testament in Greek, both in the variety of versions preserved for us in LXX manuscripts, and also in the clear variation among the styles and approaches of the translators of the different Old Testament books. How wide the variety may have been has been hotly contested, the extreme view, associated with P. Kahle, being that the very idea of a single authorised version called the Septuagint is a development subsequent to the New Testament period, and that during the first century a luxuriant variety of independent Greek 'targums' of Old Testament passages was in use.[24] Most recent scholars think Kahle went too far, and the generally uniform 'LXX' text found in most New Testament quotations indicates as much at least for Christian usage, but the idea of a single 'authorised version' of the Old Testament in Greek in the first century is almost certainly an anachronism. Matthew may therefore have had a greater variety of versions from which to choose than we know about, and may not have been left so much to his own ingenuity in finding a text-form for his quotations which would best suit the contexts into which he inserted them.[25]

However, whether by a judicious selection among existing versions, or by his own creative paraphrasing of the original, there seems no reason to doubt that the distinctive text-form of the formula-quotations could have come to us from Matthew himself rather than from an already existing collection of proof-texts. How then did these interesting versions come to be created and incorporated into Matthew's gospel?

THE ORIGIN OF THE FORMULA-QUOTATIONS

We have seen that the repetition of the striking formula, and the apparently distinctive textual phenomena of the formula-quotations,

24. P. Kahle, *The Cairo Geniza* (Oxford: Blackwell, ²1959) 209-264, Kahle's view is criticised by S. Jellicoe, *The Septuagint and Modern Study* (Oxford University Press, 1968) 59-63 and by Soares Prabhu, *Formula Quotations*, 65-67.
25. See further the comments and bibliography in the preface to the second edition of Stendahl's *School*, pp. i-iii; Stanton, 'Origin', 1933.

have inevitably resulted in the ten (or eleven) quotations so introduced being studied *as a group*. And from this practice it is a short step to the notion that they may have had some separate corporate existence prior to their inclusion in Matthew's gospel. (Cf. the 'Servant Songs' of Isaiah, where the recurrence of the distinctive Servant terminology and of certain repeated motifs has too often led, since Duhm isolated them as a group, to their study as a separate stratum with a supposedly independent origin and message, rather than as a part of the context in which we find them.) This impression is strengthened by the observation that all of them appear rather as detached comments on the narrative, rather than as an essential part of the flow of the story, so that if the formula with its quotation were removed from the text the narrative would in each case continue without noticeable interruption. Were these texts then part of a collection which Matthew found ready-made, and simply inserted into his narrative at the most appropriate point he could find?

This view has sometimes been linked with the belief of some scholars that the primitive church possessed 'testimony-books', collections of Old Testament texts for use in preaching and teaching, to demonstrate the claims of the church that in Jesus Scripture was fulfilled. If such collections existed in the first century (as they certainly did later: Cyprian compiled 'Three Books of Testimonies against the Jews', and works as early as Justin show the same tendency to collect scriptural ammunition for debate), surely Matthew's formula-quotations would be a good example of the use of such an anthology.

The 'testimony-book' theory was given its classic expression by Rendel . Harris in the early part of this century,[26] and was influential for some thirty years until C.H. Dodd argued[27] that the concentration of the New Testament writers is not so much on individual 'proof-texts' as on 'text-plots', larger areas of the Old Testament to which they frequently turned as the most productive quarries for apologetic and preaching material. Since then there has been less talk of 'testimony-books' as such,[28] despite Strecker's arguments for such a *Zitatensammlung*,[29] and more tendency to envisage a wide-ranging appeal to the Old Testament by early Christian preachers and teachers, without the restriction of a defined 'collection'. Of course there were favourite texts, but it is a remarkable fact that among Matthew's formula-quotations only a few

26. J.R. Harris, *Testimonies I & II* (Cambridge University Press, 1916, 1920).
27. C.H. Dodd, *According to the Scriptures* (London: Nisbet, 1952).
28. The discovery of two brief documents at Qumran which contained collections of related Old Testament texts with an eschatological flavour (*4QTestimonia* and *4QFlorilegium*) gave something of a boost to the theory, but *4QTest* contained only four biblical texts, while *4QFlor* is more a 'midrash on the last days' (Vermes' title for it) than a simple collection of proof-texts.
29. Strecker, *Weg*, 50, 82-85. McConnell, *Law*, 101-141 sustains a critical dialogue with Strecker on this point.

(perhaps Micah 5:2; Is. 42:1-4; 53:4; Zech. 9:9) are likely to have come in this category – most are completely ignored by the other New Testament writers, and modern interpreters remark on the oddity of Matthew's choice.[30]

But to dismiss the idea of an existing collection of 'testimonies' is not necessarily to conclude that these quotations came directly out of Matthew's own head as he wrote his story. Were they perhaps already embedded in, or at least associated with, the tradition as Matthew received it? In a few cases this might well be argued, particularly for 21:4-5, where the same quotation occurs in John's telling of the story, and while Mark and Luke contain no explicit quotation, there can be no doubt that they, and surely any early Christian teller of the story, would have seen its significance in the way Jesus' action drew attention to Zechariah 9:9 as fulfilled in his coming to the city. But while it is the obvious quotation for the story, here as in other cases it is introduced as a sort of 'aside', the removal of which would leave the story intact, and it was apparently in this form that the tradition found its way to Mark and Luke.

It has sometimes been argued that some of the narratives in which the formula-quotations occur are fictional stories or situations created out of the text itself, so that for instance Christian meditation on Zechariah 11:12-13 (together with some related Jeremiah texts) led to the conclusion that an encounter of Judas with the priests such as is narrated in 27:3-8 must have taken place 'in order that the scripture might be fulfilled', or that the slaughter of the children in Bethlehem arose out of imaginative meditation on Jeremiah 31:15. In that case the stories could never have existed without the text. Against this suggestion one must consider that there is no obvious reason why a text such as Jeremiah 31:15 should have formed the subject of Christian meditation in the first place unless there was something in the story of Jesus to suggest its relevance, while the whole *raison d'être* of the 'quotation' coined in 2:23 is the narrative to which it belongs, without which it simply did not exist! Further, the considerable ingenuity exercised in some cases in bringing the text into conformity with the 'facts' narrated would be quite unnecessary if those 'facts' were merely a reflection of what was already in the text.[31] It is altogether more likely that, as their 'separable' nature suggests, the quotations were added as comments on an already existing tradition.

But was it *Matthew* who first thought of these comments? Stendahl's theory of a 'Matthean school'[32] arose primarily from a study of these

30. For fuller discussion of the testimony-book hypothesis see Soares Prabhu, *Formula Quotations*, 67-73.

31. I have developed this argument more fully in *NTS* 27 (1980/81) 235-237, and in *Gospel Perspectives*, vol. 2 (1981) 250-252.

32. See above pp. 113-114.

quotations, whose distinctive text-form he took, as we have seen in the last section, to be evidence of the creative work of a group who in their corporate study had developed sophisticated techniques for finding (or where necessary manufacturing) scriptural support for the stories of Jesus. While the gospel was no doubt compiled by a single individual, it was the conclusions of this 'school' that he was setting down. But we have seen reasons to treat the argument from text-form with caution, and in that case the major reason for postulating the 'school' is removed. Perhaps it is ultimately impossible (and not very important) to decide where a writer is speaking only for himself and where he is the spokesman of a group, and I see no reason to think that Matthew wrote in splendid isolation. But the same considerations which tell against the formula-quotations having existed as an independent testimony collection also render it improbable that they came ready-made from the workshop of a 'school'. Whether or not Matthew learned and refined his method of using the Old Testament in the context of such a group, the relation of the quotations to their narrative contexts is such that their application to those particular stories seems to be have been worked out by the man who gave us the stories in their present form.

In that case, it is wrong to think of these ten (or eleven) quotations as forming in the author's mind a distinct group with their own peculiar characteristics. Rather he introduced references to the Old Testament as and when the narrative suggested them to him, and one, but only one, of his characteristic ways of doing so was by means of the fulfilment formula. It is modern scholarship which has found it convenient to treat them as a group, led to this both by the incidence of the fulfilment formula and also by the recognition that quotations so introduced tend to differ in their text-form from the LXX. We have seen, however, that the way in which they differ is not always the same. These quotations do not so much display a unified textual method or hermeneutical approach; rather where they agree is in the purely negative sense that most of them depart, sometimes radically, from the faithful reproduction of the LXX text which is characteristic of the formal quotations which Matthew shares with Mark and Luke (but not always of his own independent quotations).

Why then did Matthew tend to differ from the LXX particularly (but not only) on those occasions when he felt his fulfilment formula to be appropriate? The answer may lie partly in the nature of the contexts where he makes use of this formula, and partly in the character of the texts which he decides to insert into these contexts.

Most of the narrative sections in which the formula-quotations appear are peculiar to Matthew, the only significant exception being the entry to Jerusalem, in the course of which Zechariah 9:9 is introduced. Four of the other formula-quotations occur in brief summaries of some aspect of Jesus' ministry, which Matthew includes within an overall narrative context which is shared with Mark (4:13-16; 8:16-17; 12:15-21; 13:34-35); each of these summaries, whether echoing Marcan phrases or not, consists of the bare minimum of factual content needed to explain the relevance of the Old Testament passage, so that their sole *raison d'être* seems to be to introduce the quotation. The remaining six formula-quotations are associated with short stories peculiar to Matthew, most of which, like the summaries just mentioned, seem to exist solely to provide a basis for the quotation. The accounts of Joseph's dilemma (1:18-25) and of the visit of the magi (2:1-12) do indeed have a story-value of their own, so that one could imagine them occurring without the formula-quotation, and each introduces other facets of the total 'fulfilment' scene in addition to that indicated by the formal quotation. But in each of those two passages as they now appear in Matthew the quotation occupies a central place, and in the remaining pericopes (2:13-15; 2:16-18; 2:19-23; 27:3-10) the role of the quotation is so crucial that it is hard to see why the stories should have been told at all except in order to point out the fulfilment of the passage quoted.

There is, of course, a tension between this observation and the point made earlier that from a literary point of view all the formula-quotations are separable from their context. On the one hand the removal of the quotations would allow the narrative to flow on with little apparent interruption, while on the other hand the narrative in most cases seems to have little point once that quotation is removed. This suggests that the relationship between text and context is more subtle than is suggested either by those who think the narratives are fictional constructions out of the texts or by those who regard the texts as alien intrusions from a pre-existing collection. My conclusions from a study of this relationship in chapter 2 (where four of the eleven quotations occur) would, I believe, also apply *mutatis mutandis* to most of the other seven contexts:

> We have not a simple relation of either facts controlling texts or texts creating 'facts', but a more complex dialectic. The evangelist ... is aware of traditions which he believes to be factual, and which seem to him to require explanation or comment. This he achieves not only by incidental allusions and by a carefully drawn parallel with the experiences of Moses (and perhaps the story of Balaam), but by one selected proof-text for each episode of his narrative. The narrative then affects the texts, as each is adapted more or less drastically to fit its new context and to draw out the message which was the evangelist's purpose in including this incident in his account. Conversely, the text affects the narrative, in that it is structured around the text and related in such a way as to bring out the relevance of the text to that situation, so much so that in

some cases it is little more than a framework for the text. In short, the narrative tradition is the motive for the selection and shaping of the texts, but the texts have become the organizing principle for the narrative.[33]

To return, then, to the question of why Matthew departs from the LXX in these quotations, one answer is surely that he has deliberately given the texts in a form which is best adapted to bring out the relevance of the text to its narrative context, and that where an extensive 'targumising' was the best way to make his point he has not been reluctant to do so.

It is also possible, however, that the nature of the selected texts themselves has caused Matthew to quote more freely here than he does in some other cases. We have noticed above that most of the texts deployed in the formula-quotations are ones which occur nowhere else in the New Testament (the only one explicitly quoted elsewhere is Zech. 9:9, though the 'servant' passages of Isaiah quoted in 8:17 and 12:18-21 certainly influenced New Testament thought elsewhere, and Is. 7:14 is echoed in Luke 1:31), and few of them are obvious christological prooftexts (exceptions are Micah 5:2; Zech. 9:9); they were called to mind by details of the tradition which Matthew received, rather than by their own inherent suitability to the theme of messianic fulfilment. Is this then a further factor in explaining Matthew's textual freedom in these cases? 'When the evangelist introduces as a formula citation a passage that was already known in Christian usage, he is likely to have reproduced the familiar wording, but if Matthew himself was the first to see the possibilities of an Old Testament fulfilment, he is likely to have chosen or adapted a wording that would best fit his purposes.'[34]

MATTHEW THE INTERPRETER

If then it is to Matthew himself that we owe the introduction and the special characteristics of the formula-quotations, so that they are to be understood as one prominent aspect of his total aim to present Jesus as the fulfilment of the Old Testament, what does this tell us of his practice of 'christological exegesis'?

C.F.D. Moule characterises many of Matthew's special appeals to the Old Testament as 'vehicular', by which he means 'the arbitrary use of words as a vehicle, simply, for something that is derived from elsewhere'. In this he sees Matthew as engaging in a similar enterprise to that of the Qumran *pesharim*, ignoring the original meaning of the words and taking them out of context. The result is, he believes, 'to our critical eyes, manifestly forced and artificial and unconvincing',

---

33. *NTS* 27 (1980/81) 237.
34. Stanton, 'Origin', 1933.

though he goes on to argue that underlying these 'vehicular' uses (which he does not wish to defend as exegetical models) is what he calls a 'relational' understanding of Scripture, a true perception that there is to be found 'in Jesus an overall fulfilment, on the deepest level, of what Scripture as a whole reflected'. Matthew's *method* of using the Old Testament is, then, at many points unacceptable, but his *reason* for so using it is a valid and theologically significant concept of fulfilment in Jesus.[35]

I am not sure that so neat a distinction can be drawn between the hermeneutical technique and the theology of fulfilment which inspires it. It is, I believe, precisely the thorough-going nature of Matthew's conviction that in Jesus all God's purposes have come to fulfilment which has led him to use the text in the subtle ('artificial'?) way that we find in the formula-quotations, and to search for aspects of 'fulfilment' in texts which would seem to the modern interpreter to have no reference beyond their original historical setting.

Thus he sees in Isaiah 7:14, which clearly relates to the specific situation in which the prophet spoke in 735 BC, a foreshadowing of a different historical situation in which there would be a fulfilment of a different order, but one to which the wording of the text as he understands it would prove perhaps even more directly appropriate than for the original situation. (In view of the development of messianic motifs in chapters 7-11 of Isaiah, including the repetition of the name Emmanuel and the recurring motif of the child to be born, it is possible that this further reference was consciously intended by the prophet himself, though we shall see that Matthew could also discern a divinely intended 'fulfilment' where the human author had no such future reference in mind.)[36] Similarly, in his application of Hosea 11:1 to the childhood travels of Jesus, he draws on the frequent Old Testament understanding of the exodus as a prefiguration of God's eschatological act of deliverance, while his application of the phrase 'my son' (which in Hosea referred to Israel) to Jesus is not an arbitrary twisting of the meaning, but rather the outworking of the very 'relational' understanding of the Old Testament which Moule approves, in that here, as often in this gospel and in the rest of the New Testament, Jesus is seen as the one in whom all that Israel was and should have been has come to its climax.

We shall be looking more closely at this sort of 'typological' approach to the Old Testament in the next section. Many more examples could be added. But my point here is that such applications of Old Testament texts are not made on the basis of the lucky discovery of a chance verbal association, but rather derive from a deep meditation on that broad-ranging fulfilment which is the foundation of Matthew's (and, if not always so explicitly, of the other New Testament writers') Christian theology. The subtlety which Matthew's formula-quotations display (both in their boldly adapted wording and in the choice of texts which others might have failed to notice) is not that of the verbal juggler, but that of the innovative theologian whose fertile imagination is controlled by an overriding conviction of the climactic place of Jesus in the working out of the total purpose of God.

Part of the difficulty which the modern critical interpreter finds with Matthew derives from our tendency to assume that a text can have only one meaning and application. The idea of a prophecy which can be fulfilled more than once in different ways, or of a historical report which may at the same time embody a pattern of the divine activity which points forward to a subsequent fuller embodiment, is foreign to our exegetical canons. But to approach Scripture in this way, as Matthew does, is not necessarily to cast proper exegesis to the winds. Rather it is to recognise the dimension of an ongoing and consistent divine purpose, which may invest a text with a *sensus plenior*, to be perceived by those who come to it in the light of further experience and revelation. Such an interpretation may go beyond the conscious awareness of the human author of the original text, not by setting his meaning aside as irrelevant, but by seeing it in the wider context of divine activity in which it rightly belongs. While such an approach could lend itself to the artificial construction of allegory which we find at Qumran, it need not, and I would argue that in Matthew's case it does not, but rather that, however imaginative some of his 'secondary' applications of Scripture may be, they are not inconsistent with a 'proper' understanding of the original purpose of the passage.[37] The link between the original purpose and Matthew's perceived 'fulfilment' is precisely in his 'relational' concept of fulfilment in Jesus.

My study of the purpose and method of the formula-quotations of chapter 2[38] took its cue from some observations of L. Hartman[39] to the effect that in some of Matthew's uses of Scripture it is possible to distinguish between the 'surface meaning' and other nuances in the text which the less careful or less well-instructed reader might fail to notice. I argued there 'that Matthew was well aware of differing levels among his potential readership. . . . that he was a sufficiently sophisticated

37. See Gundry, *Use*, 205-234 for an extended defence of this view.
38. 'The Formula-Quotations of Matthew 2 and the Problem of Communication', *NTS* 27 (1980/81) 233-251.
39. 'Scriptural Exegesis in the Gospel of St. Matthew and the Problem of Communication', in Didier, *Matthieu*, 131-152.

author and communicator not to aim only for the lowest common denominator in his readership, nor to write an esoteric manual for initiates only, but to cater for the different levels of comprehension at the same time.'[40] In the four formula-quotations of chapter 2 I suggested that we could trace a quite sophisticated process of exploration of the ways in which Scripture found its fulfilment in Jesus, and that the degree to which any given reader would be able to follow Matthew into all the richness of his scriptural meditation would depend not only on how well he knew the Old Testament, but also on the extent to which he already shared Matthew's subtle grasp of the concept of fulfilment. I believe that the same considerations apply today, in that what one reader finds bizarre or opaque in these scriptural arguments may prove full of meaning to one who through 'sitting with' Matthew in his study and meditation has come to see that he is not playing slick word-games, but rather exploring with reverent delight the sometimes unexpected links which emerge as the same God who acted in the story of Israel and who spoke through the prophets now brings his redemptive scheme to fruition.

In the next section we shall explore some of the ways in which this hermeneutical approach can be seen in Matthew's gospel outside the formula-quotations. The fact that this is so warns us against the tendency mentioned above to treat the eleven formula-quotations as if they constituted a unique group, displaying an approach to the Old Testament which is not that of the rest of the gospel. It may be possible, as does R.S. McConnell,[41] to discover in these eleven passages alone 'an outline of Jesus' whole life and ministry', but we should not imagine that Matthew consciously singled out this particular group for this purpose, or that he would have regarded them as containing all that needed to be said about Jesus as the fulfiller. McConnell rightly observes that among these eleven passages there is no reference to the passion of Jesus, and suggests that 26:54,56, which contain the verb πληρόω but without citing any specific Old Testament text, serve to complete the picture, perhaps because Matthew found no one text adequate to convey the broad scope of fulfilment in Jesus' suffering and death. But this is too mechanical an account of Matthew's hermeneutical method. He has many ways of bringing out the fulfilment of Scripture in the passion narrative, and the fact that they are not presented as formula-quotations does not make them any less a central part of Matthew's message. The formula-quotations are simply one expression of the total fulfilment theology which undergirds Matthew's presentation of Jesus throughout, surfacing sometimes in formal quotation, sometimes in verbal echo,

---

40. *Ibid.* 250; cf pp. 240-241 for the basic idea.
41. McConnell, *Law*, 133-135.

sometimes in the way a story is told so that any reader acquainted with the Old Testament will be set thinking about ongoing patterns in the work of God. To restrict this rich hermeneutic to one particular group of quotations or to the specific occurrences of the verb πληρόω is to fail to do justice both to Matthew's theology and to his communicative skill.

C. 'TYPOLOGY'

Most, though not all, of the formula-quotations involved a text which might reasonably be interpreted as a prediction of future events, even if those events may not always have been specifically associated in their Old Testament context with the messianic consummation. The claim that something was predicted and has now happened is the most obvious expression of a fulfilment-theology, and is one which occurs frequently throughout the New Testament, including some passages of Matthew outside the formula-quotations. But Matthew's concept of fulfilment goes much further than that.

The term 'typology' has had a chequered history in biblical scholarship, sometimes occurring as a pejorative term for the *mis*use of the Old Testament, an exegetically irresponsible drawing of fanciful parallels without regard for the original meaning of the text. But, whatever the term used, it has been increasingly realised that you cannot do justice to the way the New Testament writers refer to the Old without recognising some concept of ongoing patterns in the purpose of God whereby later events may be helpfully understood in the light of the earlier. On the basis of such a concept it becomes possible to see a 'fulfilment', a theologically significant future relevance, for passages which in their original writers' apparent intention were not in any way predictive, but merely records of the way things were.

Such a conviction may or may not work itself out in a definable 'technique' for handling Old Testament texts. It is likely to find different ways of expression in different writers (and even within the same writer). But it is this conviction, however expressed in practice, which I refer to as the 'typological' understanding and use of the Old Testament. I do not expect to see in the New Testament a uniform 'typological method', nor to find there the elaborate working out of 'parallels' which we find in some patristic writing and later Christian preaching. Still less do I see this hermeneutical orientation as controlled by, or even necessarily linked to, the uses of the τύπος word-group in the New Testament. If it is felt that therefore 'typology' is not the best term by which to describe it, I shall not be greatly worried. But I know no better simple label to attach to an approach to the Old Testament which sees it as pointing forward to Jesus in much more than merely its explicitly predictive parts.[42]

Few would wish to dispute that typology, so defined, is a characteristic of Matthew's use of the Old Testament.[43] It is not of course his exclusive preserve, and several of his typological references are shared with Mark and Luke. But Matthew seems particularly ready to notice and draw attention to typological connections. A few of the more prominent examples from Matthew's special material will illustrate the point.

THE NEW MOSES

Moses occupied such a commanding position in Jewish religious and national self-consciousness that it was inevitable that Jews who followed Jesus should have to think out how their new leader was related to the law-giver and founder of the nation, particularly in view of the tendency both within the Old Testament and in later Judaism to envisage the eschatological events in terms of a 'new exodus'. How Matthew approached this question with reference specifically to the *laws* of Moses will be our subject in the next section. But the story and the role of Moses himself also provided material for typological reflection.

W.D. Davies devoted a long section of his work on the Sermon on the Mount to the question of how far Matthew intended, both in the Sermon and elsewhere in his gospel, to present Jesus as the new Moses.[44] His conclusion is cautious. It is certainly true that at a number of points in the gospel there is a comparison of Jesus with Moses, generally implicitly rather than explicitly. In the material shared with Mark and/or Luke possible New Moses or New Exodus motifs may be traced particularly in the stories of the baptism, the temptation and the transfiguration, and in each case it can be argued that Matthew is aware of the parallel. But it is also to be noted that in the first two of these incidents the more obvious typological motif is of Jesus as the new

---

42. I discussed the nature of New Testament typology, and the appropriateness of the term, in my *JOT*, 38-43, 76-80, and subsequent discussion has not caused me to want to alter the basic position there set out. See the notes there for bibliography of discussion up to 1966. For surveys of subsequent discussion see e.g. D.L. Baker, *Two Testaments, One Bible* (Leicester: Inter-Varsity Press, 1976) 239-250; J. Goldingay, *Approaches to Old Testament Interpretation* (Leicester: Inter-Varsity Press, 1981) 97-115.

43. Even A.T. Hanson, who interprets most of the generally claimed 'typological' passages of the New Testament as witnessing rather to the belief of the 'real presence' of Christ in the events of the Old Testament, and so is reluctant to allow the presence of typology as such, is nonetheless willing to grant that at least in Mt. 12:38-41 'we are actually witnessing the birth of typology (or a birth of typology) inside the NT'! See A.T. Hanson, *Jesus Christ in the Old Testament* (London: SPCK, 1965), especially 172-178; for subsequent reflections see his *The Living Utterances of God* (London: Darton, Longman and Todd, 1983) 36-38,187.

44. Davies, *Setting*, 25-93; much of the surrounding discussion also bears on this question.

Israel who undergoes the exodus experience, rather than the new Moses who leads it. In the transfiguration, where Moses himself appears on the scene to invite comparison (and Matthew's mention that Jesus' face shone emphasises the comparison with Moses in Ex. 34:29-35), Matthew's Jesus appears as 'Mosaic, and yet more-than-Mosaic'. In Matthew's own material and in his structuring of the gospel Davies finds little trace of the deliberate assertion of a Moses typology outside the first two chapters (to which we shall return) and possibly the 'mountain' scenes of the Sermon on the Mount and of 28:16-20. Even where the theme may be present, it is intertwined with, and generally overshadowed by, other christological and typological ideas. Jesus as the new Moses is thus a typology of which Matthew is well aware, but which he uses with considerable restraint. It is absorbed into a much richer conception of Jesus as Messiah. Jesus is not just 'another Moses', but something far higher.[45]

While this is a fair assessment of the relative importance of the New Moses theme in Matthew's total christological presentation, it remains a significant element in Matthew's concept of fulfilment. We have seen that the first two chapters of the gospel form a particularly striking 'manifesto' on the subject of fulfilment, and in chapter 2 the Moses typology has a determinative place. Underlying the overt scriptural argument of the four formula-quotations is a sustained parallel with the birth and experiences of Moses, which comes to the surface in the strangely inappropriate use of the plural in 2:20 to refer to Herod in the words 'those who sought the child's life are dead', in which the plural subject echoes Exodus 4:19 where Moses was offered a similar reason to return from exile.

The basic parallel is that of the wicked king's attempt to kill the future deliverer of God's people, an attempt which is thwarted by a period of self-imposed exile, even though many other children are killed. Of course the parallel with the Exodus story is not exact: Herod's plot, though indiscriminate in its effects, was directed against a specific usurper, whose birth had been supernaturally revealed, while Pharaoh ordered a general killing of all male Hebrew babies; Moses' escape as a baby was not by exile, and his subsequent exile was in response to a threat in adult life; Moses went into exile from Egypt, Jesus was taken *to* Egypt. But even so there is sufficient common ground in the king's

45. For a similar assessment of the importance of the New Moses idea see Banks, *Jesus*, 229-235; Kingsbury, *Matthew: Structure*, 89-92 (where Kingsbury, in accordance with his overall thesis, sees all the 'Moses' passages as pointing to Jesus not as a new Moses but as Son of God). Mohrlang, *Matthew and Paul*, 23 and notes, provides references to others holding similar views. See also more recently Donaldson, *Jesus*, 111-114; Donaldson's dismissal of a 'New Moses' focus especially in 5:1-2 is queried by D.C.Allison, *ExpT* 98 (1986/7) 203-205. For a more positive evaluation of the importance of the New Moses theme for Matthew see Blair, *Jesus*, 124-137.

fear, the multiple killing of children, the saviour's deliverance, the theme of exile, and the reference to Egypt to cause any Jewish reader to ponder the parallel.

In extra-biblical Jewish tradition the story of Moses had already gained important additional features, and some of these would make the parallel much closer. In the versions of the story in Josephus, in the Palestinian Targum, and in later rabbinic midrash, Pharaoh's killing of the Hebrew children was no mere strategy for population control, but was prompted, like Herod's act, by direct prophecy of the birth of Israel's liberator. The prophetic warning is variously ascribed to 'a sacred scribe', to 'astrologers', or to a dream of Pharaoh himself interpreted by his magicians, Jannes and Jambres. The same traditions record that Moses' father was prompted to rescue his son by a dream in which he was told of Moses' destiny to deliver Israel.[46] The wide attestation of such traditions in relatively early Jewish sources indicates that they were current in Matthew's day, and in that case the visit of the magi and Herod's concern specifically about the birth of a predicted rival also fit neatly into the Jesus-Moses comparison, while Joseph's dream has a direct precedent. The whole narrative structure of chapter 2 thus helps the reader to see in Jesus the divinely-preserved saviour of God's people, the new Moses of the new exodus.[47]

In discussing the formula-quotations above, we noted how the narrative of chapter 2 seemed to be designed to provide a setting for the quotations, and in particular to set out the geographical movements of the infant Messiah in which those quotations find their fulfilment. We have now seen that that same narrative has a further function in the context of Matthew's fulfilment-theology, to draw attention to Jesus as the new Moses. This theme forms a sort of sub-plot, less conspicuous to the casual reader, but full of meaning for those who are able to recognise the allusions to the Exodus story and its subsequent developments.

From the point of view of strict logic these two purposes are scarcely compatible, since one of the formula-quotations (2:15) clearly depends on the understanding of Jesus as the new *Israel*, God's son brought out of Egypt, rather than Israel's leader who returned from exile *to* Egypt in order to rescue God's 'son' (Ex. 4:22). But we are learning to see Matthew's appeal to the Old Testament as more subtle than a single systematic typological scheme. And the more closely this narrative is studied the more multi-dimensional this appeal is seen to be. To quote W.D. Davies again, the Mosaic typology in Matthew's prologue proves

---

46. Josephus, *Ant.* II 205ff; *Targum Pseudo-Jonathan*, Exodus 1:15; *Exodus Rabbah* I 18; *Sanhedrin* 101b.
47. See my notes in *NovT* 21 (1979) 105-106 for references to fuller treatments of the parallels.

to be 'one element in a mosaic of motifs, one strand in a pattern, which equally, if not more, emphasized the Christ as a new creation, the Messianic King, who represents Israel and is Emmanuel'.[48]

'SOMETHING GREATER'

Another passage where a number of typological reflections occur together and throw light on one another is chapter 12. The chapter begins with the conflict between Jesus and the Pharisees over the disciples' action in plucking and eating ears of corn on the sabbath, which we have considered above.[49] I argued there that the force of the first argument (12:3-4) depends on the relationship of Jesus to David, as at least his equal in authority, and that the subsequent argument about the priests in the temple (12:5-6) makes explicit the basic assumption that 'something greater is here'. We also noted in passing that virtually the same phrase[50] occurs twice later in the chapter (12:41,42), where Jesus is presented as 'something more than' Jonah and Solomon. The latter passage is one where the question of Jesus' authority is again central (as it has been also in the intervening Beelzebul debate, 12:22-37), in that he has been challenged to produce a sign to vindicate his ministry and refuses any sign except 'the sign of Jonah'; nonetheless those who fail to respond to his appeal will fare worse than those pagans who responded to the preaching of Jonah and the wisdom of Solomon, because they ought to have recognised the presence in Jesus of 'something more'.

Whatever the history of these pericopes in the tradition before Matthew, it can hardly be by accident that he includes the same pregnant phrase three times in a relatively short compass, the more so in view of the fact that its use in 12:6 is a Matthean insertion into a pericope which in its Marcan form probably implies the theme of 'something greater' (than David) but does not make it explicit. The fact that the same theme of the vindication of Jesus' authority over against his Pharisaic detractors runs through the whole passage indicates that these typological connections are presented in order to establish Jesus' credentials. The Old Testament 'models' selected add up to a remarkable overview of the main channels through which God's authority was formerly exercised among his people – David, the greatest king (and model of messianic expectation), the temple and its priesthood, Jonah as a representative prophet, and Solomon the wise man (and also,

48. Davies, *Setting*, 92, summarising the results of his detailed study of scriptural themes in the prologue, *ibid.* 61-83.
49. Above pp. 169-171.
50. It is not possible to discern any real difference in meaning between the 'something greater (μεῖζον)' of verse 6 and the 'something more (πλεῖον)' of vv. 41,42. The latter phrase is shared with Luke 11:31,32, while the former is peculiar to Matthew.

hardly insignificantly, the king, the son of David). To have claimed that in Jesus all these lines of authority came together and found their contemporary manifestation would have been bold enough. But he is 'greater', 'more' than all of them. 'This "more" indicates that the salvation history of the past has not only been taken up, but has been transcended; in other words this "more" has an eschatological ring. . . . God is speaking for the last and final time.'[51]

This element of 'transcendence' is found throughout Matthew's emphasis on fulfilment in Jesus. We shall return to this question in the next section, in relation to the law. But it is inherent also in Matthew's typology. He does not envisage simply a *repetition* of the patterns of God's work in the Old Testament, but a climactic 'fulfilment' of the pattern, 'something greater'.

Most of the references to the Old Testament which I have been describing as 'typological' are recognised as such not by any particular phraseology or formulae, but simply by asking what was the point of the Old Testament reference or allusive language in the gospel context in which we find it. There is also, however, in this same context in chapter 12 an explicitly drawn parallel between the Old Testament occurrence and its 'fulfilment' in Jesus, which is almost universally recognised as an example of typology even by those who are generally reluctant to use the term of New Testament phenomena. This is the statement that 'As Jonah was three days and three nights in the belly of the whale, so will the Son of man be three days and three nights in the heart of the earth' (12:40). Whatever the original relation of this statement to the preceding reference to the 'sign of Jonah' and to the following mention of Jonah's preaching to the Ninevites,[52] it is clear that for Matthew the parallel experience of Jonah and Jesus was a significant part of the scheme of fulfilment. Jonah's experience appears in the Old Testament simply as a narrative of a past event, with no hint of any future relevance, but the parallel serves to underline the continuity between Jonah and Jesus, however different the causes and nature of their three-day incarceration. The relation is, in this verse, apparently merely one of equivalence ('As . . . so . . .'); it is the following verse which makes explicit the sense of transcendence. But the establishment of the parallel here forms the basis for the more christologically significant statement of the nature of the relationship which follows.

Generally, however, Matthew's typological framework is less explicitly exposed than in these two passages, and the reader is left to ponder on the significance of the hints and allusions to a wide range of Old Testament people, events and institutions which are worked into

51. Jeremias, *NT Theology*, 82.
52. See my discussion of the issue in my *JOT* 43-45, together with the further discussion of its authenticity as a saying of Jesus, *ibid.* 80-82.

the narrative as occasion offers. As he does so, he will increasingly come to realise that for Matthew the range of the concept of 'fulfilment' is far broader than a mere study of the Old Testament's explicit predictions of God's eschatological purpose would reveal.

D. JESUS AND THE LAW

Important as Old Testament prophecy was, the part of the Old Testament which was supremely important for subsequent Judaism was the law. If Matthew is to present Jesus as the fulfilment of the whole scriptural revelation, it is essential that he deal with the relation of Jesus to the law. But, while there may be occasional hints of a future hope in the Pentateuch, the law as a whole gives no indication of a future change in the economy of God, still less of any possible alteration in the centrality of its own function as the definitive revelation of the will of God. Is there then any meaning in speaking of 'fulfilment' in this connection? And if not, is this a problem for Matthew's theological orientation as we have been discovering it?

The subject is, of course, taken up directly in the Sermon on the Mount. But the way in which it is done has led to strikingly divergent assessments of how Matthew and his church regarded the law in relation to the situation of fulfilment in Jesus.[53] Until recently the tendency has generally been to emphasise the 'conservatism' of Matthew in this regard, especially in comparison with the apparently more 'radical' attitude of Mark. Thus it is observed that whereas in Mark 7:1-23 there is a clear intention to set aside the observance not only of the scribal rules on washing but also of the Old Testament food laws themselves (focused in Mark's editorial comment, 'Thus he declared all foods clean', 7:19), the same discussion in Matthew avoids this direct breach with the food laws, and seems deliberately to restrict the issue to that of washing rituals (Mt. 15:20), which were a provision of scribal tradition, not of Pentateuchal law. Even scribal traditions seem to be acceptable to Matthew in principle (23:2-3,23), even though he, no less than the other evangelists, frequently shows Jesus in dispute with the scribes on points of the interpretation and application of the Old Testament law. And this 'conservative' attitude finds its focus in what appear to be the most extreme statements in the New Testament on the subject of continued observance of the law, with which the major discussion of the subject is introduced in 5:17-19.

A recent study which has strongly endorsed this traditional understanding of Matthew as a legal conservative is that of R. Mohrlang.[54]

53. For a useful survey of views on this subject up to 1976 see Stanton, 'Origin', 1934-1937.
54. Mohrlang, *Matthew and Paul*, 7-26, 42-47.

The point of 5:17-19, Mohrlang asserts, is that 'the entire law remains valid' (though he recognises the tension this creates with other parts of Matthew). Even 'the scribal tradition appears to retain its fundamental authority in Jesus' teaching generally'. Matthew 'stands at one with the scribes and Pharisees' in his acceptance of their role as (necessary) interpreters of the law. He is thus engaged in uneasily fending off a more 'lax' view of legal requirements deriving from some 'Pauline' Christians, while not wishing totally to condemn the Pauline perspective, which was perhaps represented within his own congregation. Matthew remains closer to traditional Judaism than Paul; for him the entire law remains authoritative, and Christian living is to be judged in terms of legal observance.

It is in the light of such apparent conservatism that some have suggested that one main focus of Matthew's book was an attack on antinomianism within the church. This view is especially associated with the name of G. Barth,[55] who sees in the background of Matthew's writing a group who believed that Christ had abolished the law, and whose consequent libertine behaviour sufficiently alarmed Matthew to provoke him to reaffirm the permanent validity of the law in the strongest terms. J. Zumstein, on the basis of a study of 'the terminology of the struggle against heresy' in Matthew, further specifies this supposed opposition group within Matthew's church as charismatics whose worship was focused on the Risen Lord to the virtual exclusion of the earthly Jesus and his teaching, the law being of still less interest to them.[56] Such hypothetical reconstructions of the Matthean church scene have not been widely agreed, but they bear witness to an undeniable tendency in Matthew to insist that following Jesus does not entail the repudiation of the law, a theme which is most prominent in 5:17-20.

But the 'conservatism' apparent in these few texts is only one side of a picture which is far from simple. The discussion introduced by 5:17-19 goes on to distinguish the 'righteousness' Jesus requires from that of the scribes and Pharisees (5:20), and to offer in 5:21-47 a series of examples of how Jesus' ethical teaching relates to the law which can hardly be described as 'conservative'. In two cases Jesus' interpretation merely points to a more demanding challenge in respect of thought and desire which underlies the literal application of the law, without in the least suggesting that the literal application of the law ceases to be important (5:21-22, 27-28). Another extends the Old Testament principle of love for the 'neighbour' (fellow-Israelite?) to cover even one's enemies, in contrast with some Old Testament passages which were far less generous (e.g. Dt. 23:3-6), but surely not in conflict with the spirit of Leviticus 19:18 (5:43-47). But in other cases there is a more radical

55. Bornkamm, Barth and Held, *Tradition*, 159-164 summarises his view.
56. Zumstein, *Condition*, 199-200.

implication. The permission for divorce which Deuteronomy 24:1-4 appears to give is withdrawn (5:31-32; and cf. 19:3-9, where the Deuteronomy text is set aside in favour of a principle of unbroken marriage based on Genesis 1:27; 2:24). The elaborate system of oaths and vows is undercut by the simple principle, 'Do not swear at all', with the implication that the legislation of the Old Testament on the subject 'comes from evil' (5:33-37). 'An eye for an eye and a tooth for a tooth' is replaced by the dangerously radical principle 'Do not resist one who is evil', which is then illustrated by striking examples of refusal to insist on legal rights and protection (5:38-42).

On each of these cases there is extensive debate as to exactly how far Jesus' reinterpretation is intended to go. It is certainly true that the opposition is on the surface more clearly against the current literal (and often minimalising) interpretation of the text than against the true bearing of the Old Testament text itself.[57] It is also true that in 5:38-42 at least the protest can fairly be seen as leveled against those who applied to personal ethics texts which were designed as a guide to judicial procedure. By such means it is possible to avert the judgement that Jesus is here shown as simply 'abrogating' the Old Testament law (which would certainly be a remarkable contradiction of what has just been said in 5:17). But it can hardly be denied that in the presentation of Jesus' ethical standards the Old Testament texts on which his contemporaries would have relied for several of these issues are at best set aside. The whole discussion seems to operate on a level different from that of the literal observance of regulations. Jesus declares, with a bold 'But I say to you. . .', the deeper principles of the will of God which underlie the specific laws of the Old Testament, and in the light of which some of those laws are found to be at least inadequate as guides to a Christian's conduct. This is a 'righteousness' so far transcending the legal rectitude aspired to by the scribes and Pharisees (5:20) that its goal is nothing less that 'perfection' (5:48).

Outside the central discussion in 5:17-48 we find Jesus in Matthew's gospel, as in Mark and Luke, in constant debate with the scribes and (especially in Matthew) Pharisees. Despite the apparently more restricted discussion in 15:1-20 as compared with Mark 7:1-23, it is as a dangerous radical that they see him. His views and practice in relation to such issues as sabbath observance, fasting, ritual purity and divorce, and his notorious association with tax-collectors and sinners, are seen as in stark opposition to the legal norms of his day. The opposition which erupts into the lengthy diatribe of chapter 23 focuses not just on a few disputed points of law, but on the whole understanding of what it is

57. B. Przybylski, *Righteousness in Matthew and his World of Thought* (Cambridge University Press, 1980) 81-84 interestingly explains this passage in the light of 'the Rabbinic principle of making a fence around Torah'.

to do the will of God by which 'scribes and Pharisees' operated and which Jesus repudiated. The difference is summed up in the text from Hosea which is twice cited by Jesus (only in Matthew's gospel) in opposition to Pharisaic protests, 'I desire mercy, and not sacrifice' (9:13; 12:7). Whatever may be the meaning of 5:17-19, the gospel as a whole forbids us to describe Matthew's Jesus as a legal conservative.[58]

In the light of this overall perspective of the gospel, several recent interpreters have returned to 5:17-19 to see whether it is in fact making so conservative a statement about the law as has traditionally been thought. The result has been a new perspective on this passage, at the centre of which is a reevaluation of what can be meant by 'fulfilment' in this connection.[59]

It may not be unimportant to notice first that the Jesus who speaks these words is apparently one who finds it necessary to rebut the charge that his mission was to 'abolish' the law![60] In this we can recognise the radical Jesus whose conflict with scribal orthodoxy we have just been noticing. The charge is firmly repudiated; nowhere is it suggested that Jesus has come to replace the old law by a new law. But the word used as the converse of 'abolish' is not to 'confirm' or 'enforce' the law, still less to 'obey' it (which would in any case be an odd converse to 'abolish', a matter of teaching rather than of practice), but to 'fulfil' it. Moreover it is not only to the law that this verb applies, but also to 'the prophets'. In relation to the prophets the verb πληρόω, as used for the formula-quotations, means to bring that to which the text pointed forward. Can it mean the same in relation to the law? An interesting pointer in this direction is the brief saying in 11:13, 'All the prophets *and the law* prophesied until John'. Such an understanding of πληρῶσαι in 5:17 would make the saying refer neither to what Jesus taught about the law nor to whether or not he observed it in practice, but to the function of the law as a pointer to a future 'fulfilment', one which has come in the ministry of Jesus. Thus, as Banks summarises this interpretation of

---

58. It must be admitted that 23:2-3 and 23:23 are apparently out of keeping with this orientation. Banks (*Jesus*, 175-180) rightly observes, however, that in each case the statement of approval of scribal teaching functions as one side of a contrast, where the emphasis falls on the other member. 23:3 could be paraphrased 'You may follow their teaching if you like, *but* don't imitate their behaviour'; and 23:23 similarly 'Go on observing their tithing rules if you wish, *but* don't let this distract you from the weightier matters of the law'.

59. This approach has been most fully worked out by Meier, *Law*, 41-124 (cf. summary, *ibid.* 160-161). It is represented (with considerable variations in detail) also by Banks, *Jesus*, 203-226 (which is virtually the same as his article in *JBL* 93 [1974] 226-242); Guelich, *Sermon*, 134-174; D.J. Moo, 'Jesus and the Authority of the Mosaic Law', *JSNT* 20 (1984) 3-49. It has been taken up in Carson, *Matthew*, as well as in my own Tyndale Commentary on Matthew.

60. Cf. the comment by C.F.D. Moule, *Essays in New Testament Interpretation*, 69, that Matthew 5:17-20, 'which sounds like extreme legalism' is better interpreted 'as a defence against anti-Christian Pharisaic allegations that Christianity lowered moral standards'.

Matthew's text, 'it is not so much *Jesus'* stance towards the Law that he is concerned to depict: it is how the *Law* stands with regard to him, as the one who brings it to fulfilment and to whom all attention must now be directed'.[61] Such an interpretation makes good sense of the contrast with 'abolition' of the law, and is consistent with the regular usage of the verb πληρόω in Matthew.

But what then of the statements in 5:18-19 about, apparently, the permanent validity of the law? W.D. Davies argued cogently in 1957 that 'until all is accomplished' does not necessarily by itself point to the end of the world, but rather to the point of fulfilment of 'all' that God has planned, and therefore that its most appropriate sense in this context is to the 'fulfilment' in Jesus as the point up to which the law remains in force.[62] 'All is accomplished' not so much by the faithful observance of the law in the same way as previously, but rather in that its preparatory function has been successfully achieved, and that to which it pointed forward has come.

5:19, however, *is* talking about the continuing validity of 'these commandments'; even within 'the kingdom of heaven' they are not to be 'relaxed', but to be 'done'. The verb translated 'relax' is λύω, which means to 'untie', i.e., presumably, to make them invalid (cf. καταλύω, 'abolish', in 5:17, which is the same metaphor); it refers to the status accorded to the commandments (cf. 'and teaches men so'), not simply to whether or not they are obeyed. (NIV 'breaks' and GNB 'disobeys' are therefore misleading translations.) But the second half of the verse refers unambiguously to 'doing' the commandments as well as 'teaching' them, so it seems that something more than a merely theoretical continuance is envisaged. Banks and others[63] have tried to avoid this conclusion by proposing that 'these commandments' in 5:19 are those of *Jesus*, not those of the Old Testament law, but this is to destroy the clear sequence of thought from verse 18 to verse 19, and also to ignore the regular usage of ἐντόλη ('commandment') in Matthew to refer to Old Testament laws.[64] Rather we should recognise that this verse does

61. Banks, *Jesus*, 226.
62. W.D. Davies 'Matthew 5:18', in *Mélanges Bibliques rédigés en l'honneur de André Robert* (Paris: Bloud & Gay, 1957) 428-456, reprinted in Davies, *Christian Origins and Judaism* (London: Darton, Longman & Todd, 1962) 31-66. Davies suggested that the point of 'fulfilment' should be identified more specifically as the cross, which was to result in our freedom from the law, and the consequent abolition of the Jew/Gentile divide. This is perhaps too specific (and too 'Pauline'?) an interpretation, but the general point of a new situation arising out of the ministry of Jesus in which 'all is accomplished' appears well grounded.
63. Banks, *Jesus*, 222-223, taking up a suggestion made earlier by Kilpatrick, *Origins*, 25-26.
64. Meier, *Law*, 106,123, attempts an uneasy compromise between these two apparently incompatible interpretations. He believes that Matthew included the verse with two purposes: first in the context of Jesus' historical ministry to 'inculcate faithfulness to the Torah while the old aeon lasts', secondly in the post-Easter church to enjoin obedience to *Jesus'* commands.

MATTHEW: EVANGELIST AND TEACHER

expect Jesus' disciples to continue to observe the law. As such it is undeniably out of keeping not only with its immediate context (where Jesus goes on to question the literal applicability of several Old Testament laws) but also with the whole New Testament, which nowhere else suggests that all the least of the Old Testament commandments (including the sacrificial laws) should continue to be observed literally in the Christian era. Few interpreters who are sensitive to the wider context in Matthew and beyond have been able to feel comfortable with this verse. It may be worth noting, however, that the question of *how* the commandments are to be 'done' is left open, and it would seem responsible to answer this question from the surrounding context, where something very different from a rule-based legalism seems to be envisaged.

An important distinction must be drawn, I believe, between the *authority* and the *function* of the Old Testament laws. To affirm that they remain authoritative, with not a jot or a tittle lost, is not necessarily to imply that they will continue to function in the same way. They remain the word of God, and none of them is to be discarded or disparaged; but does this mean that they must all continue to be obeyed in just the same way as before Jesus came? If our focus on 'fulfilment' as the key to understanding Jesus' relation to the law in Matthew 5 (and indeed throughout the gospel) is valid, then it can hardly be that the coming of that to which the law pointed forward will leave its practical application unaffected, even though it remains of permanent importance as a statement, appropriate to the 'pre-fulfilment' situation, of the will of God. Such a distinction is needed in some of the antitheses which follow in 5:21-47. Jesus' questioning of Deuteronomy 24:1-4, of the oath and vow legislation, and of the *lex talionis*, is not necessarily an attempt to 'relax' them in the sense of declaring that they can now be dispensed with, but rather a restatement of their *function* in relation to the ethics of Christian discipleship. If that is the focus of v 19, seen in the light of its context, it cannot be interpreted as an endorsement of an ultra-conservative approach to legal observance on the part of Jesus, or of Matthew unless he is to be credited with a remarkable degree of incompetence in setting side by side in his gospel two totally incompatible approaches to the law.

On this understanding of 5:17-48, Matthew presents the relation of Jesus to the Old Testament law as another aspect of the total scheme of fulfilment which I believe to be the basic orientation of his gospel. In this as in other areas Jesus has brought that to which the Old Testament pointed forward, so that the focus of God's purpose is now to be found in Jesus rather than in the Old Testament in its own right. The law remains a permanent and crucial revelation of the will of God, but its application can no longer be by the simple observance of all its precepts as literal regulations for Christian conduct. The key to its interpretation is in Jesus and in his teaching, with its sovereign declaration of the will of God at a far deeper level than mere rule-keeping. In other words, Matthew's presentation of the law is above all *christological*. That is why I have felt it appropriate to discuss the question of Matthew's view of the law in this chapter rather than (as might well be possible) in the following chapters which deal with his view of Israel and of the church. The key word on the subject in Matthew is 'fulfilment'.

E. FULFILMENT AND HISTORY

JESUS AS THE TURNING-POINT OF HISTORY

From all this it follows that for Matthew (as indeed for all other New Testament writers) the history of God's dealings with his people has reached its decisive turning-point in the coming of Jesus. In Matthew, as in Mark, Jesus' public preaching begins with the declaration of the arrival of the 'kingdom of heaven' (4:17; 10:7; cf. Mark 1:15), and the long discourse on discipleship which follows is founded on this conviction, so that a whole new way of living is demanded by the new situation of the 'kingdom of heaven' in which the law and the prophets are 'fulfilled'. The era of the prophets and the law extended 'until John' (11:13); since then 'the kingdom of heaven is subjected to violence' (11:12)[65] – but that very fact is an indication of its effective presence, as several other passages make equally clear (5:3,10; 12:28; 13:16-17 etc.).

In passing we may note that John the Baptist stands in a rather ambivalent position, as the figure of transition from the old era to the new. On the one hand he is consistently presented as Jesus' inferior, and appears as a prophet (11:9) and fore-runner (11:10), who for all his greatness yet stands outside the kingdom of heaven (11:11). On the other hand he is more than a prophet (11:9), and Matthew is at pains to stress the continuity between the ministry of John and that of Jesus.

---

65. The combination of the noun βιαστής (always elsewhere used in a bad sense, 'violent man') with the verbs βιάζομαι (also normally used of violence in a bad sense) and ἁρπάζω ('to seize, plunder') makes it very unlikely that the verse should be translated in the apparently commendatory sense of NIV 'the kingdom of heaven has been forcefully advancing, and forceful men lay hold of it'. It is arguable that βιάζομαι, understood as middle voice, should be translated thus in Luke 16:16, but there the subject of the verb is 'everyone', not 'the kingdom of heaven', and there is no reference to βιασταί who 'seize' or 'plunder' it. For a clear discussion of the exegetical options for this verse see Carson, *Matthew*, 265-268; he proposes to translate βιάζεται by 'has been forcefully advancing', but to retain the sense of violence against the kingdom of heaven in the second half of the verse. A detailed study of the use by Josephus of βιάζω, ἁρπάζω and cognates by E. Moore, NTS 21 (1974/5) 519-543, indicates that βιάζεται too is more likely to carry a bad sense.

Both of them preach in the same words (3:2 with 4:17; 3:7 with 23:33; 3:10 with 7:19);[66] the authority of Jesus' mission is the same as that of John (21:23-27; cf. v.32); both suffer the same violent response (11:12), and both are (for different reasons) unacceptable to 'this generation' (11:16-19). John, as the returning Elijah (11:14), represents the beginning of the age of fulfilment which succeeds the age of 'prophesying' (11:13), but does not live to experience its full realisation in the completed ministry of Jesus and the development of the church. Hence perhaps the otherwise puzzling contrast between the great John and the 'least in the kingdom of heaven' (11:11).[67]

STAGES IN THE HISTORY OF SALVATION?

But granted that the coming of Jesus was understood as the time of fulfilment, does this mean that Matthew saw the *Heilsgeschichte* as a simple two-stage process of promise followed by fulfilment, or is there room for a further crucial turning point in his understanding of history? Since Conzelmann's thesis that Luke saw Jesus' ministry as 'the centre of time'[68] there has been discussion of whether the evangelists saw an unbroken continuity between the ministry of Jesus and the 'age of the church', or whether they regarded these as two separate stages. Both answers have been offered with regard to Matthew.

To speak of a three-stage *Heilsgeschichte* is to postulate that Matthew made a clear distinction between the period of Jesus' ministry and the subsequent growth of the church, and looked back to Jesus' ministry as, in the words of G. Strecker,[69] 'a unique, unrepeatable, holy, and ideal epoch in the course of history'. Strecker is particularly concerned to emphasise that for Matthew the continuation of history after the time of Jesus has real significance, even though the eschatological hope remains strong. The end is delayed, and in the meantime the church is committed to carrying out the ethical implications of Jesus' teaching, the 'way of righteousness'. The church thus lives between the past event of Jesus' first coming and the indefinite future event of his parousia. For Israel too there is a new situation since the death of Jesus: the

66. For Matthew's presentation of John the Baptist as 'a preacher of the Christian congregation' see G. Bornkamm, *Tradition,* 15-16. Cf. above pp. 129-130.
67. J.P. Meier, 'John the Baptist in Matthew's Gospel', *JBL* 99 (1980) 383-405, gives a valuable summary and interpretation of the data. He explains the paradox in John's status in terms of a three-stage understanding of *Heilsgeschichte* by Matthew, a point to which we now turn.
68. H. Conzelmann, *Die Mitte der Zeit* (Tübingen: Mohr, 1953); published in English as *The Theology of St. Luke* (London: Faber, 1960).
69. Strecker's view is fully set out in *Der Weg der Gerechtigkeit*; note particularly the summary on pp. 184-188. His views are further developed and summarised in an article 'Das Geschichtsverständnis des Matthäus', *EvTh* 26 (1966) 57-74, published in English translation in Stanton, *Interpretation,* 67-84. The phrase quoted is from p. 73 of the latter publication.

earthly ministry of Jesus was directed only to Israel, but now the opportunity to respond to Jesus' message has come to an end, the gospel is preached to all nations, and the privileged position of Israel has been taken over by the (international) church.[70]

In response, J.D. Kingsbury[71] suggests that this three-stage understanding of Matthew's view of *Heilsgeschichte* results from focusing too much on Matthew's ecclesiology, and not enough on his christology. Kingsbury argues from Matthew's use of phrases like 'that day', and particularly 'in those days', that he sees the whole period from the appearance of John the Baptist to the final consummation as a single period, the 'last days'. His scheme is thus one of a two-stage *Heilsgeschichte*, the two stages being appropriately designated as those of 'prophecy' and 'fulfilment'. He sees no distinction between the pre-Easter Jesus and the exalted Lord, and thus can describe the former in terms of the latter. There is continuity between the ministries of John, of Jesus and of the disciples, the latter being the representatives of the continuing life of the church. The focus of Matthew's concept of *Heilsgeschichte* is in 'the abiding presence of Jesus with his disciples, both "then" and "now" '.[72]

There is surely an element of artificiality about this debate. Each side is affirming something true about Matthew's perspective, but that affirmation does not necessarily carry with it the negation of what the other side is affirming. To speak in terms of definable stages of *Heilsgeschichte* reflects a modern desire to systematise Matthew's thought, which seems more akin to the atmosphere of 'Dispensationalism' than to any obvious concern of the evangelist himself! Is there any improbability in the view that Matthew could equally happily affirm both that there is an essential continuity between the disciples' experience of Jesus and that of the subsequent church, that the risen Lord of the church's teaching is the same as the earthly Lord of the pre-Easter ministry, and at the same time that something has changed? The clearest focus of that change (as Meier's study effectively demonstrates) is in relation to the appeal to Israel and the mission to the Gentiles; the post-Easter mission of 28:18-20 breathes a different atmosphere from the restricted mission of 10:5-6 and 15:24. But to recognise the signifi-

---

70. Strecker's discussion has proved the most influential expression of a three-stage *Heilsgeschichte* in Matthew. Others who have supported this general approach (though with differences in detail) include Walker, *Heilsgeschichte*, and J.P. Meier, *Law*, 25-40 (reproduced in substantially the same form in *CBQ* 37 [1975] 203-215), who argues (with a conscious echo of Conzelmann?) that Matthew understood the death and resurrection of Jesus as *die Wende der Zeit*, 'the turning-point of time'.

71. *CBQ* 35 (1973) 466-474; the argument is reproduced and developed in Kingsbury, *Matthew: Structure*, 25-39.

72. Kingsbury, *Matthew: Structure*, 36. Kingsbury's argument, and his objection that Strecker, Walker and Meier have been too much influenced by Conzelmann's understanding of Luke, are supported by Donaldson, *Jesus*, 209-211.

cance of this change does not entail that the post-Easter church must regard itself as belonging to a different 'dispensation' to which the pre-Easter ministry of Jesus is of doubtful relevance. It is more typical of Matthew's method to believe that he could see both continuity and discontinuity in different respects with regard to the link between Jesus' ministry and the 'church age', just as he was able to do with reference to the continuing relevance of the Old Testament law in the time of fulfilment.

So Kingsbury is right to notice the close links between the ministry of Jesus and the concerns of Matthew's church, but Strecker is also right to insist that the application of Jesus' words and deeds will be different in the context of the Gentile mission from the period of the restricted appeal to Israel. It is perhaps significant that Donaldson, in explicitly repudiating the 'three-stage' view, nonetheless finds it appropriate to speak of the ministry of Jesus, the age of the church, and the parousia as 'three phases ("preparation", "inauguration" and "consummation") of one period of fulfilment'.[73] On the other side, there is not clear agreement between the exponents of the 'three-stage' view as to just when the second stage gives way to the third, Meier locating the turning-point firmly at the cross-resurrection of Jesus, Strecker less definitely 'at the end of the life of Jesus'[74] and Walker at the fall of Jerusalem (which Strecker designates 'a visible expression of the rejection which has already been effected'). Perhaps, then, Matthew's view of *Heilsgeschichte* is less susceptible of neat systematisation than some modern scholarship would like!

THE 'TRANSPARENCY' OF HISTORY

Another angle on this discussion is provided by U. Luz.[75] Focusing on the terms 'historicizing' (derived from G. Strecker) and 'transparency' (derived from R. Hummel), Luz asks whether for Matthew the disciples of Jesus are 'set in an unrepeatable, holy past' (Strecker) or are equated with the church of Matthew's own day, so that their experiences as recorded in the gospel are seen as 'transparent' for the present day. Luz himself finds the idea of transparency more correct. Thus 'the disciples become transparent and are models of what it means to be a Christian', while Jesus' miracles are similarly transparent of the present experiences of a disciple.[76] The terminology of 'transparency' allows

---

73. Donaldson, *Jesus*, 210-211.
74. Strecker, *Weg*, 117.
75. U. Luz, 'Die Junger im Matthäusevangelium', *ZNW* 62 (1971) 141-171, reprinted in English translation in Stanton, *Interpretation*, 98-128 (references to latter publication).
76. *Ibid*. 105-107. Here Luz draws particularly on the work of Bornkamm on the stilling of the storm and of Held on the other miracle stories in Bornkamm, Barth & Held, *Tradition*.

Luz to see in Matthew's work both a concern for the reality of the events he relates as past history and at the same time a recognition of their contemporary relevance. 'The temporal distance is bridged, but evidently not in a way that simply dissolves the historical Jesus in the community's experiences of the Spirit.'[77] Thus for Luz there is both continuity and discontinuity in Matthew's understanding of the relation between the earthly ministry of Jesus and the contemporary experience of the church. The experience of fulfilment is firmly rooted in history, but cannot remain at a purely histcrical level.

Zumstein's study of *La Condition du Croyant dans l'Evangile selon Matthieu* comes to a similar conclusion. Like Luz, Zumstein notices how the word μαθητής in Matthew serves to link the original disciples of Jesus on earth to the church of Matthew's own day. The original disciples, and indeed the other actors in the historical drama, act as 'types' of the situation of the contemporary believer. Matthew operates, then, on the assumption of 'a correlation between the history he is living and the history he is narrating'. 'So the situation of the believer is not qualitatively different from that of the first disciples. . . . The teaching which was addressed to the historical companions of Jesus is also the content of the church's message. . . . the believer must become the faithful and attentive hearer of the earthly Jesus.'[78]

This seems to be a proper insistence that Matthew sees no clean break between the period of Jesus' earthly ministry and the continuing life of the church in the post-Easter period. The fulfilment which was inaugurated with the coming of Jesus continues its course through the history of the church until it is consummated in the parousia. But this sense of continuity in no way requires that Matthew was uninterested in the historicity of the stories and teaching of the earthly Jesus which he records for the church's benefit. Even if it is not 'unrepeatable' in the sense intended by Strecker, the past remains the past. It was in the real events and teaching of the pre-Easter period that Matthew saw fulfilment taking place; and it is to those same real events and teaching of the past that the post-Easter church must continue to look for the basis of its existence and its obedient discipleship as the age of fulfilment pursues its course.

MIDRASH AND HISTORY

The preceding discussion suggests that Matthew, for good theological reasons, took the historical dimension of his task seriously, that he was interested in recording for his church the events of the life and teaching of Jesus in which he saw fulfilment as having come. To have a theology

77. *Ibid.* 111.
78. Zumstein, *Condition*, 81, 129.

of 'fulfilment in Jesus' is not incompatible with, but indeed rather demands, the careful recording of history.

In recent years, however, it has been suggested that it is precisely Matthew's interest in fulfilment which prevents our taking his narratives as factual history. The discussion has centred around the word 'midrash'. The argument has been that Matthew's fascination with tracing themes of Old Testament fulfilment in the story of Jesus was channeled into a currently familiar literary form, 'midrash', which led to the free embellishment and alteration of the stories about Jesus received from the tradition, and their supplementation with new imaginative material, to the extent of inventing whole new narrative sections in order to express in suitably scriptural terms the significance of Jesus. Such a procedure, we are told, would have deceived no-one familiar with the midrashic method; it is only modern scholars with their different canons of historicity who imagine that Matthew meant us to take all these stories as sober fact.

The use of 'midrash' in this context in gospel studies was initiated primarily by M.D. Goulder, in his important but controversial study, *Midrash and Lection in Matthew* (1974). Goulder believes that Matthew's work is best compared with that of the author of Chronicles, in his rewriting and embellishment of the stories of Samuel and Kings. For this procedure he uses the term 'midrash', justifying it from the use of this term in 2 Chronicles 13:22; 24:27 (the *only* uses of the Hebrew word *midrash* in the Old Testament) to describe not the Chronicler's own work but that of two of his predecessors. We shall consider the appropriateness of the term 'midrash' shortly, but the model of Chronicles may be assessed independently of the term.

Chronicles is, in Goulder's view, a 'rewriting' of the earlier histories, apparently not mainly on the basis of additional information, but rather in order to set them in a particular theological or ideological framework corresponding to that of the 'priestly' strand of the Pentateuch. Thus one part of scripture is used to reinterpret another, and the new stories of Chronicles are simply 'made up' on the basis of its author's understanding of the priestly law.[79]

Matthew similarly, according to Goulder, 'rewrote' Mark. His work is a 'midrash' on Mark (treated apparently already as an authoritative, if not 'canonical', text). He thus includes virtually the whole of Mark, though at many points quite drastically reworked in the interests of his own theological convictions, but has expanded it not by adding independent historical information (for Goulder does not believe in 'Q' or any other separate sources of Jesus tradition available to Matthew) but simply by making up new material on the basis of his own understanding of and meditation on the fulfilment of scripture in the

79. Goulder, *Midrash*, 28-32.

life and teaching of Jesus. If the Chronicler was justified in his creative reworking of the 'sacred' text of Kings, so is Matthew in regard to Mark and the Jesus tradition. The procedure would have been familiar and acceptable to those who shared his cultural context (which, unfortunately, his modern readers do not, hence our failure to appreciate the nature of his creative contribution). It is then a fundamental literary error to regard the non-Marcan elements in Matthew as intended to be 'history', and this precisely because of Matthew's pre-occupation with the theme of 'fulfilment'.

This is a very bald summary of a detailed and subtle discussion, but I think it is sufficient to show that the whole position is open to question on several fronts.

With regard to literary relationships and sources, our earlier discussion has indicated that the belief that Matthew made direct use of Mark would be rejected by some, and among those who accept it few would also agree that Matthew had no other sources. The denial of other sources is not of course in itself essential to Goulder's view of Matthew's method, though it gives it a sharper focus. For instance, Gundry's commentary on Matthew adopts a similar view of his 'midrashic' method and his dependence on Mark, but attributes most of Matthew's non-Marcan material to a 'Q' which Gundry believes was much more extensive than only those parts also taken up by Luke. This limits the degree of Matthew's assumed creativity, by restricting the 'midrashic' element largely to the embellishment of existing tradition rather than the wholesale creation of stories which had no factual basis.[80]

More important for our present purpose is the question whether the writing in narrative form of what is not meant to be seen as 'history' (and the recording as words of Jesus of the author's own scripturally-inspired meditations) does in fact correspond to a literary genre familiar at the time, 'midrash'.

Even within Jewish studies, definition of the term 'midrash' is not straightforward;[81] when used by New Testament scholars with reference to the different literary canons of early Christian literature it becomes even more slippery. An important article by P.S. Alexander on 'Midrash and the Gospels'[82] expresses the frustration of a specialist in Jewish literature over the misuse of the term by New Testament scholars, with special reference to Goulder. He argues that, irrespective of the different sense of the term in its two uses in Chronicles, it is properly used only

---

80. Gundry, *Matthew*, 623-640 spells out his methodological approach, and indicates how he sees it as relating to his evangelical theological position.
81. For some key contributions to the debate see R. Bloch, 'Midrash' in *Dictionnaire de la Bible, Supplément V* (Paris: Letouzey & Ané, 1957) 1263ff; A.G. Wright, *CBQ* 28 (1966) 105-138, 417-457; R. Le Déaut, *Interpretation* 25 (1971) 259-282. For convenient summaries with reference to discussion of Matthew see Soares Prabhu, *Formula Quotations* 12-16; Brown, *Birth*, 557-563.

as a technical term for that specific genre of commentary on biblical texts which developed in post-Jamnian Judaism, in which text and commentary are kept formally separate. It is thus to be distinguished from the earlier rewritings of the Old Testament such as Jubilees and from the Targums, where comment becomes part of the text. We have seen above that there is a sense in which Matthew may appropriately be described as a 'targumist'; to that degree 'midrash' would, on Alexander's terms, be an inappropriate label for his procedure.[83]

This is not the place to go into the debate over terminology. But whatever term is used, can we accept Goulder's assumption that the imaginative creation of apparently factual stories on the basis of scriptural meditation was a recognised literary practice in first-century Judaism? Much of the symposium *Gospel Perspectives*, vol. 3 (1983) is devoted to this question, including both an overview of the nature of Jewish historical writing in the period and a detailed study of a number of key examples. What emerges from that study is the variety of different types of Jewish literature in the first century, among which the sort of 'midrash' postulated by Goulder is certainly not prominent. There are a good number of examples of the rewriting of the biblical histories, often with considerable embellishment and with some clearly tendentious angling of the stories, in works such as the Palestinian Targums, Jubilees, Josephus and Pseudo-Philo (though it is seldom that it can be clearly established that the embellishments were due to the influence of other scriptural texts). But when it comes to the telling of recent history, there seem to be no clear parallels to the sort of literary approach Goulder envisages for Matthew. Indeed it is remarkable how few examples we have in Jewish literature of the narration of recent history (with the one striking exception of Josephus), or of anything like a 'biography' of near contemporaries. Indeed, as P.S. Alexander points out,[84] there simply are *no* rabbinic parallels to the gospels as a literary genre; many anecdotes and records of the teaching of rabbis were preserved in the rabbinic collections, but there is no evidence of any *biographies* of rabbis as such.

The distinction between ancient, scriptural history and recent events is significant. As I wrote in summing up the conclusions of *Gospel*

82. P.S. Alexander, 'Midrash and the Gospels' in Tuckett, *Synoptic Studies*, 1-18; cf. the more wide-ranging critique of New Testament scholars' naiveté in their appeal to Jewish literature which originally formed the first part of the same paper, published in *ZNW* 74 (1983) 237-246.

83. Bruce Chilton, in *Gospel Perspectives*, vol. 3 (1983), 9-32, similarly rebukes writers on the gospels for their misuse of the term in the light of Jewish usage. His proposal to use 'Midrash' (capital M) for the rabbinic literary genre and 'midrash' (small m) for 'the general process by which one "searches out" the meaning of scripture', while logically tidy, seems unlikely to have much influence on actual usage!

84. P.S. Alexander, 'Rabbinic Biography and the Biography of Jesus: a Survey of the Evidence', in Tuckett, *Synoptic Studies*, 19-50.

Perspectives, vol. 3, 'The development of supplementary material over many centuries within the folk-tradition of a nation is not at all the same thing as the addition within the Christian community of new material to the stories of their leader within the lifetime of many who were present during the actual events. In addition, the explicitly "scriptural" status of the Old Testament stories may be supposed to have rendered them more subject to devotional and apologetic elaboration than is likely to have been the case with the stories of Jesus.'[85]

It is therefore questionable whether a recognisable category of 'midrash' as presupposed by Goulder can be found in first-century Jewish literature, and even more questionable whether Matthew can plausibly be made to fit into it. In that case it is not legitimate to invoke the word 'midrash' as providing a ready-made key to how he set about compiling his gospel.

It is rather from the gospel itself, from its expressed interests and apparent aims, that we should try to understand how Matthew envisaged his task. We have seen reason above to believe that Matthew had a strong sense of the importance of history. And we have focused throughout this chapter on his conviction that in that history was to be found the fulfilment of God's purposes as set out in the Old Testament and the history of Israel. Fulfilment and history are not in conflict; rather the fulfilment takes place in the history. Indeed it is not easy to see quite what 'fulfilment' might mean if there is no actual history in which the pattern is fulfilled. Matthew's undoubted enthusiasm for discovering patterns of fulfilment, and the subtlety of the interpretative methods he has employed to draw attention to them, which has led to the comparison of his work with some aspects of later 'midrash', should be seen not as weakening his sense of historical responsibility, but rather as demanding a careful record of the facts on which the whole claim to fulfilment depends.

VI

MATTHEW AND ISRAEL

*The 'fulfilment' of Israel. The threat of judgement. The Jewish leaders.
A new people of God? The gospel for all nations. Matthew and anti-Judaism.*

IN THE GOSPEL OF MATTHEW, K. TAGAWA[1] FINDS 'QUITE CONTRADICTORY
attitudes concerning the problem of the Gentiles and the Jews',
and concludes that Matthew has no worked-out theological
understanding of the question. 'Matthew has a very strong
consciousness of being a member of a community, but he makes no
effort to give a historico-theological explanation of the relation of the
Church to Israel. He is clearly aware of the fact that the people Israel
and the Christian Church are not directly equal, but on the other
hand, he confuses them because both are the milieu in which he finds
his own existence.' Because of this 'undifferentiated community
consciousness' he effectively treats the church and Israel as identical.[2]

This rather extreme statement brings into focus again the question
which has already occupied us in discussing the authorship and the
setting of the gospel.[3] There is no easy answer to the apparent paradox
of Matthew's attitude to Israel, and very different conclusions continue
to be drawn from the same gospel text, as we have already seen in
chapter 3. Must we then settle, with Tagawa, for an inherent contradiction in Matthew's thought, caused by a lack of theological reflection
on the question of Israel and the church? Or is it possible to discern
some coherence in his position? And in particular does the idea of
'fulfilment' which has been the focus of our last chapter offer us any
light on the question?

A.   THE 'FULFILMENT' OF ISRAEL

In the last chapter we have seen ample evidence that for Matthew it
is in Jesus and in the events surrounding his ministry that God's purposes
for his people have reached their climax. Many different strands of Old
Testament life and thought are seen as pointing forward to him, quite

1. K. Tagawa, 'People and Community in the Gospel of Matthew', *NTS* 16 (1969/70)
149-162.
2. *Ibid.* pp. 152, 159, 162.
3. Above pp. 70-72, 95-108.

apart from explicit predictions of the coming of the Messiah. The history and religion of the people of God in the Old Testament have reached their culmination in him.

Within this general pattern of fulfilment there is one strand which is of particular importance for the theme of this chapter. Various passages in Matthew suggest that Israel itself, the people of God, is seen as finding its 'fulfilment' both in Jesus himself and in the community which is to result from his ministry. The term 'the new Israel' is indeed not used in Matthew any more than in the rest of the New Testament; P. Richardson affirms that the explicit description of either Jesus or the church as 'Israel' begins with Justin in the second century.[4] But there is a great deal in Matthew to suggest that the movement of thought which culminated in such language was already under way in his time, indeed that he was himself one of those most responsible for it.

ISRAEL-JESUS TYPOLOGY

Among the uses of the Old Testament by Matthew which are sometimes stigmatised as 'artificial' or 'irresponsible' is the formula-quotation in 2:15, 'Out of Egypt have I called my son'. Even a nodding acquaintance with Hosea 11:1 leaves no doubt that this is a reflection on past history, when God brought Israel out of Egypt in the exodus. So what can this passage have to do with Joseph's escape to Egypt well over a thousand years later, resulting from Herod's attempt to eliminate the newly-born 'king of the Jews'? Has Matthew then been misled by the very evocative word 'son' into a use of Scripture 'at which most readers today will feel discomfort and dissatisfaction because it seems to ignore the original meaning of the words and takes them out of their context'?[5]

Certainly Hosea was not referring to any future event. But our discussion of typology in the last chapter has prepared us to see Matthew claiming the 'fulfilment' of passages which had in themselves no forward reference. Among the crucial events of Old Testament history it is not surprising to see the exodus taken as a type of God's future acts of deliverance; indeed the Old Testament writers themselves sometimes so used it.[6] But a 'natural' typological use of the exodus might be to see the new people of God as parallel to the Israelite nation, and their deliverance from sin as the 'fulfilment' of the exodus event. What Matthew in fact offers is bolder than that, the proposal that Israel,

4. So P. Richardson, *Israel in the Apostolic Church* (Cambridge University Press, 1969) 1, 9-14, 205-206, etc.

5. Moule, *Origin*, 127.

6. See e.g. the discussion of Exodus typology in F. Foulkes, *The Acts of God* (London: Tyndale, 1958) and R.E. Nixon, *The Exodus in the New Testament* (London: Tyndale, 1963).

described in this connection as God's 'son' (cf. especially the use of this imagery in Ex. 4:22-23) finds its fulfilment not in a community but in an individual 'Son of God', and Israel's initial call 'out of Egypt' points forward to his literal return from Egypt.[7]

If this case stood alone, it might be written off as a rather careless misuse of Scripture on the basis of the key-word 'son'. But in the surrounding context other hints occur that Matthew sees the story of Israel taken up in that of Jesus. The preceding story of the homage of the Magi to the new king of the Jews is apparently modelled in part on the words of Isaiah 60:1-6, where it is to the people of God in Zion that the Gentiles will bring their gold and frankincense; and the immediately following formula-quotation (2:17-18) interprets the events at Bethlehem in the light of Jeremiah's words about the 'loss' of Rachel's children in the exile to Babylon (Jeremiah 31:15), a passage which sees that loss as the prelude to a joyful return and restoration of the people of God, just as Jesus is now to be restored from his exile in Egypt.[8]

This line of interpretation comes even more clearly to the surface in the account of Jesus' testing in the wilderness in 4:1-11. The repeated challenge 'If you are the son of God', in the context of privation in the wilderness, might by itself suggest the same exodus motif as was evoked by the use of Hosea 11:1. But this is put beyond doubt by the three-fold quotation of texts from Deuteronomy 6-8, a passage which focuses throughout on that episode and the lessons it contained for Israel's filial obedience. The first quotation, from Deuteronomy 8:3, takes us to the heart of this typology, for in that section Israel is called to 'remember all the way which the Lord your God has led you these forty years in the wilderness ... testing you ... As a man disciplines his son, the Lord your God disciplines you.' Israel, God's son, had lessons to learn in the wilderness before the entry to the promised land; so too has Jesus, God's son, before his mission begins in Galilee. Israel under Moses learned its lessons none too well; will Jesus prove more worthy of the title 'Son of God'?[9]

As we move into Matthew's account of Jesus' ministry and teaching similar implications arise. Jesus' presentation of his mission in terms of the Isaianic Servant of Yahweh and the Danielic Son of Man are

---

7. Gundry (*Use*, 93-94; *Matthew*, 34) points out that Matthew has not yet related the return from Egypt, only the escape and residence there, and therefore sees the point of the reference in Jesus' preservation *in* Egypt rather than his return *from* there. But this is too subtle; Jesus went to Egypt in order to return, and even the 'until' of verse 15 points to that conclusion of the episode.

8. See my remarks on the significance of this formula-quotation in *NTS* 27 (1980/81) 244-246.

9. See my *JOT*, 50-53 for this understanding of the wilderness episode as related by Matthew and Luke, and for references to other similar interpretations of the passage. This typological element is apparently absent from the much briefer account of Jesus in the wilderness in Mark 1:12-13.

of course common to all the gospels, but each of them receives special emphasis in Matthew, the former by its use in two of the formula-quotations (8:17; 12:17-21), the latter by a sequence of allusions (10:23; 16:27-8; 24:30 with 34; 26:64) to the 'coming of the Son of Man' as an event imminent within the lifetime of his hearers, leading up to the climactic claim of their fulfilment in the declaration of 28:18, with its echo of Daniel 7:14.[10] The interpretation of each of these figures in its Old Testament context poses problems precisely because each seems to blend individual with corporate aspects. The Servant, for all his in-dividual and indeed vicarious suffering, is himself 'Israel', and the 'one like a son of man' turns out in the latter part of Daniel 7 to represent 'the people of the saints of the Most High'. Matthew's Jesus is presented therefore as one who is in some sense a corporate figure. As C.H. Dodd concludes, 'The Messiah is not only founder and leader of the Israel-to-be, the new people of God; he is its "inclusive representative". In a real sense he *is* the true Israel, carrying through in his own experience the process through which it comes into being.'[11]

A similar conclusion may be drawn from other Old Testament references in the gospel. If, as is commonly suggested,[12] the origin of the 'third day' motif in the resurrection predictions is to be found in Hosea 6:2, this would involve a typology similar to that of 2:15, in that a prediction of the national 'resurrection' of Israel is transferred to Jesus, so that, to quote Dodd again, 'the resurrection of Christ *is* the resurrection of Israel of which the prophet spoke.'[13] The rejected stone of Psalm 118:22 is a figure for the vindication of Israel, but is applied in 21:42 to Jesus as the one in whom God's purpose for his people will be paradoxically fulfilled; and the same psalm forms the basis of Jesus' final appeal/threat to unrepentant Israel in 23:39. Psalm 22 gains extra prominence in Matthew's passion narrative, with likely echoes of its words in 27:35, 39, 43, 46; but this psalm too, while it is expressed in strongly individual terms, is generally understood to have been used, if not originally composed, as a psalm of national lament. Both these psalms present the ultimate vindication of the one despised and rejected by men, a pattern in Israel's national experience and hopes that Matthew apparently saw reaching its due culmination in Jesus himself.

We have seen in the previous chapter[14] how Matthew's presentation of Jesus' response to his opponents in chapter 12 focuses on the theme of 'something greater'. The elements in the Old Testament which are

10. For this interpretation of the Daniel 7 allusions see below pp. 290-292, 311, 314-316.
11. C.H. Dodd, *The Founder of Christianity* (London: Collins, 1970) 106.
12. See e.g. B. Lindars, *New Testament Apologetic* (London: SCM, 1961) 60ff; M. Black, *ZNW* 60 (1969) 4-5. The issue is discussed in my *JOT*, 53-55.
13. Dodd, *According,* 103; cf. *ibid.* 77.
14. Above pp. 189-191.

singled out to be superseded in this way include the central features of Israel's national life and constitution, her kings, prophets, wise men, priests and temple. If in Jesus there is 'something greater' than all these, even including the institution of the temple, we are not far from an explicit statement that in Jesus Israel as a corporate entity of the people of God has found its 'fulfilment'.

Some of the features noted above are not, of course, peculiar to Matthew, but are part of the common tradition which may, I believe, be traced back to Jesus' own understanding of his mission. But if the conception of Jesus as the fulfilment of Israel was not new, it has certainly achieved greater prominence in Matthew's account of Jesus than in the other gospels, and indeed than in most of the New Testament writings.

C.F.D. Moule took this theme as one of the key elements in his important discussion of 'Fulfilment-Words in the New Testament'.[15] In addition to messianic and other individual categories, he found applied to Jesus in the New Testament as a whole 'a great convergence of Israel-titles and other collectives . . . Servant of Yahweh, Son of Man, Zechariah martyr, rejected-but-vindicated stone, cornerstone, foundation stone, stumbling-stone, temple, . . . This marks him as, in the estimate of Christians, the climax of the pattern of true covenant-relationship. . . . Thus, to a unique degree, Jesus is seen as the goal, the convergence-point, of God's plan for Israel, his covenant- promise.'[16] But if this is a common New Testament theme, it is one on which Matthew's emphasis is second to none. Of the list of titles in Moule's quotation above all except the foundation stone (and the stumbling-stone if Matthew 21:44 is not considered original)[17] occur prominently in Matthew, and our discussion has indicated others which could be added to the list.

ISRAEL-CHURCH TYPOLOGY

If in the ministry of Jesus himself we are to see the fulfilment of Israel and the establishment of 'something greater than the temple', it

15. *NTS* 14 (1967/8) 293-320.
16. *Ibid.* 300-301.
17. The omission of Matthew 21:44 from some Western MSS and the Sinaitic Syriac and in some of the earlier patristic witnesses suggests it may have found its way into the text of Matthew at an early stage from the parallel in Luke 20:18; but the wording is slightly different, and it would more naturally have been inserted after v 42, so that it is possible that these texts represent an accidental omission. The editors of the UBS[3] and NA[26] texts and of the Aland *Synopsis* felt the question to be sufficiently open to justify retaining the verse in the text in square brackets, though Greeven's revision of Huck's *Synopse* has omitted it. The verse is defended as an original part of Matthew, if not of Jesus' words at this point, by some recent commentators, notably Albright & Mann, *Matthew*, 265-267 and Gundry, *Matthew*, 430-431. Beare, *Matthew*, 425-426 is more equivocal.

is not a long step to the idea that those who follow Jesus' teaching, and who are thus formed into a new community of the restored people of God, are to be seen as the true continuation of Israel. For as long as Jesus' followers were drawn entirely from the Jewish people, this might be no more than an extension of the prophetic notion of the 'remnant', and in the early stages of the growth of the Christian community this is likely to have been how they understood their role. But by the time Matthew wrote his gospel the church was far from purely Jewish, and this was a development which, as we shall see, Matthew himself welcomed. How then did he understand this new racially mixed community in relation to Israel?

One distinctive feature of Matthew's gospel is its use in two passages of the noun ἐκκλησία (16:18; 18:17). This was a familiar term to a Greek-speaking Jew, being the regular LXX translation for qahal, the 'congregation' of the people of God. Despite frequent statements to the contrary, I can see no improbability in Jesus' use of some such term to describe the group of restored Israelites which he was gathering around himself, and which he would naturally have expected to continue beyond the period of his own personal ministry.[18] But by the time Matthew included this term in his record of Jesus' teaching it had come to have for him and his readers a more developed meaning, in that they were conscious of belonging to ἐκκλησίαι which were typically composed of both Jews and Gentiles, and which were by this stage self-consciously distinct from 'their synagogues'. In the retention of so emotive a word from the Old Testament, but now defined as the ἐκκλησία of Jesus (16:18), he surely intends to indicate that the Christian church now fills the role of the Old Testament congregation of God's people.

Elsewhere in Matthew Old Testament language about Israel is similarly transferred to the disciples of Jesus. In chapter 5 Jesus demands of his disciples a righteousness exceeding that of the scribes and Pharisees (5:20), and goes on to contrast his own approach to 'righteousness' with that familiar to 'the men of old'. Six examples of Jesus' radical demand are offered in vv 21-47, and then the whole sequence is summed up in the words 'You, therefore must be perfect, as your heavenly Father is perfect' (5:48), an echo of the repeated formula of Leviticus 11:44,45; 19:2; 20:7; 20:26, 'You shall be holy, for I am holy'.[19] This formula reflects the very basis of the distinctive existence of the people of God, as Leviticus 20:26 makes clear by grounding this demand in the fact that 'I have separated you from the peoples, that you should

18. For a spirited defence of Mt. 16:17-19, and therefore of the word ἐκκλησία, as an authentic pronouncement of Jesus on the occasion of Peter's confession at Caesarea Philippi, see B.F. Meyer, The Aims of Jesus (London: SCM, 1979) 185-197.

19. The use of τέλειος, 'perfect', rather than 'holy' is probably due to the additional influence of Dt. 18:13, a similarly comprehensive demand on the people of God, where the LXX uses τέλειος,

be mine.' It is, apparently, those who follow Jesus' way who now
constitute the true people of God, separated not only from 'the peoples'
but also from the scribes and Pharisees who will not even enter the
kingdom of heaven.

Earlier in the same chapter the Matthean beatitudes describe Jesus'
disciples in terms of the 'poor' and 'meek', Old Testament descriptions
of the true 'remnant' within the nation of Israel, and the statement that
the meek 'shall inherit the earth' (5:5) takes up the promise of Psalm
37:11 addressed to the godly minority within Israel.

An important passage for understanding Matthew's theology of Israel
and the church is 8:11-12, where people 'from east and west' will come
into the messianic banquet with the Jewish patriarchs to take the place
of the rejected 'sons of the kingdom'. We shall consider this passage
more fully later, but it is relevant to note here that the gathering 'from
east and west' is often regarded as a deliberate echo of Old Testament
passages whose theme is the regathering of the scattered people of *Israel*
(Ps. 107:3; Is. 43:5; cf. 49:12). The prophecy of the gathering of the
elect 'from the four winds, from one end of heaven to the other' in
24:31 similarly echoes Deuteronomy 30:4 and Zechariah 2:10 (EVV
v.6), passages which also refer originally to the regathering of scattered
Israel. This last reference is, of course, shared with Mark, but in
Matthew's version an additional allusion may be seen in the mention
of a 'loud trumpet call', recalling Isaiah 27:13 with its 'great trumpet'
to recall the exiled Israelites to Jerusalem. This willingness to describe
the gathering of the international church by means of Old Testament
passages about the regathering of Israel further supports the suggestion
that Matthew saw the church as the true Israel.[20]

Jesus' choice of twelve disciples, with its obvious Israel-symbolism,
is not of course a purely Matthean theme, but it receives a peculiarly
Matthean emphasis in 19:28, where their place of authority on twelve
thrones judging the twelve tribes of Israel is located in the παλιγγενεσία,
the wholly new situation which will obtain 'when the Son of Man shall
sit on his glorious throne'. The combination of the themes of throne,
glory, judgement and Son of Man points irresistibly to the vision of
Daniel 7, where the dominion given to the Son of Man (vv. 13-14) finds
its counterpart in the everlasting reign of the 'saints of the Most High'
(vv. 18,22,27). But whereas in Daniel 7 it is the people of God as a
whole who are given the kingship, and their rule is apparently over all
the other nations, in Matthew 19:28 it is Jesus' twelve disciples (representing the disciple group as a whole?) who will reign over ('judge' in
its familiar Old Testament sense of 'rule') the twelve tribes of *Israel*. It
is open to question whether this refers to the nation, now seen as on
a par with the other nations in Daniel 7, or to the church seen as the

20. I have discussed these allusions more fully in *JOT*, 63-64.

ideal Israel of the new age, but in either case there can be no mistaking the implication that Daniel's vision of Israel's glory is here seen as fulfilled in the future authority given to Jesus' disciples.

The New Testament concept of the church as the true temple of the new age[21] is not explicit in Matthew any more than in the other gospels, but it is not likely that Matthew could have presented the theme of the coming destruction of the temple (to which we shall return below) together with the announcement of 'something greater' (12:6), without having this idea in mind. The primary reference of the 'something greater' is, as we have seen, to Jesus himself, but the concept of the continuation of that 'something greater' in the community of those who follow Jesus is a natural transition, and one which would be almost inevitable for a Christian writing in the period when the personal ministry of Jesus had been succeeded by the continuing Jesus-community.[22]

The idea of the church as the true fulfilment of Israel is not of course peculiar to Matthew, and is indeed more clearly stressed and more fully worked out by other New Testament writers, but we have seen reason to believe that it was not only a theme which he took for granted, but one which played a significant part in his understanding of 'Israel'. Israel reaches its culmination firstly in Jesus himself, but also derivatively in the community of those who belong to Jesus.

Fulfilment implies both continuity and discontinuity. There remains a people of God, in which the hopes and destinies of Old Testament Israel find their culmination. But the very existence of a newly constituted community of the people of God, and one which is not purely Jewish, calls in question the status of the existing Israel, the 'sons of the kingdom'. We turn, then, to the negative side of Matthew's Israel-theology, to the theme of Israel's failure.

B. THE THREAT OF JUDGEMENT

When Jesus asks his disciples who people are saying that he is, it is interesting that in Matthew's account the name of Jeremiah is included among the prophetic figures mentioned (16:14). J. Carmignac has suggested[23] that this was not a random choice, nor was it governed by

21. For this concept see esp. R.J. McKelvey, *The New Temple* (Oxford University Press, 1969).
22. For this as an aspect even of Jesus' own understanding of his mission, not just of post-Easter theology, see McKelvey, *ibid.* 58-74; B. Gärtner, *The Temple and the Community in Qumran and the New Testament* (Cambridge University Press, 1965) 105-122; Dodd, *Founder*, 89-90.
23. J. Carmignac, 'Pourquoi Jérémie est-il mentionné en Matthieu 16,14?' in G. Jeremias (ed.) *Tradition und Glaube: Festgabe für K.G. Kuhn* (Göttingen: Vandenhoeck & Ruprecht, 1971) 283-298.

any special preeminence of Jeremiah over the other prophets, but rather that there was an obvious parallel between the mission and message of the two men. Jeremiah, for all his preaching of ultimate hope for Israel, would have been characterised in the popular mind above all as a prophet of doom, the man who preached surrender to the Babylonians, who offered no hope that God would defend Jerusalem, and who even dared to predict the total destruction of the temple. As the Talmud puts it, 'Jeremiah is all destruction'![24] Christian tradition has not normally seen Jesus in any such light, and yet there is ample ground in the gospel accounts for concluding that an unsympathetic onlooker might well have been more impressed by Jesus' threats than by his promises and have felt that he, like another Jesus, son of Hananiah, a generation later,[25] was conducting a one-man crusade against the patriotic values of Israel, a crusade which focused for both Jesuses as for Jeremiah on the fate of the temple. And the gospel of Matthew gives more basis for that impression than any other.

JUDGEMENT ON THE TEMPLE

The one specific charge against Jesus (other than the High Priest's question on Messiahship) which is recorded in Mark's and Matthew's account of the examination by the Sanhedrin is his alleged threat against the temple (Mk. 14:58; Mt. 26:61). This charge clearly played a more central role than as just one among several futile attempts to incriminate Jesus, as is shown by its repetition again at the cross (Mt. 27:40) and the continuing centrality of this charge when Jesus' follower Stephen faced the same 'court' in Acts 6:13-14. Nor was the High Priest changing the subject when he followed up this charge with his question about Messiahship, for there is ample evidence that current messianic expectation included a purification, restoration, or even replacement of the temple and its worship.[26] Jesus' demonstration in the temple was apparently one of the major reasons for his arrest and trial, and it was followed, at least in private with the disciples, by his prediction of its destruction within a generation. It is increasingly being recognised that the decision of the Jerusalem establishment to eliminate Jesus was motivated in large measure by the understanding that he was a threat to the temple, the centre of national life and identity (and, hardly

24. *Baba Bathra* 14b.
25. In the procuratorship of Albinus, AD 62-64; see Josephus, *B.J.* VI 300-309.
26. The most prominent expression of such an ideology in the Old Testament is the vision of the new temple in Ezekiel 40-47. The later development of such expectation is briefly summarised by W.R. Telford, *The Barren Temple and the Withered Tree* (Sheffield: JSOT, 1980) 260-261, drawing on an unpublished dissertation by R.E. Dowda, *The Cleansing of the Temple in the Synoptic Gospels* (Duke University, 1972).

incidentally, the focus of the authority of the priestly families who controlled the Sanhedrin).[27]

All this is clear from Mark as well as from Matthew. But while Mark plainly regards the temple charge as 'false witness' (and perhaps softens the 'political' impact of the charge by the assertion that Jesus' new temple will be of a different type, 'made without hands'), Matthew phrases his account in such a way that this charge is separated from the futile search for 'false witness' in 26:59-60a, and specifies that this new charge was offered by *two* witnesses, which makes it technically admissible as evidence.[28] The High Priest's question then follows logically: Jesus' claim to Messiahship is inextricably linked with his campaign against the temple.[29]

Matthew has prepared the way for this focus even before Jesus' actual arrival in Jerusalem in chapter 21, by recording his assertion that 'Something greater than the temple is here' (12:6). The statement is not developed at that point, where its function is to underline the authority of Jesus in relation to legal issues (the sabbath), though the immediately following quotation of Hosea 6:6 with its downgrading of 'sacrifice' might well lead a Christian reader to see here already a pointer to the theology of the Letter to the Hebrews, focused on a new covenant with a new (heavenly) sanctuary and the supersession of animal sacrifice by the one sacrifice of Christ. Matthew's typological interests which we have considered in chapter 5 suggest that he would find that theology congenial, and that he shared Hebrews' understanding of the institutions of the old covenant as 'becoming obsolete, growing old, and ready to vanish away' (Heb. 8:13). The destruction of the temple in AD 70 would come as no surprise to the author of Hebrews (if, as I believe, he was writing before that event), but rather as the appropriate outworking of what was already theologically true, that 'something greater' had taken its place. And Matthew would agree.

The coming destruction of the temple is not just a case of natural obsolescence, but of judgement. Jesus' action in the temple court (21:12-13), whatever its positive 'messianic' connotations, undoubtedly includes an element of indignant repudiation of the way the temple is currently being used, and the immediately following account of the cursing of the fig-tree (21:18-19) is usually understood as a symbolic presentation of God's judgement on his unfruitful people.[30] The first

27. For the significance of Jesus' attitude to the temple as perhaps the single most important cause of his execution, see especially Meyer, *Aims*, 168-170,181-202; E.P. Sanders, *Jesus and Judaism* (London: SCM, 1985) 61-90,270-271,287,293,301-305.
28. For the difference between Mark and Matthew at this point see Senior, *Passion*, 163-168; Gundry, *Matthew*, 541-543.
29. For this link see D. Juel, *Messiah and Temple* (Missoula: Scholars' Press, 1977), particularly 197-215.
30. This significance is almost universally recognised in Mark's interwoven stories of the temple and the fig-tree, the fullest recent examination being that of Telford, *Temple*.

explicit prediction of the future desolation of the temple (23:38) comes as the climax of the extended denunciation of the scribes and Pharisees in chapter 23 (to which we shall return), and in particular the statement that the sins of the fathers have culminated in 'this generation', upon whom punishment is now at last to fall. Jesus' last, earnest appeal to Jerusalem has met with no response (23:37), and now there can be only one outcome. 'Your house is abandoned to you, desolate.'

Up to this point Jesus has been teaching in the temple, but now he 'left the temple and was going away' to the Mount of Olives (is there an echo here of the departure of the divine presence from the temple to the same mountain in Ezekiel 10:18-19; 11:22-23?), and his disciples' admiration for its magnificence is answered only by the assertion that it is to be totally destroyed (24:1-3). The extended discourse which follows in 24:4 - 25:46 is on the theme of judgement, which in the earlier part of the discourse is focused on Jerusalem and its temple, but in the later part extends to a more universal and eschatological perspective. Just how and at what point this transition is made is a matter of exegetical controversy. My own understanding is that the judgement on Jerusalem remains in focus until 24:35, with 24:36 marking a transition to the different 'day and hour' of the παρουσία, which is introduced under that term in vv 37,39 (thus answering the second part of the disciples' question in v 3),and in v 27 is clearly differentiated from the events of the siege of the city.[31] In that case the statement that the predicted judgement will take place within 'this generation' (v 34) takes up the same time-scale for the judgement on Jerusalem set out in 23:29-39. But on any understanding of chapter 24 it is clear that the future destruction of the temple is set in a context of divine judgement.

JUDGEMENT ON 'THIS GENERATION'

The Old Testament prophets frequently denounced the ungodly attitude of their contemporaries, and in Matthew we find several such denunciations picked up and redirected against the contemporaries of Jesus. Thus the opening of Isaiah's vineyard parable (Is. 5:1-2) provides the scenery for Jesus' parable of the defaulting tenants (Mt. 21:33),

In Matthew the stories are merely placed side by side, and Telford, *ibid.* 69-94, argues from this and other differences that Matthew has eliminated the symbolism, and uses the fig-tree story merely as an example of the power of faith. He therefore concludes that Matthew has a more positive attitude to the temple than Mark. But few recent commentators have been able to make sense of the fig-tree incident in Matthew without appealing to an Israel-symbolism and its proximity to the temple incident; indeed for Gundry, *Matthew*, 415-416, Matthew's alterations 'make the incident serve more dramatically its purpose of symbolizing God's rejection of the Jewish leaders in Jerusalem, whom the fig tree represents in Matthew'.

31. I have briefly defended this exegesis in my *Matthew*; see especially the general comments on pp. 333- 336. A parallel understanding of the structure of Mark 13 is set out in my *JOT*, 227-239.

which his enemies perceived as spoken 'against them' (21:45); Jeremiah's accusation of turning the temple into a 'den of robbers' (Je. 7:11) becomes the basis for Jesus' attack on the temple traders (Mt. 21:13); Hosea's attack on superficial worship (Ho. 6:6) is twice turned against the Pharisees who criticise Jesus (Mt. 9:13; 12:7); and on two occasions Jesus takes passages which express the dangerous superficiality of Isaiah's contemporaries in their approach to religion (Is. 6:9-10 and 29:13) and applies them to his own contemporaries with the formulae 'With them is fulfilled the prophecy of Isaiah' (Mt. 13:14) and 'Well did Isaiah prophesy *of you*' (15:7).

This 'contemporising' of the historical shortcomings of Israel finds fuller expression in a series of denunciations of 'this generation'.[32] The unresponsiveness of 'this generation' is like that of petulant children (11:16); it is an 'evil and adulterous generation' which demands a sign before it will believe (12:39; 16:4), and therefore 'this generation' will come off worse at the judgement than the pagan nations who listened to God's spokesmen in the past (12:41,42); Jesus' story of the wandering demon who returns to 'his' house with seven others is an illustration of the plight of 'this evil generation' (12:45); and Moses' despairing description of his people as a 'perverse and crooked generation' (Dt. 32:5) is echoed in Jesus' frustration with contemporary unbelief in Matthew 17:17.

Perhaps such things might be said, at least in less sanguine moments, about any generation. But Matthew's gospel indicates that 'this generation' is uniquely culpable, and is therefore ripe for judgement. Not only are they the sons of those who murdered the prophets, but they are 'filling up the measure of their fathers' (23:29-32). Their continued rejection and persecution of God's messengers is now getting to the point where the blood of all the martyrs will 'come upon' them (23:34-35); 'Truly, I say to you, all this will come upon this generation' (23:36). It is this statement of the culpability of 'this generation' which leads into the prediction of the fall of the temple, which will take place before 'this generation' has passed (24:34).

There is, then, a sense of urgency in the warnings issued to 'this generation'. It is heard already in John the Baptist's eleventh-hour warning: 'flee from the wrath to come'; 'even now the axe is laid to the root of the trees' (3:7,10). It is inherent in the mission of Jesus' disciples, who are to travel light and waste no time with the unresponsive (10:9-15), for they 'will not have gone through all the towns of Israel before the Son of Man comes' (10:23). Jesus' repeated attempts to 'gather together' the people of Jerusalem are now at an end, 'and you would not' (23:37). But it is not only Jerusalem which has resisted his appeal and must

32. On this theme see D. Marguerat, *Le Jugement dans l'Evangile de Matthieu* (Geneva: Labor et Fides, 1981) 266-267.

now face the consequences; for other less prominent towns in Galilee
'where most of his mighty works had been done' there is the same
expectation of judgement (11:20-24).

S. Van Tilborg concludes from his study of 23:29-39 that whereas
later Jewish writings on this theme left open the possibility of conversion,
Matthew leaves no such opportunity. 'The judgment is definitive. . . .
The measure is full, Israel has been rejected. Under the guidance of its
leaders Israel has let the opportunity to repent go by.'[33] Whether or
not one accepts his further conclusion that therefore the gospel must
belong to a non-Jewish context, he is right to notice this sense of finality.
There is no indication here that this is merely a threat designed to lead
to repentance, in the manner of some of the Old Testament prophets;
it looks, as S. Légasse argues,[34] more like the expectation of actual
events, focused in the predicted destruction of Jerusalem. But, as Légasse
goes on to point out, this recognition of the reality of judgement does
not imply the sort of 'anti-Judaism' that Van Tilborg's conclusion
assumes. Matthew's attitude, he suggests, derives not from racial
antipathy, still less from a vindictive desire for revenge, but rather from
the sort of 'holy hatred' expressed by the Old Testament psalmists and
the Qumran sectaries with regard to the enemies of God, those who
hinder the fulfilment of his purpose.[35]

But is it then *Israel* which stands under the threat of judgement, or
only an unresponsive part of Israel? In particular is it possible to draw
a distinction between the Jewish *leaders* as the object of Matthew's
'holy hatred' and the people as a whole?

C. THE JEWISH LEADERS

The most striking polemic in Matthew is that of chapter 23, which
concludes in the words about the final culpability of 'this generation'
which we have been considering. But the denunciations in 23:13ff (the
seven 'woes') are directed specifically at the 'scribes and Pharisees',
while in 23:1-12 it is the failings of those same 'scribes and Pharisees'
which are described in the third person, the audience being not only
Jesus' disciples but also 'the crowds', who are thus warned not to be
taken in by the pretentions of their leaders. Matthew seems, therefore,
to wish his readers to recognise a distinction between the people as a
whole and their leaders; it is the latter who are rejected as 'hypocrites'.
Similar distinctions can be traced at other points in the account of
the final week in Jerusalem. At Jesus' entry to Jerusalem there is a

33. Van Tilborg, *Leaders*, 71.
34. S. Légasse, 'L' "antijudaisme" dans l'Evangile selon Matthieu', in Didier, *Matthieu*,
421, responding to the argument of G. Baum, *Les Juifs et l'Evangile* (Paris, 1965).
35. *Ibid.* esp. 427.

contrast in 21:10-11 between 'the city' (who do not recognise Jesus) and 'the crowds' (the Galilean pilgrim group who introduce him as 'their' prophet). In the temple Jesus is welcomed by the blind and the lame, whom he heals, and by the 'children' who shout 'Hosanna', while 'the chief priests and the scribes' are left objecting (21:14-16). It is 'the chief priests and the elders of the people' who question his authority (21:23), but they are afraid that the crowd will be against them (21:26). The 'chief priests and the Pharisees' who are the object of his polemical parables (21:45) are unable to take action because the crowd recognise Jesus as a prophet (21:46). When the crowd heard Jesus' refutation of Sadducean theology, 'they were astonished at his teaching; but when the Pharisees heard that he had silenced the Sadducees, they came together . . .', a deliberate contrast of attitudes which is unfortunately obscured by verse and paragraph divisions (22:33-34). The focus in these chapters is on the growing confrontation between Jesus and the various groups of Jewish leaders, but the crowd remain in the background throughout as an audience more favourable to Jesus than neutral. So when Jesus begins his onslaught on the scribes and Pharisees in chapter 23 it is natural that he appeals over their heads to the crowds who can be regarded as on his side rather than theirs.

Several studies of Matthew have noted this favourable presentation of the crowds (οἱ ὄχλοι is a particularly frequent term in Matthew) as those who, while they may be vulnerable to being misled by their leaders, are at least still open to Jesus' message, and particularly in the earlier stages of the ministry are positively enthusiastic for him.[36] The recognition of this aspect of the gospel suggests caution in making blanket statements about Matthew's 'anti-Judaism' or his theology of 'the rejection of Israel'. We shall need to return to this in the next section. For the present it requires us to be careful in noting *against whom* the gospel's denunciations and warnings of judgement are directed.

'The Jewish leaders' is, of course, a very loose phrase, and one not used by Matthew himself. He uses several terms, of which the most common are 'Pharisees' (32 times), 'scribes' (21 times),[37] 'Sadducees' (8 times), 'chief priests' (18 times), and 'elders' (11 times). Very often he combines two or more of these terms, the favourite combinations being

---

36. For more lengthy surveys see Van Tilborg, *Leaders*, 142-165; P.S. Minear, 'The Disciples and the Crowds in the Gospel of Matthew', *ATR Sup.* 3 (1974) 28-44; more briefly J.D. Kingsbury, *The Parables of Jesus in Matthew 13* (London: SPCK, 1969) 24-28; Donaldson, *Jesus*, 114-115,207-208.

37. There are also two places where γραμματεύς is used of followers of Jesus, whether scribes who have 'become disciples' (so perhaps 13:52) or those who within the Christian community function as the scribes do in the Jewish (so probably in 23:34, and perhaps more likely in 13:52 as well). The γραμματεύς of 8:19 is sympathetic to Jesus, but at the point of the narrative his discipleship apparently remains only potential. The question of 'Christian scribes' in Matthew is discussed by Van Tilborg, *Leaders*, 128-141; Zumstein, *Condition*, 156-163.

220   MATTHEW: EVANGELIST AND TEACHER

'scribes and Pharisees' and 'chief priests and elders (of the people)'. These terms are not all of the same type, 'Pharisee' and 'Sadducee' being 'party' names, while scribes, chief priests and elders represent professional categories or roles in society. There is therefore room for some overlap, in that most scribes are likely to have been Pharisees, and most senior priests Sadducees. But in all these matters our historical sources leave a good deal to be desired, and any discussion of the significance of these terms in the real world of pre-70 Palestine must acknowledge that there is much that we do not know.[38]

All these terms are used also by the other synoptic evangelists (though Mark and Luke each refer only once to Sadducees) in broadly similar ways.[39] In all three the tendency is for scribes and Pharisees to be mentioned more frequently in the earlier part of the gospel, but for the chief priests and elders to come to the fore in the passion narrative, where it is they who must take official action to suppress Jesus. In certain key passages Mark uses the formidable triple combination of chief priests, scribes and elders to indicate the uniting of the whole Jerusalem 'establishment' against Jesus: in Jesus' prediction of his coming rejection at Jerusalem (Mk. 8:31), in describing the 'delegation' which questioned Jesus' authority in the temple (Mk. 11:27), and the group which brought the official charge against him before Pilate (Mk. 15:1, where he adds 'and the whole council' for good measure!). Luke agrees in all three cases, but Matthew sticks to only the chief priests and elders except in 16:21.

Apart from the unexpected combination of 'Pharisees and Sadducees' in 3:7 and 16:1-12, which we have considered earlier,[40] the most distinctive features in Matthew's presentation of the Jewish leaders are the sustained polemic against the 'scribes and Pharisees' in chapter 23 (corresponding to only three verses at this point in Mark and Luke, though incorporating also some material shared with Luke 11:39-52), and the increased prominence of the Pharisees throughout (including the period in Jerusalem preceding Jesus' arrest, when Mark mentions them only once and Luke not at all). Thus while Matthew presents all the categories of leaders listed above as generally hostile to Jesus, and as involved in the process of his rejection by 'Israel', it seems that he wishes to emphasise the role of the scribes and, particularly, the Pharisees.

Matthew's 'anti-Pharisaism' has been frequently commented on,[41] and explained in terms of the situation in which the gospel was written.

38. This point is emphasised by D.A. Carson, *JETS* 25 (1982) 163-167; Stanton, 'Origin', 1919.
39. The uses in all three Synoptics are conveniently set out in tabular form in Garland, *Intention*, 218-221.
40. Above pp. 106-107. These are the only passages in which Matthew mentions Sadducees, apart from the discussion about the resurrection in 22:23-34, where Mark and Luke also mention them.
41. E.g. Strecker, *Weg*, 137-143; Davies, *Setting*, 290-292.

Thus D.R.A. Hare concludes from a study of Matthew 23:29-39 that whereas Luke expresses anti-Pharisaic attitudes as 'a matter of literary convention', Matthew has deliberately intensified this element, to the extent that 'some kind of unhappy contact with Pharisaism is required to explain the hostility of the author'.[42] He goes on to explain this by the origin of Matthew's gospel in a church which had experienced persecution directed against Christian missionaries specifically by Pharisees.[43] But since there are several indications in the New Testament that there was no general hostility of Pharisees to the Christian movement as such in the period before AD 70,[44] it is often concluded that Matthew is reading a later situation back into the period of Jesus' ministry, and in so doing has contributed to the caricature of first-century Pharisaism which in recent years has been increasingly repudiated by both Jewish and Christian scholars.[45] On this view Matthew, in lumping together all that he finds objectionable under the title of 'Pharisees' or 'scribes and Pharisees', simply reveals his own prejudices and his distance from the situation of Jesus' ministry.

In response to this commonly held view, D.E. Garland[46] points out that it is not only Matthew who introduces the Pharisees as opponents of Jesus (though his statement that 'Luke mentions the Pharisees even more often in his gospel' hardly matches the evidence set out in the preceding tables). It is not so much, he argues, following the studies of R. Walker and S. Van Tilborg, that Matthew has a grudge against the Pharisees *as such*, but rather that he makes no careful distinction between the various Jewish groups in the period of Jesus' ministry, but 'treated all of them as a homogeneous group'. His use of 'Pharisees' and of 'scribes and Pharisees' is therefore a general term for 'the genus, false leaders of Israel'.[47]

---

42. Hare, *Persecution*, 96, summarising pp. 80-96.
43. *Ibid.* 126-129. Hare suggests that this experience would fit the situation in a Syrian church in the period after the Jewish war when the Jamnian authorities were beginning to crack down more seriously on the Christian movement, *ibid.* 165-169.
44. See S. Brown, *NovT* 22 (1980) 212-215.
45. For Jewish comment see P. Winter, *On the Trial of Jesus* (Berlin: de Gruyter, ²1974) 174-6, 185-189; more recently J. Neusner, *Judaism in the Beginning of Christianity* (Philadelphia: Fortress, 1984) 45-61, a distillation from his fuller study, *From Politics to Piety: The Emergence of Pharisaic Judaism* (New York: KTAV, 1979); more stridently, H. Maccoby, *The Mythmaker: Paul and the Invention of Christianity* (London: Weidenfeld & Nicolson, 1986) 19-44. From the Christian point of view, the works of E.P. Sanders have signaled a new appreciation of Pharisaic Judaism: see his *Paul and Palestinian Judaism* (London: SCM, 1977) *passim*, and particularly his *Jesus*, where a full survey of the 'State of the Question' (23-58) focuses on the way Christians and Jews have hitherto differed in their estimate of Jesus' attitude to Judaism and to Pharisees in particular; Sanders' own view, developed in different ways throughout the book, is summarised in the conclusion (290-292) that there was 'no substantial conflict between Jesus and the Pharisees'. A detailed bibliography of discussion of the relation between Jesus and the Pharisees is supplied by M.J. Cook, *Mark's Treatment of the Jewish Leaders* (Leiden: Brill, 1978) 80 n. 6.
46. *Intention*, 221.
47. *Ibid.* 41-46.

Yet Matthew was not totally unaware of such distinctions. He, along
with Mark and Luke, records Jesus' dialogue with the Sadducees on a
matter which related specifically to their theology at a point where it
differed markedly from that of the Pharisees (22:23-33), and the editorial
comment which he adds in 22:34 indicates that he saw Sadducees and
Pharisees as distinct groups, despite his mention that they were jointly
represented in the two 'delegations' of 3:7 and 16:1.[48] On the other
hand, it is entirely appropriate that he presents Jesus' disputes over
matters of religious law as conducted with scribes and/or Pharisees,
whose interest was in these areas. Even the sustained polemic against
the scribes and Pharisees in chapter 23 maintains this distinction, for
the focus there is on matters of religious observance, ritual and ethics,
and the issues raised highlight the problem of an excessive concern with
form and ceremony which is the occupational hazard of the specialist
in religious law. The 'hypocrisy'[49] with which the seven 'woes' charge
them is not so much a matter of the deliberate adoption of a false
public image as of a casuistical concern for the minutiae of external
behaviour which obscures rather than clarifies the essentials of how a
man should aim to please God.[50] Matthew has focused on the Pharisees
not so much because this is a convenient term of abuse for any religious
opponent (this would rather reflect modern usage), but because he sees
the essence of Jesus' conflict with the official religion of his time as
falling in those areas of theology and ethics which were (and continued
to be in his day) the special concern of the Pharisees (and particularly
of those of them who were scribes).[51]

There is, then, a rough *prima facie* verisimilitude about the way
Sadducees, Pharisees and scribes appear in Matthew, as well as in the
way he, like Mark and Luke, includes the chief priests and elders in
the plot (and allows the Pharisees to disappear from the scene) from
the point where official disciplinary action takes over from theological
and ritual debate. His more frequent singling out of scribes and Pharisees
for dishonourable mention may well reflect something of the situation
in which he and his church found themselves some decades later, but
this emphasis does not seem to have eroded his awareness of the role
of the various elements in 'the Jewish leadership' in the rejection of
Jesus.

48. See above pp. 106-107.
49. For extended discussions of this very prominent Matthean term see, in addition
to Albright & Mann (next note), U. Wilckens, *TDNT* IX 559-571; Van Tilborg, *Leaders*,
8-26; Garland, *Intention*, 91-123.
50. Albright and Mann have usually translated ὑποκριτής in Matthew as 'casuist',
though in the woes of chapter 23 they offer 'Away with you, you pettifogging Pharisee
lawyers!'. They offer an extended justification of this interpretation in *Matthew*, CXV-
CXXIII.
51. See Mohrlang, *Matthew and Paul*, 20-21.

And over against any or all of these groups there remains the crowd, those ordinary Jews who seem at several points in this gospel to represent not so much the opposition to Jesus as the uncommitted majority for whose allegiance the messianic proclamation of Jesus must compete with the 'leaven of the Pharisees and Sadducees' (16:6-12). May we then conclude that Matthew has no concept of the failure and judgement of *Israel* as such, but only of its unworthy leaders? Must we then speak not of a 'rejection of Israel', but rather of the imposition of a new leadership (that of Jesus and his disciples) on the continuing people of God? Is the alleged 'anti-Jewishness' of Matthew a misunderstanding based on the failure of some of his readers to distinguish between leaders and people?

D. A NEW PEOPLE OF GOD?

LEADERS AND PEOPLE

Even before the great diatribe of chapter 23, Jesus' repudiation of the Jewish leadership has reached a climax in the three parables with which he responds to their challenge, 'By what authority . . .?'. That question was an official challenge from 'the chief priests and the elders of the people' (21:23). Jesus responds first with a diplomatically evasive answer which in fact stakes his claim to the same authority as that by which John the Baptist had operated (21:24-27), and then continues without any expressed change of audience to offer three parables of rejection and replacement. The reluctant son proves ultimately to be the one who does the will of his father, despite his brother's profession of loyalty – and so 'the tax-collectors and the harlots go into the kingdom of God before you' (21:28-32). The irresponsible tenants of the vineyard will be thrown out and 'put to a miserable death', and the vineyard given to other tenants (21:33-43). The invited guests who exclude themselves from the banquet will be destroyed, and their place taken by last-minute recruits from the streets, 'both good and bad' (22:1-10).

Mark and Luke also include the parable of the tenants of the vineyard at this point, with obvious polemical intent, but Matthew has powerfully increased the effect by compiling this sequence of parables. The immediate reference of the parables is clear enough from the narrative context, and Matthew spells it out in 21:45: 'When the chief priests and the Pharisees heard his parables, they perceived that he was speaking about them.' The current leadership, which has set itself against the mission of John and of Jesus, has thereby failed in its trust and is doomed. It is to be replaced by those who *have* responded (21:31-32), by tenants 'who will give him the fruits in their seasons' (21:41,43). The wedding hall will be filled with guests (22:10), but they will not be those who had the first claim on the invitation; for them there remains only destruction and the burning of their city (22:7).

But it is 'their city' which will be burned. The judgement falls not only on the recalcitrants themselves, but apparently on the community to which they belong. Is this to wring too much significance out of a narrative detail in a parable, the very fault of which we are constantly warned by modern parable interpreters? But this detail, and the military campaign which leads up to it, are emphatically not part of the narrative scenery of a royal wedding feast. Their presence in the parable adds a ludicrously incongruous touch to the story. They are meant to be noticed. Whatever the history of the tradition of this parable, Matthew wants his readers to be aware that the Jewish leaders' rejection of God's invitation will result in the burning of 'their city'. So in one of the parables arising out of Jesus' conflict with the Jewish *leadership* we find the theme of the destruction of *Jerusalem*. The coming judgement on Jerusalem and its temple is bound up with the fault of Jerusalem's leaders.

In the parable of the tenants the vineyard is depicted in terms drawn from Isaiah 5:1-7, where the vineyard is explicitly interpreted as 'the house of Israel'. In Jesus' parable, unlike Isaiah's, it is not the vineyard itself which fails, but its tenants who refuse to hand over its fruit. The fault is in the leaders rather than the nation. And yet here too the judgement seems to fall more broadly, for 'the kingdom of God will be taken away from you and given to a *nation* producing the fruits of it' (21:43). Not just new leaders, but a new 'nation'. It is frequently observed that Matthew uses the singular ἔθνος rather than the plural ἔθνη, which would normally indicate 'the Gentiles' as opposed to the Jews; so this is not a crude theory of the total replacement of the Jewish nation by the Gentiles. But nonetheless the fact that Matthew uses such a term in describing God's intended replacement suggests that something more radical is in view than just a change of leadership.[52]

What is suggested in these parables is spelled out, as we have seen, in other parts of the gospel, in the warnings of judgement on 'this generation' (a term which is not on the face of it limited only to the Jewish leadership) and on the temple, itself not only the centre of the priestly establishment but also the heart of the religious life of the nation. It is Jerusalem, not just its leadership, which has failed to respond to Jesus' appeal and for which time has now run out (23:37); and, as we have seen, Jerusalem is not the only community to which this verdict can be applied (11:20-24). When Jesus speaks of 'the sons of the kingdom' being excluded from the messianic banquet in favour of 'many from east and west' (8:11-12), there is nothing in the context

52. Note the detailed discussion of Mt. 21:43 and its place in Matthew's theology by Marguerat, *Jugement*, 314-324.

to suggest that he is speaking only of the Jewish leadership; the background to this pronouncement is the declaration that 'no-one in Israel' (not just the leaders) can match this Gentile's faith.[53]

So what about the apparently sympathetic 'crowds' of chapters 21-23 and elsewhere? Are they to be involved despite themselves in the downfall provoked by their leaders' failure? D.E. Garland,[54] while recognising the positive attitude to the crowd in the earlier part of the gospel, argues that in chapters 21ff Matthew has prepared the ground for this unhappy conclusion. The crowd's acclamation of Jesus as 'Son of David' (21: 15-16) is shown to be inadequate (22:41-46); their enthusiasm has not reached the point of full acceptance of Jesus as God's son. If they continue to follow their 'blind guides' (23:16,24), both will fall into the pit together (15:14). For so long as the crowds remain potentially winnable, they are presented as distinct from their leaders, but if Jesus' warnings are not heeded they cannot avoid being judged along with them. So, despite all the earlier favourable language about the crowd, when we come to the passion narrative it seems that their choice has been made; they have 'sided with the wrong camp'. Thus Jesus at his arrest addresses 'the crowds' as those who have now turned against him (26:55), and by the time of the trial before Pilate the chief priests and elders have the crowd firmly on their side, calling for the release of Barabbas and the death of Jesus (27:15-23).

Historically speaking, of course, not all these various 'crowds' would have been composed of the same people. So it is gratuitous to imagine that the hostility of the Jerusalem crowd indicates that the crowds who had listened eagerly to Jesus' teaching in Galilee had now 'changed sides'. And it shows a regrettable lack of historical realism when some preachers suggest that the same 'crowds' who welcomed Jesus into the city in 21:9 had turned against him by chapter 27, particularly since Matthew himself so carefully distinguishes in 21:10-11 between 'the city' who did not recognise Jesus and the Galilean pilgrim 'crowds' who introduced him to them. In considering such questions it is important to bear in mind the sustained contrast between Galilee as the place of light and Jerusalem as the place of darkness which is a marked feature of Matthew's narrative.[55]

But in terms of the narrative development of chapters 21-27 we cannot help noticing the movement of the Jerusalem crowd from sympathetic detachment to active hostility, from being at least open to Jesus' claims to casting in their lot with his opponents. Matthew seems

53. Most recent editions and commentaries agree that this reading is more likely to be original than the majority reading 'not even in Israel', an assimilation to the Lucan parallel.

54. Garland, *Intention*, 39-41 (cf 213f).

55. See above pp. 138-139.

to be saying by this means that the judgement which Israel's leaders are bringing on themselves will not affect only them, but those who have cast in their lot with them. The effect of this will be the destruction not just of the establishment, but of Jerusalem itself. And the loss of the nation's capital and centre of its religious life is more than the rejection of a failed leadership. Whatever the status of individual Jews, the nation of Israel as officially constituted cannot survive its leaders' downfall.[56]

If this conclusion can be drawn even from the development of the narrative, it is put beyond doubt by the terrible conclusion to which the trial scene is brought when Pilate, 'before the crowd', disclaims personal responsibility for Jesus' death, and 'all the people answered, "His blood on us and on our children" ' (27:24-25). The shocking character of this pronouncement is made worse by the unfortunate tendency of English versions to translate it in the form of a wish, 'His blood *be* on us and on our children'. This is quite unjustified. No verb is expressed in the Greek, and the sequence of the passage indicates a simple indicative verb: Pilate asserts that he *is* innocent of this man's blood, and the people respond, 'His blood *is* on us and on our children', i.e. we accept the responsibility which you disclaim.[57] But even so it is a startling statement. This verse more than any other is the basis of Matthew's reputation for anti-Judaism, and has been used repeatedly over the centuries to justify Christian persecution of Jews.

The breadth of scope of this declaration is emphasised both by the attribution to '*all* the people' (emphatically not just the chief priests and elders) and by the extension of responsibility to 'our children'.[58] Moreover, 'the people' does not here represent ὄχλος, the normal term for 'crowds', but λαός, which in Matthew is generally used with special reference to Israel as the 'people of God'.[59] In contrast with the Gentile governor, the λαός declares its acceptance of responsibility.

This is Matthew's way of indicating that what happened in Jerusalem that Passover was not the capricious wish of a volatile *ad hoc* crowd under the temporary influence of the wicked priests, but a deliberate decision by a representative group of Israel which was to have lasting consequences for the nation. In view of the emphasis on the coming judgement on Jerusalem which we have seen above, it seems likely that Matthew had the events of AD 70 particularly in mind when he included

---

56. For a similar assessment see Hare, *Persecution*, 151-152; Légasse, in Didier, *Matthieu*, 418-420.
57. The phrase is a familiar Old Testament idiom for responsibility for someone's death: see e.g. Lv. 20:9; Dt. 19:10; Jos. 2:19; 2 Sa. 1:16; etc.
58. Similarly in the Old Testament such responsibility was sometimes understood to be hereditary, 2 Sa. 3:29; 1 Ki. 2:33; it could even affect a whole city, Je. 26:15.
59. See Senior, *Passion*, 258-259 with references to many other discussions of Matthew's use of λαός.

this conclusion to the trial scene; the nation which has rejected its Messiah will have to face the consequences within 'this generation' (when the 'children' of that Jerusalem crowd would bear the brunt). While it cannot be too strongly emphasised that Matthew 27:25 must not be twisted into a tool for continuing anti-Jewish prejudice and worse,[60] it clearly marks Matthew's conviction that the rejection of Jesus was to usher in a radical new stage in the *Heilsgeschichte*, as a result of which the special status of the Jews as the people of God could not continue unaffected.

CONTINUITY AND DISCONTINUITY

We have noted that the reference to a new nation, ἔθνος (singular), in Matthew 21:43 is generally taken to indicate something less crude than a mere substitution of the Gentiles for the Jews as the people of God. In the next section we shall be considering the place of the Gentiles in Matthew's vision of the kingdom of heaven, and I shall there take issue with the suggestion of some interpreters that Matthew sees no further hope for Jews and therefore no need to preach the gospel to them.[61] But if that is not the implication of the message of 'judgement on Israel' which we have been considering above, what does it mean, and what is the nature of this new ἔθνος?

Earlier in this chapter I have referred to C.H. Dodd's careful delineation of the nature of the continuity and discontinuity between Israel and Jesus, Israel and the church. The following passage from Dodd, commenting on Jesus' alleged saying about the destruction and restoration of the temple, seems to me to focus the issue admirably. 'The manifest disintegration of the existing system is to be preliminary to the appearance of a new way of religion and a new community to embody it. And yet, it is the *same* temple, first destroyed, that is to be rebuilt. The new community is still Israel; there is continuity through the discontinuity. It is not a matter of replacement but of resurrection.'[62]

Not replacement, but resurrection. A resurrection *is* in one sense a replacement. The new body is not the same as the old; indeed it needs to be very unlike it if it is to function adequately in a new sphere of existence. But there is a continuity of identity; the resurrected person is the same person as the one who died. In one sense all is new; in another sense there is no change. Is this then a suitable model for understanding Matthew's view of the new people of God?

It may be worth noting in passing how Dodd's language echoes in

---

60. See especially the passionate repudiation of this misuse of the passage by H. Kosmala, ' "His Blood on us and on our Children" (The Background of Mat. 27,24-25)', *ASTI* 7 (1970) 94-126; also J.A. Fitzmyer, *TS* 26 (1965) 667-671.
61. Below pp. 235-237.
62. Dodd, *Founder*, 90.

other imagery the thought expressed in Paul's famous allegory of the olive-tree in Romans 11:17-24, where the loss of many branches of the original tree and the inclusion of new branches from another stock results in a different and better (more fruitful) tree, but the identity remains; it is still the olive tree, still Israel, so that any of the original branches which are grafted back will find it still 'their own olive tree'. Not that Matthew must be made to speak the language of Paul, of course, but the fact that one other early Jewish Christian could come to this assessment of God's plan for his people suggests that it is not perverse to look for a similar tension between continuity and discontinuity in Matthew's view of Israel.

In a passage entitled 'The end of Israel's privilege', D. Marguerat sets out the basic Jewish understanding of election. 'The fact of belonging genealogically to God's chosen people gives every Jew the right to avail himself of the blessing given to the patriarchs. Envisaged as a corporate personality, Abraham incorporates every Israelite in his own righteousness and makes him a beneficiary of his own merits. *The guarantee of salvation offered by descent from Abraham will never be truly gainsaid* in the amazingly varied range of eschatological schemes offered by later Judaism.'[63] John the Baptist was therefore making a direct assault on essential Jewish theology with his denial that being a 'son of Abraham' could be a guarantee of salvation (Matthew 3:9), and the same shock would be felt by those who heard Jesus' words about the inclusion of 'many from east and west' with the Jewish patriarchs at the messianic banquet, while 'the sons of the kingdom' are excluded (8:11-12). Here is a radical challenge to the whole concept of what it means to be 'the people of God'. If membership is not by physical descent, what is to take its place?

In the case of the centurion, which gives rise to Jesus' radical words in 8:11-12, it is *faith* which has taken the place of racial descent as the basis of membership in the messianic banquet; and that faith has been presented in the centurion's story as a practical reliance on the authority and compassion of Jesus. In the strikingly similar story of the Canaanite woman (15:21-28) Jesus' initial reluctance to share the privileges of Israel with a Gentile 'dog' is overcome by a similar 'faith' in Jesus' power and willingness to heal. So, in line with Matthew's presentation of Jesus as himself the true Israel, those who respond to Jesus, even if not Jews, find through him the blessings of Israel.

Conversely, Jesus' whole appeal, like that of John, is based on the assumption that salvation is not guaranteed to Jews as such, but to those who repent and produce 'fruit that befits repentance' (3:8; for the important theme of such 'fruit' in Jesus' teaching cf. 7:16-20; 12:33-37; 21:41,43), those who enter the 'way of righteousness' in

63. Marguerat, *Jugement*, 268-269; his italics.

response to the preaching of John and Jesus (21:31-32). But this is not a simple matter of ethical reformation; it involves a response to *Jesus*. A superficial claim to follow him is not enough, and will merit the ultimate sentence pronounced by Jesus himself, '*I* never knew you; depart from *me*' (7:21-23). What makes the difference between those who ultimately stand or fall is their response to *Jesus'* words (7:24-27). The criterion at the eschatological judgement will be what men have done to *him*; indeed he himself will be the judge (25:31-46).

We shall be thinking further in the final chapter about the christo-logical implications of this focus on Jesus in the context of salvation and judgement. At this point we must notice that Matthew's under-standing of the new constitution of the people of God is focused in Jesus. So those who belong to Jesus, whatever their racial origin, become part of the people of God, and conversely those who are born Jews must nonetheless find their salvation in him rather than in their genealogy. There is therefore a real discontinuity, a new beginning. But because Matthew has been at pains to show that Jesus is himself the true fulfilment of Israel, there is continuity as well. Jesus' primary appeal is therefore to Israel (15:24), and his first disciples are all Jews, with a mission to other Jews (10:5-6). Israel is expected to welcome its Messiah and to find in him the fulfilment of its Old Testament destiny. But while many Jews have done so, so that in them the true Israel continues to find its expression, official Judaism has failed to respond, and Matthew has no doubt that it has thereby stepped outside the bounds of the true people of God, and lost its place at the centre of the *Heilsgeschichte*. He finds no pleasure in recording the fact, but the centrality of Jesus in his theology of fulfilment leaves him no alternative.

This tension between continuity and discontinuity needs to be carefully stated. Thus while D.R.A. Hare is right in one sense in saying that according to Matthew 'God has rejected Israel',[64] and that for him 'Israel is no longer the People of God',[65] he is going too far in speaking of this as a 'permanent and complete rejection of Israel', which involves Matthew in ruling out any further mission to Jews. The end of Israel as an institutional 'people of God' does not rule out the reconstitution (or 'resurrection', to use Dodd's word) of 'Israel' in Jesus, and the inclusion in this reconstituted Israel of many individual Jews. Similarly in his presentation of Matthew's view of 'Israel replaced by the church'[66] while Hare recognises a 'tension between continuity and discontinuity' in the rest of the New Testament, he finds this tension 'almost non-existent in Matthew's view of Israel and the church'; Matthew is not presenting a theology of a 'True Israel', nor even of a 'New Israel', but

64. This is the heading of a section of Hare, *Persecution*, 152-156.
65. *Ibid.* 156.
66. *Ibid.* 156-162.

rather of a 'new people of God' which is not Israel. But in stating that
'for Matthew there is no continuity between Israel and the Church'[67]
he fails to do justice to the fulfilment motif which we have considered
earlier. This new people of God is indeed the 'Congregation of the
Messiah', as he rightly states, but that Messiah is the Messiah *of Israel*,
and is himself the fulfilment of Israel.

A less one-sided picture emerges from G.N. Stanton's interesting
comparison, which we noted earlier,[68] between the theology of Matthew
and that of the second-century Christian text conventionally known as
5 Ezra. Stanton sees in 5 Ezra the continuation of a distinctively
Matthean strain of Christianity. Its main theme is the replacement of
Israel by a 'people soon to come' (from the point of view of the
pseudonymous author, Ezra) which is to inherit all the privileges which
Israel has lost by its disobedience. Matthew 21:43 (and its surrounding
context) is clearly drawn on for this theology of transfer to 'another
people' (*gens altera*). So there is a clear sense of discontinuity; Israel
has been rejected. And yet for the author of 5 Ezra while this 'people',
the Christian church, is now irrevocably separated from Israel,
nonetheless both church and Israel have the same 'mother', Jerusalem,
and various characteristics of Old Testament Israel continue to be
attributed to the church. 'There is a complete rupture between the
church and Israel, but there is also continuity. The church is neither
the new Israel nor the true Israel, nor the new people of God, but
simply "the people". . . . 5 Ezra is at the opposite end of the theological
spectrum from Marcion.' In all this Stanton sees 5 Ezra as in basic
agreement with the theology of Matthew, who also 'cannot mask the
rupture which has taken place, but in his redaction of his sources he
takes pains to stress the continuity of the church and Israel'.[69]

'IT COULD HAPPEN TO YOU TOO'

But if Matthew has a strong conviction that Israel faces judgement
and the loss of its privileged position as the people of God, he will not
allow his church to hold this view with a smug, 'holier-than-thou' kind
of complacency. Israel's failure has come about through its unwillingness
to respond to God's initiative in Jesus, and such unresponsiveness could
happen again. In the same way that Paul warned the newly-ingrafted
branches of the olive-tree against assuming that their place in the tree
was any more guaranteed than that of their predecessors (Rom.
11:20-22), Matthew wants his readers, belonging as they do to the newly
reconstituted people of God, to realise that they too could lose their

67. *Ibid.* 170.
68. See above pp. 104-105, referring to Stanton's article in *JTS* 28 (1977) 67-83.
69. *Ibid.* 76,79.

place of privilege. ' "It happened to the Jews; it could happen to you."
This is the constant refrain.'[70]
Thus Israel's failure is not simply a matter of history; it is also a
warning. The kingdom of God is taken away from them and given to
another nation *producing its fruits* (21:41,43), and the following parable
of the wedding feast concludes with the sobering account of the expulsion
from the feast of one of the 'replacement' guests who proved not to be
properly attired (22:11-13). Entrance to the feast may be free and
unexpected, but it is not without conditions. The tenure of the vineyard
may be lost by its new tenants as well as by the old ones. It all depends
on continued faithfulness to God and response to Jesus (7:24-27), on
a faith which remains alive, and a righteousness which continues to
exceed that of the scribes and Pharisees.

In many of the accusations directed against the Jewish leaders it is
not difficult to detect at least a side-glance at tendencies in the church
of Matthew's own day which seemed to him to threaten its continued
status as the people of God. Just as we have seen that the historical
disciples of Jesus function for Matthew as 'transparent' for the church
of his own day,[71] so it is also for Jesus' Jewish opponents. The scribes
and Pharisees are attacked for their love of title and position (23:5-7),
but they are a warning to 'you', who have one teacher, one Father,
and one master, the Christ (23:8-12). Similarly the examples of
ostentatious religious observance in 6:1-18 are offered so that 'you'
may not be like those 'hypocrites'; and in fact it is not only unbelieving
Jews who are stigmatised as 'hypocrites', but also disciples of Jesus
who prove unworthy of the name (7:5; 24:51).[72]

We shall be considering further in the next chapter the remarkable
emphasis in Matthew on the church as a *corpus mixtum*, which comes
to a climax in the parables of the weeds and of the net, but is present
in several passages.[73] Here Matthew's theology of the church seems to
be closely related to his theology of Israel. 'Israel' has not ceased to
exist, but the majority of the apparent members of Israel have failed
to fulfil their place in the purpose of God, resulting in the paradoxical
presence of 'sons of the kingdom' in the 'outer darkness' which they
had understood to be the place of non-Israelites (8:11-12); but among
the many from east and west who come to take their place it appears
that there is no more automatic guarantee of enjoying the promised
blessings than for their predecessors – for them too the 'outer darkness'
remains a possibility (22:13; 25:30; cf. 13:42,50). Professed membership

70. S.Neill, *The Interpretation of the New Testament, 1861-1961* (Oxford University
Press, 1964) 277.
71. See above pp. 200-201.
72. See Légasse, in Didier, *Matthieu,* 426-427.
73. See below pp. 275-278.

of the people of God has always been a privilege which requires an appropriate response to God if it is to retain any meaning and any promise of God's blessing. In this sense, nothing has changed with the reconstitution of Israel in Jesus. Repentance still requires appropriate fruit (3:8-9); it is the son who does his father's will who is the true son, rather than the one who proclaims his loyalty (21:28-32). Even those who address Jesus as 'Lord, Lord' may prove in the event to be those whom he never knew (7:21-23).

So Israel's failure is no excuse for complacency on the part of the church; rather it is a solemn warning of what it means to be, and to continue, the people of God. 'It happened to them; it could happen to you.'[74]

E. THE GOSPEL FOR ALL NATIONS

MATTHEW'S UNIVERSALISM

In an earlier chapter we considered the view of Clark, Strecker and others that only a Gentile could have produced a gospel which takes so negative a view of Israel.[75] In addition to the suggestion (which I there called in question) that at certain points the gospel betrays its author's unfamiliarity with Jewish matters, the basis of this view lies in an attempt to account for the twin features of Matthew's theology, his hostility to official Judaism and his enthusiasm for the inclusion of non-Jews in the people of God. I proposed there that the paradox of 'Jewishness' and 'anti-Jewishness' in this gospel is better accounted for by the reaction of a Jewish follower of Jesus to the fact that the majority of his fellow-Jews have gone the other way than by Gentile authorship, and I believe that the discussion of Matthew's theology of Israel in this chapter has provided support for that proposal.

We need not return now to the question of authorship, but it is important in this chapter that we recognise that Matthew's theology of the 'rejection of Israel' carries as its counterpart an openness to Gentiles and a consequent acceptance that the gospel must be preached to all nations. We have seen in the last section that he envisages a people of God reconstituted by the admission of 'many from east and west', in which racial origin is no longer the basis of belonging.

Already very near the beginning of his gospel Matthew has given notice of this theme, in that the first worshippers of the new 'King of the Jews' are not Jews but men from the East, who come, as the Queen of Sheba came to the son of David, 'bearing spices and very much

74. Cf. Garland, *Intention*, 214-215; Marguerat, *Jugement*, 322-324, 404-405.
75. See above pp. 102-108.

gold' (1 Ki. 10:2,10). Nor is the story of the magi the only part of the introduction to the gospel which points outside Israel; the infant Messiah immediately goes off to Egypt (2:13-15), and after his return the impact of his ministry spreads outside Jewish territory to Syria and the Decapolis (4:24-25), while even the chosen location of his ministry is deliberately dubbed 'Galilee of the *Gentiles*' (4:15). The Jesus who is so carefully introduced in 1:1-17 as the Messiah of Israel (though perhaps significantly the four women included in vv. 3-6 were all probably non-Israelites!) is thus shown even before the account of his ministry is properly under way to belong not only to Israel but also to the nations around.[76]

After the account of Jesus' teaching in chapters 5-7, the narrative resumes with two miracles of healing which again serve together to underline the universality of his mission. The strongly Jewish colouring of the healing of the leper in 8:1-4 ('Show yourself to the priest' . . . 'Moses commanded' . . . 'a proof to them [the Jews?]') is immediately offset by the response to a Gentile centurion in 8:5-13. Comparison of Matthew's handling of this story with Luke's makes it clear that for Matthew its main focus is on the fact that the man was not a Jew.[77] The narrative alone might have sufficed to make this point, but Matthew goes out of his way to underline it by the way he tells the story. Jesus' testing question, 'Shall *I* come and heal him?',[78] raises the issue of the appropriateness of a Jewish healer being called to a Gentile patient, or even entering a Gentile house, and the centurion's judicious reply evokes the comment 'With no-one in Israel have I found such faith'. Matthew's inclusion at this point of the saying about 'many from east and west' puts beyond doubt the significance which he saw in the event. It depicts the Jewish patriarchs sharing the messianic banqueting table with these 'many', while the 'sons of the kingdom' find themselves excluded and experiencing the fate which Jewish orthodoxy assigned to the Gentiles ('outer darkness . . . weeping and gnashing of teeth'). This saying sums up Matthew's theology of the people of God: the membership has been both widened and narrowed (by the exclusion of some Jews); there is both continuity (it remains the messianic banquet of Israel) and discontinuity; and the key to membership has been clearly indicated in the preceding verse as a *faith* in Jesus which may be found in a Gentile as well as (or better than!) in Israel.

A closely similar story of Jesus' response to Gentile faith occurs in 15:21-28. There is the same sequence of emphasis on the suppliant's non-Jewish origin, testing question by Jesus on the appropriateness of

76. I have developed this theme in relation especially to chapter 2 in *NTS* 27 (1980/81) 237-240.
77. See my discussion of the passage in I.H. Marshall (ed.), *New Testament Interpretation* (Exeter: Paternoster, 1977) 253-264.
78. See *ibid.* 256-257 for the reasons for punctuating v 7 as a question.

his extending his ministry outside the 'house of Israel', a refusal to be put off and a humble but insistent reply by the woman, which evokes Jesus' commendation of her *faith*, resulting in instant healing by a word alone. It is important to note that it is precisely in this context that we find the one clear statement in Matthew's gospel that Jesus' mission was limited to 'the lost sheep of the house of Israel' (15:24). It is remarkable how often this verse is quoted out of context as a proof-text for the 'parochialism' of Matthew, but it is nothing of the sort. While it is indicative in form, it functions in the dialogue more as a question, a test of faith, a statement of position which invites (and receives) a counter-proposal, and it is that counter-proposal which wins Jesus' assent and carries the day. The narrative itself negates the apparent absoluteness of 15:24. Jesus *is* sent to lost sheep outside the house of Israel; there is plenty of bread for the 'dogs' as well! The whole story is one which, if read with wooden literalism, gives good reason to complain of the 'chauvinistic' attitude it displays,[79] but which, if read within its total literary context and with a due openness to a dialogue conducted not so much by sober propositions as by verbal fencing, fits well into Matthew's theology of Jesus as the Messiah of Israel – *and* of all those who respond in faith.

Nor does 15:21-28 stand in isolation. It follows the debate with scribes from Jerusalem, which includes Jesus' fundamental pronouncement (15:11) undercutting the whole basis of the ritual purity which made practical separation between Jew and Gentile inevitable. His encounter with the Canaanite woman gives practical expression to this declaration of principle, and it is succeeded by further ministry among presumably Gentile crowds who 'glorified the God of Israel' (15:31). Among them, as previously among the Jews (14:13-21), he shares the blessing of miraculous feeding, as Moses had done for Israel in the wilderness (15:32-38). Nor was this the only time Jesus ventured into Gentile territory during his ministry according to Matthew (cf 8:28-34; 16:13ff).

So when in the parables of chapters 21-22 Jesus speaks of replacement by 'another nation' and of the invitation to the wedding feast of a motley crowd ('both bad and good') from the thoroughfares in place of the originally invited guests, the ground has been well prepared. The blessings of Israel are not to be for Israel alone. The mission of the disciples which Jesus had initially deliberately restricted to Israel (10: 5-6,23) is soon to be 'preached throughout the whole world, as a testimony to all nations' (24:14), and the devotion of the woman who anoints Jesus' head before the passion will be remembered 'wherever this gospel is preached in the whole world' (26:13).

Against this background the culmination of the gospel comes as no surprise. The risen Jesus has been given all authority in heaven and on

---

79. See especially the remarkably hostile comments of Beare, *Matthew*, 340-344.

earth, and so his followers are now to go and make disciples of all nations (28:18-19). It is the outcome to which the gospel, for all its focus on Jesus' mission to Israel, has been pointing throughout. And it is important to notice that the basis of this universal discipleship is spelled out in terms not of the rites and duties of Israel, circumcision and the keeping of the law,[80] but in terms related specifically to Jesus himself, baptism into the name of Father, *Son*, and Holy Spirit, and obedience to the commands of *Jesus*; it must be so, for it is Jesus who has the universal authority, and it is Jesus himself who will be with them in carrying out their task. Thus the focus of the people of God is now explicitly and exclusively not in racial descent or in solidarity with a political community but in relationship with the Son of God. On that basis of belonging, the Gentile stands on the same footing as the Jew, and Matthew can look forward to the completion of the truly universal ἐκκλησία which he has already begun to experience.

ARE THE JEWS INCLUDED?

'All nations' sounds about as inclusive as anyone might wish. But 'nations' represents τὰ ἔθνη, which in this plural form often has the technical meaning of 'the Gentiles'. Is it possible, then, that it has that meaning here, and that the so-called Great Commission is for the preaching of the gospel to 'all the Gentiles', thus excluding the Jews from potential membership of the reconstituted people of God? This view has been put forward especially by D.R.A. Hare and D.J. Harrington.[81]

Their case is based on the general usage of ἔθνος in biblical Greek, where they have little difficulty in showing that 'Gentiles' is its more frequent meaning; this applies to its uses in Matthew as a whole as well. They are aware, however, that the fuller phrase πάντα τὰ ἔθνη occurs four times in Matthew, and that it is at least arguable that this idiom has a different focus. These passages are 24:9,14; 25:32 and 28:19. In each case they are able to offer an interpretation which is consistent with the phrase excluding Jews, but it is not at all clear that this is the most natural interpretation in any of these cases. In particular they find it necessary to restrict the application of 24:9 to hostility experienced by Christians in their mission to the *non-Jewish* world, and to take the great judgement scene of 25:31-46 as depicting only the judgement of Gentiles, that of Jews being made on a different basis. These proposals

80. Meier, *Law*, 28-29, emphasises the radical significance of the dispensing with circumcision at this point.
81. D.R.A. Hare & D.J. Harrington, ' "Make Disciples of all the Gentiles" (Mt 28:19)', *CBQ* 37 (1975) 359-369. This interpretation was already proposed in Hare, *Persecution*, 148, and had been put forward also by K.W. Clark, *JBL* 66 (1947) 166, and by Walker, *Heilsgeschichte*, 111-113.

are possible, but few commentators have taken these texts in this way, and it looks rather as if the interpretation is required in order to fit the thesis. Underlying the linguistic argument is the conviction already spelled out at length in Hare's dissertation that Matthew's theology of the rejection of Israel is such that there can be no place for any further mission to Israel by the Christian church. If, as I have suggested above,[82] this is an excessively negative interpretation of Matthew's theology, then there is less reason to suppose that πάντα τὰ ἔθνη in 28:19 (and in its other Matthean uses) should be interpreted as excluding Israel.

Already before the writing of Hare and Harrington's article W. Trilling[83] had argued strongly for the inclusion of Israel in πάντα τὰ ἔθνη, and their article was framed partly in response to his arguments. Their article in turn provoked a response from J.P. Meier,[84] who reconsiders in detail the Matthean use of ἔθνος, and concludes that in all the passages where Matthew is not simply repeating tradition found in Mark or 'Q' but is either introducing new material or significantly modifying the tradition (and this category includes all the uses of the full phrase πάντα τὰ ἔθνη) it is at least doubtful whether the meaning 'Gentiles' is intended, and in most cases highly improbable. Meier therefore concludes from general Matthean usage alone that in 28:19 the right translation is 'all peoples', which includes the Jews within the Christian missionary perspective.[85]

Meier's argument is set up purely on the basis of Matthew's linguistic usage. It would be strengthened if he added also the general theological perspective of the gospel, which, as we have seen, embraces both the conviction of the end of Israel's privileged status as the people of God and the hope, indeed the assumption, that individual Jews will respond to their Messiah. It is Matthew's regret that their number is not larger, that they remain only a remnant while the majority of Israel has rejected God's appeal in Jesus, but there is no indication that the church should not continue to seek, and to expect, Jewish converts. It is, after all, in Galilee that the mission to all nations is launched, and the characterisation of Galilee as the place of dawning light (4:12-16) has not been revoked but rather reinforced throughout the gospel;[86] and those sent out are themselves all Jews. If it is true that membership of the people of God is no longer to be seen as based on racial descent, neither can it be thought to be precluded by racial descent. To be a Jew in itself

82. See above pp. 229-230.
83. Trilling, *Israel*, 26-28. Cf. a briefer discussion by B.J. Hubbard, *The Matthean Redaction of a Primitive Apostolic Commissioning: an Exegesis of Matthew 28:16-20* (Missoula: Scholars' Press, 1974) 84-87.
84. J.P. Meier, 'Nations or Gentiles in Matthew 28:19?', *CBQ* 39 (1977) 94-102.
85. Gundry, *Matthew*, 595-596, while he makes no specific reference to this debate, offers further reasons for understanding πάντα τὰ ἔθνη here as including Israel.
86. See above pp. 138-139.

neither makes a person a member of the people of God nor excludes him from it. What matters, as 28:18-20 makes very clear, is his relationship with Jesus, and that is open to all.

A FUTURE FOR ISRAEL?

At the end of the passage which more clearly than any other expresses Matthew's conviction of the final loss of Israel's privilege, brought about by the climactic guilt of 'this generation' and symbolised by the desolation of 'your house', and preceding the more detailed discourse on judgement focused again on the destruction of the temple, there occurs an enigmatic statement about the future: 'You will not see me from now on until you say, "Blessed is he who comes in the name of the Lord" ' (23:39).

The immediate focus in context is surely on the first part of the statement, 'You will not see me from now on . . .'. The last phrase represents ἀπ' ἄρτι, a significant phrase introduced by Matthew also in 26:29,64 to indicate the beginning of a new situation. This is the end of Jesus' direct appeal to Israel; he is leaving, and they will find themselves abandoned. The fact that chapter 24 follows immediately indicates that it is the impending judgement that is primarily in mind. But why is the 'until' clause added, and to what does its quotation of the greeting of Psalm 118:26 refer? This same greeting has already been used on Jesus' first arrival in Jerusalem (21:9); does he then expect to enter the city again? If so, when, and with what result?

Commentators offer a wide variety of interpretations of this verse, apparently based not so much on a necessary meaning in the words themselves, but on their understanding of Matthew's theology of Israel as a whole. Some see here the prospect of a future change of mind by Israel, perhaps in line with Paul's vision of the ultimate salvation of 'all Israel' (Rom. 11:25-26); others go so far as to find here a future reversal of the verdict of 21:43, 'a return of the kingdom to Israel at the parousia'.[87] Some wish to leave the outcome open: 'The quotation of Psalm 118 keeps open the way Jesus will be received – as consuming Judge or welcomed King';[88] others feel that the context of condemnation and judgement is decisive against any hope that Israel as a whole will ever again welcome Jesus: 'From now on, Israel will know Jesus only as judge. The *Heilsruf* can only be viewed as a greeting for the final judge.'[89]

---

87. So Gundry, *Matthew*, 474.
88. Carson, *Matthew*, 487-488.
89. Garland, *Intention*, 208. Garland provides, *ibid.* 204-209, a full bibliography of discussions of this verse up to 1979.

A recent dicussion by D.C. Allison[90] rightly points out that the words
ἕως ἂν εἴπητε ('until you say') express not so much a conviction that
this will happen, as an indefinite possibility, so that the sentence functions
as a conditional prophecy, 'You will only see me on condition that you
say . . .'. Thus while Allison, unlike Garland, understands the greeting
as one of positive acceptance, he believes that the verse leaves open
whether it will ever be spoken by Israel. 'The date of the redemption
is contingent on Israel's acceptance of the person and work of Jesus.'
Thus the verse 'was evidently formulated to give expression to the
conviction that, if Israel would repent, the end would come'. So far
that repentance has not taken place; until it does, the judgement which
so clearly fills the horizon in this section of the gospel is all that can
be expected.

Thus while this verse in no way revokes the judgement pronounced
on unbelieving Israel, it does not exclude the possibility of future
repentance. But it makes no promise that this will ever happen, and
Israel's stance both in the period of Jesus' ministry and at the time of
Matthew's writing gives no ground for optimism. The gospel which is
for all nations is open to Israel too, but Israel as a community has as
yet shown no sign of accepting it.

F. MATTHEW AND ANTI-JUDAISM

We have noted the way Christian prejudice against Jews, and often
direct persecution of them, has frequently found its justification, however
unfairly, in the cry of the people in 27:25, which only Matthew reports.
But that verse is part of a general sense of hostility and rejection towards
at least the leaders of the Jews in Jerusalem, and sometimes clearly
extending beyond only the leadership, which seems to grow in intensity
as the gospel progresses and the rejection of the Messiah by his own
people becomes more final. How far, then, may Matthew be charged
with responsibility for the shameful story of Christian anti-Judaism?

In particular it is worth asking how he compares in this respect with
other New Testament writers, with John's constant diatribe against 'the
Jews'[91] as the enemies of Jesus, with the writer of Hebrews whose
scholarly discussion of the relation of the old covenant with the new
seems to leave little room for a continuing place for Judaism in the
purposes of God, and especially with Paul, whose agonised reflections
on the fate of his own nation range from the dismissive judgement of

90. D.C. Allison, 'Matt. 23:39 = Luke 13:35b as a Conditional Prophecy', *JSNT* 18
(1983) 75-84.
91. See however M. Lowe, *NovT* 18 (1976) 101-130, for the proposal that John uses
οἱ 'Ιουδαῖοι to mean specifically 'the Judaeans', not Jews as a whole; his proposal is taken
up by Schillebeeckx, *Christ*, 335-336 and 872-873, n. 36.

1 Thessalonians 2:14-16 to the elaborate scenario for the ultimate
salvation of 'all Israel' worked out in Romans 9-11. How far do they
speak with the same voice?

D. Marguerat pronounces the viewpoints of Matthew and of Paul
'irreconcilable', since the very proposal ('Have they stumbled so as to
fall?') which Paul dismisses in Romans 11:11 with a firm μὴ γένοιτο
seems to express exactly the view of Matthew. Paul is at pains to
maintain, despite appearances, that God's promises and election of
Israel as his own people have not been revoked; but for Matthew Israel
is no longer the people of God. Paul wants his Gentile readers to grasp
their solidarity with Israel; Matthew, writing at a time when the conflict
with the synagogue has reached the point of separation, presents Israel
only as a figure of disobedience, disinherited by God.[92]

A similar contrast between Paul and Matthew is drawn by D.R.A.
Hare. Whereas Paul saw the rejection and replacement of Israel as
partial and temporary, for Matthew it was complete and permanent.
Paul stresses the continuity of the church with Israel, whereas Matthew
can see only discontinuity: for him the church is not True Israel, or
even New Israel, but a 'third race'. The difference of viewpoints is to
be explained by the different historical situations to which the two
writers belong: Paul writes before the Jewish War, and in the context
of a successful Gentile mission, Matthew after the destruction of
Jerusalem, and in the light of the failure of his church's attempted
mission to Jews.[93]

Both Hare and Marguerat rightly emphasise the difference in situation
and aims between Paul and Matthew. But it is questionable whether
that difference of perspective has led to such 'irreconcilable' attitudes
to Israel as they suggest. It is instructive to turn from these writers who
compare Matthew with Paul from the point of view of their ecclesiology,
to another who compares them at the ethical level. R. Mohrlang's
conclusions are remarkably different: looking at their respective attitudes
to the (Jewish) law, he characterises Matthew as the one who remains
closer to his Israelite heritage, and Paul as the one who breaks away.
For Matthew the church is 'still under the jurisdiction of the Mosaic
law (albeit as now interpreted by Jesus)', whereas for Paul 'the question
of legal authority has ceased to be of central concern'. From the point
of view of their attitude to the law, then, 'it can only be concluded that
Matthew's viewpoint is closer to that of traditional Judaism, while
Paul's represents a more radical break with it.'[94]

The questions of Israel as the people of God and of the continuing
relevance of Israel's law for the Christian church are, of course, not

92. Marguerat, *Jugement*, 381-398.
93. Hare, *Persecution*, 152-153, 156-157, 164-166.
94. Mohrlang, *Matthew and Paul*, 42-47.

the same. But these differing accounts of the relation between Matthew and Paul show that any assessment of how 'pro-Jewish' or 'anti-Jewish' the New Testament writers were will depend on the kind of questions asked.

If by 'anti-Judaism' is meant the view that the unbelief of the majority of the Jewish people has forfeited their privileged position as the unique people of God, that there is now a new basis of membership in the people of God based not on racial descent but on relationship with Jesus, then Matthew would be anti-Jewish. But so also surely would Paul, with his allegory of the olive-tree which has both lost many of its former branches and gained many new ones from a 'wild olive'. In this change of membership Paul is able to see the purpose of God, fulfilling his promises to Israel. But so can Matthew, if we were right in tracing out at the beginning of this chapter his view that in Jesus and in his people 'Israel' finds its true fulfilment. This is not 'anti-Judaism'. Matthew no less than Paul accepts and welcomes the Israelite basis of the people of God in its reconstituted form, as Mohrlang's study shows. The church is, in Dodd's phrase, the 'resurrection' of Israel; it is Israel reborn.

But what of the (larger) part of the old Israel which remains outside? Their failure to respond to God's initiative reflects many similar failures of Israel in Old Testament times, when it was only a remnant in which the 'Israel-ideal' continued. But this time there is a more ultimate dimension to the pattern: it is the Messiah himself they have rejected, and so repentance now must involve not only a return to covenant obedience as before, but the acceptance of Jesus as the new focus of the people of God. The continuing mission to Jews is aimed at precisely this end, and we have seen no reason to believe that Matthew was other than enthusiastic about that continuing mission. But as long as it has not succeeded, it is hardly 'anti-Judaism' to record the fact, and to continue to warn of the consequences (for the new people of God as well as for the old) of not responding to Jesus.

A sensitive study of 'L "antijudaisme" dans l'Evangile selon Matthieu' by S. Légasse,[95] to which I have already referred, makes no attempt to lessen the severity of Matthew's emphasis on the judgement of unrepentant Israel (not merely its leaders), and on the loss of Israel's place of privilege: Israel, by rejecting the Messiah and accepting the responsibility for his death, 'blots itself out from salvation-history', so that 'Israel as such has nothing more to look forward to from God than his judgement and condemnation'.[96] But, he insists, this is not the whole picture, and he goes on to defend Matthew against the charge of 'anti-Judaism'. This is not a 'gospel against the Jews', but a gospel

95. In Didier, *Matthieu*, 417-428.
96. *Ibid.* 424.

for the church, to warn it by Israel's example. Moreover, his theological conviction of Israel's failure does not spring from personal animosity or a desire for revenge, for the same gospel preaches love for enemies. Matthew, far from gloating over the fate of the Jews, longs for them to be saved, to come to Jesus and accept his yoke, so that they may find his rest from the 'heavy loads' of rabbinic requirements (11:28-30; cf. 23:4).

Légasse believes that Matthew has given up any idea of active mission to Jews, and is merely asking the church 'to keep the doors wide open towards Israel' to welcome individual Jews who may wish to avail themselves of Jesus' offer of 'rest'. If, as I have argued, 28:19 does envisage active mission to Jews as well as to other nations, his argument is strengthened. While it is sadly possible (and has often been done) to use Matthew's theology of Israel as a pretext for prejudice and even persecution against the Jews, that was not Matthew's intention, nor may he be fairly charged with incitement to 'anti-Judaism'. He faithfully records the sad fact, no doubt as poignant to him as it was to Paul, of the wrong choice made by the majority of his 'kinsmen by race' and its disastrous consequences for their place in the purpose of God. But he takes no pleasure in it, and evidently hopes that, while the nation as such can no longer claim a place of special privilege, the expanding Christian mission will ensure that Jews will continue to take their place along with 'many from east and west' in the newly reconstituted people of God, in which 'Israel' finds not its rival but its fulfilment.

Matthew does not have cause, as Paul does, to offer an extended discussion of the theology of Israel's election and of what might be the future course of God's dealings with the nation as such. He makes no specific pronouncement about the future salvation of 'all Israel'. It seems likely that his own experiences of Jewish hostility and unresponsiveness to the Christian message leave him less optimistic than Paul about whether a time will ever come when Jerusalem will be willing to say 'Blessed is he who comes in the name of the Lord'. But the man who included 23:39 in his gospel cannot be said to have had no desire for such an outcome, or to have felt that it was incompatible with his theology of judgement. To have lost their special place as the (racial) people of God does not entail that Jews, whether individually or as a community, are denied the opportunity of salvation if they are prepared to respond to their Messiah, and thus to become part of *his ἐκκλησία*, now drawn from 'all nations'.

MATTHEW'S GOSPEL AND THE CHURCH

The ecclesiastical gospel? The pastoral function of the gospel. Matthew's vision of the church.

THE LAST CHAPTER HAS ALREADY INTRODUCED US TO MATTHEW'S UNDERstanding of the church. The fulfilment in Jesus not only of specific hopes and patterns of the Old Testament but also of the very concept of Israel as the people of God has resulted in the formation of a new body which at the same time is and yet is distinct from Israel. In the community of those who belong to Jesus, himself the true fulfilment of Israel, is to be found the new focus of the people of God. Matthew's ecclesiology is thus closely linked with, and dependent on, his christology. Indeed J.P. Meier goes so far as to say, 'The nexus between Christology and ecclesiology is one of the most typical characteristics of Matthew's gospel, yes, even its specificity.'[1]

When we consider Matthew's christology in the next chapter this link will again be in view. In this chapter, however, I want not so much to focus on Matthew's theoretical model of the church, but rather to consider in what way his gospel was designed to contribute to the life and ministry of the church as he knew it. In the process we shall naturally give further consideration to his understanding of the nature of the church as the community of God's people, but if I was right in earlier chapters in picturing Matthew as primarily a pastor and teacher in his church rather than an academic theoretician, we may expect to discern his ecclesiology most effectively as it is applied to the issues of church life.

A. THE ECCLESIASTICAL GOSPEL?

Matthew has traditionally been characterised as 'the ecclesiastical gospel'.[2] How appropriate this designation is depends on what content

---

1. Meier, *Vision*, 216.
2. E.g. F.V. Filson, *The Gospel according to St. Matthew* (London, A & C Black, ²1971) 41. L.T. Johnson, *The Writings of the New Testament* (Philadelphia: Fortress, 1986) 172, begins his discussion of Matthew with the pronouncement, 'Matthew is the gospel of the church'.

is given to the term 'ecclesiastical'. If all that is meant is that Matthew, unlike the other gospels, contains the noun ἐκκλησία, this is hardly a suitable basis for categorising the whole gospel, especially as the word occurs only twice (16:18; 18:17).

I have mentioned above[3] that ἐκκλησία has an obvious background in LXX usage, where it signifies the assembly of God's people, and that therefore its occurrence in Matthew's gospel is not in itself surprising, nor does it necessarily carry with it any sophisticated ecclesiology. In 18:17 its use requires only that the local group of followers of Jesus is understood to be capable of coming together to reach a joint decision on a case involving unacceptable conduct among its membership. In 16:18 its scope is apparently broader, envisaging a single ἐκκλησία resulting from Jesus' ministry, and daringly describing it as *his* rather than God's ἐκκλησία. But, even though the other gospels offer no specific parallel to this sort of language, it is entirely in keeping with what was already familiar usage for Paul, who could speak of himself as having persecuted 'the ἐκκλησία' (Phil. 3:6), and could describe Christian groups corporately as 'the ἐκκλησίαι of Christ' (Rom. 16:16), not to mention the more 'mystical' language of the ἐκκλησία as Christ's body, of which he is the head (Col. 1:18,24). The fact that Matthew is prepared on occasion to use terms which seem to have been widely used in a similar way in the church of his time hardly justifies us in labeling his the 'ecclesiastical gospel'.

Matthew's two uses of ἐκκλησία do not, then, require us to believe that he knew, or even envisaged, a highly developed ecclesiastical organisation. Nor is this impression given by the gospel as a whole. We have noted earlier that, on the contrary, E. Schweizer has called attention to the remarkably *unstructured* and informal character of the Christian community envisaged in the gospel, as one which 'seems to know neither elders nor bishops nor deacons' and operates instead through the recognition of prophets and teachers on the basis of gift rather than of formal office.[4] The seminal essay of G. Bornkamm, 'Enderwartung und Kirche im Matthäusevangelium',[5] while declaring that 'No other Gospel is so shaped by the thought of the Church as Matthew's, so constructed for use by the Church', nevertheless goes on to observe that 'only the most meagre beginnings of a real ecclesiology, centred in the Church as an independent, empirically circumscribed

3. See above p. 211.
4. See above pp. 118-119, summarising Schweizer's 1974 article reproduced in Stanton, *Interpretation*, 129-155.
5. First published in W.D. Davies & D. Daube (ed.), *The Background of the New Testament and its Eschatology: in honour of C.H. Dodd* (Cambridge University Press, 1954) 222-260. It was then revised to become the foundation of the joint volume of Bornkamm with G. Barth and H.J. Held, *Überlieferung und Auslegung im Matthäusevangelium* (1960), published in English as *Tradition and Interpretation in Matthew* (London: SCM, 1963), where the essay appears as pp. 15-51.

entity, are to be found in Matthew's Gospel'.[6] He observes not only the lack of self-designations of the community ('the true Israel', 'the elect', etc.) such as one finds at Qumran, but also the fact that, again in contrast to the Qumran community, there is no mention of 'special offices . . . in an exactly graded hierarchical structure', even where matters of congregational discipline are under discussion. A strong sense of the distinctiveness and theological significance of the new community of the people of God which is being brought into being through the ministry of Jesus does not in itself entail the early development of sophisticated structures for church government and organisation. Important as the church is for Matthew, he does not seem to be either concerned with or even very much aware of the formal structures which the word 'ecclesiastical' conjures up for us.[7]

But if it is wrong to exaggerate the importance of Matthew's use of the word ἐκκλησία in itself, it must nevertheless be noticed that in each of the two passages where it occurs the focus is on the *authority* vested in this ἐκκλησία (or, more exactly in 16:18-19, in Peter as its foundation and representative), an authority which is defined as that of 'binding' and 'loosing', and which operates not only on earth but in heaven. The occurrence in these two passages of almost the same pronouncement of authority (16:19; 18:18) must surely indicate that Matthew has a distinctive understanding of the role of the ἐκκλησία, and one which is important to him.

THE ROLE OF PETER

The most striking difference between the two verses is, of course, the fact that while the singular pronouns and verbs of 16:19 mark this as a pronouncement to Peter himself, in 18:18 they have become plural, indicating the corporate responsibility of the ἐκκλησία. It may be appropriate, therefore, to say a word at this point about the role of Peter in Matthew's gospel.

Recent discussion of the question has tended to operate between two poles.[8] On the one hand, the *unique* role of Peter has been emphasised,

---

6. *Tradition*, 38-39.
7. Cf. Bornkamm's account (in Stanton, *Interpretation*, 92) of how the Matthean church is distinguished from Judaism: 'no longer Temple and sacrifices, ritual laws and circumcision (the latter is not once mentioned in Matthew's gospel), nor the rabbinical teaching of the synagogue, but neither a new cultic or hierarchical order; rather discipleship'.
8. A thorough study of 'The Figure of Peter in Matthew's Gospel as a Theological Problem' has been offered by J.D. Kingsbury, *JBL* 98 (1979) 67-83, including a survey of earlier discussion, in which the two competing approaches are documented. Also of particular interest in view of the traditional polarisation between Catholic and Protestant interpretation over the significance of Mt. 16:17-19 is the ecumenical study of *Peter in the New Testament*, edited by R.E. Brown, K.P. Donfried and J. Reumann (Minneapolis: Augsburg / New York: Paulist Press, 1973) 75-107 ('Peter in the Gospel of Matthew').

a position for which the key text is obviously 16:17-19; Peter stands apart from the other disciples as not only the leader of the group but also the one who occupies a special and unrepeatable position as the foundation-stone of the church. On the other hand, Peter has been seen as *typical*, as *primus inter pares*, and this position finds an appropriate basis in the other of our ἐκκλησία-passages, in that in 18:18 Peter's apparently unique personal 'power of the keys' is found after all to be shared with the community as a whole. But it is hardly likely that Matthew would include two such striking passages, both peculiar to his gospel and the second clearly intended to remind the reader of the almost identical wording in the first, in order to establish two opposite and incompatible views of the role of Peter! Are these positions really so opposite?

Matthew is not alone in stressing the role of Peter. Much of his Peter material is closely paralleled in Mark, where also Peter plays a leading role, particularly as spokesman of the disciple group.[9] In Matthew this role, which is in any case obvious from the various mentions of Peter in the narrative, is made more explicit by the further inclusion of questions from Peter as 'prompts' for pronouncements by Jesus in 15:15 and 18:21, by the focus on Peter as the spokesman of the group in 17:24-27, and particularly by the description of Peter as πρῶτος in 10:2. But the willingness to recognise Peter's fallibility which is so striking in Mark is present in Matthew too.

Two incidents in particular highlight this more critical attitude to Peter. The story of his attempt to walk on the water in 14:28-31 combines a recognition of Peter's leading role (he is not only the one to respond on behalf of the rest to Jesus' reassurance, but also the only one to attempt to do what Jesus can do) with his abject failure as a man of 'little faith'. At the end of the incident it is hard to be sure whether Matthew wants his readers to admire Peter for the boldness of his faith, inadequate though it proved to be, or to condemn him for his foolhardiness. Similarly in 16:13-23, while Peter is the one to make the great messianic confession, and thus receives the ringing accolade of 16:17-19, recognising his unique role, Matthew not only retains the tradition of Peter's misunderstanding and Jesus' rebuke of him in 16:22-23, but sharpens it by the inclusion of the remarkable words 'You are a stumbling-block to me'. The paradox that the same rock on which the ἐκκλησία is to be built can also prove a few verses later to be a σκάνδαλον provides a uniquely Matthean focus on the complexity of the role of Peter. The holder of the keys of the kingdom of heaven is no superman, but rather one who in his fallibility provides a warning

9. See e.g. E. Best, 'Peter in the Gospel according to Mark', *CBQ* 40 (1978) 547-558, reprinted in his *Disciples and Discipleship* (Edinburgh: T. & T. Clark, 1986) 162-176.

and a model for other fallible disciples. Indeed, while Mark 16:7 ensures that the dismal failure in the high priest's courtyard is not the last that we hear of Peter, Matthew offers no such explicit ground for hope, having no mention of Peter by name after that event (though the very specific 'eleven disciples' of 28:16 allows us to read hope between the lines!).

In the light of this complexity in Matthew's presentation of Peter, there seems to be good ground for concluding that neither of the two competing views mentioned above has a monopoly of the truth. Thus Kingsbury argues[10] that Matthew both sets Peter in a unique position, which he describes as a 'salvation-historical primacy', and at the same time regards him as the typical disciple, who both in his failures and in his role of leadership offers a model for other disciples. As a matter of historical fact no-one else could occupy the position of 'foundation-stone'; as leader of the initial disciple group Peter was called upon to exercise the office of 'key-holder' after the death of Jesus both as the leading preacher of the Jesus movement in the early days in Jerusalem, and in taking the initiative in matters requiring decision for the life and discipline of the community (e.g. Acts 1:15-23; 5:1-11; 8:14-25; 10:1 - 11:18). Yet even in these incidents Peter is not acting alone (notice the inclusion of John in Acts 8:14ff), nor as a dictator with unquestionable authority. He is answerable not only to the other members of the twelve, but also to the church as a whole (Acts 11:1-18), and is not the only one initiating new developments in the church's organisation and mission. This historical role of Peter as recorded in Acts seems to mirror well the tension we have seen in Matthew's presentation, between on the one hand the 'salvation-historical primacy' of the foundation-stone and on the other a leadership which operated as that of *primus· inter pares*, leaving Peter as an appropriate model for the 'typical disciple'.

In this light, then, the development from the singulars of 16:19 to the plurals of 18:18 is not surprising, but rather represents accurately Matthew's view of the role of Peter. The special authority which it was appropriate for Peter to exercise in a personal capacity in the process of the initial development of the Jesus movement was one which was· not in principle his alone, but exercised by him on behalf of the community as a whole, and equally capable of being exercised by the community corporately. How in practice that corporate authority might be exercised (through appointed leaders or by democratic vote?) Matthew, with his 'meagre beginnings of a real ecclesiology', does not spell out.

---

10. Kingsbury, *JBL* 98 (1979) 67-83, esp. pp. 80-83. Cf., more briefly, E. Schweizer, in Stanton, *Interpretation*, 135-137.

'BINDING AND LOOSING'

The 'authority', both of Peter and of the ἐκκλησία, which we have been considering is described as that of 'binding' and 'loosing' on earth that which will also prove to have been 'bound' and 'loosed' in heaven.[11] The verbs are customarily, and surely rightly, explained in the light of the frequent rabbinic usage of 'binding' in the sense of declaring what is required or forbidden by law. These terms thus refer to a teaching function, and more specifically one of making halakhic pronouncements which are to be 'binding' on the people of God.[12] In that case Peter's 'power of the keys' declared in 16:19 is not so much that of the doorkeeper, who decides who may or may not be admitted to the kingdom of heaven, but that of the steward (as in Is. 22:22, generally regarded as the Old Testament background to the metaphor of keys here), whose keys of office enable him to regulate the affairs of the household. Thus the sense of declaring who is or is not a member of the kingdom of heaven, or more specifically of pronouncing personal absolution or condemnation, which has often been read into this passage under the influence of the apparently similar language of John 20:23, does not represent the primary meaning of these terms, even though it is of course true that halakhic pronouncements will ultimately result in the recognition of who are and are not 'sinners' against those particular laws. The authority in view here is more immediately one of teaching than of disciplinary judgement.

But if this is quite widely agreed with reference to 16:19, it is interesting to note that some interpreters discern a shift in the use of the 'binding'

11. I have deliberately reproduced the rather clumsy, and therefore noticeable, future perfects of Matthew 16:19 and 18:18, which are more normally rendered into English by a simple future passive, 'will be bound', 'will be loosed'. Despite frequent statements of commentators that perfect forms in *koine* Greek do not always carry a perfect sense, I remain convinced that the choice of verb form is significant here. If Matthew had wished to use future passives he could have done so; his choice of the periphrastic future perfect form, consistently maintained for the two relevant verbs in both passages, suggests that he wished to say something rather different. It is sometimes suggested that this tense could be understood to indicate that things bound on earth will subsequently be found in heaven to have been bound (by means of their binding on earth). But this interpretation would differ little from the sense of a simple future passive. It would be more appropriate to the future perfect form to understand that things bound on earth will already have been bound in heaven prior to the earthly decision; and since this offers a meaning more clearly distinct from that of the simple future passive which Matthew avoided, it seems more likely that this was what he intended. In that case he has used the periphrastic tense to avoid the idea that there is an automatic heavenly rubber stamp on any decision made on earth; on the contrary, the authority of the earthly pronouncement consists precisely in the fact that it is passing on a decision which has already been made in heaven. There is a detailed discussion of both the grammatical and the exegetical issues involved here by Carson, *Matthew*, 370-374, with references to the main studies of the grammatical issue.
12. See e.g. the evidence from the Palestinian targums presented by Thompson, *Advice*, 192-193, and the more wide-ranging discussion of similar terminology in different Semitic cultural and legal contexts by J.D.M. Derrett in *JBL* 102 (1983) 112-117.

and 'loosing' terminology when they come to 18:18. Thus G. Bornkamm simply states, 'It is certain that Matt. 18:18 refers to disciplinary authority, and not, as Matt. 16:19, primarily to teaching authority'.[13] It is not that the terminology has changed, but that the context of chapter 18, and the plural subject of v.18, is felt to require a more 'disciplinary' sense. F.W. Beare thus sees a progression from 16:19 to 18:18, with John 20:23 as a further development in the same direction: in 16:19 'bind' and 'loose' denote 'the authoritative declaration that an action or course of conduct is permitted or forbidden', so that the verse 'has nothing to do with the power of absolution, though it may carry with it the authority to expel an offender from the synagogue or to readmit him'; in 18:18 this latter sense has taken over, and 'the power of discipline is assigned to the assembled church'; while John 20:23 'appears to be an interpretation of this saying precisely in the sense of conferring the power of absolution'.[14]

But is it legitimate to interpret Matthew in terms of John (where in any case the Matthean 'bind' and 'loose' terminology is not used)? And in Matthew there is cause to hesitate over using the language of 'church discipline' even with regard to 18:18, if by this is meant the exclusion or inclusion of members in the disciple community. The objects of the 'binding' and 'loosing' in 18:18 no less than in 16:19 are expressed as *neuter* pronouns, whereas if the focus had in fact shifted to the binding and loosing of *people* in chapter 18 one might have expected masculine pronouns. In rabbinic usage it is things (rules, prohibitions, etc.) that are bound onto people, not people who are bound, and Matthew's neuter pronouns suggest the same idea. The context in chapter 18 does indeed indicate that these authoritative pronouncements will affect the coherence and membership of the disciple community, but the actual terminology of binding and loosing seems still to be used in the 'rabbinic' way. Just as Peter was given in 16:19 the right to declare what is or is not the will of God, so that right is also to be exercised in 18:18 (in the context of ruling on the conduct of an individual member who 'sins') by the whole assembled ἐκκλησία.

I mentioned above that the main reason why commentators discern a change of focus between 16:19 and 18:18 is that the context of the latter is concerned with 'church discipline'. The relevance of this observation depends on what is understood by 'church discipline'. The issue in 18:15-17 is that one 'brother' is concerned about the 'sin' of another.[15] The whole section is expressed in the singular, what 'you'

13. Bornkamm, in Stanton, *Interpretation*, 88. Cf. E. Schweizer, *The Good News according to Matthew* (ET. Atlanta: John Knox, 1975) 371: 'One might say that Matthew 16:19 refers more to the teaching magisterium, 18:18 to church discipline'.
14. Beare, *Matthew*, 355-356.
15. If the words εἰς σέ ('against you') are included in v 15, the focus is more on a personal dispute between two members of the community. But these words are absent

(singular) should do about your brother's sin, even in v 17, where the result of his refusal to listen to the ἐκκλησία is to be that 'you' (singular) treat him as an outsider. The ἐκκλησία as a whole has been involved in the process, but the ultimate issue is one of personal relationship rather than of official excommunication. The plural pronouns of 18:18 therefore build on the role of the ἐκκλησία as the final court of appeal rather than on the single disciple's duty to ostracise his erring brother. The declaration by the ἐκκλησία of what is right or wrong (which is what the 'binding' and 'loosing' is about) is the basis on which the individual disciple acts towards his brother, and no doubt other members of the ἐκκλησία may be expected to follow suit. But this is 'church discipline' only in a very informal and unstructured sense, very different from what that phrase is likely to conjure up in a modern ecclesiastical context. The whole focus of interest in vv 15-17 is not on the punishment of an offending brother, but on the attempt to 'gain' him, by a process involving the minimum public exposure necessary to achieve the positive end of his restoration to fellowship. The atmosphere throughout is one of pastoral concern and appeal rather than of pronouncing judgement, even though in an extreme case the personal separation of the offender may result.[16]

THE AUTHORITY OF THE CHURCH

I believe, then, that it is inappropriate to read the language of 'binding' and 'loosing' as denoting the official exercise of discipline over members of the community by a formally constituted leadership; still less does it suggest that some officially constituted body is entitled to exercise quasi-priestly powers of excommunication or absolution. But even if the church context envisaged in chapter 18 is much less formal and the focus of the passage is primarily on pastoral care, it remains true that the formula of 16:19 and 18:18 accords an awesome degree of authority to the halakhic pronouncements of the disciple community, and of Peter as its leader and steward, the holder of the keys. For the keys are those not of an earthly organisation, but of 'the kingdom of heaven', and there is apparently an unbroken continuity between the pronouncements made on earth and the verdict of 'heaven'. It looks dangerously. like a *carte blanche*. Does Matthew intend by this formula to confer

from some important early witnesses. The focus of the passage has so far been on the pastoral concern of the disciple for each individual 'little one' in the community, rather than on personal grievances, and the introduction of these words in v 15 unnecessarily anticipates the subsequent change of focus in v 21, from which they probably found their way into the text of v 15. Cf. Thompson, *Advice*, 176.

16. For this 'pastoral rather than disciplinary' emphasis in 18:15-17 see especially the discussion by Thompson, *Advice*, 175-188.

unquestionable authority on the decisions of fallible members of the disciple community? Or is there implicit here a promise of infallibility? Two considerations suggest caution here. First, there is the obvious fallibility of the disciples in general and of Peter in particular, a prominent feature of the Marcan tradition which Matthew does not gloss over, and even goes out of his way to emphasise by his distinctive use of terms like ὀλιγόπιστος ('of little faith') and διστάζω ('to hesitate, doubt') with reference both to the disciples in general (6:30; 8:26; 16:8; 17:20; 28:17) and to Peter (14:31), by the striking juxtapositʼon already mentioned of the special role of Peter as foundation-stone with his actual performance as stumbling-stone, σκάνδαλον (16:18,23), and by the recognition in the verses preceding 18:18 that the same disciples who constitute the ἐκκλησία to which the pronouncement is made are quite capable of proving themselves to be σκάνδαλα to one another (18:6-9).

Secondly, in 16:18-19 the ἐκκλησία is not that of Peter, but that of Jesus, built by him; it is he who has given Peter the keys. And 18:18 is immediately followed by an explanation of the basis of their authority to bind and loose, in that their united requests will be granted by 'my Father in heaven', and that in their assembly Jesus himself is present (18:19-20). The phrasing of these verses suggests that they may originally have existed independently of their present context, but that in no way diminishes the fact that Matthew, by placing them after 18:18, has created a theological context in which his readers are to understand the link between binding and loosing 'on earth' and 'in heaven' (both of which phrases are noticeably repeated in v 19). Far from being autocrats on earth, they are suppliants to Jesus' Father in heaven, and the basis of that approach is the fact of his own presence in the disciple group which has met 'in his name'. Here we see the practical applicability of the christological perspective already hinted at in 1:23 ('God with us') and brought into triumphant clarity by the final words of the gospel, 'I am with you always, to the close of the age'. The authority of the church, then, is not independent. It is the authority of Jesus, delegated to his people among whom he himself continues to be the focal point. The decisions of the church, and of Peter, are the decisions of Jesus, already made in heaven and pronounced through the channel of his representatives on earth.[17] Theirs is not a static authority vested in an institution, but the dynamic authority which derives from a living and continuing relationship with the Lord of the church. Here again, ecclesiology is a function of christology.

There is an inevitable tension between these two factors, the frightening responsibility of passing on the decrees of heaven and the all too clear fallibility of the actual people to whom this responsibility is

17. See above n. 11 for the significance of the tenses used.

delegated. Matthew does not offer a direct resolution of this tension, but the fact that he allows the two factors to stand side by side suggests that we should be cautious of assuming that he held so naive a view of the authority of the church that he saw no problem in endorsing any and every pronouncement made by a group of disciples. The ideal of the clear communication of the will of heaven through the presence of Jesus among his people must always be balanced by the fallibility and self-interest to which those people continue to be prone, and the recognition that it is not always easy in practice to discern where the true people of God is to be found (a problem of which Matthew was well aware, as we shall see later in this chapter).

So, for all Matthew's 'high' view of the authority delegated to Peter and the church, the overall perspective of his work does not encourage us to see this as a primarily 'ecclesiastical' gospel in the sense that it focuses attention on an institutional church as itself the locus of authority. Ecclesiology is subordinate to christology, and the 'church' which emerges is not a shining army with banners, but a relatively unstructured gathering of 'little ones' who belong to Jesus, a body which impresses the reader more with its vulnerability and need of correction than with a sense of awe. It is rather in the sense that Matthew's book aims to strengthen, and where necessary correct, the continuing life of this disciple community that it can appropriately be called the church's gospel. It is to that aspect of Matthew's work that we shall devote the rest of this chapter.

B. THE PASTORAL FUNCTION OF THE GOSPEL

THE FUNCTION OF THE 'FIVE DISCOURSES'

In considering Matthew 18:18, we have noticed how the pronouncement on the authority to bind and loose occurs in the course of a passage which deals with practical issues of church life. While the first part of the discourse of chapter 18 may be seen as developed from the tradition recorded in Mark 9:34-37,42-48, and the remainder contains rough parallels to Luke 15:3-7 and 17:3-4, the bulk of its material is peculiar to Matthew, and, more significantly, the structure of the discourse taken as a whole is entirely Matthew's own.

The focus of chapter 18 is on relationships within the community of Jesus' disciples. Beginning with the question of status, Jesus declares that the essential prerequisite for life in the kingdom of heaven is the acceptance of the position of the child, the lowest rung in the social structure (vv 1-4); to welcome 'one such child' in his name is to welcome him (v 5), and from this point on the literal child used as a symbol in v 2 fades from view and the focus is on one's fellow-disciples in general as 'little ones' (vv 6,10,14); as such they are vulnerable, and he stresses the importance of avoiding σκάνδαλα, since disciples are responsible for one another (vv 6-9);[18] none is to be undervalued, but rather the members of the community must share the concern of their Father in heaven that not one should be lost (vv 10-14); so the individual disciple who sees his brother sin must take action to bring about his restoration, action in which in an extreme case it may be necessary to involve the whole local congregation (vv 15-17); if so, the united voice of the congregation carries the authority of heaven itself, since its basis is the presence of the risen Jesus among his people (vv 18-20); in such a community there is no place for grudges or for self-righteous indignation, but rather there must be unlimited forgiveness (vv 21-22), and a concluding parable grounds this demand for forgiveness in the fact that each disciple owes what he is to the forgiving grace of God; they are a community of the forgiven (vv 23-35).

The portrait of the church which thus emerges is an attractive one. Status-consciousness and formally constituted authority have no place. The focus is on the relationship and mutual responsibility of all members of the community, each one of whom matters, and yet all of whom must regard themselves only as 'little ones'. The resultant pastoral concern and action is not the preserve of a select few, but is the responsibility of each individual disciple, and, where necessary, of the whole group together. The structure is informal, but the sense of community is intense. And overarching it all is the consciousness of the presence of Jesus and of the forgiveness and pastoral concern of 'your Father in heaven'.

Matthew's compilation of such a chapter must indicate something of the perspective and purpose of his gospel. Chapter 18 is often described as a *Gemeindeordnung*, a 'community rule', on the analogy of the Qumran document often known by that name, 1QS.[19] Perhaps this suggests too comprehensive and regulative a role for what is in fact a treatment of a limited range of congregational issues, and those more in general principle than in halakhic detail, but the term aptly indicates the use for which the chapter is appropriate, and for which it seems likely that Matthew intended it. While it is not necessarily true

18. Vv 8-9, which focus on σκάνδαλα in one's own life rather than in the context of the community, are attached to vv 6-7 by the catch-words σκάνδαλον/σκανδαλίζω, and seem out of place in a chapter which otherwise concentrates single-mindedly on the community. The same connection is found in Mark 9:42-48, and it is possible that Matthew left these apparently intrusive verses in the discourse simply because they were already there in the tradition. But he was not generally averse to reducing traditional material to what he considered the essentials for his purpose, so it may be that he included these verses here because σκάνδαλα in the life of an individual disciple are likely, if left unchecked, to have an effect on others within the community.

19. Typically G. Bornkamm, in Stanton, *Interpretation*, 85-97 *passim*.

that every piece of New Testament paraenesis must reflect an actual problem to which it is a deliberate corrective, there seems good reason in this case to approve the title given to W.G. Thompson's sensitive discussion of the chapter, *Matthew's Advice to a Divided Community*.[20] Matthew writes out of pastoral concern for a Christian group whose weaknesses and temptations he knows well. His book is intended to help the followers of Jesus as he knows them to live up to their Master's intentions.

What is true of chapter 18 is also true of much of the other material in the gospel. In particular, each of the other four of the 'five discourses'[21] may plausibly be seen as angled towards areas in the life and thinking of the church for which Matthew writes which he perceives to be in need of strengthening or correction.

The wide range of material included in that magnificent collection of teaching which we call the Sermon on the Mount[22] is united by its focus on the nature and demands of discipleship. It deals with the true character and rewards of discipleship (5:3-10), the distinctiveness of the disciple (5:11-16), the ethics of discipleship in relation to current understanding of the ethical demands of the law (5:17-48), the disciple's religious observance (6:1-18) and his choice of priorities between the claims of God and of earthly concerns (6:19-34), his attitude to fellow-disciples (7:1-6,12) and to God as his Father (7:7-11); it then concludes with four contrasts between true and false discipleship (7:13-27), which serve to challenge the readers to examine their own standing as followers of Jesus as well as to discern the genuine and the spurious among those who are attached to the church. The appropriateness of this collection for use in teaching in the church was quickly recognised; it remains to this day a favourite resource of preachers and teachers who wish to turn the attention of their congregations to what it means to live consistently as a follower of Jesus, and there can be little doubt that Matthew so intended it.[23]

20. Thompson summarises on pp. 259-264 the nature of the 'dissension and disunity' which he supposes, on the basis of the contents and tone of the gospel as a whole, to have existed in Matthew's church. Mutual distrust, betrayal and hatred have resulted from the experience of persecution and of rival teachers ('false prophets'). Zumstein, *Condition*, 171-200, sees the divisions within the Matthean community as essentially doctrinal, with Matthew opposing a 'charismatic' group attached to certain 'enthusiastic prophets' who preach antinomian doctrine; but Stanton ('Origin', 1909-1910) is sceptical of this estimate: 'It is difficult to find traces of a group of Christians either within or outside Matthew's community about whose *doctrinal* views the evangelist is concerned.' The 'divisions' which Thompson rightly notes, while they may in part have been caused by doctrinal deviations, are manifested, and are tackled by Matthew, primarily in the area of personal relationships in the community.

21. See above pp. 154-165.

22. For the compilation of the 'Sermon' see above pp. 160-163.

23. A conveniently brief and quite up-to-date summary (with reference to fuller discussions) of the history of the interpretation and use of the Sermon on the Mount is given by Guelich, *Sermon*, 14-22. Guelich also goes on, *ibid.* 24-33, to discuss the role of the Sermon in Matthew's purpose for his gospel.

It is true, of course, that the tendency of some interpreters to lift the
Sermon totally out of its context, and to present it as an independent
ethical code irrespective of Matthew's wider purpose in his gospel, has
led to serious misunderstanding.[24] The Sermon is about the life and
values of those who hear and obey the words of *Jesus*, and who recognise
God as their 'Father in heaven' (a constant refrain in these chapters),
not a treatise on secular ethics. It comes to us as part of Matthew's
portrait of Jesus, and in that sense must be seen as a *christological*
document. 'The Sermon on the Mount compels us, in the first place,
to ask who he is who utters these words: they are themselves kerygmatic.'[25] The concluding comments in 7:28-29 confirm that this is a
true assessment of Matthew's intention. But, having recognised that
the passage must not be read without reference to its context in Matthew's
total project, it remains true that it can effectively function, as surely it
was intended to do, as a guide to living as a follower of Jesus, and it
is likely that at least some of the selection of material included in these
chapters was prompted by perceived weaknesses or potential problems
in the church as Matthew knew it.

The suitability of the other discourses as teaching resources in the
context of the developing church is also clear. 10:5-15 gives directions
for their evangelistic enterprise, while 10:16-42 prepares them for the
opposition and division which would result (and which were presumably
already the experience of those for whom Matthew was writing). The
parables of chapter 13 focus on the themes of division in men's response
to the word of God, the growth of the kingdom of heaven in spite of
opposition, and the radical demands of discipleship, all matters of
obvious concern to the followers of Jesus in the period when the new
movement was becoming increasingly conscious of itself as a new and
distinct community, and facing up to the problem of the hostility and
unbelief of those around them. And chapters 24-25 focus on the sort
of eschatological questions which we know from other New Testament
writings to have been matters of great concern in the developing churches
(notably in the striking concentration of the two Thessalonian letters
on questions arising from the expectation of an early parousia, resulting
in teaching which at many points recalls some of the material in Matthew
24-25).[26]

OTHER INDICATIONS OF A PASTORAL FUNCTION

It is not only the five discourses which offer material suitable for the
teacher in the church of Matthew's day. Sayings and dialogues through-

24. See above pp. 164-165.
25. Davies, *Setting*, 435. Cf. Guelich, *Sermon*, 27ff.
26. See the detailed study of such links by D. Wenham, 'Paul and the Synoptic
Apocalypse', *Gospel Perspectives* vol. 2 (1981) 345-375.

out the gospel would have obvious relevance to issues arising in the developing life of the Christian communities, such as the right use of the sabbath (12:1-14), the authority of tradition (15:1-9) and the nature of true purity (15:10-20), the appropriate attitude to taxation both religious (17:24-27) and secular (22:15-22), marriage and bereavement (22:23-33), divorce and singleness (19:3-12), wealth and poverty (19: 16-30), the danger of concern for status within the disciple group (20:20-28), the acceptance of the unacceptable (8:5-13; 9:10-13; 15:21-28), the priority of discipleship over other loyalties (8:18-22; 12:46-50; 16:24-28). The list could be extended considerably, expecially if we take account of the fact that many of the stories of Jesus (e.g. 4:1-11; 26:36-44) or of the disciples (e.g. 8:23-27; 14:22-33) would lend themselves easily to use as examples or warnings concerning true discipleship.

Of course not many of the items mentioned in the preceding paragraph are peculiar to Matthew. It is, generally speaking, in the five discourses that his distinctive contribution to the teaching material of the church is concentrated. But even in those pericopes which he shares with one or both of the other synoptic evangelists, there are sometimes distinctive elements which suggest the author's concern for the practical usefulness of his gospel in the context of church life. The divorce pericope in 19:3-12 is an obvious example, in that it is only Matthew who includes here and in 5:32 the recognition that Jesus' prohibition of divorce may not apply to cases of πορνεία. We cannot here do justice to the lively arguments both over the meaning of πορνεία and over the relation of this exceptive clause to the apparent absoluteness of Jesus' prohibition as recorded by Mark and Luke,[27] but the fact that Matthew includes the phrase suggests that he had an eye not only to the general statement of principle but also to the applicability of this teaching in a real-life situation. A similar concern probably underlies his continuing the pericope to include (in response to the disciples' dismay over the ruling on divorce) some comments on marriage and singleness in relation to the calling of the individual disciple (19:10-12).

Another section of the gospel where Matthew's special interest in the practical issues of church life is not far from the surface is the diatribe against the scribes and Pharisees which precedes the eschatological discourse. Its primary focus is, of course, as we have seen in the last chapter, on the Jewish leaders who confronted Jesus during his earthly ministry, and on the judgement which was to result from their failure to respond to God's initiative in Jesus. But it is not hard to discern behind the careful listing of their failings the possibility that Matthew is warning also against similar attitudes which might exist, or already

---

27. I have discussed these issues briefly in my *Matthew*, 123-124, 281-282. A fuller discussion along similar lines, with reference to the more important recent contributions to the debate, is offered by Carson, *Matthew*, 413-418.

did exist, also within Christian circles. Their desire to be noticed and applauded (23:5-7) is closely parallel to the ostentatious religious practice against which disciples are warned in 6:1-18, and their preoccupation with the niceties of permissible oaths (23:16-22) reflects 5:33-37 where disciples are warned against the same lack of proportion. Their inconsistency (23:3) and inconsiderateness (23:4), their preoccupation with ritual detail to the exclusion of more important matters of principle (23:23-26) and the superficiality of their religious reputation (23:27-28), these are not the exclusive faults of one specific group, but the dangers into which members of any religious community too frequently fall. In all these aspects of chapter 23 the application to the Christian community remains below the surface, but in 23:8-12 it breaks into full view, as the bad example set by the scribes and Pharisees in the matter of ostentation and desire for status is directly applied to 'you', who are not to go the same way. And the identity of the 'you' is not left in doubt: they are 'brothers', who have 'one Father who is in heaven', and whose master is 'the Christ'.

Matthew's gospel is about Jesus, and about how in him God's purposes have come to fulfilment. But the story is told not only for information or to satisfy historical interest, but with an eye to those who wish to follow Jesus, and whose life as Christians, both individually and especially in community, Matthew wishes to mould to the pattern established by his life and teaching.

'THE TEACHER'S GOSPEL'

P.S. Minear entitles his study *Matthew: the Teacher's Gospel* because he believes that 'The author of this Gospel was a *teacher* who designed his work to be of maximum help to *teachers* in Christian congregations.'[28] He pictures the author as a church leader with a special gift for teaching, applying what he knew of Jesus' teaching to the specific issues which arose in the life of the church. 'Each crisis faced by this community, each debate with hostile groups, each internal altercation among family members would have provided an occasion for a teacher to give specific advices drawn from the legacy of Jesus.' Matthew's book is designed by one such professional teacher for use by his colleagues, the leaders in the churches of his region.[29]

While it goes beyond the evidence to assign to Matthew the professional status of a teacher, and we may hesitate to restrict his intended readership specifically to other teachers, Minear is surely right to emphasise that the gospel is designed to provide guidance for the practical issues of church life. While this may not be the only use for

28. Minear, *Matthew* 3.
29. *Ibid.* 6, 9-10.

which the book was intended, it was apparently an important factor
in Matthew's compilation of the discourses and in the selection and
angling of much of the other material. Whatever his professional status,
Matthew displays the interests and methods of a Christian teacher.

It is of course true that Matthew is considerably less lavish than
Mark in his use, in speaking of *Jesus'* ministry, of the specific vocabulary
of teaching, the verb διδάσκω 'to teach' and the nouns διδαχή 'teaching'
and διδάσκαλος 'teacher'.[30] Indeed Matthew seems quite deliberately to
avoid allowing disciples to use the title διδάσκαλος of Jesus, preferring
them to use the more exalted title κύριος 'Lord'; it is outsiders and
opponents who address Jesus merely as 'teacher' in Matthew. But,
however inadequate διδάσκαλος may be as a title for Jesus, teaching
(and particularly teaching in relation to matters of law, as a 'rabbi')[31]
was a part of his ministry according to Matthew, and the relatively less
prominent use of that specific word-group must be balanced against
the prominence of actual teaching material in the structure and content
of the gospel. Then at the end of Matthew's gospel comes a significant
change; hitherto it has been Jesus, not his disciples, who has been
described as teaching, but in 28:20 the risen Jesus commits to his
disciples the responsibility of 'teaching them to observe all that I have
commanded you'. It can be only a delegated authority, since in the last
resort the community has only one teacher (23:8); but it is the commands
of that one teacher that are to form the content of their teaching, and
it is he who has promised to be with them always in the carrying out
of this commission (28:20). It is this delegated teaching authority which
is the basis of Matthew's understanding of his own task and of the
importance of the role of teaching in the church.

A CHRISTIAN HALAKHAH?

It would be a mistake, however, to suggest that Matthew saw his
task as simply parallel to that of a Jewish rabbi making halakhic
pronouncements to regulate the life of his congregation. While there
may be some sayings in his gospel which could function in this way as
halakhah, its general approach is much more at the level of principles

---

30. The statistics, with reference to Jesus, are: διδάσκω – Mark 15, Matthew 9, Luke
15; διδαχή – Mark 5, Matthew 2, Luke 1; διδάσκαλος – Mark 12, Matthew 9, Luke 13.
In view of the difference in length between the gospels, this indicates that it is Mark
rather than Matthew who emphasises this aspect of Jesus' activity (at least in so far as
the use of this word-group can indicate). See my fuller discussion in *Gospel Perspectives*
vol. 1 (1980) especially pp. 103-112.
31. G. Bornkamm, *Tradition*, 38 n. 1, points out the typically Matthean combination
of διδάσκω with κηρύσσω 'preach' in summary accounts of Jesus' ministry, and argues that
the two are not equivalent, διδάσκω being restricted in the rest of the gospel to contexts
where Jesus 'is clearly designated Rabbi' and is dealing specifically with the law; διδάσκω
is thus related to the law, κηρύσσω to the kingdom of God.

and values than at that of detailed regulation. As R. Mohrlang observes, 'Those who interpret Matthew's formulation of Jesus' teachings primarily in terms of Christian halakoth tend to overestimate the halakic element in the Gospel, and fail to recognize the vast difference between the bulk of Jesus' teachings and genuine rabbinic halakoth. . . . They lack the comprehensive specificity of halakah and its preoccupation with the letter of the law.' He goes on to quote T.W. Manson to the effect that Jesus' teaching is 'a compass rather than an ordnance map . . . the object is to give direction rather than directions.'[32] As we have seen in discussing his view of Jesus and the law,[33] Matthew wishes his readers to see Jesus as preaching the 'fulfilment' of the law in himself and his teaching, a fulfilment which, while it does not result in the abolition of the law, leads to an ethic which operates on a different level from 'the righteousness of the scribes and Pharisees', and is so far from legalistic that it can even envisage the setting aside of the letter of certain Old Testament laws (not to mention sitting very lightly to later Jewish elaboration of those laws) in favour of the underlying principles of the will of God.

If, then, there is any truth in von Dobschütz's famous description of Matthew as 'a converted Jewish rabbi',[34] it is found as much in the word 'converted' as in the title 'rabbi'! The basis of von Dobschütz's characterisation is not that Matthew offers a detailed halakhah for the church, but that the *style* of his writing is rabbinic, making constant use of the devices of repetition, stereotyped formulae, 'the schematic use of numbers', etc. These are teaching devices, and von Dobschütz properly ascribes them to 'the clearly catechetical interest of the author'. The wide popularity of Matthew's gospel in the life of the developing churches, which we noted in chapter 1, was in large part due to the fact that his style of presenting Jesus' teaching proved so well suited for use in the instruction of the members of a Christian congregation. Thus 'the Jewish rabbi had become a Christian teacher and now used his catechetical skills in the service of the gospel.'[35]

If von Dobschütz is right, Matthew's conversion has involved a radical break from his rabbinic past, at the level of the content of his teaching, if not of its technique. But it is in any case hardly legitimate to conclude from Matthew's familiarity with effective teaching methods, such as the rabbis often used, that he had himself been such a rabbi. His skills may as well have been learned through his experience after his conversion as a teacher in a Christian congregation which oper-

32. Mohrlang, *Matthew and Paul*, 23-24, quoting T.W. Manson, *The Sayings of Jesus* (London: SCM, 1949) 37.
33. Above pp. 191-197.
34. E. von Dobschütz, in Stanton, *Interpretation*, 24,25.
35. *Ibid.* 26. The data from the gospel in which von Dobschütz discerns Matthew's 'inclination towards stereotype and formula' are set out on pp. 20-24.

ated in an environment where rabbinic teaching was familiar. Von Dobschütz's appropriate description of him as 'catechist' does not entail the additional title of 'rabbi'.

Rather than legislate for the details of life as rabbinic halakhah was designed to do, Matthew's Jesus offers us broad principles of conduct. Sometimes the principle is illustrated by examples of real-life application, as in 5:38-42, where the general principle of non-resistance to evil is illustrated by the three cameos of the blow on the cheek, the law-suit for possession of the garment, and the soldier's requisitioning of a porter, together with the much broader demand to refuse no request for help! But few interpreters have been able to accept these as literal rules of conduct, the last in particular being plainly unworkable in a society where begging is a way of life. The reader of Matthew who has understood and accepted the teaching of 5:38-42 is still going to face the need to work out the practical application of this teaching in relation to any specific situation in which he finds himself, and he cannot expect Matthew's book to undertake this task for him. Matthew the teacher aims to provide the reader not so much with ready-made answers, but with the raw materials from which an answer can be constructed.

Prominent among those broad principles is the demand of love. Much has been written on the place of the love-commandment in early Christian teaching,[36] and this cannot of course be claimed as a uniquely Matthean focus of interest. But the call to 'love your enemies' (5:43-47) occupies a prominent place as the culmination of Matthew's distinctive presentation of the demands of discipleship in 5:21-48. Matthew, like the other evangelists, records Jesus' summary of the law in terms of love, but he also adds the comment 'On these two commandments depend all the law and the prophets' (22:34-40). It is only Matthew who includes 'love your neighbour as yourself' as the final item in 'the commandments' presented by Jesus to the rich enquirer (19:19).

Even when the word 'love' is not used, the theme is prominent. The ethical teaching of the Sermon on the Mount culminates in the famous 'Golden Rule' (7:12), which, while it does not use the word 'love', is properly recognised as encapsulating in a nutshell what love means in practice; and this too is presented as a summary of 'the law and the prophets'. R. Mohrlang[37] also rightly points out that the theme of love is expressed in Matthew's use of the terminology of mercy (ἔλεος), which is one of the 'weightier matters of the law' omitted by the scribes and

36. In addition to discussions of the issue in more general studies of New Testament theology and ethics, see the more specialised monographs of V.P. Furnish, *The Love Command in the New Testament* (Nashville: Abingdon, 1972) and of J. Piper, *'Love Your Enemies': Jesus' Love Command in the Synoptic Gospels and in the Early Christian Paraenesis* (Cambridge University Press, 1979), with the references they give to further literature.
37. Mohrlang, *Matthew and Paul*, 96-97. Pp. 94-100 survey Matthew's focus on love.

Pharisees (23:23), and is the focus of the repeated quotation from Hosea (uniquely in Matthew), 'I desire mercy, and not sacrifice' (9:13; 12:7). The commendation of the righteous at the last judgement, while it uses no specific 'love'-terminology, focuses on acts of 'loving your neighbour as yourself' (25:35-36).

It is possible to find rabbinic passages which in some way 'parallel' the Golden Rule[38] or Jesus' summary of the law and the prophets in terms of love,[39] but the contrast between the essential focus of the ethics of Matthew's Jesus and that of the Pharisees is well summed up in his repeated quotation of Hosea 6:6, 'I desire mercy and not sacrifice', a focus not on the details of ritual observance or of rules of conduct, but on the broader principle of love which operates at the level of motives and relationships rather than of halakhic prescription. J. Piper summarises his discussion of Matthew's presentation of the command to love your enemies as follows: 'The obedience Mt is calling for . . . is an obedience which consists in a radical transformation of the deepest spring of man's being.'[40] These 'radical, impracticable commands', as Piper calls them, point not to a new code of behaviour, but to the new values of the kingdom of heaven. This is not halakhah, but gospel.

C. MATTHEW'S VISION OF THE CHURCH

If Matthew was aware of failings in the church as he knew it, and designed his gospel, at least in part, to help to correct those failings by an appropriate selection and presentation of the teaching of Jesus, it should be possible from the study of the book he has produced to gain some idea of what he felt the church *ought* to be. We have already noted in chapter 3 a variety of suggestions as to what his church may actually have been like, both in its structures and in the tendencies which Matthew may be understood to be trying to correct.[41] But correction implies a standard. What then was the pattern in Matthew's mind of the true nature and the proper functioning of the community of the followers of Jesus?

38. Rabbi Hillel: 'What is hateful to you, do not do to your neighbour. That is the whole law; the rest is commentary' (*Shabbath* 31a). This is, of course, a negative formulation; no direct rabbinic parallel to Jesus' positive version is known.

39. Both the texts singled out by Jesus (Dt. 6:5 and Lv. 19:18) were frequently mentioned in rabbinic discussion. And there are several examples of attempts to select one or more Old Testament passages as 'summaries of the law' (see especially *Makkoth* 23b-24a). But there is no parallel to the bringing together of these two commandments in this connection, though certain passages in the Testaments of the Twelve Patriarchs which speak of loving God and man ('neighbour') might have been derived from these passages (Issachar 5:2; 7:6; Dan 5:3); it is, however, possible that these passages themselves reflect Christian influence. See further J.B. Stern, *CBQ* 28 (1966) 312-316.

40. Piper, '*Love Your Enemies*', 145. Matthew's presentation of the love-commandment is discussed specifically on pp. 141-152.

41. See above pp. 108-119.

DISCIPLESHIP

Matthew's most frequent term for those who follow Jesus is μαθητής, 'disciple'. It has been argued, particularly by G. Strecker,[42] that Matthew restricts this term to the inner circle of the Twelve, but there are several passages where special pleading is needed to maintain this restriction on the meaning of the noun, notably 8:21 (with the implied reference back to another μαθητής in the scribe of 8:19), 10:24f and 10:42. On this basis B. Przybylski[43] effectively counters Strecker's argument, and goes on to point out that the three uses of the verb μαθητεύω in Matthew (a verb used elsewhere in the New Testament only in Acts 14:21) allow no such restriction. In particular, it is this verb which describes the continuing mission of Jesus' followers in 28:19; unless there is a strange lack of coherence between Matthew's use of the noun and the verb, μαθητής describes not only those who followed Jesus during his earthly ministry (including the 'eleven μαθηταί' to whom 28:19 is addressed), but also those who will be won to him through the continuing mission of the church. Μαθητής seems, then, to be a term appropriate to all who follow Jesus, past, present and future. The μαθηταί who were with him during his earthly ministry are not in principle distinct from those who come later. They are, indeed, to use Luz's term,[44] 'transparent' for the subsequent followers of Jesus in Matthew's day. 'One of the evangelist's prime concerns in writing the Gospel is to spell out what it means to be a μαθητής of Jesus.'[45]

The command to 'make disciples' in 28:19 offers a useful summary of what Matthew understands discipleship to involve. The imperative μαθητεύσατε is not followed here by an explicit indirect object, but its meaning is 'unpacked' in the two following participial clauses: a disciple is one who is 'baptised into the name of the Father and the Son and the Holy Spirit', and one whose responsibility it is to 'observe all that Jesus has commanded'. Both clauses focus on a relationship. In the first clause it is a relationship of allegiance to the triune God (a form of expression which we shall have to discuss in the next chapter from the point of view of its christological implications); in the second clause it is more specifically to Jesus, whose earthly teaching is to form the basis of the disciple's way of life. A similar focus is found in Matthew's other two uses of μαθητεύω, where the indirect object is expressed simply as 'Jesus' (27:57) or less personally as 'the kingdom of heaven' (13:52), a phrase which, however, functions (especially in chapter 13)

42. Strecker, *Weg*, 191-193. Cf. Albright & Mann, *Matthew*, LXXV-LXXVII.
43. Przybylski, *Righteousness*, 108-110. On the relationship of μαθητής to μαθητεύω see also the remarks of U. Luz in response to Strecker, in Stanton, *Interpretation*, 109.
44. See above pp. 200-201.
45. Mohrlang, *Matthew and Paul*, 74. He discusses Matthew's view of discipleship ibid. 74-78.

virtually as a slogan for the whole scope of the ministry of Jesus. The three uses of μαθητεύω therefore encourage us to see discipleship as essentially a matter of relationship with Jesus. It must, of course, involve membership of a community ('baptising into') and a distinctive life-style (observing all that Jesus has commanded), but these are the products of an antecedent acceptance of Jesus himself as master.[46] In the light of this focus on relationship it is therefore appropriate that the passage concludes with Jesus' promise to be 'with you always'. While it is Mark, not Matthew, who defines the role of the Twelve in the first place as 'to be with him' (Mark 3:14), Matthew too would apparently have regarded this as the essence of discipleship.[47]

Another prominent term is the verb ἀκολουθέω 'to follow'. When the first disciples are called in 4:18-22, it is this verb which describes their response, and in many places it seems to be almost a technical term for belonging to the disciple group (see e.g. 8:19,22; 9:9; 19:21,27f). Twice 'following Jesus' is paired with 'taking up the cross' as a description of the demand of discipleship (10:38; 16:24; and in both these cases, as in 4:19f, it is suggestively linked with the adverb ὀπίσω 'behind'). On the other hand, the verb can have a purely literal sense, as in 21:9 where it is paired with 'going in front', or in 9:19 where it is Jesus and his disciples who 'follow' the ruler in order to attend to his daughter. Between the clearly 'technical' use and the literal sense there are a number of interesting passages where people apparently outside the disciple group are said to 'follow' Jesus. The crowds follow him in 4:25; 8:1; 12:15; 14:13; 19:2; 20:29, and while this 'crowd' is distinguished from the 'disciples' (5:1; 14:15), it is clear that they are there out of enthusiasm for Jesus, whether out of appreciation of his teaching or the hope of healing. Then there are the blind men who 'follow' Jesus as a result of being healed (20:34; others 'followed' him *in order to* be healed, 9:27!). Does the use of the verb in such cases indicate that they became 'disciples'? Or were there different degrees of 'following'? Or is the whole discussion trying to squeeze too much out of a verb which has a naturally wide range of possible usage, literal and metaphorical? J.D. Kingsbury suggests that what distinguishes the 'technical', discipleship sense of the verb from its more literal or neutral uses is the presence in context of the twin motifs of 'personal commitment' to Jesus and

---

46. Mohrlang, *ibid.*, emphasises the nature of discipleship in Matthew as submission and obedience, to God first, but also to Jesus as κύριος, expressed in practical observance of his teaching. He goes on (pp. 76-78) to illustrate the importance of the theme (though not the language) of the *imitatio Christi* in Matthew.
47. J.D. Kingsbury, *JBL* 98 (1979) 76-78 (following the lengthy discussion by H. Frankemölle, *Jahwe-Bund*, 7-83) makes much of Matthew's rather varied uses of 'with' in order to underline this point. While the point being made reflects a true insight into Matthew's view of discipleship, it is questionable whether the usage of 'with' is a sufficiently clear basis for it!

of 'cost'.[48] On this basis he concludes that the uses of the verb with regard to the crowds and those who are healed does not carry the sense of discipleship, despite the tendency of most commentators to take it in this sense at least in 20:34. I believe he is right to suggest caution: the verb on its own cannot be held to be a technical term for discipleship where the context does not otherwise suggest it, even if Kingsbury's contextual criteria for discerning the metaphorical sense may be too tightly drawn. But where the metaphorical sense is clearly intended, this verb, like the noun μαθητής, focuses our attention on the personal commitment to Jesus which is the essence of discipleship.[49]

One particularly interesting use of ἀκολουθέω is in 8:23, where the embarkation for the crossing of the lake is described in a way which seems from the narrative point of view rather clumsy and unnecessary: 'When he got into the boat, his disciples *followed* him.' At the narrative level this is a literal use of the term, but it follows immediately after the encounter with two potential 'followers' in 8:18-22, in the course of which the verb ἀκολουθέω has twice appeared as a term for discipleship. Matthew's introduction of this term in v 23 has therefore been taken to indicate that the following story of the stilling of the storm is included not only, or even primarily, as a miracle-story to show Jesus' supernatural power, but as an allegory of discipleship.[50] H.J. Held has traced this aim in other miracle-stories in Matthew,[51] and it is now widely accepted that Matthew's miracle-stories are intended not only to give historical information, but also to provide models of how a disciple may relate to and depend on his Lord in the crises of life. B. Gerhardsson has argued that this applies particularly to the *nature*-miracles: 'As opposed to the therapeutic miracles which are worked throughout for the people outside the group of the disciples, ... the non-therapeutic miracles are always worked for *the disciples* (or for one of them). They happen, so to speak, within the church.'[52] Those

48. J.D. Kingsbury, *JBL* 97 (1978) 56-73. The distinction is introduced on p. 58, and worked out on pp. 58-62.
49. For a wide-ranging and stimulating study of the idea of 'following' and 'coming behind' in the world of Jesus' day (arising out of an exegetical study of Matthew 8:21-22), see M. Hengel, *The Charismatic Leader and His Followers* (ET. Edinburgh: T & T Clark, 1981). Hengel believes that the model of the personal disciples of a rabbi, often cited as the basis of this terminology, is inadequate to explain such language in the context of Jesus' historical ministry, and that the focus is more on the radical commitment involved in being called to throw in their lot with a prophetic or charismatic figure, to participate in his mission and authority and in the conflict and renunciation which that must entail.
50. See the classic essay of G. Bornkamm in *Tradition*, 52-57; cf. e.g. B. Gerhardsson, *The Mighty Acts of Jesus according to Matthew* (Lund: Gleerup, 1979) 54-55, and most recent commentators.
51. Much of Held's dissertation as reproduced in Bornkamm, *Tradition*, 165-299 pursues this theme. See especially pp. 181-192, 200-206 for Held's suggestions as to how Matthew has deliberately reshaped the tradition with this aim.
52. Gerhardsson, *Mighty Acts*, 54.

who followed Jesus (literally as well as metaphorically) during the time of his ministry thus provide a model for those who will continue to follow him as members of the disciple group.

Those who are related to Jesus as disciples and followers find themselves brought by that relationship into a community with one another. They become *brothers*. Thus in 23:8 those who follow the one teacher are all 'brothers'. When mutual relationships within the disciple community are under discussion, it is the term 'brother' which focuses the nature of the relationship in 18:15-17,21,35. A disciple's conduct is judged in terms of his relationship with his 'brother' (5:22-24; 7:3-5). But this is not merely the language of camaraderie; the basis of their brotherhood is that they are first of all brothers *of Jesus*. This is declared in the remarkable passage where Jesus contrasts his literal family with the true family of his 'mother and brothers' who do the will of his Father in heaven (12:46-50), and is presupposed when the risen Jesus outside the tomb sends a message to 'my brothers' (28:10). The under-standing of the phrase 'one of the least of these my brothers' in 25:40 is a matter of exegetical dispute, but I am inclined to the view that here too 'brother' carries the same sense, so that the passage refers to acts of kindness specifically towards the least of Jesus' followers, rather than to the needy in general.[53]

The further designation of the 'brothers' in this last passage as 'the least' recalls another distinctively Matthean expression, 'the little ones'.[54] Indeed in 25:45 the term 'brothers' has been dropped, and 'one of these least' serves alone to designate those in whom the Son of Man is served or rejected. There is a close parallel here to the thought of 10:40-42, where to receive 'you' (the disciples) is to receive Jesus, and an act of kindness offered to 'one of these little ones' $εἰς$ $ὄνομα$ $μαθητοῦ$ (RSV,

53. There has been an increasing reaction in recent years against the assumption of most earlier commentators that Matthew 25:31-46 refers to general humanitarian concern, though among those who have proposed a more specifically Christian focus there has been a variety of views as to whether the reference is to needy Christians in general, to a specific class of 'little ones', or to those engaged in Christian mission and thus recognised as representatives of Jesus among the nations. For this specifically 'Christian' exegesis see e.g. J.R. Michaels, 'Apostolic Hardships and Righteous Gentiles', *JBL* 84 (1965) 27-37; J. Manek, 'Mit wem identifiziert sich Jesus (Matt. 25:31-46)?' in B. Lindars & S.S. Smalley (ed.), *Christ and Spirit in the New Testament: in honour of C.F.D. Moule* (Cambridge University Press, 1973) 15-25; G.E. Ladd, 'The Parable of the Sheep and the Goats in Recent Interpretation' in R.N. Longenecker & M.C. Tenney (ed.), *New Dimensions in New Testament Study* (Grand Rapids: Zondervan, 1974) 191-199; G. Gay, 'The Judgment of the Gentiles in Matthew's Theology', in W.W. Gasque & W.S. LaSor (ed.), *Scripture, Tradition and Interpretation: essays presented to E.F. Harrison* (Grand Rapids: Eerdmans, 1978) 199-215; R.H. Stein, *An Introduction to the Parables of Jesus* (Philadelphia: Westminster, 1981) 137-140; Gundry, *Matthew*, 514f; Carson, *Matthew*, 518-523.

54. The importance of this phrase in Matthew's view of the church has been drawn out especially by E. Schweizer in the article 'Matthew's Church' published in English translation in Stanton, *Interpretation*, 129-155. For interesting examples of its continuing use in circles apparently influenced by Matthew see G.N. Stanton, *JTS* 28 (1977) 80-82.

'because he is a disciple')[55] will receive a reward. Here we should probably see μικρός 'little one' as virtually a synonym of μαθητής.[56] That conclusion is reinforced by the very prominent use of the same term in chapter 18, where disciples are urged to recognise and care for one another as μικροί (18:6,10,14).

Here the term arises naturally out of the first few verses of the chapter, where Jesus has used a child as an illustration of true greatness in the kingdom of heaven (18:1-4), and has gone on to talk (in terms reminiscent again of 10:40-42) of the need to 'receive one such child in my name' (18:5). From that point on the literal child of v 2 is left behind, and it is the disciples as 'little ones' who are the focus of the chapter.[57] This term for disciples therefore calls attention to the theme of true greatness, the demand that disciples should not ape the world's ideas of status and importance, a theme which recurs in different forms e.g. in 6:1-18; 20:25-28; 23:2-4,9-12.

Disciples, then, are people who first and foremost belong to Jesus. They are personally committed to him, with a loyalty which transcends even natural family ties. It is their relationship with him which forms the basis of their community with one another, and in this community they are therefore able to recognise one another as brothers, and to care for one another with all the concern of members of the same family. Indeed they are themselves 'little brothers' of Jesus. None of them can claim pre-eminence in terms of status in the community, but all must recognise themselves, and each other, as 'little ones'. Whether or not Schweizer is right to see in this portrait a reflection of what Matthew's church was actually like,[58] it is clear that this is how Matthew wanted it to be.

DOING THE WILL OF GOD

In recent years, especially since G. Strecker chose as the title of his monograph on the theology of Matthew *Der Weg der Gerechtigkeit*, students of Matthew have focused on his use of the term δικαιοσύνη

55. The same rather unusual construction has been used twice in the preceding verse: εἰς ὄνομα προφήτου, εἰς ὄνομα δικαίου, where in each case the person so received has just been described by the same term, προφήτης and δίκαιος; it seems clear then that εἰς ὄνομα must be understood not as an appeal to someone else, but as designating the category in which the person concerned is recognised. Albright and Mann explain it on the basis of a Semitic idiom 'al shem. (They see the 'Prophet' and 'Righteous One' of v 41 as Jesus, not the disciple, but this does not affect the meaning of the idiom, and in v 42 they agree with the RSV rendering.)

56. See the comments of U. Luz in Stanton, *Interpretation*, 110 and n. 21 (p. 120), in response to Strecker's argument that εἰς ὄνομα μαθητοῦ should be understood as 'on appeal to the name' of one of the Twelve.

57. Pace S. Agourides, ' "Little Ones" in Matthew', *The Bible Translator* 35/3 (1984) 329-334. who envisages a distinction, indeed a 'tension', between the disciples in general and the μικροί. who are 'a group of young disciples who were not held in great esteem in some circles in the church'.

58. See above pp. 118-119.

'righteousness'. This may seem surprising in view of the fact that the noun occurs only seven times in the gospel, but most of these uses bring it into sharp focus. Thus the purpose of Jesus' baptism is to fulfil all δικαιοσύνη (3:15); the subjects of the beatitudes are those who are hungry and thirsty for δικαιοσύνη (5:6) and are persecuted on account of it (5:10); disciples are called to exercise a δικαιοσύνη greater than that of the scribes and Pharisees (5:20); they must beware of exercising it merely for human approval (6:1); rather it is God's kingdom and his δικαιοσύνη that they are to concentrate on (6:33); and the teaching of John, which Jesus endorses, is described as the 'way of δικαιοσύνη' (21:32). Such uses suggest that δικαιοσύνη was for Matthew a term which aptly summed up what was distinctive about following Jesus.

In view of the prominence of this term in Paul's letters, it is not surprising that discussion has focused on the relation between its use by Matthew and by Paul. Strecker insisted that Matthew's use is quite different, in that for him δικαιοσύνη is an ethical quality, a way of life, and is not to be interpreted on the basis of its Pauline use to denote God's saving action. It is a demand upon man, not a gift from God.[59] R. Mohrlang's extended comparison of the ethical perspectives of Matthew and Paul modifies this conclusion at least to the extent that he emphasises that δικαιοσύνη for Matthew 'embraces both being and doing'; it is as much a matter of inward motivation as of outward performance. But it remains 'a strictly ethical concept' involving 'thoroughgoing and determined obedience to the deepest intent of the law', not a forensic soteriological term.[60]

The most exhaustive recent discussion of *Righteousness in Matthew* is by B. Przybylski. He too insists that Matthew must not be interpreted in the light of Paul. Rather he must be understood against the background of current Jewish usage as illustrated by Qumran and Tannaitic literature. Przybylski's very detailed study of this background[61] indicates that *tsedeq* (which became increasingly distinct in meaning from its cognate *tsedaqah*) is a matter of behaviour, not of soteriology. It is the norm by which man's behaviour is measured in the sight of God. It is a demand on man, not a gift to him. It is, Przybylski argues, *tsedeq* rather than *tsedaqah* which forms the basis of Matthew's use of

59. Strecker, *Weg*, especially 149-158, 179-181, 187. This aspect of Strecker's view is usefully summarised in his article 'The Concept of History in Matthew' translated in Stanton, *Interpretation,* 74-77, Przybylski, *Righteousness,* 1-2, provides a useful summary of the contrasting views on offer in recent study of δικαιοσύνη in Matthew, ranging from Strecker's purely ethical understanding of the term to a thoroughly 'Pauline' interpretation by M.J. Fiedler (in an unpublished dissertation).
60. Mohrlang, *Matthew and Paul,* 45, 98-99, 113-114. Mohrlang's notes, especially those relating to pp. 113-114, provide a useful guide to significant recent discussions of the subject.
61. Przybylski, *Righteousness,* 13-76; pp. 3-12 justify this approach.

δικαιοσύνη. It means 'man's conduct in accordance with the will of God'. But since the law, which is man's guide to right conduct, can be differently interpreted, there may be degrees of righteousness, and the 'greater righteousness' of Matthew 5:20 is 'that which corresponds to the interpretation of the law given by Jesus'. Matthew's use of δικαιοσύνη, then, is with reference to right living; it is not, like Paul's use, an indication of his belief that salvation is the gift of God.[62]

But, Przybylski goes on to argue,[63] it is therefore incorrect to suggest that δικαιοσύνη is the key term in Matthew's theology. For, even if he does not use this term to express the idea, Matthew does believe that salvation is the gift of God, not merely earned by human effort. So δικαιοσύνη is not synonymous with discipleship. Indeed Jewish piety exhibits its own δικαιοσύνη, so that a 'greater δικαιοσύνη' is needed to mark out the followers of Jesus. Rather, 'it must be concluded that for Matthew the terminology which expresses the essence of discipleship is *doing the will of God*.[64] This term, prominent especially in 7:21 and 12:46-50 as the mark of a true disciple, gives positive expression to Matthew's understanding of discipleship; δικαιοσύνη, on the other hand, is a more polemical term, used with reference to 'properly religious Jews'. In his final chapter Przybylski goes further and argues that δικαιοσύνη functions in Matthew as a provisional concept, a bridge between Jewish religious ideas and the teaching of Jesus. It is therefore ultimately inadequate to express true discipleship, which goes beyond Jewish piety to observing all that Jesus commanded (28:20, a passage where Przybylski finds the absence of the term δικαιοσύνη significant); this is now, for the followers of Jesus, the way to 'do the will of God'.

I believe that Przybylski is right to question the centrality of the term δικαιοσύνη for Matthew; his usage is too varied to be focused in a single term. But the demotion of δικαιοσύνη to a 'provisional' and 'inadequate' status goes too far. While it is certainly true that Matthew 5:20 and 6:1 contain a polemical element, contrasting two levels of δικαιοσύνη, that of outward religious observance and that of the disciple who aims to please his Father in heaven, it takes some ingenuity to find a similar polemical thrust in its use in 5:6,10 and 6:33, in each of which δικαιοσύνη appears to function precisely as a designation of the highest values of a true disciple. Readers of the Sermon on the Mount would not naturally suppose that to 'do the will of my Father' (7:21) is intended to represent a higher level of discipleship than the δικαιοσύνη of these verses (or the 'greater δικαιοσύνη' required in 5:20). True δικαιοσύνη (as opposed to the superficial type castigated in 5:20 and 6:1) *is* 'doing the will of God',

62. *Ibid.* 105-107.
63. *Ibid.* 107ff.
64. *Ibid.* 112-115.

and that is what Matthew wishes to see as the distinguishing mark of
those who belong to the disciple community.[65]

GRACE AND REWARD

A character portrait of the disciple who 'does the will of God' is
offered by the 'beatitudes' which open the Sermon on the Mount. The
eight brief characterisations of 5:3-10 add up to a total way of living
(and indeed of being) which render disciples so distinctive (and therefore
persecuted, vv 11- 12) that they are able to function as salt to the earth
and light in a dark world (vv 13-16). But the beatitudes are not only
a catalogue of ethical virtues.[66] Each of them carries an explanation of
the 'blessedness' of those so described, introduced by ὅτι 'because',
and expressed in the future tense (except for the first and last, where
'theirs is the kingdom of heaven' may be understood either of a present
experience or of a future expectation – if indeed it is right to tie it down
temporally at all). It would seem then that to do the will of God is not
only good in itself, but carries the prospect of reward, whether that
reward be understood in terms of resultant blessings in the present
situation or of an eschatological recompense.

The subject of the 'rewards' of discipleship in Matthew is important,
but easily misunderstood. Zumstein discusses whether the beatitudes
answer the question 'What must I do to be saved?' or rather 'By adopting
what way of life am I to respond to the gracious offer of eschatological
blessing?' – and argues strongly for the latter as the true interpretation.[67]
Guelich points out that the beatitudes are addressed to those who
already are disciples; they are not an inducement to respond to Jesus'
message so much as the assurance that the radical new way of life on
which they have embarked will not prove to be in vain. 'These promises
are given as assurance rather than as reward.'[68] His remark seems to
be theologically correct; Matthew does see salvation as something given,
not earned.[69] But at the level of terminology it must be recognised that
Matthew does not seem to share the coyness of many modern Christians
with regard to rewards. Μισθός 'reward' is not an unworthy concept.
True, those whose piety is mere outward show are dismissed with the
withering comment that they 'have received their reward' (6:2,5,16),

65. The use of the adjective δίκαιος (which is not discussed in this connection as often
as might be expected) exhibits a similar range of reference. It denotes Jewish piety (true
or pretended) in e.g. 1:19; 9:13; 13:17; 23:28,29,35; but in 10:41 the context requires that
it refers specifically to disciples, and in 13:43,49; 25:37,46 it denotes those who are saved
in the context of final judgement.
66. For a survey of some recent discussions which have focused too exclusively on
this ethical aspect of the beatitudes see Zumstein, *Condition*, 306.
67. *Ibid.* 307, concluding his extended discussion of the beatitudes, pp. 284-308.
68. Guelich, *Sermon*, 111, part of the conclusion to a lengthy study, pp. 62-118.
69. See Przybylski, *Righteousness*, 106-107.

but the contrasting destiny of the true disciple is not to have no reward
at all, but to be able to look forward to one which is really worth
having, a reward from 'your Father who is in heaven' (6:1); he 'will
repay you' (6:4,6,18). The following verses similarly ground the call for
earthly poverty in the promise of 'treasure in heaven' (6:19-21). It is
assumed that doing the will of God will result in a 'reward' (5:12,46;
10:41- 42; cf., not using μισθός, 19:29; 25:21,23), and this is something
to be glad about (5:12). J. Jeremias[70] recognises the prominence of the
reward theme, but goes on to emphasise rightly that there is no question
of acquiring merit; it is not so much 'reward' as 'recompense'. 'Merit
has an eye to human achievement; recompense looks to God's faithfulness.' No-one will be a loser, in any ultimate sense, by becoming a
disciple.

R. Mohrlang also recognises the importance of the theme of rewards
in Matthew, but points out that more prominent than the positive
aspect is the negative: 'the danger of failing to attain the kingdom, and
the fearful prospect of judgement that implies'. It is this that 'serves as
the dominant motivating force for ethics throughout the Gospel'.[71]
D. Marguerat has devoted a whole doctoral dissertation to the theme
of judgement in Matthew, and has no difficulty in showing how
important this theme is in the gospel, notably in the placing of the
vision of the last judgement as the final section of the final discourse
(25:31-46).[72]

But again it would be a travesty of Matthew's theology to suggest
that he advocates a discipleship based on fear. Rather the disciple is
one who increasingly experiences the love and provision of his 'Father
in heaven' – this key phrase occurs ten times in the Sermon on the
Mount alone. It is that relationship which is the context of discipleship,
and it is a relationship which is not earned by obedience, but given by
grace. Jesus' mission is 'to save his people from their sins' (1:21), and
the theme of God's undeserved forgiveness recurs throughout the gospel,
until it is focused in the important inclusion in Matthew's version of
the words at the last supper of the phrase 'for the forgiveness of sins'
(26:28).[73] The parable of the two debtors in 18:23-35 emphasises that
the disciple owes all that he is to God's lavish forgiveness – but the
point of the parable is that this grace of God must be the basis for
the disciples' corresponding forgiveness of each other. In that parable

70. Jeremias, NT Theology, 215-217.
71. Mohrlang, Matthew and Paul, 48-52. He goes so far as to describe Matthew's
'concept of reciprocity' in God's dealings with men as a jus talionis, ibid. 52- 54.
72. Marguerat, Jugement; see especially the chart of the occurrence of judgement-
language on p. 31. He complains that while many have noted the importance of the
theme, it has never before been the subject of a detailed study in its own right (p. 55).
73. See Mohrlang, Matthew and Paul, 78-81 for the theme of the grace of God in
Matthew.

there is a fascinating blend of the motive of fear of punishment (vv 34-
35) with the more fundamental motive of gratitude and imitation of
the grace of God. That blend is typical of the gospel as a whole, in its
presentation of what it means to do the will of God.

Mohrlang[74] therefore concludes that the commonly drawn contrast
between Matthew and Paul as one between law and grace is incorrect.
While it is true that Matthew's primary focus is on ethics rather than,
as in Paul, on 'the theological dynamics behind ethics', and he therefore
'portrays the life of discipleship as one of submission and radical
obedience to the will of God (as expressed in the law and interpreted
by the life and teachings of Jesus)', while Paul aims to free his readers
from the law, nonetheless there is 'not an absolute dichotomy'. Similarly,
Marguerat[75] concludes that while Paul presents salvation as *preceding*
ethics, and as independent of law, Matthew makes no such distinction,
but understands grace and obedience, salvation and ethics, as part of
a single whole. And underlying the whole is the disciple's relationship
with Jesus; it is only on this basis that true δικαιοσύνη can be accomplished. It is precisely in 'the bringing together of grace and demand'
that Matthew's theological originality is to be discerned.[76]

UNDERSTANDING THE MYSTERY

While Matthew's Jesus is depicted as teaching in the synagogues and
to the crowds in the open air, the discourses which form the core of
Jesus' teaching in the gospel are addressed primarily, and in some cases
exclusively, to his disciples. They form 'the privileged audience of
Christ's teaching'.[77] Of the five great discourses three (chapters 10, 18,
24-25) are introduced specifically as spoken to disciples alone. One of
the others, the Sermon on the Mount, is indeed spoken in the presence
of the crowds (5:1; 7:28), but Matthew makes it clear that the target
audience is the disciples who 'came to him' in 5:1 and to whom he
'opened his mouth' in 5:2, and the content of the Sermon, with its
repeated contrast between 'you' and society at large, presupposes this
more restricted audience; the crowds appear almost as eavesdroppers!

In chapter 13, however, we do see Jesus deliberately addressing his
parables to 'great crowds' from a boat on the lake (13:1-3). Yet it is
this chapter which in fact brings out the privileged situation of the

74. *Ibid.* 126-128.
75. Marguerat, *Jugement,* 212-235, discusses the issue of 'salvation by works' in
Matthew in comparison with Paul.
76. *Ibid.* 235.
77. Zumstein, *Condition,* 31. He analyses the way the major discourses (including
chapter 23) are presented on pp. 29-36, showing that this privileged position of the
disciples is a matter of deliberate redactional design.

disciples most forcefully, for whereas the parables are presented as public teaching, they are interspersed with passages where Jesus, alone with the disciples, explains both his teaching method and the meaning of some of the parables (13:10-23,36-43), while v 34 stresses that the crowds received nothing but the parables alone; v 35 then goes on to explain this teaching method as a 'fulfilment' of Psalm 78:2, which makes it appear a matter of deliberate policy. It is not clear how wide the audience is for the remaining parables of vv 44-50 (which include another explanation of a parable, vv 49-50), but the concluding verses 51-52 seem again to be addressed specifically to the disciples, with their depiction of a scribe who 'has become a disciple of the kingdom of heaven'. The distinction between the wider audience and the privileged inner circle is thus even more clear here than in chapters 5-7, and the contents of the parables themselves underline the fact, by drawing out the divisions which exist between different levels of hearing and response leading to an ultimate division between the fruitful and unfruitful soil, the wheat and the weeds, the good and bad fish.

It is in this context that Matthew includes a remarkable passage about the disciples' privilege, 13:10-17. Part of this passage is shared with Mark and Luke, including the clear distinction between 'you' to whom the knowledge of the 'mysteries' of the kingdom of heaven is 'given' and other people ('those outside', Mark; 'the rest', Luke), and an explanation of this fact in terms drawn from Isaiah 6:9-10. But Matthew's version is considerably expanded and the impact thereby strengthened. The unprivileged position of 'them' is bluntly stated: to them the knowledge of the mystery is 'not given' (Mark and Luke speak of their having parables). This is followed immediately in v 12 by a saying which occurs in a separate position in Mark and Luke: 'To him who has will more be given, and he will have abundance; but from him who has not even what he has will be taken away.' The allusion to Isaiah 6:9-10 is then included in a similar form to that found in Mark and Luke, but is immediately followed by a full quotation of the LXX text of those verses, introduced by the formula, 'With them indeed is fulfilled the prophecy of Isaiah'. This in turn is followed in vv 16-17 by a saying found also in Luke 10:23-24 which explicitly underlines the special privilege of the disciples as those who now see and hear what many prophets and righteous people have longed to experience. These seven verses appear then to be a collection of material deliberately composed to underscore the theme already apparent in Mark 4:11f, of the privileged position of the disciples, as opposed to 'those outside', as the recipients of special revelation, a revelation which is described as 'knowing the mysteries of the kingdom of heaven'.

This privilege is seen in other passages which are either peculiar to Matthew or significantly adapted by him. Matthew 11:25-27 celebrates the special revelation given to 'babies' (the same idea as the 'little ones' considered above?) but hidden from the wise and understanding (v 25). Again this privilege is grounded in the will of God (v 26; cf. the 'given', 'not given' of 13:11), but it is more specifically traced in v 27 to the Son's decision to pass on God's truth to certain people (and by implication not to others). So far is Q material, but Matthew goes on to record Jesus' call to the weary and burdened to come and learn from him, a passage which unmistakably echoes Ben Sira 51:23-27, but with the important difference that Jesus appears not (like Ben Sira himself) as Wisdom's prophet, but as the one who offers himself in the role of the divine Wisdom.[78] The special knowledge granted to the 'babies' is therefore grounded in their relationship with Jesus as those who have 'come to him', and to whom he is willing to pass on the secrets of the knowledge of God; it is specifically as disciples that they have access to the Wisdom of God.

The most emphatic statement of this special revelation granted to disciples is in 16:17, where Peter's declaration of Jesus as Messiah and Son of God is greeted with the beatitude 'Blessed are you, Simon Bar-Jona! For flesh and blood has not revealed this to you, but my Father who is in heaven.' While the following verses go on to spell out Peter's unique role, we have seen above[79] that he speaks here as the representative of the whole disciple group. The privilege of revelation from 'my Father in heaven' is one which all disciples share, and which thus sets them apart from the rest of 'flesh and blood'.

But it is this same passage which goes on to record the inadequacy of Peter's grasp of what the revelation means, leading to the fierce rebuke, 'Get behind me, Satan! You are a σκάνδαλον to me; for your thoughts are not those of God but of men' (16:23). To receive divine revelation is not necessarily to understand it, and this tension runs throughout the gospel, as the privilege of the disciples is set off against their failure to respond adequately to the 'mysteries' which they have been given. The disciples' failure to understand is frequently singled out as a specifically Marcan emphasis, and it is often pointed out that Matthew seems more reluctant than Mark to allow the disciples (and especially Peter) to appear in a bad light, at least with regard to the extent of their understanding.[80] G. Barth[81] in particular has carefully analysed the uses of συνίημι 'understand' in Mark and Matthew in

78. On the christological implications of this use of Wisdom language see below pp. 302-306.

79. See above pp. 244-246.

80. Indeed, U. Luz (in Stanton, *Interpretation*, 101-102) argues that it is *only* on this issue that Matthew has consistently 'improved' the picture of the disciples; on other matters such as their faith or fear he is not consistent, sometimes setting the disciples in a good light in comparison with the crowds, sometimes presenting them as failures.

81. In Bornkamm, *Tradition*, 106-112. Cf Blair, *Jesus*, 102-106; Luz, in Stanton, *Interpretation*, 102-105.

relation to the disciples, and shows that Matthew not only omits some of the Markan statements about the disciples' failure to understand (e.g. Mark 6:52; 8:17b; 9:6a,10,32), but also sometimes makes a point of recording that they did in fact come to understand (e.g. Mt. 13:51; 16:12; 17:13). This is true, and an important element in the total picture. But Matthew has not carried out a complete whitewash. In addition to 16:23 mentioned above, he records other places where Jesus is frustrated by the disciples' lack of understanding (15:16; 16:9,11), or where they find it necessary to ask for explanation (13:36; 15:15).[82] But in such passages Jesus goes on to explain more carefully, and it is thus that understanding eventually results. It may be a long process, as they gradually come to terms with a whole new way of thinking. Their ultimate understanding is not a natural endowment, but a matter of privileged instruction, sometimes painfully assimilated.

Disciples are then, for Matthew, those to whom a special revelation of God's truth and purpose has been entrusted, but to whom a full understanding of this revelation does not come automatically. They must be aware of the possibility of thinking 'men's thoughts', and must aim to grow in understanding of the 'mysteries of the kingdom of heaven' which it is their privilege to be given. For this purpose, they have available Matthew's record of the teaching of Jesus, to lead them on to that eventual degree of understanding which will enable them to 'observe all that I have commanded you' (28:20).

But response to the revelation is not merely a matter of understanding. Matthew may be more concerned than Mark to give a positive account of the disciples' *understanding*, but he is much less complimentary about their *faith*. Several times he has Jesus apply to them the striking adjective ὀλιγόπιστος, usually translated 'of little faith' (6:30; 8:26; 14:31; 16:8; and the noun ὀλιγοπιστία in 17:20; all except 6:30 are peculiar to Matthew). The context in each case is a situation of need or danger which requires the supernatural power of God (or of Jesus) to solve it, and in each case their πίστις, practical trust, proves unequal to the situation.[83] Even the Gentile centurion of Capernaum trusted Jesus to heal his servant with a word, but the disciples frequently fail to match his πίστις, which was beyond that of any in Israel (8:8-10). Indeed, the traditional translation, 'little faith', is apparently too complimentary, for in 17:20 it is *contrasted* with 'faith like a grain of mustard seed', a proverbial

82. H.J. Held, in Bornkamm, *Tradition*, 291-292, draws out clearly Matthew's continued insistence on the limited understanding of the disciples.
83. J. Zumstein, *Condition*, 239 rightly points out that it is to disciples alone that Matthew applies the term ὀλιγόπιστος. Ὀλιγοπιστία is therefore defined as 'a moment of unbelief in the very midst of living as a believer'; it characterises 'the disciple whose faith fails to stand the test'. For the whole subject of Matthew's use of ὀλιγόπιστος and its relation to rabbinic use cf. H.J. Held in Bornkamm, *Tradition*, 291-296. Cf. also Gerhardsson, *Mighty Acts*, 62-65.

expression for the smallest imaginable amount.[84] Even such faith will achieve what the disciples cannot; their ὀλιγοπιστία therefore appears to be for all practical purposes no faith at all.[85] 'Ολιγοπιστία achieves no results; it merits only a rebuke.[86]

Some interpreters draw a sharp distinction at this point between understanding and faith. Whereas 'faith' for Mark contained more of an intellectual element, Matthew has transferred this intellectual element to the verb συνίημι 'understand', and uses πίστις by contrast for practical trust.[87] He can then treat the disciples differently with regard to these two concepts: 'Faith and understanding are separated in Matthew. The disciples are men of little faith, but they do understand.'[88] But we have seen above that Matthew does not have such a sanguine view of the disciples' understanding as this dichotomy suggests; their understanding, no less than their faith, is in need of correction and development. Indeed it is in one of the passages where they are rebuked for ὀλιγοπιστία (16:8) that their intellectual failure is also commented on ('Do you not yet perceive?'; 'How is it that you fail to perceive?', 16:9,11), and it seems likely that with the new 'understanding' which results from Jesus' explanation (16:12) we are to understand that their ὀλιγοπιστία in this instance is also corrected. The 'mysteries of the kingdom of heaven' are so new and so far-reaching that disciples can hardly be expected to achieve a full grasp of their implications all at once. The Peter to whom God revealed the truth about Jesus (16:17) is the same as the one who both failed to walk on the water through ὀλιγοπιστία (14:31) and was rebuked by Jesus for thinking 'men's thoughts' (16:23). Neither his faith nor his understanding matched up to the privilege of the revelation he received, and in this he is typical of other disciples.

Matthew's vision of the church, then, is of a uniquely privileged body of people, to whom the heavenly mysteries have been revealed, but who are not thereby rendered infallible in either thought or faith. They may misunderstand, and their faith may fail any number of tests. But, for all their weakness, they have launched on a course of training in understanding the mysteries, both intellectually and practically, a process in which Matthew's gospel is designed to assist both by the examples (positive and negative) provided by the original disciples and by the

84. Cf. 13:31; Mishnah, *Niddah* 5:2.

85. It is in this same context (17:17) that Jesus complains of the 'unbelieving and perverse generation'. While it may be that this description is meant to reach further than the disciples themselves, it seems clear that in the first instance it is they who have in this situation proved to be not just ὀλιγόπιστοι, but ἄπιστοι 'faithless'.

86. A similar charge is implied in 21:20, where the disciples' 'amazement' over Jesus' powerful word is contrasted with what would be the case 'if you have faith, and do not doubt', and in 28:17, where the verb διστάζω is the same one which described Peter's ὀλιγοπιστία in 14:31.

87. So G. Barth in Bornkamm, *Tradition*, 114-115.

88. U. Luz in Stanton, *Interpretation*, 103.

careful teaching by which Jesus led them towards a faith and an understanding appropriate to their God-given privilege.

WHEAT AND WEEDS

We noted in the last chapter[89] that Matthew's observation of the failure of God's people Israel to live up to the privilege of their God-given status finds its counterpart also in his view of the reconstituted people of God. Under the new covenant, as under the old, it is possible that some of those who profess allegiance to Jesus will prove to have been spurious disciples. 'Many are called, but few are chosen' (22:14). The immediate context of that epigrammatic statement is the story of the man ejected from the wedding banquet because he proved to be inappropriately attired; even if 22:1-14 is composed of originally independent traditions, it is clear from the text as it now stands that Matthew envisages this man as one of those who replaced those originally invited to the banquet, i.e. as one of the new people of God. Indeed, he has given a hint of the mixed character of those brought in from the streets by describing them as 'both bad and good' (22:10).

That last phrase recalls the focus of the two parables of ultimate separation in chapter 13, that of the weeds and that of the net. Each is interpreted in almost exactly the same words, to the effect that the angels at the close of the age will gather the bad together and 'throw them into the fiery furnace, where there will be weeping and gnashing of teeth' (13:40-42,49-50). But what is emphasised in each parable is that until that time the wheat and the weeds grow together indistinguishably in the field, and the net catches good and bad fish together, so that the ultimate separation must involve the removal of the wicked 'out of his [the Son of Man's] kingdom' (13:41) and 'from among [literally 'out of the middle of'] the righteous' (13:49). The Christian community must therefore be understood to contain 'both bad and good'. Until the final judgement it remains a *corpus mixtum*,[90] and the prospect of judgement remains a reality for its members.

What distinguishes the bad from the good is expressed in a variety of ways. In Matthew's version of the interpretation of the parable of the sower, while it remains true as in Mark and Luke that all four types of soil represent those who 'hear the word' (13:19,20,22,23), Matthew twice includes the motif of 'understanding' (συνίημι); it is the lack of understanding which marks out the first and most hopeless category

---

89. See above pp. 230-232.
90. This term has been frequently used in studies of Matthew since Bornkamm introduced it into his discussion of Matthew's ecclesiology, *Tradition*, 19 (where the Latin phrase used in the German text has been translated as 'a mixed body'). Bornkamm's essay draws attention to this theme at several points. It is discussed also e.g. by Zumstein, *Condition*, 381-385.

of hearers (13:19), while the fruitful soil represents those who 'hear and understand' (13:23). This reflects the idea of the appropriate response to revelation which we considered in the previous section, where the importance of συνίημι in Matthew's vocabulary was noted. Joyful acceptance of the word (13:20) is not enough.

The contrast between true and false discipleship is most forcefully brought out in the series of four vignettes which conclude the Sermon on the Mount. The first (7:13-14) sets up a clear opposition between saved and lost, and contains no suggestion that that division runs through the professing church (unless it be in the 'many' who go by the broad way). The second is more threatening to the 'insider', in that the false prophets are dressed as sheep, and it takes discernment to recognise them, to distinguish the true from the false (7: 15-20). But at least in this case too there is no doubt of the hostile character of those concerned, however well disguised; 'false prophets' and 'ravenous wolves' do not sound like descriptions of those of indeterminate position! The third contrast, however, is even more unsettling, for those who are rejected here are those who not only insistently call Jesus 'Lord', but also claim to have prophesied, exorcised and worked miracles in his name (7:21-23); and there is nothing to indicate that the claim is insincere. A professed allegiance to Jesus, and even successful 'charismatic' activity in a Christian context, are no guarantee of proving ultimately to be among the saved. The key lies rather in a relationship with Jesus ('I never knew you', 7:23), which expresses itself in an appropriate way of life, 'doing the will of my Father in heaven' (7:21). The same point is picked up finally in 7:24-27 where the contrast is, as in the parable of the sower, between two men who equally 'hear' what Jesus says; the difference in this case, however is expressed not in terms of 'understanding' but of 'doing'. The focus on 'doing' in both 7:21-23 and 7:24-27 (and implied in the testing by 'fruit' in 7:15-20) shows that true understanding will be expressed in the way a disciple lives, and the test of that is his practical response to 'these words of mine' (7:24,26; cf. 28:20, 'to observe all that I have commanded you'). In this connection it is probably also significant that the parable of the sower is immediately preceded by the declaration that the true member of the Jesus family is the one who 'does the will of my Father in heaven' (12:50).

If 'doing the will of God' and 'understanding' are the marks of a true disciple (as we have seen in preceding sections), it follows that mere professed membership of the Jesus group is no guarantee of salvation. The parable of the two sons (21:28-32), while it is aimed in context at the failure of traditional Judaism to respond to God's initiative through John and Jesus, surely serves also to warn the members of Matthew's church that the 'son' who says 'I go' but does nothing cannot presume that his profession will bring him into the kingdom of God.

The 'righteousness exceeding that of the scribes and Pharisees' is the entrance requirement (5:20), and it seems that even one who has responded favourably to Jesus may fail to exhibit it.

Judgement is not, then, in Matthew's understanding, a theme of relevance only to those outside the church. The insider too remains vulnerable, and in danger of 'stumbling' and being lost (18:6-14). The one who proves ultimately impervious to the appeals of his fellow-disciples, and must therefore be treated 'as a Gentile and a tax-collector', is introduced as 'your brother' (18:15-17). Even the one who causes the little ones to stumble is apparently himself envisaged as being within the Christian community, and the threat of judgement which hangs over him is expressed in the most extreme terms (18:6-7). And the same chapter finishes with the uncomfortable prospect of the previously forgiven debtor being given up to the 'torturers' (18:34), and the explicitly drawn moral that the unforgiving cannot expect to experience forgiveness.

There is, then, no room for complacency in Matthew's church. Only at the final judgement will it be ultimately clear who are the saved and who the lost (13:40-43,49-50), and there will be some surprises (25:37-39, 44). 'So the question of salvation is contingent on the final judgement. The ultimate separation will run through the church, and this perspective takes away any soteriological security behind which believers might have sheltered.'[91]

That is why the insistent warnings to be ready for the coming of the end which sound through chapters 24-25 are not directed only, or even primarily, towards those outside the disciple community. Disciples are still vulnerable to impostors, whose targets will include 'even the elect', and many will be deceived (24:4-5,10-12,23-26); it is only the one who stands firm to the end who will be saved (24:13). If there were no danger, there would be no need for the disciples to be exhorted so urgently to 'watch' (24:42,44; 25:13). But even for the master's servant there remains the possibility of being 'dichotomised' and finding himself among the hypocrites, where there is weeping and gnashing of teeth (24:51). The two parables which follow in chapter 25 focus on the same point. All ten 'bridesmaids' (25:1-13) expect to be part of the wedding celebrations, all ten have lamps, and indeed all ten go to sleep, but only those who are ready for his arrival go in; for the others the door remains shut, despite their plea of 'Lord, Lord' (cf. 7:21-23). The provision of oil, which represents the preparedness of the other five, remains uninterpreted, but the next parable (25:14-30) takes up the point. Of the three men who are at the beginning equally servants of the master, two finish up in the 'joy of their master', the other in outer

91. Marguerat, *Jugement*, 447, concluding a careful discussion of the whole theme of the mixed nature of the church as it relates to Matthew's view of judgement, *ibid.* 424-447.

darkness, weeping and gnashing of teeth. The difference lies in how they have made use of what was entrusted to them. Preparedness for the judgement seems then to consist in action appropriate to the privilege the disciple has received, not merely in the receipt of that privilege in itself. So when the parables of preparedness are followed by the awe-inspiring tableau of the last judgement (25:31-46), it comes as no surprise that the criterion of judgement is one not of profession but of practice. The true disciple is not the one who says 'Lord, Lord', but the one who does the will of his Father.

But for the time being, the two exist side by side, and the parable of the weeds makes it clear that the final judgement should not be anticipated. The mixed nature of the church, however theologically inconvenient, is a fact of life. Those who will be saved and those who will be lost share in the same community, and it is not the business of that community or of its leaders to try to separate them. Both must be allowed to grow together until the harvest.

For all his idealism with regard to what the church should be, Matthew remains a realist with regard to what it actually is, and so continues to warn its members, as they contemplate what has happened to the chosen people of the Old Testament, 'It could happen to you too.'

VIII

MATTHEW'S PORTRAIT OF JESUS

Christological titles. Beyond the Christological titles. The climax of the gospel.

I T IS NO DOUBT A TRUISM TO SAY THAT THE THEOLOGY OF MATTHEW'S GOSPEL is focused on Jesus. His book is after all a gospel, and that means that it is a book about Jesus. But the fact that the point is obvious does not mean that it is not important. Any study of Matthew's thought must necessarily consider how he understands who Jesus is, and how he wishes his readers to respond to this Jesus whom he sets before them. And such a study is likely to take us to the heart of what the book is about.

To talk about 'Matthew's christology', however, runs the risk of assuming that Matthew necessarily had a worked out 'christology', in the sense of a systematic doctrine of the person and work of Jesus, and that his gospel may therefore be expected to provide us with a rounded account of his thinking which will relate straightforwardly to the questions which occupy the pages of a modern discussion of christology, even of 'New Testament christology'. But in our study of other aspects of Matthew's thought we have repeatedly found that Matthew was not aiming to present a systematic doctrinal statement (or at least that if that was his aim he has not obviously succeeded in it!). Different insights and emphases may be discerned at different points in his work, and may fairly be taken to represent aspects of his total understanding; but when the attempt is made to integrate them into a rounded theological scheme, the pieces do not always fit very neatly, and there are areas where we have to admit that the book does not allow us to reconstruct with any confidence a total 'Matthean theology'.

But while Matthew may not have been aiming to write a systematic doctrinal treatise, he clearly was trying to help his readers to understand Jesus as he himself had come to understand him. And while he may not have been concerned to tie up all the loose ends, we should at least do him the courtesy of assuming that he is not wilfully expressing contradictory ideas about Jesus side by side. So while I am reluctant to entitle this chapter 'Matthew's christology', there does seem to be good reason for attempting to discern from his book what were the main lines which went to make up Matthew's portrait of Jesus.

A. CHRISTOLOGICAL TITLES

Until fairly recently one might have been forgiven for assuming, on the basis of the way books on 'New Testament christology' have been presented, that the study of 'titles' *was* the study of christology. More specifically, the four titles 'Christ', 'Lord', 'Son of Man' and 'Son of God' have provided the focus for most significant discussions of New Testament christology in the last thirty years.[1] Recently L.E. Keck has mounted a spirited protest against what he calls 'this fascination with the palaeontology of christological titles'. He goes on, 'To reconstruct the history of titles as if this were the study of christology is like trying to understand the windows of Chartres cathedral by studying the history of coloured glass.'[2] His objection is not only, however, that the historical study of the use of titles can be no more than prolegomena to ascertaining what those titles are intended to convey, but that in any case such titles are not the only, or indeed the most fruitful, indicator of the christological beliefs of the writers. The study of titles in fact 'by-passes christology itself, because it does not respect either its formal grammar or its material contents'.

There may be an element of over-reaction in Keck's protests, but his main point is surely right (and would probably not have been contested in theory by those who have devoted themselves to the study of titles, whatever their practice may have suggested). The use of titles is not the whole of christology, not even the heart of it. But it is nonetheless an indicator (among others) of how a writer thought about Jesus. In this chapter we shall therefore consider briefly some of the titles of Jesus used by Matthew, before going on to set them in the wider context of Matthew's overall view of Jesus in so far as his book allows us to discover it.

We shall focus on the four titles which have been at the centre of modern discussion of New Testament christology, together with 'Son of David' which achieves a greater prominence in Matthew than in the rest of the New Testament. But we shall do so with the recognition that we cannot assume that Matthew thought in terms of established 'christological titles', still less that he was presented with a ready-made catalogue of such titles from which he must draw. Such catalogues are

---

1. The main impetus to this approach to New Testament christology was O. Cullmann, *Die Christologie des Neuen Testaments* (Tübingen: J.C.B. Mohr, 1957). Cullmann's work dealt with a wider range of titles than has since become fashionable (though not as wide as those surveyed in V. Taylor, *The Names of Jesus* [London: Macmillan, 1953]). The important study by F. Hahn, *Christologische Hoheitstitel* (Göttingen: Vandenhoeck & Ruprecht, 1963) narrowed the scope to five titles (Son of Man, Lord, Christ, Son of David, Son of God), and subsequent study has generally been restricted to these, with the exception that 'Son of David' has not generally been treated as so centrally important.
2. L.E. Keck, 'Toward the Renewal of New Testament Christology', *NTS* 32 (1986) 362-377. He deals with the question of titles, pp. 368-370.

the work of modern scholars, writing with hindsight. That Matthew
uses one title and not another does not necessarily mean that he was
'devaluing' the other, or that the one used represents his chosen
nomenclature *in preference to* what others might have used.[3] It is just
that these are the terms in which he himself felt it appropriate to refer
to Jesus in the context of his gospel narrative.

CHRIST

The modern reader of Matthew's gospel tends to read the opening
verse as containing a name, 'Jesus Christ', and two titles, 'son of David,
son of Abraham'. But the combination 'Jesus Christ', functioning
virtually as a double name, is one which is almost unknown in the
gospels; outside Matthew it occurs only at Mark 1:1 and John 1:17;
17:3, and in Matthew there are just two other places (1:18; 16:21) where
some manuscripts have this combination, in both of which it is likely
that it derives not from Matthew but from later scribes to whom this
form was familiar.[4] It is likely, then, that in 1:1 as well the term Χριστός
is used as a title, and thus is the first title applied to Jesus at the very
beginning of the gospel. Moreover, the genealogy which it introduces
traces the Davidic (and therefore messianic) line, and concludes triumphantly with 'Jesus, who is called Χριστός' (1:16), and in the next verse
the final point of the genealogy is given as ὁ Χριστός, without even
the name Jesus to identify him. So when the 'story' begins in 1:18 with
'The origin of the Χριστός[5] was like this', there can be no doubt that
Χριστός is the title Matthew has chosen to express at the outset his
understanding of the significance of Jesus.

3. This tendency to play off one title against another, and apparently to assume that
Matthew would have been conscious of so doing, seems to lie behind the sustained
arguments of J.D. Kingsbury that 'Son of God' is the dominant title in Matthew (and
in Mark; see his *The Christology of Mark's Gospel* [Philadelphia: Fortress, 1983]), for
which other titles function as 'surrogates'. See especially chapter 3 of Kingsbury, *Matthew:
Structure*.
4. Textual critics are divided over these two texts. In 1:18 the reading 'Christ' (without
'Jesus') seems to have been predominant in the early Western and Syriac churches, and
in 16:21 'Jesus' (without 'Christ') has even wider attestation. In view of the likelihood
that scribes would expand a single name to the more familiar double form rather than
omit one of the names, I prefer the shorter reading in each case ('Christ' in 1:18; 'Jesus'
in 16:21); cf. Brown, *Birth*, 123 on 1:18. But even if the longer form is preferred in 1:18
(as it is tentatively by the UBS[3] and Nestle-Aland[26] texts), it is clear that Χριστός
must be understood there as an independent title ('Jesus, the Messiah'), since it follows
immediately on the use of ὁ Χριστός alone (without 'Jesus') in 1:17, which was itself
prepared for by the deliberately titular use in 1:16, 'Jesus, who is called Messiah'. Similarly
if the longer reading is adopted in 16:21, this must be as a conscious echo of Peter's
prominent use of ὁ Χριστός as a title for Jesus in 16:16, verse 21 functioning as a
comment on the significance of that title.
5. See previous note for this reading of the text. The Greek word order places even
greater emphasis on the title: 'Of the Χριστός the origin . . .', with the opening phrase
clearly picking up the title established by the preceding genealogy.

Once this point has been established, the title is surprisingly little used in the rest of the gospel. It does occur, however, in three episodes where the question of who Jesus is comes explicitly to the forefront of the narrative. In the first case the questioner himself uses 'the coming one' (11:3), but Matthew's editorial introduction has made it clear that it is the deeds of the Χριστός which have provoked the enquiry (11:2); does he perhaps regard the title Χριστός as too 'definite' to be used by John, as one who stands still outside the kingdom of heaven?[6] In the second Peter uses the title (16:16), and Matthew confirms in his narration that it is rightly applied (16:20), even if misunderstood (16:21-23). In the third case the High Priest offers the title to Jesus (26:63), but it is quickly swept aside (and occurs thereafter only as a taunt or accusation, 26:68; 27:17,22) while Jesus goes on to set out his destiny in terms which apparently exceed anything the High Priest may have intended the title to convey. In none of these passages does Matthew allow Jesus himself to utter the title, or directly claim it for himself. Yet Matthew clearly believes that it is a correct designation.

In this he differs little from Mark. The 'messianic secret' debate has focused on Mark, who likewise begins his gospel with a clear statement that Jesus is the Χριστός (Mark 1:1), but does not allow Jesus to say so in so many words; but the same features may be seen in Matthew. If Jesus in Matthew is more welcoming to Peter's use of the title than he seems to be in Mark (Mt. 16:17-19), he is no less decisive in his rejection of Peter's false view of Messiahship (16:21-23). And in the final confession before the High Priest it is Mark rather than Matthew who allows Jesus the more explicit acceptance of the title (Mark 14:62; compare Mt. 26:64).[7]

This is not the place to try to resolve the complex debate over the 'messianic secret'.[8] But at the risk of being naively simple, I would like to say of Matthew what I believe to be also true of Mark, that the most economical explanation of the strange ambivalence with which the title Χριστός seems to be treated is to be found not in a sophisticated cover-up by second-generation Christians of the fact that their 'Messiah' never in fact saw himself as such, but in the ambiguity of the title itself within the historical context of Jesus' ministry, an ambiguity which is clearly illustrated in the Caesarea Philippi narrative in either its Marcan or its Matthean form. The title which Peter correctly offered, and which Jesus did not refuse, conveyed different implications with regard to the

6. For the place of John the Baptist in relation to the time of fulfilment see above pp. 197-198.
7. The different forms of Jesus' reply are usefully discussed by D.R. Catchpole, NTS 17 (1970/71) 213-226.
8. Among the many discussions arising out of Wrede's proposals, one of the best seems to me to be that of J.D.G. Dunn in TynB 21 (1970) 92-117, reprinted (with the notes heavily reduced) in C.M. Tuckett, ed., The Messianic Secret (London: SPCK, 1983) 116-131 (together with a number of other important essays on the same subject).

nature of the Messiah's task to the popular mind (in which Peter at this point shared) and to Jesus (whose radical new understanding of Messiahship subsequently came to be the accepted doctrine of the churches in which the gospels were written). What the term means to Mark and Matthew, the sense in which they use it in the introductions to their gospels, is therefore something very different from what it would have meant if Jesus had used it openly in the pre-Easter situation, which would have been to invite Peter's misunderstanding on a grand scale. The title by which the gospel writers can describe Jesus without fear of misunderstanding is one which he himself could not safely use, however rightly it should have conveyed the significance of his mission to those who did not share Peter's 'human thoughts'.

It is therefore appropriate that, in Mark no less than in Matthew, the only time Jesus introduces the topic for discussion it is as a matter of 'objective' debate, and with a view to questioning the nature of Messiahship as generally understood in terms of a Son of David (22:41-45; cf. Mark 12:35-37). We shall return to that episode in the next section. For now we may note that while Matthew and Mark will no doubt have expected their readers to understand the question as relating to the status of Jesus himself, their awareness of the difference between their understanding of Χριστός and that of the period of Jesus' ministry was sufficient to prevent their making it at the narrative level into a public claim by Jesus about himself.

Beyond that, for all the importance of the title in Matthew's own understanding as witnessed to by the opening verses of the gospel, it is scarcely used in the narrative context of Jesus' ministry. Twice Matthew's Jesus warns of impostors who will claim the title for themselves (24:5,23). Only once does he speak to his disciples of the Χριστός whom they follow, and there only cryptically in the third person, though there is no doubt how Matthew intended his readers to understand it (23:10; cf. Mark's one similar third person use, 9:41).

What Matthew claims about Jesus in his opening section by means of the title Χριστός will in fact come to expression in the rest of the gospel in other ways, which are less formal perhaps, but more imaginative and distinctive of Matthew's style. We have already considered this theme in chapter 5, where we saw the rich variety of ways in which Matthew draws out the theme of 'fulfilment' in Jesus, and we shall return to this theme later in this chapter. Here then is a clear case where Keck's warning must be taken seriously; it would be very wide of the mark to imagine that a study of the uses of the title Χριστός will offer an adequate understanding of Matthew's view of Jesus as the Messiah in whom God's purposes have come to fruition. Indeed, a study of the title alone would produce a serious distortion of this aspect of Matthew's portrait of Jesus.

SON OF DAVID

Alongside the prominent use of Χριστός to introduce Jesus, the theme of his Davidic descent and the actual title 'Son of David' are no less emphasised in Matthew's prologue. The title 'Son of David' stands alongside Χριστός in the first verse, and David 'the king' plays a key role in the structure of the genealogy (1:6,17), which is in fact a tracing of the line of Davidic kings of Judah, actual or presumptive. The following narrative focuses on Joseph, the final name in the list, and explains how he came to accept Jesus into his family, and the theological point of this opening scene is underlined when the angel addresses Joseph as 'son of David' (1:20). It is his obedience to the angel's instructions that enables Jesus too to bear this title. Jesus' birth in the royal town of Bethlehem thus appropriately fulfils the Davidic prophecy (2:6).

While statistics alone can be deceptive, it is worth noting that the title 'Son of David' occurs more frequently in Matthew's gospel than in the whole of the rest of the New Testament, and that seven of his nine uses of it are peculiar to his gospel. Mark and Luke both share the double use of the title in the story of Bartimaeus, and the discussion about whether the Messiah is the Son of David, but otherwise make no use of the title as such, even though Luke's introductory chapters emphasise the fact of Jesus' Davidic descent no less than Matthew does (Luke 1:27,32,69; 2:4,11). John raises the issue only as a matter of public speculation (John 7:42). It is clear that Jesus' Davidic origin was a feature of early Christian preaching (Acts 2:29-36; 13:22f; Rom. 1:3), but other New Testament references to Jesus' Davidic origin are very few (2 Tim. 2:8; Rev. 3:8; 5:5; 22:16). It seems clear then that Matthew had an unusually strong interest in this issue.

When we look at the way the title is used in Matthew's narrative, we note that as in the case of Χριστός Jesus nowhere uses it of himself, and introduces it in discussion only to question its adequacy (22:41-45). But it seems nonetheless to be a title freely used by others of Jesus, and there is no indication in this case that he demurred at that use. Indeed, he is prepared to defend its use when this is challenged by the religious authorities (21:15f).[9] It is used not only by his enthusiastic followers (21:9,15),[10] and by the crowds who discuss the secret of his power (12:23), but especially by those who come to him expecting healing (9:27; 15:22; 20:30,31), one of whom is not even an Israelite.

---

9. This passage in particular renders doubtful J.D. Kingsbury's suggestion (*JBL* 95 [1976] 593) that according to Matthew Jesus is more favourably inclined to the title Χριστός than to 'Son of David'.

10. The use of 'Son of David' in 21:15 serves also to point out a favourable *contrast* between the 'son' who heals the blind and lame in the temple and David himself who banned those same categories from 'the house' in Jerusalem (2 Sa. 5:8).

It is especially noticeable that almost every use of the title in Jesus' ministry is in direct connection with his healing power, either requested (9:27; 15:22; 20;30f) or experienced (12:22f; 21:14f).[11] There is almost a standard formula in such cases, involving the appeal to 'Have mercy', and the titles 'Son of David' and 'Lord' (compare the wording of 9:27-28; 15:22,25; 17:15; 20:30-33).[12] Mercy and healing are apparently understood to be the proper activities of the son of David (cf. 11:2-6 where the 'deeds of the Messiah' similarly consist in works of healing and mercy). Little evidence has been adduced from non-Christian sources for such an expectation,[13] and it is not immediately clear why Matthew has chosen to link healing so specifically with the 'Son of David' motif.[14] But there is no doubt that he intends his readers to understand Jesus' ministry, including especially his response to physical need, as that of the Son of David.

It is clear then that Matthew, more than any other New Testament writer, presents this title as both appropriate and important in understanding who Jesus is.[15] Yet it is this title which Matthew's Jesus, no less than in Mark and Luke, singles out for apparent rejection in 22:41-45. In view of his own positive evaluation of the title, it can hardly be that he wishes his readers to understand Jesus as repudiating its use altogether, and it is widely agreed that the point of the pericope is not that Jesus is *not* Son of David, but that he is *more than* Son of David. The explicit contrast is with being David's *Lord*, which at least implies someone superior to David rather than a mere replica of the former king of Israel, but probably also carries the wider connotations which we shall see to be part of Matthew's use of κύριος 'Lord' elsewhere.[16] It was only too possible, as we saw above in relation to

11. The connection with healing has been emphasised in most recent discussions of Matthew's use of 'Son of David', notably by C. Burger, *Jesus als Davidssohn* (Göttingen: Vandenhoeck & Ruprecht, 1970), followed by D.C. Duling, 'The Therapeutic Son of David: an Element in Matthew's Christological Apologetic', *NTS* 24 (1977/8) 392-410. Also B. Nolan, *The Royal Son of God* (Göttingen: Vandenhoeck & Ruprecht, 1979) 158-215.

12. Cf J.M. Gibbs, *NTS* 10 (1963/4) 449-450.

13. D.C. Duling, *NTS* 24 (1977/8) 407-410, suggests that Matthew's usage should be understood against the background of the tradition of Solomon as an exorcist (attested e.g. by Josephus, *Ant*. VIII 45-49). Duling has set out the evidence for this tradition in Judaism in *HTR* 68 (1975) 235-252, and argues that it is possible that this is the background to Mark's stress on the exorcistic activity of Jesus, which Matthew has then deliberately modified by extending Jesus' ministry to a broader 'therapeutic' pattern, and associating the 'son of David' title with this. This seems a rather tortuous explanation for what appears in Matthew to be a positive interest in Jesus' healing activity as 'Son of David' rather than a reaction against an alternative view (which itself is in any case not clearly visible in Mark). Moreover, Duling's survey shows that the evidence for a wide-spread belief in Solomon as exorcist before the time of Josephus is not impressive.

14. This, according to Stanton, 'Origin', 1923-1924, 'remains something of an enigma'.

15. The importance of the title for Matthew is well presented by D.J. Verseput, *NTS* 33 (1987) 533-537.

16. J.D. Kingsbury, *JBL* 95 (1976) 595-596, in accordance with his general thesis that Matthew's emphasis is throughout on Jesus as 'Son of God', argues that the contrast is

Χριστός, for messianic language (and 'Son of David' is decidedly
messianic language) to be interpreted at the level of human achievement
and triumph, of the fulfilment of Israel's hopes for national political
restoration, the return of the great kingdom of David. No doubt the
'Son of David' acclamations in 21:9,15, in connection with the first
coming of the Galilean prophet to the Jewish capital, carried something
of this flavour. That Jesus' 'devaluation' of the title in 22:41-45 follows
on this popular acclamation suggests that he may have been as concerned
over this possible misunderstanding of his mission as he was over Peter's
'human thoughts' at Caesarea Philippi. If Matthew so understood him,
it may therefore be suggested that it was to counter-balance any
triumphalistic notion of the messianic role that he emphasised the link
between the title 'Son of David' and Jesus' concern for the suffering
and oppressed; the healing of blind and dumb men, and the relief of
a demon-possessed Gentile girl, are not the 'deeds of the Messiah' which
would have been the natural connotations of 'Son of David' in many
Jewish minds. Perhaps, then, Matthew emphasises this connection not
because it was already an established datum of Jewish messianic
expectation, but precisely because it was not.[17]

A related line of thought is developed by J.M. Gibbs[18] and slightly
differently by J.D. Kingsbury.[19] Those who use the title 'Son of David'
in Matthew are predominantly people of no social or theological
importance, the blind, the lame, the dumb, the demon-possessed
daughter of a Canaanite woman ('Canaanite' is much more emotive
than merely 'Gentile' to Jewish ears!). It is these 'no-accounts' (to use
Kingsbury's term) who correctly perceive who Jesus is, while Israel's
leaders attribute his power to Satan, and are moved to anger when his
healings in the temple lead to enthusiastic praise. What is clear even
to the blind and the Gentiles is hidden from them (cf. 11:25); in fact it
is they who are truly blind. The association of 'Son of David' language
with the healing of the 'no-accounts' thus serves an apologetic purpose,
as part of Matthew's repudiation of the unbelief of Israel's leaders.

---

not with 'Lord' but with 'Son of God' (implied in the questions 'Whose son is he?', 'How
is he his son?'). I see no need for this either/or (see my remarks above on the danger of
playing off titles against each other): as David's 'Lord', Jesus is clearly the son of someone
higher, and so there seems no problem in suggesting that 'Lord' here points to 'Son of
God'. For Matthew he is both!

17. D.J. Verseput, NTS 33 (1987) 541-549 also emphasises 'Matthew's redefinition of
the Davidic Messiah', but sees this as achieved primarily by his presentation of Jesus as
not only Davidic Messiah but also the Son of God, obedient to his Father's purpose.
'His was a gentle mission blessed by God to call men to himself, in stark contrast to the
imperial and triumphal traits of Jewish Davidic expectation.'

18. J.M. Gibbs, NTS 10 (1963/4), especially the summary, 463-464.

19. JBL 95 (1976) 598-601. Kingsbury's account is accepted and developed by W.R.G.
Loader, CBQ 44 (1982) 570-585.

LORD

This title may be dealt with even more briefly, not because it is unimportant, but because there has been a large measure of agreement on its significance for Matthew since G. Bornkamm[20] drew attention to Matthew's consistent use of κύριε as a term of address to Jesus by the disciples (and sometimes by others) where Mark and Luke use a wider variety of terms, including διδάσκαλε 'teacher' and ἐπιστάτα 'master' (Luke only). Particularly noticeable is Matthew's avoidance of διδάσκαλε (and the roughly equivalent Aramaic terms ῥαββί and ῥαββουνί) as terms of address used by the disciples, while allowing them to be used by Jesus' opponents, to the extent that 'it is hardly enough to describe "teacher" language as inadequate in Matthew's view — it is almost derogatory'.[21] Κύριε, by contrast, is the right term for a disciple to use, 'with its overtones of power and authority demanding submission and obedience'.[22]

It remains a question, however, whether Matthew's preference for this term of address necessarily indicates that it is for him 'a divine Name of Majesty'.[23] Matthew does indeed make frequent use of ὁ κύριος as a title, but this is in its standard LXX usage as the name of God, generally in Old Testament quotations and allusions, and not with reference to Jesus. In the one case where Matthew's Jesus appears to describe himself as ὁ κύριος (21:3), the startling novelty of the usage leads commentators to question whether Matthew could have expected his readers to think that the questioner in Bethphage (who is not even presented as a disciple) would have understood it of Jesus rather than of God, or even of the donkey's 'owner' (κύριος).[24] Otherwise, the 25 cases where κύριος is applied directly to Jesus are all in the vocative,[25] and one does not need to go outside Matthew's gospel to discover that κύριε was an appropriate form of respectful address in contexts where

20. Bornkamm, *Tradition*, 41-43.
21. This is the conclusion to a comparative discussion of the synoptic uses of such language in my 'Mark and the Teaching of Jesus', *Gospel Perspectives* vol. 1 (1980) 106-109.
22. Mohrlang, *Matthew and Paul*, 74, part of a useful summary of the data, which relates the use of this term to Matthew's view of discipleship.
23. So Bornkamm, *Tradition*, 43.
24. See most commentaries. The question is complicated by the uncertainty whether Jesus was here giving a pre-arranged 'password', and by the possibility that Matthew is exploiting the different uses of κύριος to hint at a christological significance which is not appropriate to the actual narrative context.
25. Excluding 12:8, where the statement that the Son of Man is κύριος of the Sabbath does not involve a title; and 24:42, where 'your κύριος' draws on the imagery of the following parable of the servants waiting for their master which uses ὁ κύριος, as often in the parables, to denote an earthly 'master', whose parabolic function is to represent God or Jesus. Such passages, and others such as 10:24-25 which involve κύριος-language, undoubtedly contribute to the reader's understanding of Jesus as Lord, but they are not properly described as using ὁ κύριος as a title of Jesus.

no idea of divine majesty is present (13:27; 21:30; 25:20,22,24; 27:63)!
It is possible, then, to argue that there is no christological significance
in the use of this form of address, except merely that those using it
recognise Jesus as in some sense superior or in authority over them.[26]
But it seems clear that Matthew saw more in the term than mere
politeness. It is addressed to Jesus as the one who is expected to save
the suppliant from illness or danger (sometimes in conjunction with
'Son of David', as noticed above), with the assumption that he possessed
more than ordinary power, and sometimes in circumstances where
human politeness was clearly out of place (8:25; 14:30; 17:4). In
particular, it is the way Jesus expects to be addressed when he comes
as judge, when the Son of Man comes in his glory with all the angels
and sits on his glorious throne (7:21,22; 25:11,37,44). Even if κύριε
alone cannot be said to imply divine majesty, the contexts in which it
is used with reference to Jesus indicate that it conveys for Matthew a
unique degree of authority, and there seems no reason to doubt that
it was for this reason that he has so consistently included it in his story
as the appropriate form of address by those who accept the authority
of Jesus. It would be going beyond the evidence to suggest that Matthew
intended the use of κύριος in relation to Jesus to be understood as a
direct application of the LXX divine title ὁ κύριος; but it is likely that
he saw and even exploited the appropriateness of the fact that it was
the same Greek word which was used for each.

THE SON OF MAN

The voluminous recent discussion of the title 'the Son of Man' has
generally focused on questions of the origin and meaning of the term,
and its tradition-history considered in the gospel tradition as a whole.
Comparatively little attention has been paid to any distinctive features
of its use in the gospels individually, except in the case of John. A
bibliography on the study of 'the Son of Man' would be immense, but
one on Matthew's use of the title would be brief.[27] This is due, no
doubt, to the fact that by and large the same range of uses of the term

---

26. See the cautious comments of Moule, *Origin*, 35-36.
27. See the introductory comments to M. Pamment's article on 'The Son of Man in
the First Gospel', *NTS* 29 (1983) 116-129. Strecker, *Weg*, 125 dismisses the title as being
of no significance for Matthean redaction (except for the idea of 'the kingdom of the
Son of Man', to which he devotes a footnote on pp. 166-167). There has been a recent
exchange of articles on Matthean christology between J.D. Kingsbury and D. Hill in
JSNT, the sections dealing with this title being especially vol. 21 (1984) 22-32 (Kingsbury)
and 48-51 (Hill); vol. 25 (1985) 68-74. Cf. subsequently Kingsbury, *Matthew as Story*,
95-102. Other discussions of the title 'the Son of Man' specifically in Matthew include
A.J.B. Higgins, *Jesus and the Son of Man* (London: Lutterworth, 1964) 97-118; Albright
& Mann, *Matthew*, LXXXVIII-XCIX; Kingsbury, *Matthew: Structure*, 113-122; B.
Lindars, *Jesus Son of Man* (London: SPCK, 1983) 115-131.

may be found in all the gospels, each of which offers examples of the three traditional categories of 'Son-of-Man sayings', relating to the earthly condition of Jesus, to his suffering and death, and to his future vindication and glory (to which John adds the theme of the Son of Man who has come down from heaven). And of course it is equally true in all the gospels that the title occurs (in striking contrast with the titles so far considered) only as a self-designation by Jesus, never as a form of address or of christological speculation by others (except in John 12:34, where it is directly taken up from Jesus' own use of the term). It is not surprising then to find that Matthew can use the title 'the Son of Man' where Mark uses 'I' (16:13; cf. Mark 8:27) and a few verses later reverse the process (16:21; cf. Mark 8:31); it comes to the same thing.

It is on this basis that Kingsbury has argued that 'the Son of Man' does not function like the other christological titles. It is, in his terms, not 'confessional', but a 'public' title.[28] By this he means that whereas other titles serve to identify who Jesus is (and thus may be used as predicates to such phrases as 'You are . . .', 'This is . . .', or 'I am . . .'), 'the Son of Man' is never so used. Jesus uses the phrase to refer to himself, but neither he nor others use it to explain who he is. The question still remains 'Who do men say that the Son of Man is?' (16:13). Kingsbury further asserts that it is used always in relation to those who are not his followers; it is indeed used in conversation with his disciples, but only to speak of how other people think of him, or will treat him, or of how he will in due course be vindicated over them. There is thus always a sense of distance when Jesus uses this term; it sets him apart from those who oppose and reject him. 'It is principally with an eye to the "world", Jews and Gentiles and especially opponents, that Jesus designates himself as the Son of Man.'[29]

Kingsbury's observations are generally correct, I believe, though not all the Matthean uses of 'the Son of Man' fit as neatly into the scheme as he would wish.[30] But these features are not particularly distinctive

28. Kingsbury, *Matthew: Structure*, 114-117; *JSNT* 21 (1984) 22-27.
29. *Ibid.* 28. This aspect of 'distancing' in the use of the title is at first sight in conflict with the argument of M. Pamment, *NTS* 29 (1983) 116-129, that it was the role of the human figure of Daniel 7:13 as 'a representative and exemplary figure' which particularly appealed to Matthew. Pamment's argument is not, however, that the Son of Man is seen as representing men in general, but only those who, as his disciples, are identified with his mission. 'What is said about the work and destiny of the Son of man is also said about the disciples'. 'He presents Jesus as the Son of man who calls men to follow his example and to share his destiny.' It is as the disciples, together with him, stand apart from the unbelief of people in general that they can be a part of his special role to restore man in the image of God. This association of the disciples with the Son of Man is particularly clear in 19:28, but Pamment shows that it is also implied in other Son of Man sayings, even if there is an element of special pleading in her attempt to trace this theme in *all* such sayings.
30. See the remarks of D. Hill, *JSNT* 6 (1980) 2-3.

of Matthew; they could equally be discerned in the usage of the other gospels. They may help to explain why this title occurs only as Jesus' own self-designation; there would be little point in others using it about him if it does not tell us who he is. But the question remains, why this particular self-designation? Even if it originates historically in Jesus' usage along the lines Kingsbury indicates (and I see no reason to doubt this), did Matthew see in it no more than a colourless label?

This is not the place to go into the very complex debate over how the term may have been understood against the background of Old Testament and later Jewish usage.[31] I remain convinced that the primary background must be found in the vision of 'one like a son of man' in Daniel 7:13-14, and that Matthew's use of the term, like that of Jesus before him, derived from the conviction that those verses provided a pattern which it was Jesus' mission to fulfil. A similar conviction led the author of the Similitudes of Enoch to use the title 'that Son of Man' for the heavenly deliverer and judge around whom his vision is centred, but it remains an open question whether the title had yet been coined and passed into common use at the time of Jesus, or indeed of Matthew; I think it more likely that it had not, and that 'Enoch' derived his title independently from the same source.[32] In that case the title as used by Jesus was for his hearers a new and potentially puzzling development, but one which allowed him to express his own under-standing of his mission without fear that existing and inappropriate connotations of the term would lead to misunderstanding. But the title, once coined, could not be used by Jesus or by those who followed him without a vivid awareness of Daniel's vision. Even if it is not a 'confessional' title, in Kingsbury's term, it is far from an empty label, as Kingsbury himself recognises.[33]

Whatever special significance the title had for Matthew is likely to be indicated by those Son of Man passages where he alone includes the title, or where his version is significantly different. What is im-

31. A convenient brief summary of the debate may be found in Carson, *Matthew*, 209-213; more fully (but less up-to-date) see the article of O. Michel, copiously supple-mented by I.H. Marshall, in *NIDNTT* vol. 3 (1978) 613-634.

32. The date of the composition of the Similitudes of Enoch (1 Enoch 37-71) remains under dispute. The recent edition by E. Isaac in J.H. Charlesworth (ed.), *The Old Testament Pseudepigrapha* vol. 1 (London: Darton, Longman & Todd, 1983) p.7 rejects Milik's very late dating, but records an increasing consensus that the Similitudes date from the first century AD rather than from pre-Christian times. An up-to-date discussion reaching the same conclusion is found in G.R. Beasley-Murray, *Jesus and the Kingdom of God* (Exeter: Paternoster, 1986) 63-68. In that case this work cannot be seen as the direct source of Jesus' usage. The apocalyptic tradition of interpretation of Daniel 7 on which it draws may reasonably be assumed to be considerably older than the composition of the work as we know it, but there is no evidence that this tradition had resulted in a titular use of 'the Son of Man' before the Similitudes were written.

33. *JSNT* 21 (1984) 27. D. Hill (*ibid.* 49-51) is right, however, to object that Kingsbury has not sufficiently taken into account the connotations of the phrase in the light of its background in Daniel 7.

mediately obvious is that in terms of the three traditional categories of such sayings, the majority of Matthew's distinctive uses fall in the group which focus on the future vindication and glory of the Son of Man (the exceptions are 13:37, where the sower of good seed is identified as the Son of Man; 16:13, where 'the Son of Man' is substituted for 'I', as noted above; and 26:2, an additional but not strongly marked passion prediction).

And in many of these passages the echoes of Daniel 7:13-14 are unmistakable not only in the title itself but also in references to clouds, heaven, coming, glory, kingdom, judgement and the like. These elements are present in some of the Son of Man sayings in Mark and Luke as well, but in Matthew they are more frequent and more strongly marked. Thus Matthew includes an additional prediction of the coming of the Son of Man before the disciples' mission to the towns of Israel is complete (10:23); he depicts Jesus as looking forward to 'the regeneration, when the Son of Man shall sit on his glorious throne' and his disciples will share with him in 'judging' Israel (19:28); and he pictures the final judgement as the time when the Son of Man will send his angels to gather the wicked for destruction (13:41). These passages are found only in Matthew, and so also is the stupendous climax in the vision of the last judgement, 'when the Son of Man comes in his glory, and all the angels with him', when 'he will sit on his glorious throne' and all the nations will be gathered before him for judgement (25:31-33).

In this last passage we see the culmination of a peculiarly Matthean theme, that of the Son of Man as 'the King' (25:34). Much has been made in some twentieth-century scholarship of the lack of connection in the teaching of Jesus between the Kingdom of God and the Son of Man,[34] but in Matthew there is no reticence in speaking of the kingdom of the Son of Man (13:41; 16:28; 19:28; 25:31-34; cf 20:21 for the 'kingdom' of Jesus). Thus where Mark speaks of the future coming of the kingdom of God, Matthew has 'the Son of Man coming in his kingdom' (16:28; cf. Mark 9:1 [Luke 9:27]). The angels who accompany the Son of Man or whom he sends out in Mark (Mark 8:38; 13:27), and who are described in Luke as the 'angels of God' (Luke 12:8-9), appear in Matthew as 'his angels' (13:41; 16:27; 24:31). It is Matthew alone, too, who includes sayings about the 'παρουσία of the Son of Man' (24:27,37,39) – and παρουσία is a term for the king's visitation. But even

34. This lack of connection was argued especially by H.B. Sharman, *The Son of Man and the Kingdom of God* (New York: Harper & Row, 1943) and by P. Vielhauer in W. Schneemelcher (ed.) *Festschrift für Günther Dehn* (Neukirchen, 1957) 51-79 (reprinted in Vielhauer's *Aufsätze zum Neuen Testament* [München: Kaiser, 1965] 55-91), and has since been a dominant idea especially in German scholarship. It is a healthy sign of disrespect for this dogma that G.R. Beasley-Murray devotes nearly 100 pages of his *Jesus and the Kingdom of God* to 'The Son of Man and the Kingdom of God' (though the design of the book as a collection of distinct exegetical studies does not offer a discussion of the issue in general). The essential connection between the two concepts is comprehensively demonstrated in C.C. Caragounis' recent work (see note 36 below).

292 MATTHEW: EVANGELIST AND TEACHER

before that παρουσία the Son of Man is seen as vindicated and enthroned, and given all authority in heaven and on earth (28:18, a passage appropriately described by W.D. Davies[35] as 'the enthronement of the Son of Man' on account of its use of the imagery of Daniel 7:14, even though the actual title 'the Son of Man' is not used), and the inclusion by Matthew of the phrase ἀπ' ἄρτι 'from now on' in 26:64 makes it clear that he understood the vindication and glory of the Son of Man as not merely an event of the distant future.

It seems clear then that Matthew saw in this title, and expected his readers to see, not just a self-designation of Jesus but a pointer to the ultimate goal of his mission. After his humiliation and suffering, Jesus will receive from his Father the vindication, enthronement, glory and judgement which are given to 'one like a son of man' in Daniel 7. We shall return later to the significance of Daniel 7 for Matthew's christology, but for now we may conclude that he recognised that it was from that passage that Jesus derived his favourite self-designation, and that in his recording of the title he took pains to draw out the implications of the source from which it came. It is undoubtedly for Matthew primarily a title of majesty, not of humiliation. The later patristic use of this title to focus on Jesus' humanity and humiliation *in contrast to* his divinity and glory ('Son of God') would have had no appeal for Matthew.[36]

THE SON OF GOD

Few are likely to quarrel with the assertion that the presentation of Jesus as the Son of God is central to Matthew's christological enterprise.[37]

35. Davies, *Setting*, 197.
36. Two recent studies of 'the Son of Man' have particularly emphasised the majestic implications of the title, not only for Jesus and the New Testament writers but also in the original intention and subsequent Jewish interpretation of Daniel's vision. C.C. Caragounis, *The Son of Man: Vision and Interpretation* (Tübingen: J.C.B. Mohr, 1986) argues that Daniel's 'one like a son of man' was intended to be understood as representing not the nation of Israel but a majestic spiritual deliverer (and that the Similitudes of Enoch were therefore correct in developing such a figure on the basis of Daniel 7), and that Jesus boldly identified himself with this exalted being, even though he also recognised and accepted his role as representative and leader of the suffering people of God. Caragounis therefore repudiates the modern dogma that the Son of Man and the Kingdom of God are not connected in the teaching of Jesus; the two 'are in Jesus' teaching indissolubly connected with each other, as they were in Daniel, and that in conjunction with Jesus' fight against the powers of darkness' (p. 243). A briefer but tightly argued study by S. Kim reveals its thesis in its title, *'The "Son of Man" ' as the Son of God* (Tübingen: J.C.B. Mohr, 1983); Kim is prepared to speak of the 'one like a son of man', both in Daniel's intention and in Jesus' interpretation, as a divine figure. Both these studies present a bold challenge to currently accepted views of Daniel 7, as well as of the use of the title in the gospels, but I suspect that Matthew would have been more in sympathy with them than with more conventional twentieth-century interpretation!
37. J.D. Kingsbury's sustained effort (*Matthew: Structure*, 40-127, supplemented by *JSNT* 21 [1984] 3-36; and in other articles) to establish this point has met with little opposition, though his tendency to find 'Son of God' cryptically present when other titles

In this, of course, he is not alone – it could be said of all four gospels (though the theme is not so prominent in Luke, despite its striking introduction in 1:32,35), and indeed of other New Testament writings, especially Hebrews and 1 John. Indeed in terms of sheer statistics Matthew does not use the term more freely than Mark, given the relative lengths of their books, while John leaves both far behind. But vocabulary statistics are a poor guide to theological concerns.

Presumably the definitive statement of who Jesus is must be found in the direct declaration by God himself recorded by all three synoptic gospels as part of the baptism and transfiguration stories, and in each case it is a declaration that Jesus is the Son of God, though the words also contain an echo of the description of the Servant of Yahweh in Isaiah 42:1 (3:17; 17:5). Other such pivotal declarations are also shared with Mark, in 8:29 where Jesus is recognised as Son of God, presumably with supernatural insight, by the demons, in 26:63 where 'Son of God' (or the equivalent) is part of the designation offered by the high priest and accepted by Jesus himself, and in 27:54 where it is the centurion's term to express what he has seen in the death of Jesus. And Matthew shares with Mark also two passages where Jesus presents himself as God's son, obliquely in public in the imagery of a parable (21:37) but clearly in private with his disciples (24:36).

The significance of these Marcan passages is sufficient to establish how central the idea was for Mark, even without his clear statement in the heading to his gospel (Mark 1:1, accepting the longer text). But in Matthew the impact is increased both by his development of the narratives already noted and by additional uses of the title. Thus the divine declaration of 3:17 is taken up and reinforced by the devil's use of 'Son of God' in 4:3,6, and the whole narrative of the testing in the wilderness focuses on the nature of the filial relationship. Jesus' acceptance of the title 'Son of God' in 26:63f is taken up as a taunt against him at the cross, where a remarkable sequence of christological themes and titles used ironically by the bystanders (including two further uses of 'Son of God', 27:40,43) serves to inform the reader of who Jesus really is. Then follows, as in Mark, the centurion's declaration of the truth which the others failed to see, but it is given added weight in Matthew both by a fuller description of the supernatural events which provoked it and by the extension of the confession to include the whole guard.

are used has been treated more sceptically, especially when it reaches the point of claiming that this is the dominant theme in large sections of the gospel where the title is in fact virtually absent (e.g. 4:17-10:42, on which see Kingsbury, *Matthew: Structure*, 53-63; if in a pericope like 4:18-22 'Matthew alludes to Jesus as the Son of God' [p. 56], of what sort of pericope could this not be true?). To agree that it is a central concept is not necessarily to accept that it dominates all other themes and titles in the way Kingsbury suggests. See the criticisms by D. Hill, *JSNT* 6 (1980) 2-16.

In two other Marcan pericopes Matthew has introduced the title
'Son of God'. Peter's declaration of who Jesus is (16:16) includes both
'Christ' and 'Son of God', and so offers a parallel to the declaration
to be made by Jesus himself in 26:63f. But here, unlike in Mark, it is
a disciple who has been brought by God (16:17) to this recognition of
Jesus' true nature even during his ministry. Indeed, even this is not a
totally new perception, because it was in the same language that the
disciples had already responded to the impact of Jesus' numinous power
and authority on the lake (14:33).

There are three other uses of Son of God language in Matthew with
reference to Jesus. In 2:15 the application of Hosea 11:1 to the infant
Jesus depends on the recognition that Jesus is God's son, and so can
appropriately be prefigured by God's 'son' Israel.[38] In 11:27 (a Q
passage) Jesus himself declares the unique privilege and authority of
'the Son' in his exclusive relationship with 'the Father'.[39] And in 28:19
the whole Son of God christology of the gospel comes to its remarkable
climax in the association of 'the Son' with the Father and the Holy
Spirit as the joint object of the allegiance of those who are to be made
disciples. We shall have more to say on both these last two passages.

But, as 11:27 reminds us, a son implies a father, and son-language
alone gives us only one side of the total picture. Matthew's Jesus refers
to God as 'Father' some 44 times (compared with 4 in Mark and 17
in Luke). Half of these uses (mostly in the Sermon on the Mount)
describe God as the Father of the disciples, but the rest refer to him
specifically as the Father of Jesus. Four of them are direct address in
prayer, 'Father' or 'my Father'; four of them mention 'the Father' in
direct connection with 'the Son' (11:27; 24:36; 28:19, all passages
mentioned above); the rest describe God specifically as 'my Father'
(except where Jesus speaks of 'his [the Son of Man's] Father' in 16:27).
This usage, with its clear distinction between 'your Father' and 'my
Father', indicates that underlying the Son of God language we have
considered there is a strongly developed sense of a unique relationship
between Jesus and God, and one which Matthew wishes to emphasise.

38. See above pp. 182-183, and my comments in *NTS* 27 (1980/1) 243-244, for the
hermeneutical principles underlying this use of Scripture. It is the agreed understanding
of Jesus as Son of God which provides the 'trigger', even though a more sophisticated
typology underlies Matthew's argument.
39. J. Jeremias, *NT Theology*, 59-61, has argued that the definite articles should be
taken as generic, so that the statement is a quite general observation about the mutual
knowledge of any father and son; in that case 'the son' is not to be taken as a title of
Jesus. In reply we might first ask whether such a general observation would in fact be
true: some sons are much better known by others than by their fathers and vice versa!
Secondly, even if Jeremias is right, it is hard to see what other function such a 'parable'
might be intended to serve in this context than as a basis for understanding the mutual
relationship of Jesus and his Father, particularly in the light of the clearly personal
reference of v 27a. In that case precisely the same christological point would be being
made, though in a less direct way.

While it is true that in this gospel (unlike John) the title 'Son of God' or 'the Son' is applied to Jesus more by others than by himself, the freedom with which he speaks of God as his Father shows that Matthew has no doubt that Jesus not only was but was conscious of being the Son of God.

There is no doubt then of the importance for Matthew of the fact that Jesus is the Son of God. But the title alone could be interpreted in different ways. It was not, after all, a totally new development for an individual to be called a son of God, even in Jewish culture.[40] Two ways in which such language could be used by Jews seem particularly relevant to understanding what it may have meant to Matthew.

There are occasional references in the Old Testament to the king (David or a successor) as the son of God (2 Sa. 7:14; Ps. 2:7; 89:26-27). In view of the clear relevance of these passages to the development of the hope of a Messiah of the line of David, it is remarkable that later Jewish writings do not generally take up the term and refer to the Messiah as the son of God. The only evidence for this is in a few fragments from Qumran: 1QSa 2:11-12 *possibly* refers to the Messiah as begotten by God (this depends on a disputed restoration of a damaged text); 4QFlor 1:10-13 interprets 2 Samuel 7:11-14 as referring to the Messiah, but without making any specific comment on the father-son language; 4QpsDanA[a] says that *someone* will be hailed as Son of God and called Son of the Most High, and while the state of the text does not allow us to see who this is, it is a good guess that it is the Messiah.[41] These few fragments from an isolated community hardly add up to a convincing proof that 'son of God' was familiar as a messianic title in first-century Judaism in general. But they do show that the Davidic Son of God texts of the Old Testament were not forgotten, and the frequent reference to Psalm 2:7 in the New Testament suggests that this was an important element in their description of Jesus as the Son of God.

Another potentially relevant Jewish use of son of God language is one which developed after the Old Testament period, the idea of righteous or holy men being 'sons of God'. The evidence for this too is not great, but it is more widely distributed, being found in pre-Christian wisdom books (Ben Sira 4:10; Wisd. 2:16-18; 5:5; Ps. Sol. 13:9) as well as in rabbinic tradition which probably goes back to the first century AD.[42] This usage seems to have made at least some contribution to

40. For a survey of both pagan and Jewish uses of such language see e.g. M. Hengel, *The Son of God* (ET. London: SCM, 1976) 21-56; J.D.G. Dunn, *Christology in the Making* (London: SCM, 1980) 13-22.
41. On this last passage see J.A. Fitzmyer, *NTS* 20 (1973/4) 391-394. On the three Qumran fragments together, see Hengel, *Son of God*, 43-45; Dunn, *Christology*, 15-16.
42. See Hengel, *Son of God*, 42-43, n. 85 for relevant texts. Some of the impressive-looking collection of material by Vermes, *Jesus the Jew*, 194-213 is not directly relevant to the

Matthew's understanding of 'Son of God', since his striking inclusion of the title twice in the scene of the mocking of Jesus on the cross (27:40,43) comes in a passage which reads like a deliberate echo not only of Psalm 22:7-8 but also of the passage in Wisdom 2:10-20 (itself inspired by Psalm 22?) where the righteous man is mocked by his persecutors for his claim to be the 'Son of God'.

But this meagre Jewish evidence for existing usage of son of God language is clearly quite inadequate to explain its very prominent and theologically loaded use in the New Testament generally and in Matthew in particular. In Christian language it has taken on far richer meaning, and all the gospel writers indicate that the source of this is to be found in Jesus' own awareness of his special relationship with God.[43] Matthew is heir to this tradition much more than to any prior Jewish usage, and it would therefore be wrong to attempt to limit the significance of the term simply to Jesus' role as Messiah and as the persecuted righteous one. These themes may properly be discerned in his use of 'Son of God', but they are far from exhausting its significance.

This point is correctly emphasised in a recent and valuable study of 'The Role and Meaning of the "Son of God" Title in Matthew's Gospel' by D.J. Verseput.[44] He notes the relevance of the Jewish usage we have considered, but sees Matthew's use of the title as 'distinctively shaped by the milieu of its Christian usage', involving a unique, intimate relationship with God which goes far beyond the Jewish model. It is, he believes, this relationship, rather than any speculation about Jesus' origin, which is in view. The function of this language is therefore to define more clearly the nature of Jesus' messianic role, in particular as it relates to the equally prominent title Son of David. Unimpressed by Kingsbury's assertion that 'son of God' is the superior title, Verseput demonstrates that the assertion of Jesus' Davidic Messiahship is central to Matthew's purpose, particularly in establishing the guilt of the Jewish leadership in failing to recognise him as Son of David. By contrast with the powerful assertion of this truth at the outset of the gospel, the title 'Son of God' comes into the gospel 'in a casual, almost inadvertent manner', and is assumed rather than argued as a proper description of Jesus. Its function, Verseput argues, is to redefine the nature of Messiahship by emphasising Jesus' filial obedience. In contrast with 'the imperial and triumphal traits of Jewish Davidic expectation', Jesus follows out

christological use of 'Son of God', since it speaks of Israelites in general as sons of God, not of specific individuals to whom the title is distinctively applicable.
43. The historical probability of this explanation has been impressively demonstrated by J.D.G. Dunn, *Jesus and the Spirit* (London: SCM, 1975) 11-40, 62-67. Cf his *Christology*, 22-33. Dunn is perhaps excessively cautious in using only what he regards as critically unimpeachable evidence, and has accordingly made virtually no use of the Johannine tradition, but it is therefore the more significant that his limited range of evidence has produced so strong a case for the historical origin of this language with Jesus himself.
44. *NTS* 33 (1987) 532-556.

the divine plan of a gentle mission to call men to God. The Son of God thus proves to be 'the "unmessianic" Messiah' as he works out the hidden plan of God. But Israel's leaders fail to recognise this divine pattern of Messiahship, and so they put him to death; it is thus precisely because he is the Son of God, the gentle, rejected Messiah, that he must die.

This is a stimulating and important article. It seems to me to be right in most of what it affirms, particularly in its integration of what are often seen as separate, even imcompatible, emphases of the gospel into a coherent account of the author's purpose. I cannot help wondering, however, whether Verseput's recognition of the Christian distinctiveness of Matthew's use of Son of God language has gone far enough. It is interesting that the two elements in the Jewish usage (the Messiah and the righteous man) which he sets aside as inadequate to explain that of Matthew do in fact correspond quite closely to what he finds in Matthew, the use of 'Son of God' to emphasise Jesus' obedience to the Father as the fulfilment of his messianic role. Is that *all* Matthew intends?

Jesus is introduced, after the genealogy, as one born by direct divine creation. It is true, as Verseput notes,[45] that this is not made by Matthew into an explicit basis for calling Jesus 'Son of God' (contrast Luke 1:32,35), but it seems improbable that he failed to see how appropriate such an origin would be for one whose unique relationship with God he wishes to emphasise. The virgin conception, even if not the explicit basis of the use of 'Son of God', *is* a part, and not an unimportant part, of Matthew's whole christological viewpoint. Indeed perhaps the 'casual, almost inadvertent manner' in which the title 'Son of God' is first introduced in 2:15 is to be accounted for precisely by the fact that Matthew has already established Jesus' right to this designation in 1:18-25.

As long as attention is focused only on the title itself, the full extent of the divine christology which lies behind 'Son of God' cannot be appreciated. We shall consider this fuller evidence in a later section. But in three of the 'Son' passages Matthew goes far beyond simply redefining the nature of Jesus' Messiahship. In 11:27 there is the idea not only of a unique relationship with God, but also a unique status of authority ('all things have been entrusted to me by my Father'), which anticipates the ringing declaration of 28:18, while the following verses (11:28-30) go on, as we shall see, to present Jesus in terms of the eternal Wisdom of God. If this is not a clear statement of his personal pre-existence,[46] it undoubtedly goes far beyond the concept

45. *Ibid.* 532-533.
46. Verseput, *ibid.* 539-540, comments on Matthew's lack of interest in the pre-temporal existence of Jesus. But even Dunn, whose thesis is that no New Testament writer except

of one who obediently does the Father's will. In 24:36 the Son is placed above the angels and next to (though not equal in knowledge with) the Father. And in 28:19 the Son is actually placed on a level with the Father and the Holy Spirit.

The man who began his gospel with the divine origin of Jesus and concluded it with the triadic formula of 28:19 and the assurance of the continued presence of Jesus with his disciples after the end of his earthly life could hardly have used the title 'Son of God' with no more in mind than the correction of triumphalistic ideas of Messiahship. When the disciples on the lake 'worship' Jesus as 'Son of God' (14:33) they are recognising someone who is much more than a human servant of God, or even Son of David.[47]

B. BEYOND THE CHRISTOLOGICAL TITLES

Our brief study of Matthew's use of those terms which modern scholarship has isolated as 'the christological titles' was undertaken with the recognition that his use of these particular expressions will not necessarily take us to the heart of his understanding of Jesus. Each in its different way points us towards an important aspect of Matthew's thought, but none of them alone (nor even all of them together) is sufficient to encapsulate all that Matthew wants his readers to understand about Jesus. In this section I hope to indicate something of this broader background against which we need to set Matthew's use of the titles studied above.

The areas of thought to which these titles point may be roughly summed up under two basic questions, 'What was Jesus' mission?', and 'Who is Jesus?'. Of course the answers to these questions will overlap, as all attempts to draw up a systematic christology soon discover, but in principle they are different questions, and it may clarify our discussion if we attempt to keep them both in view.

The titles 'Christ' and 'Son of David' are primarily concerned with the first of these questions. They take up the hopes of God's eschatological action for his people, and portray Jesus in terms of the one through whom he was expected to act. The title 'the Son of Man' raises similar issues, but not in so straightforward a way, since it was not, I believe, a title with a ready-made meaning before Jesus himself introduced it; its background in the vision of God's future purpose in Daniel

John had a full doctrine of the pre-existence of Jesus, sees the idea as 'but a step away' here (*Christology*, 49-50).

47. For some valuable comments on the relation of the title 'Son of God' to Jesus' miraculous activity see Gerhardsson, *Mighty Acts*, 88-91.

7 makes it potentially a 'messianic' title, but one which in itself conveys as much mystery as enlightenment, and which, in view of the way the 'one like a son of man' is described in Daniel, also raises, if it does not answer, the question, 'Who is this?'. But if the question 'Who is Jesus?' is raised at least implicitly by 'the Son of Man', it is clearly the central issue underlying the use of 'Son of God' (and the associated language of intimate relationship with God as 'Father'). While 'Son of God' *may* have 'messianic' connotations, its main focus is on the status and nature of the one so described, and it raises the issue of whether Jesus is adequately described in purely human terms as a deliverer sent by God. The same issue too underlies the use of 'Lord', in so far as this goes beyond a merely polite address to an important human person.

Both 'Christ' and 'Son of David' are terms which focus on Jesus as the fulfilment of the hopes of Israel, as expressed in the Old Testament and developed in subsequent Jewish eschatological thinking. We have considered in chapter 5 the importance of this theme for Matthew, both in his explicit claims to 'fulfilment' and in the more subtle but far more pervasive conviction that in Jesus the whole pattern of God's work among his people is coming to its destined climax (a conviction which we considered under the title of 'typology', but which is far too rich and varied to be treated as a single interpretative 'technique'). In contrast to the marked reserve with which we have seen Matthew's Jesus treating those two titles, the overall theme of fulfilment is one which is en- thusiastically developed both in Matthew's editorial comments and adaptations and in his record of the teaching of Jesus. Whatever the possible misunderstandings of 'Christ' and 'Son of David', there is no doubt that Jesus is 'he who is to come'. His role is not confined to one or more existing stereotypes, but can be expressed in terms of many Old Testament themes and models which Matthew's 'typological' ingenuity delights to explore, even where they were not themselves the subject of explicit prophetic prediction. He is the new Moses, and the new Israel experiencing a new exodus; he is one greater than Solomon, greater than Jonah, greater than the temple and its priesthood. In him all that was central to Israel's life and calling as the people of God has reached its perfect embodiment.

There is no need to repeat here the material surveyed in chapter 5. But it may be appropriate here to draw attention to two further models which we have not yet considered, which seem important for Matthew's understanding of the role of Jesus. One is a prophetic construct (the Servant of Yahweh), one a poetical way of describing God's relation with his world (Wisdom); but both, together with the various prophetic and typological models already noted, form part of the kaleidoscope of Matthew's scripturally inspired understanding of what Jesus came to do.

THE SERVANT OF YAHWEH

The importance of Isaiah's vision of the Servant of Yahweh (particularly as set out in Is. 42:1-4 and 52:13 – 53:12) for the New Testament understanding of the mission of Jesus is generally recognised;[48] and the fact that two of Matthew's formula-quotations are drawn from these passages indicates that he was no exception in this. Most of Matthew's probable allusions to this theme are shared with Mark (and less clearly Luke): the description of Jesus by the heavenly voice at his baptism and transfiguration in words drawn from Isaiah 42:1, the series of dramatic announcements of the necessity of Jesus' suffering, the words at the last supper about his blood shed for many, and the ransom saying of 20:28 (cf. Mark 10:45), with its suggestive echoes of the wording especially of Isaiah 53:10,12.[49] But Matthew also includes in 3:15 the statement that Jesus' baptism was intended 'to fulfil all righteousness', which, in the light of the following echo of Isaiah 42:1 as God's response to his decision, has plausibly been explained as an allusion to the Servant's role as 'the righteous one who makes many to be accounted righteous' (Is. 53:11).[50] It is possible too that his description of Joseph of Arimathea as 'rich' is intended to recall Isaiah 53:9, 'they made his grave . . . with a rich man in his death'.

It is far from certain that Matthew intended these last two allusions to Isaiah 53. But the importance of the theme for Matthew is shown by the fact that two of his distinctive group of formula quotations are drawn from these passages. Both 8:16-17 and 12:15-21 are summaries of Jesus' ministry designed to present it as the fulfilment of the two quoted Servant passages, Isaiah 53:4 and 42:1-4 (of which the latter is the longest Old Testament quotation in the gospel). In view of the concentration elsewhere in the New Testament (including the allusions in Matthew noted above) on the theme of vicarious suffering and redemption in Isaiah's vision of the Servant, it is remarkable that neither of these two quotations focuses on this theme, either in the specific

---

48. M.D. Hooker, *Jesus and the Servant* (London: SPCK, 1959) represents a 'minimalising' approach to the New Testament references to the Servant. The plan of her book does not allow for a specific study of Matthew's use of the idea, though she does commit herself to the view that the significance of Matthew's two formula-quotations from Isaiah 42 and 53 'lies in his desire to find passages which foreshadow particular events, and not in any intention to identify Jesus with the Servant of the Songs' (p. 149). Hooker's book, and other studies which offered a similar approach by C.F.D. Moule, C.K. Barrett and others, have perhaps led to more caution in discerning deliberate references to the Isaiah passages, but have not, as far as I can see, resulted in a serious questioning of the importance of this theme for New Testament christology.

49. See my discussion of these passages (except the voice at the baptism and temptation, which fell outside the scope of my book) as indications that Jesus saw his own mission in the light of Isaiah 42 and 53, in *JOT*, 116-132.

50. E.g. Gundry, *Matthew*, 50-51; Carson, *Matthew*, 107-108.

words quoted or in the context of Jesus' ministry to which they are related.

In 8:16-17 it is Jesus' healing ministry which 'fulfils' Isaiah's vision, and the 'infirmities' and 'diseases' mentioned in Isaiah 53:4 are understood more literally perhaps than even Isaiah intended.[51] In the light of the widespread ancient conviction that sickness is the result of sin, it is possible that the modern distinction between physical healing and spiritual salvation is inappropriate to the thought of Isaiah or of Matthew, so that a reference to physical healing would not be out of place in the account of the Servant's redemptive work.[52] At any rate, Matthew's understanding of how Jesus fulfilled the role of the Isaianic Servant is broader than that of many modern theologians.

In 12:15-21 the scene has changed. The section of the gospel which begins after the mission discourse of chapter 10 has revealed a variety of responses to Jesus and an increasing weight of opposition, leading up to the Pharisees' determination to destroy Jesus (12:14). In 12:22ff that opposition will be more vehemently expressed in the charge that Jesus is in league with Beelzebul. The brief pericope which separates these sections contains no specific incident, unless it be Jesus' 'tactical withdrawal' in a situation of likely confrontation in v.15 (a repeated theme of the gospel: cf. 4:12; 14:13; 15:21); the introductory verses serve rather to emphasise the non-confrontational character of Jesus' behaviour in this threatening situation, withdrawing from the scene of conflict, and preventing his enthusiastic followers from provoking hostile reactions by excessive publicity. Isaiah 42:2-3 provides a scriptural pattern for this attitude, but it is there presented not just as the proper demeanour of any man of God, but as the specific role of the Servant whom he has chosen, in whom he delights, and on whom his Spirit has come – a role which is clearly ascribed to Jesus, with reference to the same Old Testament text, in 3:17 and 17:5. Matthew therefore quotes the whole paragraph, and in so doing sets out not only the Servant's gentleness but also the goal of his mission, in bringing forth justice for the whole earth, a mission in which he will not fail whatever the opposition. It seems clear therefore that here we have more than a

51. The Hebrew nouns are used elsewhere both of physical suffering and in a metaphorical sense. The rabbinic tradition that the Messiah was to be a leper appears to have been based on such a literal understanding of Isaiah 53:4 (see J. Jeremias, *TDNT* V, 690, 697). But the LXX and the Targum Jonathan translate the terms as referring to 'sins' rather than physical complaints, and in view of the clear emphasis of the whole surrounding context on the Servant's role in relation to the 'iniquities', 'transgressions' of God's people it is hardly surprising that Christian interpretation has also regularly taken these terms in v 4 to have a metaphorical sense. Matthew's independent rendering of the Hebrew (see Stendahl, *School,* 106f; Gundry, *Use,* 109,111) seems then to be a deliberate exploitation of the ambiguity of the language, in order to draw out a subsidiary, but nonetheless important, aspect of the total delivering ministry of Jesus as the Servant.
52. See e.g. Gundry, *Use,* 230-231, and more fully Carson, *Matthew,* 205-206.

convenient proof-text; the role of the Servant of Yahweh is the model for the mission of Jesus.[53]

If that is so, and if we may assume that Matthew, like other ancient interpreters, would have understood the description of the Servant in Isaiah 42 to be filled out in the subsequent chapters, especially chapter 53, there seems good ground for affirming that the allusions to the redemptive role of the Servant which we noted above represent not a slavish following of tradition but a significant aspect of Matthew's total understanding of what Jesus came to do.

It remains true, however, that it is not *only* in his passion and death that Matthew saw Jesus as fulfilling the role of Isaiah's Servant of Yahweh. B. Gerhardsson has drawn attention to the way the theme of service runs through the gospel, quite apart from the discernible references to Isaiah 42ff.[54] As Son of God, he is obedient to his Father, and in this way he not only provides a model for the obedient service required of his disciples, but also makes his whole life an offering of obedience, which culminates in his self-giving on the cross as a ransom for many. Example and atonement are woven together in a total mission to 'save his people from their sins' (1:21). Thus the Isaianic Servant model operates for Matthew at a more fundamental level of his christological understanding than that of a few convenient proof-texts.

WISDOM

It is a matter for debate how far Jewish thought in the New Testament period had developed from the poetical personification of the Wisdom of God in Proverbs 1-9 and Ben Sira (and its 'objectification' in Job 28) to the concept of an actual 'being', Wisdom, who was thought to have existed alongside God since before the creation of the world and to be capable of coming to earth. The personal language used of Wisdom becomes even more vivid in the Wisdom of Solomon (especially 6:12 – 11:1), including the prayer that God would send her from heaven to work at the author's side (9:10), a prayer which is taken up in the idea of Baruch 3:37 that Wisdom has come down to earth and lives among men (cf. already Ben Sira 24:8-12), or the less optimistic view of 1 Enoch 42 that she tried to find a home among men but failed, and had to return to her place in heaven. But modern interpreters are cautious

---

53. D. Hill, *JSNT* 6 (1980) 9-12 usefully discusses the wider christological implications of Matthew's use of Isaiah 42 in 12:17-21. He approves the suggestion of O.L. Cope, *Matthew: a Scribe Trained for the Kingdom of God* (Washington: CBQ Monographs, 1976) 36-52, that Matthew has structured the remainder of chapter 12 around themes in Isaiah 42:1-4. Cf. Gerhardsson, *Mighty Acts*, 25-27.

54. B. Gerhardsson, 'Gottes Sohn als Diener Gottes: Messias, Agape und Himmelsherrschaft nach dem Matthäusevangelium', *ST* 27 (1973) 73-106; *idem*, 'Sacrificial Service and Atonement in the Gospel of Matthew', in R.J. Banks (ed.), *Reconciliation and Hope: New Testament Essays on Atonement and Eschatology presented to L.L. Morris* (Exeter: Paternoster, 1974) 25-35.

of reading into such language any more than the use of lively personal imagery for what remains an abstract quality, a poetical way of speaking of God's wise creation and ordering of his world, and of men's need to become attuned to the divine perspective.[55]

It is clear, however, that several New Testament passages use language reminiscent of this Jewish Wisdom tradition with reference to Jesus (though generally not the title 'Wisdom' itself, perhaps for the rather obvious reason that σοφία is a feminine noun!), and in so doing import an inevitably personal dimension into it.[56] How far has Matthew been influenced by this way of thinking?[57]

M.J. Suggs tells us that he had thought of giving to his monograph *Wisdom, Christology and Law in Matthew's Gospel* the subtitle 'A Footnote to Matthean Christology', but refrained from doing so because he felt it was time 'to lift the Wisdom motif out of the footnotes of scholarly discussion' and to recognise it as more than tangential to Matthew's purpose.[58] Since then discussion of the subject has focused on three passages of the gospel, and in particular on the comparison in each case of Matthew's wording with that of Luke.

In 11:19 Matthew's Jesus concludes his attack on the unresponsiveness of 'this generation' to the ministry of John and Jesus with the epigram, 'Wisdom is justified by her deeds,' whereas the last word in the Lucan parallel is 'children'. If the Lucan version (generally thought to be more original) presents John and Jesus as the 'children of Wisdom', this would be saying no more than that they have acted in accordance with God's wisdom. But it is suggested that 'deeds' in Matthew is a deliberate

55. A representative recent statement of this view is Dunn, *Christology*, 168-176.

56. It is beyond the scope of this study to go into the debate about how this language relates to the idea of Jesus' pre-existence. Dunn has not convinced most scholars that such language as Col. 1:15-20 ('The firstborn of all creation; all things were created through him and for him; he is 'before all things, and in him all things hold together' etc.) involves no more than the recognition than in Jesus the eternal wisdom of God is fully expressed. See especially A.T. Hanson, *The Image of the Invisible God* (London: SCM, 1982) chapter 3, a direct response to Dunn's *Christology*. It is widely agreed that, even if there is no clear Jewish precedent for envisaging the actual, personal existence of Wisdom as an eternal 'being', the New Testament writers who used such language about Jesus *were* talking about one who personally existed from eternity and who became incarnate, a development of doctrine which Dunn recognises in the New Testament only in the writings of John.

57. The most significant recent studies of the theme in Matthew are M.J. Suggs, *Wisdom, Christology, and Law in Matthew's Gospel* (Cambridge, MA: Harvard University Press, 1970) and F. Christ, *Jesus Sophia: Die Sophia-Christologie bei den Synoptikern* (Zürich: Zwingli-Verlag, 1970). The latter studies the relevant Synoptic sayings (all of which occur in Matthew) from a tradition-historical perspective, so that the focus is not specifically on Matthew, as it is in Suggs' work. Dunn, *Christology*, 197-206, offers a convenient overview of the discussion. M.D. Johnson, *CBQ* 36 (1974) 44-64 gives a detailed critique of Suggs' thesis, and concludes that he has considerably overplayed his hand. C. Deutsch, *Hidden Wisdom and the Easy Yoke: Wisdom, Torah and Discipleship in Matthew 11:25-30* (Sheffield: JSOT Press, 1987) provides a more detailed study of the most important passage for Matthew's Wisdom christology.

58. Suggs, *Wisdom*, 1-2.

reference back to 'the deeds of the Messiah' in v 2 (and forward to the 'mighty works' of Jesus which form the basis of the accusation in v 20), and that Matthew is thus identifying 'the Messiah' and 'Wisdom', both as designations of Jesus himself, whose 'deeds' form the basis of judgement throughout 11:2-24. For Matthew, then, Jesus is not just Wisdom's messenger; he *is* Wisdom.[59]

Immediately after this passage comes Matthew's most generally acknowledged allusion to Wisdom, in 11:25-30. In the first part of this passage, which is shared with Luke, several commentators have seen the influence of the Wisdom tradition both in the idea of 'hidden wisdom', to which the wise of this world have no access, and in the exclusive mutual knowledge of Father and Son, which echoes statements that only God knows Wisdom (especially Job 28) and only Wisdom knows God and can reveal his truth (e.g. Wisd. 9).[60] But it is in the following verses, peculiar to Matthew, that the parallel with Wisdom language rises to the surface, as one word or phrase after another recalls the appendix to Ben Sira, with its appeal to the distressed to 'Come to me' to find instruction in the house of learning, and to accept the 'yoke' under which by means of a 'little labour' great 'rest' is to be found (Ben Sira 51:23-27, a passage which draws on similar language about Wisdom's yoke in 6:23-30).[61] The wording is familiar, but the sense is new: in Ben Sira it is the sage who calls his hearers to take on Wisdom's yoke in order to find the rest which she has to offer, and which he himself has experienced; but in Matthew Jesus offers his own yoke and will himself give rest to those who learn from him. Jesus is not merely Wisdom's messenger, but himself fills the role of Wisdom.

The third passage is 23:34-39, which again divides into two parts, corresponding to two separate passages in Luke, each of which has been interpreted as showing the influence of Wisdom language. In 23:34-36 it is, paradoxically, the non-mention of Wisdom which is taken to indicate Matthew's development of the theme. In the Lucan parallel (11:49-51) the statement about sending messengers whose murder will lead to the punishment of 'this generation' is attributed to 'the Wisdom of God',[62] but in Matthew the same pronouncement occurs

59. So Suggs, *Wisdom*, 55-58; Dunn, *Christology*, 197-198.

60. Deutsch, *Hidden Wisdom*, 103-107, summarises the parallels she has found between Mt. 11:25-27 and these themes in Jewish literature (which she has set out at length in the preceding pages; NB especially 64-70 on the theme of hidden wisdom and of mystery in the Pseudepigrapha).

61. It is clear as a result of Deutsch's survey of Jewish 'parallels' to Mt. 11:28-30 (*Hidden Wisdom*, 113-130) that the only true parallel is in fact Ben Sira 51:23-30 (with the associated passage in chapter 6).

62. Where and when 'the Wisdom of God' is supposed to have made this statement remains a matter of debate. See Dunn, *Christology*, 201-202 for a brief account of possibilities, favouring the view that it is a general summary of a theme of Wisdom literature (especially of the Wisdom of Solomon 10-11), the sustained appeal to Israel and its rejection, rather than a specific quotation.

without specific attribution as part of the diatribe uttered by Jesus himself against the scribes and Pharisees. Again, therefore, where Jesus appears in Luke as Wisdom's spokesman, in Matthew he utters Wisdom's appeal as his own. It may be questioned, however, whether Matthew's readers, not having access to the text of Luke, could have been expected to discern this point in the absence of any mention of Wisdom in Matthew's text.

The theme of a repeated appeal to the people of God, and their disastrous refusal to listen, is continued in 23:37-39 (parallel Luke 13:34-35), and again it is Jesus himself, rather than Wisdom, who is presented as having made the appeal (in Luke as well as in Matthew this time). Since Bultmann's discussion of this text[63] it has been usual to understand these verses also as an allusion to 'the Wisdom Myth',[64] but it is not clear that they contain any verbal reminiscence of known Wisdom passages, and Bultmann finds it necessary to defend the reference merely as 'quite intelligible in the context of the myth' in the absence of any specific parallel among 'the fragments of Jewish Wisdom speculation that have survived for us'. If it had not been for the juxtaposition (in Matthew, not Luke) of these words with what is in Luke (not Matthew!) a saying of the 'Wisdom of God' there might have been less enthusiasm for identifying verses 37-39 as 'Wisdom language'. The mother bird in v 37 is more easily understood in the light of Old Testament usage as an image for God himself than for Wisdom (e.g. Ps. 17:9; 91:4; Is. 31:5),[65] and the Old Testament passages underlying vv 38-39 (Jer. 12:7; 22:5; Ps. 118:26) do not indicate a Wisdom context. These verses are not, therefore in themselves a firm foundation for postulating a Wisdom christology in Matthew.

It seems clear, then, that in 11:25-30 Matthew shows his awareness of Wisdom ideas, and is deliberately using echoes of one famous Wisdom passage in order to draw out the significance of Jesus as the one in whom God's wisdom speaks. And in the other passages considered it is at least possible that Matthew's way of handling the tradition of Jesus' words reveals a similar interest. If so, Matthew (in common with the other New Testament writers who drew on the Wisdom tradition) must be aware of the boldness of what he is doing, in taking a poetical personification of God's wisdom, however elaborately worked up into

63. R. Bultmann, *The History of the Synoptic Tradition* (ET. Oxford: Blackwell, 1963) 114-115.
64. The reconstruction of this 'Wisdom Myth' by Bultmann, and its development by Suggs, is criticised by M.D. Johnson, *CBQ* 36 (1974) 46-53; Johnson particularly aims to show that 'there was no pre-Christian Jewish motif of the goddess Sophia sending her envoys with revelation for man'.
65. Suggs' discussion of the imagery (*Wisdom*, 66-67) makes it clear how frequent such language was with reference to God, and can offer no example of the description of Wisdom in such terms, but merely the suggestion that it is 'appropriate in the mouth of maternal Sophia'.

the story of a supernatural visitor to the earth, and applying it to a
historical human person. The implications of such an idea for the
question of who Jesus is could hardly have escaped him, even though
the developed doctrine of the incarnation of a pre-existent divine being
is not explicit in the three 'Wisdom' passages we have considered.[66]

I suspect, however, that Suggs' first instinct was correct, that the
Wisdom motif is better described as a 'footnote to Matthean christology'.
It is important that this aspect of Matthew's thought should be
recognised, but it is not in itself a prominent feature of his gospel. If
this alone were the basis for arguing that Matthew portrays a more-than-
human Jesus it would be a not very impressive body of evidence. Its
significance lies rather in the way it fits in, as an admittedly minor
theme, with a whole way of thinking about Jesus which emerges in
other ways throughout the gospel, a view of his significance which is
not tied to any specific title or motif (though perhaps 'Son of God'
comes nearer to summing it up than any other).

It is this less clear-cut but ultimately more important aspect of
Matthew's portrait of Jesus which I want to focus on in the remainder
of this chapter, a conviction of who Jesus is which comes to expression
in varied ways as the story proceeds, and which reaches its climax in
the triumphant proclamation by the risen Lord in 28:18-20.

'THE MAN WHO FITS NO FORMULA'

This was the title of a chapter in E. Schweizer's study, *Jesus*.[67] It
expresses well the aspect of Matthew's thought which we need to
consider if we are to get 'beyond the christological titles', his presentation
of the disciples' total experience of Jesus which could not be confined
within any existing label or set of 'messianic' categories. Matthew's
christology is not primarily a matter of deploying familiar language in
creative ways to take account of a remarkable person (though he does
of course do this, as we have seen), but rather a presentation of a wholly
new type of experience, which began with the impact which Jesus made
on his first disciples, and has continued and developed in the life of
the church up to Matthew's time. It is an experience of Jesus which

---

66. Dunn, *Christology*, 204-206, argues in the case of Matthew, as he has previously
in the case of Paul, that the christological implications which are so obvious to us would
not have been apparent to the author, whose thought moved more in the functional than
the ontological sphere. When Dunn states that 'Matthew betrays no consciousness on
his part that he is taking such a dramatic step', it is appropriate to ask what sort of
evidence Dunn requires for Matthew's consciousness other than what he has in fact
written. It should be noted that Dunn's similar argument in relation to Paul has not
carried conviction (see above n. 56). Matthew does not use as extravagant language as
Paul in regard to Christ's eternal existence and cosmic role (how could he in a gospel?),
but his conviction that Jesus is more than human emerges strongly in other ways, as we
shall see below.
67. E. Schweizer, *Jesus* (ET. London: SCM, 1971) 13.

could find no adequate expression short of making him an object of worship. In a Jewish environment, where to accord divine honours to a man was the height of blasphemy, such an unheard-of conclusion could not be reached lightly, and Matthew's gospel gives us an illuminating insight into the factors which produced this remarkable result.[68] The **authority** of Jesus is clearly a central theme of Matthew's portrait.[69] In chapters 8-9 this authority is prominently displayed in Jesus' mighty works, and commented on in 8:8-9; 8:27; 9:6; 9:8; 9:33.[70] But this presentation of Jesus' authority in deed follows the balancing presentation of his authority in word in chapters 5-7, culminating in the crowd reaction of 7:28-29. It is Jesus' authority which provides the focus of the concluding scene (28:18), suitably summing up the impression which has been increasingly conveyed throughout the gospel.[71] Jesus is quite simply different from other men: he can teach in a way their scribes cannot match; he issues authoritative commands to evil spirits and they come out, to illnesses and they are cured, to the elements and they acknowledge his control; he calls men and women to give him an undivided allegiance, and they leave everything and follow him. The question 'Who is this?' is an inevitable result, and Matthew expects his readers to reach an appropriate answer.

Within this broader theme of Jesus' unique authority, his **miracles** play a special role. B. Gerhardsson has drawn attention to the importance of the quite frequent summaries of Jesus' healing activity in the development of Matthew's work, as a necessary part of the total christological presentation, which might otherwise become unbalanced by the large amount of discourse material to suggest that Jesus was primarily a prophet, a speaker for God. Jesus' authority is more all-embracing than that.[72] Gerhardsson's fine study goes on to show the breadth of the significance of the theme of the 'mighty acts' of Jesus in Matthew, which far transcends any explicit christological titles.[73]

68. For this subject more generally see R.J. Bauckham, 'The Worship of Jesus in Apocalyptic Christianity', *NTS* 27 (1980/81) 322-341; also my essay 'The Worship of Jesus: a Neglected Factor in Christological Debate?' in H.H. Rowdon (ed.) *Christ the Lord* (Leicester: IVP, 1982) 17-36. The same theme is discussed with specific reference to Peter's sermon in Acts 2 by M.M.B. Turner in the same volume, pp. 168-190.
69. So Blair, *Jesus, passim*, especially pp. 45-47. Also Mohrlang, *Matthew and Paul*, 72-74.
70. Gerhardsson, *Mighty Acts*, returns frequently to this theme; see pp. 37, 45-49, 59, 60-62.
71. A recent study by O.S. Brooks, *JSNT* 10 (1981) 2-18, notes the importance of the twin themes of *authority* and *teaching* in the concluding paragraph (28:16-20), and goes on to argue that these two themes 'have controlled the design of the entire gospel'. We have noticed in chapter 4 the danger of proposing that any theme or pattern can totally account for the structure of the gospel, but Brooks has no difficulty in showing how important these themes are.
72. Gerhardsson, *Mighty Acts*, 20-37, especially pp. 36-37.
73. *Ibid.* 91-92.

They challenge those who witness them to a response of faith in Jesus not just as 'the Messiah', but as the one in whom they are confronted with the power of God displayed in a way they have not known before. Along with Jesus' supernatural power goes his **supernatural knowledge**. As in the other gospels, Jesus is aware of unspoken thoughts (9:4; 12:25; 22:18). The point is not emphasised; it is simply assumed as appropriate to the Jesus Matthew portrays, the Jesus who has at his disposal, if he cares to make use of them, the armies of heaven (26:53-54).

These and other such traits of the Matthean Jesus might be understood merely as the privileges granted by God to a supremely holy man. Other men worked miracles, and were in some degree privy to the mind of God. The God of Israel had worked throughout their history by means of prophets, wise men and miracle workers who had not on that account been regarded as in themselves different in kind from their fellow-men. It was possible to be a man of God without being thought to be God! But there is a further development in Matthew's portrait of Jesus which seems to raise the issue to a new level, the presentation of Jesus as himself acting *as God.*

JESUS IN THE PLACE OF GOD

Matthew never says directly that Jesus is divine. (Neither do most of the writers of the New Testament books!) But there are occasional indications that it was natural for him to speak of Jesus where Jewish orthodoxy would have spoken of God, and to apply to Jesus without comment passages of the Old Testament which originally spoke of God. The fact that such language occurs quite incidentally as if it needs no argument but could simply be taken for granted, is some indication of how far Matthew's perception of Jesus had gone beyond seeing him as merely a man of God.

In one passage, indeed, the narrative does focus on the christological implications of such a transfer of the prerogative of God to Jesus, in that the scribes' objection to Jesus' declaration of forgiveness in 9:2 is couched in terms of blasphemy. The sequel indicates that Jesus, far from apologising for the boldness of his language, reinforces it by a display of authority in a physical healing. The issue is not spelled out in Matthew (he has no equivalent to Mark's 'Who can forgive sins except God alone?'). But he can hardly have thought that his readers would miss the implicit claim.

Generally such claims are not presented in an explicitly controversial context; the reader must discern them from the language used, understood against a background of Old Testament and current Jewish usage. For instance, in discussing 11:28-30 above we saw how Matthew's Jesus utters in his own name an invitation and an offer of rest under his yoke which echoes the language of Wisdom in Jewish thought. If, as we noted there, the Jewish personification of Wisdom is properly to be understood as a pictorial way of talking about God himself in his wise dealings with his world (rather than as describing a 'person' separate from God) then the placing of such language in the mouth of Jesus has obvious and startling christological implications.

A similar assumption of a more than human authority is seen in Jesus' demand for the total allegiance of his followers (10:37-39), and in the declaration that men's ultimate destiny rests on their relationship with him (7:21-23). Indeed, this last passage indicates that in the final judgement it is he, not God, who will pronounce the verdict, and that the essence of their fate consists in being separated from him! The same themes emerge even more majestically in the vision of the last judgement in 25:31-46, where again it is the Son of Man who is the judge, people are judged on the basis of the way they have responded to him, and blessing or punishment consist in coming to him or departing from him.

In the last judgement scene the Son of Man is presented as sitting on 'his glorious throne', and is in fact described as 'the king' (25:31,34). Such ideas have already occurred earlier in the gospel, the throne of the Son of Man in 19:28 (again in a context of judgement) and his kingship in the passages noted earlier when we were considering the title 'the Son of Man' (13:41; 16:28; 20:21; cf. 28:18).[74] But in 25:31ff the theme comes to its climax when, as we shall see shortly, a series of Old Testament texts are woven together into the portrayal of the end-time judge, texts which in the Old Testament context describe the role of Yahweh as the judge and king of the nations. The firm Jewish conviction of the unique kingship of God has been expanded to allow for the kingship (in no inferior sense) of the Son of Man.

Such passages assume, rather than state, some sort of 'equivalence' between Jesus and God. In the light of this assumption elsewhere in the gospel it seems possible that when Matthew records Jesus' declaration that 'He who receives me receives him who sent me' (10:40) he was presenting Jesus as more than simply the *representative* of God (though the preceding clause, 'He who receives you receives me', shows that such language does not necessarily carry ontological implications!). More explicit is 11:27, where Jesus' statement (in a context of revelation) that 'All things have been delivered to me by my Father', leads to the declaration of the exclusive mutual knowledge between 'the Father' and 'the Son' (followed, as we have just seen, by his speaking in 11:28-30 with the voice of divine Wisdom). Here the special status of Jesus already embodied in the Son of God title is more fully spelled out, and

74. See above pp. 291-292 for further aspects of this assumption of divine glory for the Son of Man.

'the Son' is seen to be in a unique relationship with God which is his by virtue of who he is, in contrast with the knowledge of the Father which others may indeed come to share, but only as a result of his mediation. As in 24:36 'the Son' is placed in a special category apart from people in general and even the angels, next only to God himself, so also in 11:27 we see the Son as distinct indeed from the Father, but yet related to him in a way which is different from other men's relationship with God not only in degree but also in kind. What we have here is not perhaps a fully worked out doctrine of the divinity of Jesus, but surely at least the raw materials out of which the climactic formula of 28:19 ('the Father and the Son and the Holy Spirit') could be formed.

One special way in which Matthew's Jesus gives expression to his own unique status is in the way he uses certain Old Testament passages. In identifying John the Baptist as the 'messenger' of Malachi 3:1 and the returning Elijah of Malachi 4:5-6 (Matthew 11:10,14; 17:11-13) he invites his hearers to reflect on the fact that both these figures are introduced in Malachi as forerunners of the coming of God himself to judgement.[75] When the Jerusalem authorities object that the children are welcoming Jesus with cries of 'Hosanna to the Son of David', he responds with a quotation from Psalm 8:2 about the praise of the creator God being sung by children (21:16). In 21:44 (if this is an original part of the text of Matthew)[76] the image of falling on the stone and being shattered is drawn from Isaiah 8:14-15, where it is Yahweh who is the stone, yet the stone in Matthew 21:42-44 is surely Jesus, exalted by God to the supreme position. In 24:35 Jesus declares the permanent validity of his words in terms which remind the reader of what Isaiah 40:8 says about the word of God.

It is in the visions of the future authority and glory of the Son of Man that this tendency is most pronounced. The language is typically the Old Testament language of theophany. The Son of Man will come with, or will send out, 'his' angels (13:41; 16:27; 24:31; 25:31) to carry out the work of judgement which in the Old Testament was the divine prerogative. Several striking Old Testament theophanic passages are clearly echoed in such pronouncements in the gospel. In 13:41 the gathering out of 'his' kingdom of 'the stumbling-blocks and those who

75. In Malachi 4:5-6 this is clear. In Malachi 3:1 the series of descriptive phrases has led some to see a third ('messianic') figure intermediate between the messenger and the Lord. See my discussion of Malachi 3:1 in *JOT*, 91-92, n. 31. I argued there that *ha-adon* in the second clause is an alternative title for the *malach* of the first and third clauses. That identification is disputed by P.A. Verhoef, *The Books of Haggai and Malachi* (Grand Rapids: Eerdmans, 1987) 287-290, who sees the *malach* of the third clause as different from the *malach* of the first; but the point being made here is not affected, as Verhoef's interpretation identifies this second *malach* with *ha-adon* taken to refer to God, and thus still allows for no third figure. Cf. further for the christological implications, *JOT*, 155.
76. See above p. 210, n. 17.

practice lawlessness' echoes Zephaniah 1:3 where God will sweep away 'the stumbling-blocks with the wicked'. In 25:31 'all the angels with him' (cf. 16:27 'with his angels') is close to the wording of Zechariah 14:5, 'The Lord your God will come, and all the holy ones with him'. The gathering of all the nations for judgement before the Son of Man in 25:32 echoes the great judgement scene in Joel 3:2, where the judge is God himself.

But the most striking echo of Old Testament theophany is in the frequent allusion to Daniel's vision of the judgement scene where the 'one like a son of man' appears (Daniel 7:9-14). It is not only v 13, with the coming of the one like a son of man in the clouds, which is taken up in the gospel, but the whole scene with its thrones, its angelic court, its clouds and glory, and its judgement pronounced over all nations. But whereas in Daniel 7 it is the Ancient of Days who sits on the throne and pronounces judgement in favour of the one like a son of man, in Matthew the Son of Man himself sits on 'his glorious throne' surrounded by 'his angels' and pronounces judgement on the nations (19:28; 25:31ff). Jesus, the Son of Man, has assumed the sovereignty predicted for him in Daniel 7:14, and is seen as occupying the very throne of God the judge.

This presentation of Jesus as fulfilling the role of God himself reaches its climax in 25:31ff, where themes from various Old Testament theophanies (noted above) are woven together into a majestic vision of his divine glory. But this is not a new idea which has suddenly occurred to Matthew as he comes to the end of his gospel; it has been implicit in occasional turns of phrase and scriptural allusions throughout the work.[77] It will come to expression again, as we shall see, in the final scene of 28:16-20, and surely here if anywhere Matthew is choosing his words carefully, in order to leave the reader with a true impression of Jesus as he understands him. If Matthew does not call Jesus 'God' *tout simple*, his gospel leaves little room for doubt what his answer would have been if we could have asked him whether Jesus was more than just a man of God.

'GOD WITH US'

Right at the beginning of the gospel Matthew has already put in a pointer in this direction. The inclusion of the name Immanuel in 1:23 in the formula-quotation from Isaiah 7:14 was not necessary to his narrative, indeed it was even potentially an embarrassment, since the name the child was given was not in fact Immanuel but Jesus! But

---

77. Gundry, *Use*, 209 gives a summary of references to the Old Testament which he has interpreted in his preceding discussion as indicating that for Matthew 'Jesus fills the role of Yahweh'. Several of them coincide with those we have considered, but they range more widely.

Matthew not only includes it, but also translates it to ensure that his readers do not miss the point. Of course it is true that 'Immanuel' as an Old Testament name need mean no more than 'God *is* with us', and need no more suggest the divinity of the one so called than the many other 'El-' and 'Yahweh-' names of the Old Testament. But Matthew's translation does not opt for this 'weaker' meaning; μεθ' ἡμῶν ὁ θεός translates the component parts of the Hebrew name literally and in sequence, and at least leaves open the startling idea that this baby is himself God, present among men.

It is a hint which the rest of the gospel will allow the keen-eyed reader to fill out as he works through the text, thinking about the implications of the language used (especially the Old Testament language). As he goes on he will find the 'with us' motif returns twice in relation to Jesus and his people. In 18:20 Jesus grounds his promise that the agreed prayer of 'two or three' disciples on earth will be granted by 'my Father in heaven' on the assurance that 'where two or three are gathered in my name, there I am among them'. The fact that the gathering is 'in my name', and that it is specifically 'on earth' as opposed to 'in heaven', suggests that he is speaking of a situation beyond that of his physical presence during the ministry – to comment on his being literally 'among them' in that context would be banal, and in any case could hardly be true of *every* gathering of two or three! Here then the Jesus who through his physical birth became 'God with us' continues to fulfil that role even after his earthly presence is withdrawn.[78]

The same point becomes even clearer, of course, when the concluding verse of the gospel picks up the opening 'God with us' theme in the assurance of the risen Jesus, 'I am with you always, to the close of the age'. Where Paul or John would speak of the presence of the Spirit as the means of God's continuing involvement with his people, for Matthew it seems more natural to speak of the presence of Jesus; it is the risen Lord who remains for his people 'God with us'.[79]

C. THE CLIMAX OF THE GOSPEL

In discussing Matthew's christology we have increasingly had to refer to themes which reach their climax in the closing scene of the gospel, where the risen Jesus appears to his disciples in Galilee and

78. If it is right to read this pronouncement in the light of the rabbinic maxim, 'If two sit together and words of the law are between them, the Shekinah dwells between them' (*Aboth* 3:2), the christological implications are the more direct, in that Jesus takes the place of the Shekinah. See Davies, *Setting*, 224-225.
79. Frankemölle, *Jahwe-Bund*, 7-83, presents this theme of 'being with' as the key to both Matthew's ecclesiology and his christology. As God's 'being with' his people was the focus of the covenant theology of the Old Testament, so Jesus' 'being with' his people lies at the heart of the new covenant.

commissions them to continue and extend his ministry to all nations. It has become a commonplace in Matthean studies to refer to this pericope as the key to the whole plan and purpose of the gospel.[80] Just as the opening two chapters set out the fulfilment theme which is to be the context for understanding Jesus' ministry as the story unfolds, so the final pericope draws together the christological implications which have come to light in the course of the narrative, and enables the reader to recognise that the person he has been reading about has emerged as far more than just a human Messiah sent by God to deliver his people.

It will therefore be appropriate to conclude this study of the gospel with a brief account of some of the main emphases of its final scene.

It is set in the hills of Galilee, the scene of Jesus' earlier training of the disciples, to which he has directed them to return (26:32; 28:7,10). Much is sometimes made of the phrase τὸ ὄρος, as a reference to a specific 'mountain', understood as the appropriate location for revelation, perhaps on the model of Mount Sinai.[81] Alternatively, T.L. Donaldson has constructed a whole thesis around the theme of *Jesus on the Mountain*, arguing that six scenes in which Matthew depicts Jesus 'on a mountain' (4:8; 5:1; 15:29; 17:1; 24:3; 28:16) are pointers to a typology not of Mount Sinai but of Mount Zion, with Jesus as himself now the focus of a 'Zion-theology' of the eschatological restoration of the people of God. It seems hazardous to derive so much theology from a simple statement of location, particularly since only three of these passages refer to a specific mountain, which is in one case (24:3) the Mount of Olives (*not* Mount Zion!) and in the others an unidentified 'high mountain' (4:8; 17:1). In the other three cases the phrase εἰς τὸ ὄρος need mean no more than 'into the hills', the general area of Jesus' 'out of town' ministry, without reference to a specific location.[82] The theology of 28:16-20 is better interpreted from its

80. E.g. O. Michel, 'Der Abschluss des Matthäusevangeliums' *EvTh* 10 (1950/1) 16-26, reprinted in English translation in Stanton, *Interpretation*, 30-41; Trilling, *Israel*, 21-51; G. Bornkamm, 'Der Auferstandene und der Irdische. Mt. 28,16-20' in E. Dinkler (ed.) *Zeit und Geschichte: Festschrift für R. Bultmann* (Tübingen: Mohr, 1964) 171-191, reprinted in English translation in J.M. Robinson (ed.), *The Future of our Religious Past* (London: SCM, 1971) 203-229; J.P. Meier, *JBL* 96 (1977) 407-424; O.S. Brooks, *JSNT* 10 (1981) 2-18; Donaldson, *Jesus*, 170-190 (and see *ibid.* 275-276 n. 1 for fuller bibliography on the passage).
81. For a cautious assessment of this interpretation see Davies, *Setting*, 85-86.
82. Donaldson, *Jesus*, 9-11, recognises this objection. His response that Matthew could have indicated this meaning by using ὀρεινός or ὀρεινή hardly meets the force of the argument, since while these terms did indeed exist in Greek vocabulary, they are not used by New Testament writers, with the sole exception of two uses of ὀρεινός by Luke. Εἰς τὸ ὄρος was the natural way for Matthew to say 'into the hills', and to argue that this meaning is nowhere 'contextually required' suggests special pleading, since the 'contextual requirement' for it to refer in three cases to a specific mountain seems to arise more from Donaldson's thesis than from anything inherent in the narrative. It is interesting that where εἰς τὸ ὄρος occurs in a context which is less promising for the thesis (14:23), it is not accorded the same weight in Donaldson's discussion (p. 12).

narrative and discourse content than from its location in the Galilean hills.

The combination of worship and 'hesitation'[83] with which the disciples greet the risen Jesus establishes a majestic and numinous context for Jesus' declaration which is to follow. They are in the presence of someone who is far from ordinary. The scene is thus set for Jesus' declaration in v.18, which recalls 11:27, but goes further in that the Father's endowment is now spelled out as 'all authority in heaven and on earth'. The 'all' of v.18 will be insistently repeated in the following verses: 'all nations', 'all that I have commanded you', 'I will be with you all the days' (literally). O. Michel concludes his article on 'The Conclusion of Matthew's Gospel' by drawing attention to the inclusiveness of this language, which marks this out as 'a *cosmic* event'.[84] There is something final and all-embracing about the authority of Jesus. And this authority is not something for the distant future; it has already been given, and is to be used as the basis for an immediate mission to all nations. The eschatological glory and authority of the Son of Man glimpsed in such passages as 13:41-43; 16:27f; 19:28; 24:30-31; 26:64, and especially 25:31-46 is now already, after the resurrection, a present reality.

My reference in the last sentence to the Son of Man seems justified by the idea of universal authority alone, even if there were no specific allusion to Daniel 7 in these verses. But in fact most interpreters have recognised in the pronouncement of v.18, together with the authority over 'all nations' which follows in v.19 and the promise of his presence 'to the close of the age' in v.20, an echo of Daniel 7:14:

And to him was given dominion and glory and kingdom,
that all peoples, nations, and languages should serve him;
his dominion is an everlasting dominion, which shall not pass away,
and his kingdom one that shall not be destroyed.

The title 'the Son of Man' is not used in Matthew's final scene, but the theme of the ultimate kingship of the Son of Man is one which the reader of Matthew has long had held before him, and no title is necessary for the allusion to be grasped. Here we have 'a christological reshaping of the Daniel saying',[85] 'the enthronement of the Son of Man'.[86]

83. Διστάζω, often translated 'doubt' in 28:17, refers not to intellectual uncertainty but to the disorientation produced by an unfamiliar and overwhelming situation; cf. its only other New Testament use in 14:31. For the mixture of emotions produced by the resurrection event see Jeremias, *NT Theology*, 303; J.D.G. Dunn, *Jesus*, 123-125. For more specific discussion of διστάζω in 28:17, suggesting more subjective grounds for the 'hesitation', see K. Grayston, *JSNT* 21 (1984) 105-109.
84. In Stanton, *Interpretation*, 39-40.
85. O. Michel, *ibid.* 36.
86. Davies, *Setting*, 197.

The recognition of a Daniel 7 model here has been disputed on the grounds that references to Daniel 7 relate to the parousia, whereas this passage clearly refers to the situation already obtaining after the resurrection.[87] But this is to miss the whole point of Matthew's subtle use of the Danielic tradition. It is true that he understands Daniel 7:13-14 (or rather the whole judgement scene in which it is set) as pointing forward to the authority Jesus will exercise as king and judge in the final judgement (so most clearly 25:31-46). But that will be only the culmination of an authority exercised progressively from the moment of his vindication through the resurrection. It is widely accepted that when Jesus declares to the High Priest that *'from now on* you will see the Son of Man sitting at the right hand of power and coming on the clouds of heaven' (26:64), the phrase ἀπ' ἄρτι 'from now on' means exactly what it says (cf. the Luke parallel ἀπὸ τοῦ νῦν), and refers not to some distant event but to the imminent vindication of Jesus which will shortly be obvious to those who have sat in judgement over him. Once it is recognised that 'coming on the clouds' is not necessarily parousia-language, but rather a reference to the 'coming' of the one like a son of man *to God* to receive vindication and sovereignty as envisioned in Daniel 7:13f, we are freed from the dogma that there can be only one point of reference of such language. Certainly Matthew was free of any such restriction. The 'coming' of the Son of Man is envisaged both within the living generation (10:23; 16:28; 24:30-34) and as a part of the ultimate consummation (19:28?; 25:31ff). But its basis lies in the imminent vindication predicted in 26:64 and fulfilled already by the time Jesus utters the declaration of 28:18.[88]

The universal authority of the now enthroned Son of Man is the basis for the universal mission of his disciples, which is launched in v 19. The sovereignty predicted in Daniel 7:14 was that of the one like a son of man, and later in the chapter this is interpreted as 'the people of the saints of the Most High' to whom judgement is given over those who have oppressed them. But this still nationalistic vision undergoes in Matthew's use a striking change, for the ambassadors of this newly installed king are to call all nations not to submit to the authority of

---

87. So G. Bornkamm in J.M. Robinson (ed.), *The Future of our Religious Past* 207-208, following H.E. Tödt, *The Son of Man in the Synoptic Tradition* 287-288; A. Vögtle, 'Das christologische und ekklesiologische Anliegen von Mt. 28,18-20', in F.L. Cross (ed.), *Studia Evangelica II* (Berlin: Akademie-Verlag, 1964) 266-294. Donaldson, *Jesus*, 176-177, 181, while recognising the weakness of Vögtle's argument, wishes to set aside the Daniel 7 background to the language in favour of a 'Zion-theology', on the grounds that the language of Matthew 28:18-20 does not echo the wording of Daniel 7:13f exactly nor include all of its elements. It is not clear why either of these conditions need be met.
88. I have spelled out this understanding of the uses of Daniel 7 in the tradition of Jesus' sayings in *JOT*, 139-148. While the material considered there was drawn from the whole synoptic tradition, it is noticeable that all the relevant texts occur in Matthew, and some of them only in Matthew.

Israel, but to become themselves disciples of the one in whom Israel has found its true embodiment, the Son of Man. Thus the temporary restriction of the period of Jesus' ministry (10:5-6; 15:24) is swept aside, and the insistent indications throughout the gospel that Jesus is more than merely the Messiah of Israel[89] are focused in the command from now on to make disciples of all nations.

The command is then further focused in two participial clauses, 'baptising . . . and teaching . . .', and each of these clauses again gives further evidence of the universal authority of the one wh'ɔ issues the command. The second clause, 'teaching them to observe all that I have commanded you', grounds this new discipleship not in obedience to the commandments of God as revealed to Israel, but in obedience to the commandments of Jesus. And the first specifies the allegiance into which they are to be baptised as 'into the name of the Father and of the Son and of the Holy Spirit'.

This famous clause has been much debated, not least because it seems to reflect the liturgical language of the post-apostolic church (Didache 7:1,3; Justin, *Apol. I* 61:3,11,13) rather than the New Testament period, when baptism was, according to Acts, simply in the name of Jesus (Acts 2:38; 8:16; 10:48; 19:5). But whatever the tradition-process which brought these to Matthew as words of Jesus,[90] there is no manuscript evidence that the text of the gospel ever existed without them. It is true that Eusebius sometimes (in his pre-Nicene writings) quotes Jesus' commission in the form 'go and make disciples in my name', but Eusebius did not always quote the New Testament exactly, and there are five passages in his later writings where he quotes Matthew 28:19 in the form in which we know it. There is little doubt then that Matthew included this 'formula' in his final scene, and that this is the source from which the Didache derived its liturgical practice.[91] It is not necessarily true that Matthew intended this clause specifically for use as a set formula; he may have been simply spelling out the theological basis of baptismal allegiance, but in doing so used a form of words which in fact lent itself to subsequent liturgical adoption. But there is no doubt that it represents the theology he wanted his readers to follow.

As a climax to Matthew's christology the trinitarian formula is remarkable. Here all the hints of a more than human status for Jesus come together, and the 'Son' who has earlier been declared to be in a unique relationship with the Father (11:27; 24:36) is coolly linked with Father and Holy Spirit as three equal persons, who together constitute

---

89. See above pp. 232-235.
90. I have discussed this question in C. Brown (ed.), *History, Criticism and Faith* (Leicester: IVP, 1976) 130-131.
91. The case against the formula as part of the text of Matthew is argued e.g. by H. Kosmala, *ASTI* 4 (1965) 132-147. The case for its authenticity is presented e.g. by Hubbard, *Redaction*, 151-175.

the (singular) 'name' which is to be the object of the disciple's allegiance. We cannot know how far Matthew had thought through the implications of such language, but he has unambiguously posed the problem which lies at the heart of all subsequent trinitarian debate, the recognition, in a monotheistic context, that Jesus, who is clearly understood to be distinct from the Father, is himself no less than God.

After that, the assurance in v 20 of Jesus' continuing presence with his disciples can cause no surprise. Is that not what God has always been able to promise his people when they obey his commands? B.J. Hubbard's study of the literary character of this final scene[92] has drawn attention to the many Old Testament commissioning scenes where God appears to his servants (Abraham, Moses, Gideon, Isaiah, Jeremiah, Ezekiel and others) and sends them out with a task to perform; when they hesitate and hold back, he assures them of his sovereignty, and of his continuing presence with them. Against this background, Matthew's Jesus comes to his worshipping but hesitant disciples as God came to the prophets in the past, and offers them the same divine assurance and authority for the task on which he sends them out.

Matthew's concluding scene has splendidly brought into the open much that the reader has been increasingly aware of as the portrait of Jesus has developed throughout the gospel. It has lifted us above the scene of earthly conflict and rejection to the ultimate authority in heaven and earth, the risen Lord who sits enthroned as the Son of Man. But the scene is still set in the hills of Galilee, among real disciples whose mission will drive them back into the cut and thrust of human conflict, with a gospel for real men and women in the nations of the world. A scene which in itself might have been worthy of one of the later Gnostic treatises, an otherworldly meeting with a heavenly figure to receive the enlightenment which sets us free from the sordid reality of life in the flesh, comes to us in fact as the climax of a *gospel*, a story of a real man who lived and suffered and died among men on earth. Matthew will not allow his readers to divorce the heavenly Lord from the Jesus of the Galilean hills, and thus to allow their discipleship to lose touch with the realities either of the past of Jesus' earthly life or of the present of their practical obedience to his commands.[93] That is why he has written a gospel, rather than a theological treatise or a tract for the times. His subject is ultimately not 'a theology', but Jesus.

92.   Hubbard's dissertation (*Redaction*) has been sympathetically criticised by J.P. Meier, *JBL* 96 (1977) 421-424. Meier is right to argue that the question was wrongly set up when scholars set out to define the 'form' (*Gattung*) of a passage whose genius lies in the fact that it does not fit into any stereotype. But, for all the originality of Matthew's conception, the Old Testament parallels to which Hubbard draws attention are surely a central aspect of the whole background of thought which enables the scene to make such a dramatic impact.
93.   This is emphasised especially by Zumstein, *Condition*, 104-106; cf. also 127, 151-152 etc.

BIBLIOGRAPHY

of modern works referred to in this book

Where there are published English translations of foreign works, these are listed rather than the originals.

E.L. Abel, 'Who Wrote Matthew?' *NTS* 17 (1970/1) 138-152.

S. Agourides, ' "Little Ones" in Matthew' *The Bible Translator* 35/3 (1984) 329-334.

W.F. Albright & C.S. Mann, *Matthew*. Anchor Bible; New York: Doubleday, 1971.

P.S. Alexander, 'Rabbinic Judaism and the New Testament' *ZNW* 74 (1983) 237-246.

'Midrash and the Gospels', in Tuckett, *Synoptic Studies* (1984) 1-18.

'Rabbinic Biography and the Biography of Jesus: a Survey of the Evidence', *ibid.* 19-50.

W.C. Allen, *The Gospel according to S. Matthew*. ICC; Edinburgh: T. & T. Clark, [3]1912.

D.C. Allison, 'Matt. 23:39 = Luke 13:35b as a Conditional Prophecy' *JSNT* 18 (1983) 75-84.

'Jesus and Moses (Mt 5:1-2)' *ExpT* 98 (1986/7) 203-205.

J.-P. Audet, *La Didachè: Instructions des Apôtres*. Paris: Gabalda, 1958.

D.E. Aune, 'The Problem of the Genre of the Gospels: a Critique of C.H. Talbert's *What is a Gospel?*', in *Gospel Perspectives* vol. 2 (1981) 9-60.

B.W. Bacon, 'The Five Books of Matthew against the Jews' *The Expositor* 15 (1918) 56-66.

Studies in Matthew. London: Constable, 1930.

D.L. Baker, *Two Testaments, One Bible*. Leicester: Inter-Varsity Press, 1976.

R.J. Banks, 'Matthew's Understanding of the Law: Authenticity and Interpretation in Matthew 5:17-20' *JBL* 93 (1974) 226-242.

Jesus and the Law in the Synoptic Tradition. Cambridge University Press, 1974.

R.J. Bauckham, 'The Worship of Jesus in Apocalyptic Christianity' *NTS* 27 (1980/1) 322-341.

F.W. Beare, *The Gospel according to Matthew*. Oxford: Blackwell, 1981.

G.R. Beasley-Murray, *Jesus and the Kingdom of God*. Exeter: Paternoster, 1986.

E. Best, 'Peter in the Gospel according to Mark' *CBQ* 40 (1978) 547-558; reprinted in Best's *Disciples and Discipleship: Studies in the Gospel according to Mark* (Edinburgh: T. & T. Clark, 1986) 162-176.

H.D. Betz, *Essays on the Sermon on the Mount*. Philadelphia: Fortress, 1985.

M. Black, *An Aramaic Approach to the Gospels and Acts*. Oxford: Clarendon, [3]1967.

'The "Son of Man" Passion Sayings in the Gospel Tradition' *ZNW* 60 (1969) 1-8.

E.P. Blair, *Jesus in the Gospel of Matthew*. Nashville: Abingdon, 1960.

R. Bloch, 'Midrash', in *Dictionnaire de la Bible, Supplément V* (Paris: Letouzey & Ané, 1957) 1263ff.

G. Bornkamm, G. Barth & H.J. Held, *Tradition and Interpretation in Matthew*. ET, London: SCM, 1963.

G. Bornkamm, 'Der Auferstandene und der Irdische. Mt. 28,16-20', in E. Dinkler (ed.), *Zeit und Geschichte: Festschrift für R. Bultmann* (Tübingen: Mohr, 1964) 171-191; reprinted in English translation in J.M. Robinson (ed.), *The Future of our Religious Past* (London: SCM, 1971) 203-229.

'The Authority to "Bind"and "Loose"in the Church in Matthew's Gospel', in D.G. Miller (ed.), *Jesus and Man's Hope*, vol. 1, 37-50; reprinted in Stanton, *Interpretation*, 85-97.

S.G.F. Brandon, *The Fall of Jerusalem and the Christian Church*. London: SPCK, 1951.

O.S. Brooks, 'Matthew xxviii 16-20 and the Design of the First Gospel' *JSNT* 10 (1981) 2-18.

R.E. Brown, K.P. Donfried & J. Reumann (ed.), *Peter in the New Testament*. Minneapolis: Augsburg / New York: Paulist Press, 1973.

R.E. Brown, *The Birth of the Messiah*. London: Chapman, 1977.

'Not Jewish Christianity and Gentile Christianity but Types of Jewish/Gentile Christianity' *CBQ* 45 (1983) 74-79.

S. Brown, 'The Matthean Community and the Gentile Mission' *NovT* 22 (1980) 193-221.

R. Bultmann, *The History of the Synoptic Tradition*. ET, Oxford: Blackwell, 1963.

C. Burger, *Jesus als Davidssohn*. Göttingen: Vandenhoeck & Ruprecht, 1970.

C.F. Burney, *The Poetry of Our Lord*. Oxford University Press, 1925.

B.C. Butler, *The Originality of St. Matthew*. Cambridge University Press, 1951.

C.C. Caragounis, *The Son of Man: Vision and Interpretation*. Tübingen: Mohr, 1986.

C.E. Carlston, 'Betz on the Sermon on the Mount – a Critique' *CBQ* 50 (1988) 47-57.

J. Carmignac, 'Pourquoi Jérémie est-il mentionné en Matthieu 16,14?', in G. Jeremias (ed.), *Tradition und Glaube: Festgabe für K.G. Kuhn* (Göttingen: Vandenhoeck & Ruprecht, 1971) 283-298.

P. Carrington, *The Primitive Christian Calendar*, vol. 1. Cambridge University Press, 1952.

D.A. Carson, 'The Jewish Leaders in Matthew's Gospel: a Reappraisal' *JETS* 25 (1982) 161-174.

Matthew, in F.E. Gaebelein (ed.), *The Expositor's Bible Commentary*, vol. 8 (Grand Rapids: Zondervan, 1984) 1-599.

D.R. Catchpole, 'The Answer of Jesus to Caiaphas (Matt. XXVI.64)' *NTS* 17 (1970/1) 213-226.

J. Chapman, *Matthew, Mark and Luke: a Study in the Order and Interrelation of the Synoptic Gospels*. London: Longmans, Green, 1937.

B. Chilton, 'Varieties and Tendencies of Midrash', in *Gospel Perspectives*, vol. 3 (1983) 9-32.

F. Christ, *Jesus Sophia: die Sophia-Christologie bei den Synoptikern*. Zürich: Zwingli-Verlag, 1970.

D.J. Clark & J. de Waard, 'Discourse Structure in Matthew's Gospel', *Scriptura*, special issue 1 (Stellenbosch, 1982).

K.W. Clark, 'The Gentile Bias in Matthew', *JBL* 66 (1947) 165-172.

H.J.B. Combrink, 'The Structure of the Gospel of Matthew as Narrative' *TynB* 34 (1983) 61-90.

H. Conzelmann, *The Theology of St. Luke*. ET, London: Faber, 1960.

M.J. Cook, *Mark's Treatment of the Jewish Leaders*. Leiden: Brill, 1978.

O.L. Cope, *Matthew: a Scribe Trained for the Kingdom of God*. Washington: CBQ Monographs, 1976.

O. Cullmann, *The Christology of the New Testament*. ET, London: SCM, ²1963.

N.A. Dahl, 'The Passion Narrative in Matthew' in *Jesus in the Memory of the Early Church* (Minneapolis: Augsburg, 1976) 37-51; reprinted in Stanton, *Interpretation*, 42-55.

J. Daniélou, *Théologie du Judéo-Christianisme*. Paris: Desclée, 1958; English version published as vol. 1 of *A History of Early Christian Doctrine* (London: Darton, Longman & Todd, 1964).

W.D. Davies, 'Matthew 5:18', in *Mélanges bibliques rédigés en l'honneur de André Robert* (Paris: Bloud & Gay, 1957) 428-456; reprinted in Davies' *Christian Origins and Judaism* (London: Darton Longman & Todd, 1962) 31-66.

  The Setting of the Sermon on the Mount. Cambridge University Press, 1963.

J.D.M. Derrett, *Law in the New Testament*. London: Darton, Longman & Todd, 1970.

  'Binding and Loosing (Matt 16:19; 18:18; John 20:23)' *JBL* 102 (1983) 112-117.

C. Deutsch, *Hidden Wisdom and the Easy Yoke: Wisdom, Torah and Discipleship in Matthew 11.25-30*. Sheffield: JSOT Press, 1987.

M. Didier (ed.), *L'Evangile selon Matthieu: Rédaction et Théologie*. Gembloux: Duculot, 1972.

E. von Dobschütz, 'Matthäus als Rabbi und Katechet' *ZNW* 27 (1928) 338-348; reprinted in English translation in Stanton, *Interpretation*, 19-29.

C.H. Dodd, *According to the Scriptures: the Substructure of New Testament Theology*. London: Nisbet, 1952.

  The Founder of Christianity. London: Collins, 1970.

T.L. Donaldson, *Jesus on the Mountain: a Study in Matthean Theology*. Sheffield: JSOT Press, 1985.

D.C. Duling, 'Solomon, Exorcism, and the Son of David' *HTR* 68 (1975) 235-252.

  'The Therapeutic Son of David: an Element in Matthew's Christological Apologetic' *NTS* 24 (1977/8) 392-410.

D.L. Dungan & D.R. Cartlidge, *Source-Book of Texts for the Comparative Study of the Gospels*. Missoula: Society of Biblical Literature, 1971. Revised edition under the title *Documents for the Study of the Gospels*, London: Collins, 1980.

J.D.G. Dunn, 'The Messianic Secret in Mark', *TynB* 21 (1970) 92-117.

  Jesus and the Spirit: a Study of the Religious and Charismatic Experience of Jesus and the First Christians as reflected in the New Testament. London:

SCM, 1975.
Christology in the Making: a New Testament Inquiry into the Origins of the Doctrine of the Incarnation. London: SCM, 1980.
R.A. Edwards, *Matthew's Story of Jesus.* Philadelphia: Fortress, 1985.
P.F. Ellis, *Matthew: his Mind and his Message.* Collegeville: Liturgical Press, 1974.
C.F. Evans *et al, The New Testament Gospels.* London: BBC, 1965.
'The New Testament in the Making', in P.R. Ackroyd & C.F. Evans (ed.), *The Cambridge History of the Bible,* vol. 1 (Cambridge University Press, 1970) 232-284.
W.R. Farmer, *The Synoptic Problem.* New York: Macmillan, 1964; second edition, Dillsboro: Western North Carolina Press, 1976.
'Modern Developments of Griesbach's Hypothesis', *NTS* 23 (1976/7) 275-295.
(ed.) *New Synoptic Studies: the Cambridge Gospel Conference and Beyond.* Macon: Mercer University Press, 1983.
A.M. Farrer, 'On Dispensing with Q', in D.E. Nineham (ed.), *Studies in the Gospels* (Oxford: Blackwell, 1955) 55-88.
F.V. Filson, *The Gospel according to St. Matthew.* London: A. & C. Black, ²1971.
J.A. Fitzmyer, 'Anti-Semitism and the Cry of "All the People"(Mt. 27:25)' *TS* 26 (1965) 667-671.
'The Contribution of Qumran Aramaic to the Study of the New Testament' *NTS* 20 (1973/4) 382-407.
F. Foulkes, *The Acts of God: a Study of the Basis of Typology in the Old Testament.* London: Tyndale Press, 1958.
R.T. France, *Jesus and the Old Testament.* London: Tyndale Press, 1971.
'The Authenticity of the Sayings of Jesus', in C. Brown (ed.), *History, Criticism and Faith* (Leicester: Inter-Varsity Press, 1976) 101-141.
'Exegesis in Practice: Two Samples', in I.H. Marshall (ed.), *New Testament Interpretation* (Exeter: Paternoster, 1977) 252-281.
'Herod and the Children of Bethlehem' *NovT* 21 (1979) 98-120.
'Mark and the Teaching of Jesus', in *Gospel Perspectives,* vol. 1 (1980) 101-136.
'The Formula-Quotations of Matthew 2 and the Problem of Communication' *NTS* 27 (1980/1) 233-251.
'Scripture, Tradition and History in the Infancy Narratives of Matthew', in *Gospel Perspectives,* vol. 2 (1981) 239-266.
'The Worship of Jesus: a Neglected Factor in Christological Debate?', in H.H. Rowdon (ed.), *Christ the Lord: Studies presented to D. Guthrie* (Leicester: Inter-Varsity Press, 1982) 17-36.
The Gospel according to Matthew: an Introduction and Commentary. Leicester: Inter-Varsity Press, 1985.
H. Frankemölle, *Jahwe-Bund und Kirche Christi: Studien zur Form- und Traditionsgeschichte des "Evangeliums" nach Matthäus.* Münster: Aschendorff, ²1984.
S. Freyne, *Galilee from Alexander the Great to Hadrian, 323 B.C.E. to 135 C.E..* Wilmington: Michael Glazier, 1980.

V.P. Furnish, *The Love Command in the New Testament*. Nashville: Abingdon, 1972.

A. Gaboury, *La Structure des Evangiles synoptiques*. Leiden: Brill, 1970.

P. Gaechter, *Die literarische Kunst im Matthäusevangelium*. Stuttgart: Katholisches Bibelwerk, 1966.

G. Gander, *L'Evangile de l'Eglise*. Aix-en-Provence: Faculté Libre de Théologie Protestante, 1970.

D.E. Garland, *The Intention of Matthew 23*. Leiden: Brill, 1979.

B. Gärtner, *The Temple and the Community in Qumran and the New Testament*. Cambridge University Press, 1965.

L. Gaston, 'The Messiah of Israel as Teacher of the Gentiles: the Setting of Matthew's Christology' *Interpretation* 29 (1975) 24-40.

G. Gay, 'The Judgment of the Gentiles in Matthew's Theology' in W.W. Gasque & W.S. LaSor (ed.), *Scripture, Tradition and Interpretation: essays presented to E.F. Harrison* (Grand Rapids: Eerdmans, 1978) 199-215.

B. Gerhardsson, 'Gottes Sohn als Diener Gottes: Messias, Agape und Himmelsherrschaft nach dem Matthäusevangelium' *ST* 27 (1973) 73-106.

'Sacrificial Service and Atonement in the Gospel of Matthew', in R.J. Banks (ed.), *Reconciliation and Hope: New Testament Essays on Atonement and Eschatology presented to L.L. Morris* (Exeter: Paternoster, 1974) 25-35.

The Mighty Acts of Iesus according to Matthew. Lund: Gleerup, 1979.

'Confession and Denial before Men: Observations on Matt. 26:57 - 27:2' *JSNT* 13 (1981) 46-66.

J.M. Gibbs, 'Purpose and Pattern in Matthew's Use of the Title "Son of David" ' *NTS* 10 (1963/4) 446-464.

J. Goldingay, *Approaches to Old Testament Interpretation*. Leicester: Inter-Varsity Press, 1981.

D.W. Gooding, Structure Littéraire de Matthieu XIII,53 à XVIII,35', *RB* 85 (1978) 227-252.

E.J. Goodspeed, *The Formation of the New Testament*. University of Chicago Press, 1926.

Matthew, Apostle and Evangelist. Philadelphia: J.C. Winston, 1959.

M.D. Goulder, *Midrash and Lection in Matthew*. London: SPCK, 1974.

The Evangelists' Calendar: a Lectionary Explanation of the Development of Scripture. London: SPCK, 1978.

'On Putting Q to the Test', *NTS* 24 (1977/8) 218-234.

F.C. Grant, *The Gospels, their Origin and their Growth*. New York: Harper and Row, 1957.

K. Grayston, 'The Translation of Matthew 28.17' *JSNT* 21 (1984) 105-109.

H.B. Green, 'The Structure of St. Matthew's Gospel', in *Studia Evangelica IV* (TU 102. Berlin: Akademie-Verlag, 1968) 47-59.

R.A. Guelich, *The Sermon on the Mount: a Foundation for Understanding*. Waco: Word Books, 1982.

R.H. Gundry, *The Use of the Old Testament in St. Matthew's Gospel, with special reference to the Messianic Hope*. Leiden: Brill, 1967.

'Recent Investigations into the Literary Genre "Gospel" ', in R.N. Longenecker & M.C. Tenney (ed.), *New Dimensions in New Testament Study* (Grand Rapids: Zondervan, 1974) 97-114.

Matthew: a Commentary on his Literary and Theological Art. Grand Rapids: Eerdmans, 1982.

M. Hadas & M. Smith, *Heroes and Gods.* New York: Harper & Row, 1965.

F. Hahn, *The Titles of Jesus in Christology: their History in Early Christianity.* ET, London: Lutterworth, 1969.

A.T. Hanson, *Jesus Christ in the Old Testament.* London: SPCK, 1965.
The Living Utterances of God. London: Darton, Longman & Todd, 1983.
The Image of the Invisible God. London: SCM, 1982.

D.R.A. Hare, *The Theme of Jewish Persecution of Christians in the Gospel according to St. Matthew.* Cambridge University Press, 1967.

D.R.A. Hare & D.J. Harrington, ' "Make Disciples of all the Gentiles" (Mt 28:19)', *CBQ* 37 (1975) 359-369.

J.R. Harris, *Testimonies I & II.* Cambridge University Press, 1916, 1920.

L. Hartman, 'Scriptural Exegesis in the Gospel of St. Matthew and the Problem of Communication', in Didier, *Matthieu*, 131-152.

M. Hengel, *The Son of God.* ET, London: SCM, 1976.
The Charismatic Leader and his Followers. ET, Edinburgh: T. & T. Clark, 1981.
Studies in the Gospel of Mark. ET, London: SCM, 1985.

D. Hill, 'Son and Servant: an Essay in Matthean Christology' *JSNT* 6 (1980) 2-16.
'The Figure of Jesus in Matthew's Story: a Response to Professor Kingsbury's Literary-Critical Probe', *JSNT* 21 (1984) 37-52.

A.J.B. Higgins, *Jesus and the Son of Man.* London: Lutterworth, 1964.

M.D. Hooker, *Jesus and the Servant: the Influence of the Servant Concept of Deutero-Isaiah in the New Testament.* London: SPCK, 1959.

B.J. Hubbard, *The Matthean Redaction of a Primitive Apostolic Commissioning: an Exegesis of Matthew 28:16-20.* Missoula: Scholars' Press, 1974.

R. Hummel, *Die Auseinandersetzung zwischen Kirche und Judentum im Matthäusevangelium.* München: Kaiser, ²1966.

J. Jeremias, *New Testament Theology, vol. 1: The Proclamation of Jesus.* ET, London: SCM, 1971.

S. Jellicoe, *The Septuagint and Modern Study.* Oxford University Press, 1968.

L.T. Johnson, *The Writings of the New Testament: an Interpretation.* Philadelphia: Fortress, 1986.

M.D. Johnson, 'Reflections on a Wisdom Approach to Matthew's Christology' *CBQ* 36 (1974) 44-64.

D. Juel, *Messiah and Temple: the Trial of Jesus in the Gospel of Mark.* Missoula: Scholars' Press, 1977.

P. Kahle, *The Cairo Geniza.* Oxford: Blackwell, ²1959.

L.E. Keck, 'Toward the Renewal of New Testament Christology' *NTS* 32 (1986) 362-377.

T.J. Keegan, 'Introductory Formulae for Matthean Discourses' *CBQ* 44 (1982) 415-430.

G.D. Kilpatrick, *The Origins of the Gospel according to St. Matthew.* Oxford: Clarendon, 1946.

S. Kim, *The "Son of Man" ' as the Son of God.* Tübingen: Mohr, 1983.

R. Kimelman, '*Birkat ha-Minim* and the Lack of Evidence for an Anti- Christian

Jewish Prayer in Late Antiquity', in E.P. Sanders, A.I. Baumgarten & A. Mendelson (ed.), *Jewish and Christian Self-Definition*, vol. 2 (London: SCM, 1981) 226-244.

J.D. Kingsbury, *The Parables of Jesus in Matthew 13.* London: SPCK, 1969.
'The Structure of Matthew's Gospel and his Concept of Salvation-History', *CBQ* 35 (1973) 451-474.
'Form and Message of Matthew' *Interpretation* 29 (1975) 13-23. ·
Matthew: Structure, Christology, Kingdom. Philadelphia: Fortress, 1975.
'The Title "Son of David" in Matthew's Gospel' *JBL* 95 (1976) 591-602.
'The Verb *akolouthein* ("to follow") as an Index of Matthew's View of his Community' JBL 97 (1978) 56-73.
'The Figure of Peter in Matthew's Gospel as a Theological Problem' *JBL* 98 (1979) 67-83.
The Christology of Mark's Gospel. Philadelphia: Fortress, 1983.
'The Figure of Jesus in Matthew's Story: a Literary- Critical Probe', *JSNT* 21 (1984) 3-36.
'The Figure of Jesus in Matthew's Story: a Rejoinder to David Hill', *JSNT* 25 (1985) 61-81.
Matthew as Story. Philadelphia: Fortress, 1986.

A.F.J. Klijn, 'The Study of Jewish Christianity' *NTS* 20 (1974) 419-431.

H. Kosmala, 'The Conclusion of Matthew' *ASTI* 4 (1965) 132-147.
' "His Blood on us and on our Children" (The Background of Mat. 27, 24-25)' *ASTI* 7 (1970) 94-126.

H. Köster, *Synoptische Überlieferung bei den apostolischen Vätern.* Berlin, 1957.

R.A. Kraft, 'In search of "Jewish Christianity" and its "Theology". Problems of Definition and Methodology', in *Judéo-Christianisme: Recherches historiques et théologiques offertes en hommage au Cardinal Jean Daniélou* (Paris: Recherches de Science Religieuse, 1972) 81-92.

E. Krentz, 'The Extent of Matthew's Prologue' *JBL* 83 (1964) 409-414.

W.G. Kümmel, *The New Testament: the History of the Investigation of its Problems.* ET, London: SCM, 1973.

J. Kürzinger, 'Das Papiaszeugnis und die Erstgestalt des Matthäusevangeliums' *BZ* 4 (1960) 19-38.
'Irenäus und sein Zeugnis zur Sprache des Matthäusevangeliums' *NTS* 10 (1963/4) 108-115.

G.E. Ladd, 'The Parable of the Sheep and the Goats in Recent Interpretation' in R.N. Longenecker & M.C. Tenney (ed.), *New Dimensions in New Testament Study* (Grand Rapids: Zondervan, 1974) 191-199.

W.L. Lane, *The Gospel according to Mark.* Grand Rapids: Eerdmans, 1974.

R. Le Déaut, 'Apropos a Definition of Midrash' *Interpretation* 25 (1971) 259-282.

S. Légasse, 'L' "antijudaisme" dans l'Evangile selon Matthieu', in Didier, *Matthieu*, 417-428.

E. Levine, 'The Sabbath Controversy according to Matthew' *NTS* 22 (1975/6) 480-483.

R.H. Lightfoot, *Locality and Doctrine in the Gospels.* London: Hodder & Stoughton, 1938.

B. Lindars, *New Testament Apologetic: the Doctrinal Significance of the Old Testament Quotations.* London: SCM, 1961.

Jesus Son of Man: a Fresh Examination of the Son of Man Sayings in the Gospels in the Light of Recent Research. London: SPCK, 1983.

W.R.G. Loader, 'Son of David, Blindness, Possession, and Duality in Matthew' *CBQ* 44 (1982) 570-585.

E. Lohmeyer, *Galiläa und Jerusalem*. Göttingen: Vandenhoeck & Ruprecht, 1936.

C.H. Lohr, 'Oral Techniques in the Gospel of Matthew' *CBQ* 23 (1961) 403-435.

M. Lowe, 'Who were the *Ioudaioi?' NovT* 18 (1976) 101-130.

U. Luz, 'Die Junger im Matthäusevangelium' *ZNW* 62 (1971) 141-171; reprinted in English translation in Stanton, *Interpretation*, 98-128.

H.K. McArthur, *Understanding the Sermon on the Mount*. London: Epworth, 1961.

R.S. McConnell, *Law and Prophecy in Matthew's Gospel*. Basel: Reinhardt, 1969.

N.J. McEleney, 'Mt. 17:24-27 – Who Paid the Temple Tax?' *CBQ* 38 (1976) 178-192.

R.J. McKelvey, *The New Temple: the Church in the New Testament*. Oxford University Press, 1969.

A.H. McNeile, *The Gospel according to St. Matthew*. London: Macmillan, 1915.

H. Maccoby, *The Mythmaker: Paul and the Invention of Christianity*. London: Weidenfeld & Nicolson, 1986.

B.J. Malina, 'Jewish Christianity or Christian Judaism: Toward a Hypothetical Definition' *JSJ* 7 (1976) 46-57.

J. Manek, 'Mit wem identifiziert sich Jesus (Matt. 25:31-46)?' in B. Lindars & S.S. Smalley (ed.), *Christ and Spirit in the New Testament: in honour of C.F.D. Moule* (Cambridge University Press, 1973) 15-25.

T.W. Manson, *The Sayings of Jesus*. London: SCM, 1949.

D. Marguerat, *Le Jugement dans l'Evangile de Matthieu*. Geneva: Labor et Fides, 1981.

R.P. Martin, *Mark, Evangelist and Theologian*. Exeter: Paternoster, 1972.

W. Marxsen, *Mark the Evangelist*. ET, Nashville: Abingdon, 1969.

E.Massaux, *Influence de l'Evangile de saint Matthieu sur la littérature chrétienne avant saint Irénée*. Louvain/Gembloux: Publications Universitaires de Louvain/Duculot, 1950; reprinted with supplement and introduction by F. Neirynck, Leuven University Press, 1986.

F.J. Matera, 'The Plot of Matthew's Gospel' *CBQ* 49 (1987) 233-253.

J.P. Meier, 'Salvation-History in Matthew: in Search of a Starting Point' *CBQ* 37 (1975) 203-215.

Law and History in Matthew's Gospel. Rome: Biblical Institute Press, 1976.

'Nations or Gentiles in Matthew 28:19?' *CBQ* 39 (1977) 94-102.

'Two Disputed Questions in Matt 28:16-20' *JBL* 96 (1977) 407-424.

The Vision of Matthew: Christ, Church and Morality in the First Gospel. New York: Paulist Press, 1979.

'John the Baptist in Matthew's Gospel' *JBL* 99 (1980) 383-405.

B.M. Metzger, *The Text of the New Testament: its Transmission, Corruption and Restoration*. Oxford University Press, ²1968.

The Canon of the New Testament: its Origin, Development and Significance. Oxford: Clarendon, 1987.

B.F. Meyer, *The Aims of Jesus*. London: SCM, 1979.

E.M. Meyers & J.F. Strange, *Archaeology, the Rabbis and Early Christianity*. London: SCM, 1981.

J.R. Michaels, 'Apostolic Hardships and Righteous Gentiles' *JBL* 84 (1965) 27-37.

O. Michel, 'Der Abschluss der Matthäusevangeliums' *EvTh* 10 (1950/1) 16-26; reprinted in English translation in Stanton, *Interpretation*, 30-41.

D.G. Miller (ed.), *Jesus and Man's Hope*. Pittsburgh Theological Seminary, 1970-1971.

P.S. Minear, 'The Disciples and the Crowds in the Gospel of Matthew', *Anglican Theological Review*, Supplement 3 (1974) 28-44.

Matthew: The Teacher's Gospel. London: Darton, Longman & Todd, 1984.

J. Moffatt, *An Introduction to the Literature of the New Testament*. Edinburgh: T. & T. Clark, 1911.

R. Mohrlang, *Matthew and Paul: a Comparison of Ethical Perspectives*. Cambridge University Press, 1984.

D.J. Moo, *The Old Testament in the Gospel Passion Narratives*. Sheffield: Almond, 1983.

'Tradition and Old Testament in Matt 27:3-10', in *Gospel Perspectives*, vol. 3 (1983) 157-175.

'Jesus and the Authority of the Mosaic Law' *JSNT* 20 (1984) 3-49.

E. Moore, 'Βιάζω, ἁρπάζω and Cognates in Josephus' *NTS* 21 (1974/5) 519-543.

L.L. Morris, 'The Gospels and the Jewish Lectionaries', in *Gospel Perspectives* vol. 3 (1983) 129-156.

C.F.D. Moule, 'Fulfilment Words in the New Testament: Use and Abuse' *NTS* 14 (1967/8) 293-320; reprinted in Moule's *Essays in New Testament Interpretation* (Cambridge University Press, 1982) 3-36.

'St. Matthew's Gospel: some Neglected Features', in F.L. Cross (ed.), *Studia Evangelica* II (TU 87. Berlin: Akademie-Verlag, 1964) 90-99; reprinted in Moule's *Essays in New Testament Interpretation*, 67-74.

The Origin of Christology. Cambridge University Press, 1977.

The Birth of the New Testament. London: A. & C. Black, ³1981.

R. Murray, 'Defining Judaeo-Christianity' *Heythrop Journal* 15 (1974) 303-310.

'Jews, Hebrews and Christians: some needed Distinctions', *NovT* 24 (1982) 194-208.

F. Neirynck, *The Minor Agreements of Matthew and Luke against Mark*. Leuven University Press, 1974.

P. Nepper-Christensen, *Das Matthäusevangelium: ein judenchristliches Evangelium?*. Aarhus: Universitetsforlaget, 1958.

J. Neusner, *From Politics to Piety: the Emergence of Pharisaic Judaism*. New York: KTAV, 1979.

Judaism in the Beginning of Christianity. Philadelphia: Fortress, 1984.

S. Neill, *The Interpretation of the New Testament, 1861-1961*. Oxford University Press, 1964.

R.E. Nixon, *The Exodus in the New Testament*. London: Tyndale Press, 1963.

B. Nolan, *The Royal Son of God*. Göttingen: Vandenhoeck & Ruprecht, 1979.

J.B. Orchard, *Matthew, Luke and Mark*. Manchester: Koinonia Press, 1976.

J.B. Orchard & T.R.W. Longstaff (ed.), *J.J. Griesbach: Synoptic and Text-*

Critical Studies 1776-1976. Cambridge University Press, 1978.

H. Palmer, 'Just Married, Cannot Come', *NovT* 18 (1976) 241-257.

M. Pamment, 'The Son of Man in the First Gospel' *NTS* 29 (1983) 116-129.

R. Pesch, 'Levi-Matthäus (Mc 2ı4/Mt 9ᵩ 10ᵌ)' *ZNW* 59 (1968) 40-56.

W. Pesch, 'Theologische Aussagen der Redaktion von Matthäus 23', in P. Hoffmann *et al* (ed.), *Orientierung an Jesus: zur Theologie der Synoptiker.* Für J. Schmid (Freiburg: Herder, 1973) 286-299.

C.S. Petrie, 'The Authorship of "The Gospel according to Matthew": a Reconsideration of the External Evidence' *NTS* 14 (1967/8) 15-33.

J. Piper, *'Love Your Enemies': Jesus' Love Command in the Synoptic Gospels and in the Early Christian Paraenesis.* Cambridge University Press, 1979.

A. Plummer, *An Exegetical Commentary on the Gospel according to St. Matthew.* London: Robert Scott, 1909.

I. de la Potterie (ed.), *De Jésus aux Evangiles.* Gembloux: Duculot, 1967.

B. Przybylski, *Righteousness in Matthew and his World of Thought.* Cambridge University Press, 1980.

B. Reicke, 'Synoptic Prophecies on the Destruction of Jerusalem', in D.E. Aune (ed.), *Studies in New Testament and Early Christian Literature: Essays in honor of A.P. Wikgren* (Leiden: Brill, 1972) 121-134.

K.H. Rengstorf, 'Die Stadt der Mörder (Mt 22.7)', in W. Eltester (ed.), *Judentum, Urchristentum, Kirche: Festschrift für J. Jeremias* (Berlin: Töpelmann, 1960) 106-129.

P. Richardson, *Israel in the Apostolic Church.* Cambridge University Press, 1969.

S.K. Riegel, 'Jewish Christianity: Definitions and Terminology' *NTS* 24 (1978) 410-415.

J.M. Rist, *On the Independence of Matthew and Mark.* Cambridge University Press, 1978.

J.A.T. Robinson, 'The Parable of the Wicked Husbandmen: a Test of Synoptic Relationships' *NTS* 21 (1974/5) 443-461.

Redating the New Testament. London: SCM, 1976.

The Priority of John. London: SCM, 1985.

W. Rothfuchs, *Die Erfüllungszitate des Matthäus-Evangeliums.* Stuttgart: Kohlhammer, 1969.

E.P. Sanders, 'The Argument from the Order and the Relationship between Matthew and Luke', *NTS* 15 (1968/9) 249-261.

The Tendencies of the Synoptic Tradition. Cambridge University Press, 1969.

'Priorités et dépendances dans la tradition synoptique', *Recherches de Science Religieuse* 60 (1972) 519-540.

'The Overlaps of Mark and Q and the Synoptic Problem' *NTS* 19 (1972/3) 453-465.

Paul and Palestinian Judaism. London: SCM, 1977.

Jesus and Judaism. London: SCM, 1985.

E. Schillebeeckx, *Christ: the Christian Experience in the Modern World.* ET, London: SCM, 1980.

E. Schürer (ed.), *The History of the Jewish People in the Age of Jesus Christ,* new edition ed. G. Vermes, F. Millar. Edinburgh: T. & T. Clark, 1973-1987.

E. Schweizer, 'Observance of the Law and Charismatic Activity in Matthew' *NTS* 16 (1969/70) 213-230.

Jesus. ET, London: SCM, 1971.

Matthäus und seine Gemeinde. Stuttgart: Katholisches Bibelwerk, 1974.

'Matthew's Church', translated from the above, in Stanton, *Interpretation*, 129-155.

The Good News according to Matthew. ET, Atlanta: John Knox, 1975.

D.P. Senior, *The Passion Narrative according to Matthew.* Leuven University Press, 1975.

H.B. Sharman, *The Son of Man and the Kingdom of God.* New York: Harper & Row, 1943.

P.L. Shuler, *A Genre for the Gospels: the Biographical Character of Matthew.* Philadelphia: Fortress, 1982.

M. Silva, 'Ned B. Stonehouse and Redaction-Criticism', *Westminster Theological Journal* 40 (1977/8) 77-88, 281-303.

M. Simon, 'Réflexions sur le Judéo-Christianisme', in J. Neusner (ed.), *Christianity, Judaism and other Greco-Roman Cults. Vol. 2, Early Christianity* (Leiden: Brill, 1975) 53-76.

H.D. Slingerland, 'The Transjordanian Origin of St. Matthew's Gospel' *JSNT* 3 (1979) 18-28.

E.M. Smallwood, *The Jews under Roman Rule.* Leiden: Brill, 1976.

G.M. Soares Prabhu, *The Formula Quotations in the Infancy Narrative of Matthew.* Rome: Biblical Institute Press, 1976.

G.N. Stanton, *Jesus of Nazareth in New Testament Preaching.* Cambridge University Press, 1974.

'5 Ezra and Matthean Christianity' *JTS* 28 (1977) 67-83.

(ed.), *The Interpretation of Matthew.* London: SPCK, 1983.

'The Origin and Purpose of Matthew's Gospel: Matthean Scholarship from 1945 to 1980', in H. Temporini & W. Haase (ed.), *Aufstieg und Niedergang der römischen Welt*, Teil II (Principat), Band 25 (Religion), Teilband 3 (Berlin: de Gruyter, 1985) pp. 1889-1951.

'The Origin and Purpose of Matthew's Sermon on the Mount', in G.F. Hawthorne & O. Betz (ed.), *Tradition and Interpretation in the New Testament: Essays in honor of E.E. Ellis* (Grand Rapids: Eerdmans, 1987) 181-192.

R.H. Stein, *An Introduction to the Parables of Jesus.* Philadelphia: Westminster, 1981.

K. Stendahl, *The School of St. Matthew, and its Use of the Old Testament.* Uppsala 1954; second edition, Philadelphia: Fortress, 1968.

'Quis et Unde? An Analysis of Matthew 1-2', in W. Eltester (ed.), *Judentum, Urchristentum, Kirche: Festschrift für J. Jeremias* (Berlin: Töpelmann, 1960) 94-105; reprinted in Stanton, *Interpretation*, 54-66.

J.B. Stern, 'Jesus' Citation of Dt 6,5 and Lv 19,18 in the Light of Jewish Tradition' *CBQ* 28 (1966) 312-316.

H.-H. Stoldt, *History and Criticism of the Marcan Hypothesis.* ET, Edinburgh: T. & T. Clark, 1980.

N.B. Stonehouse, *The Witness of Matthew and Mark to Christ.* London: Tyndale Press, 1944.

Origins of the Synoptic Gospels. Grand Rapids: Eerdmans, 1963.

G. Strecker, *Der Weg der Gerechtigkeit: Untersuchung zur Theologie des Matthäus*. Göttingen: Vandenhoeck & Ruprecht, ³1971.

'Das Geschichtsverständnis des Matthäus', *EvTh* 26 (1966) 57-74; reprinted in English translation in Stanton, *Interpretation*, 67-84.

B.H. Streeter, *The Four Gospels: a Study of Origins*. London: Macmillan, 1924.

M.J. Suggs, *Wisdom, Christology and Law in Matthew's Gospel*. Cambridge MA: Harvard University Press, 1970.

K. Tagawa, 'People and Community in the Gospel of Matthew' *NTS* 16 (1969/70) 149-162.

C.H. Talbert, *What is a Gospel? The Genre of the Canonical Gospels*. Philadelphia: Fortress, 1977.

V. Taylor, *The Names of Jesus*. London: Macmillan, 1953.

W.R. Telford, *The Barren Temple and the Withered Tree*. Sheffield: JSOT Press, 1980.

W.G. Thompson, *Matthew's Advice to a Divided Community: Mt. 17,22 - 18,35*. Rome: Biblical Institute Press, 1970.

H.E. Tödt, *The Son of Man in the Synoptic Tradition*. ET, London: SCM, 1965.

C.C. Torrey, *Our Translated Gospels*. London: Hodder & Stoughton, n.d.

W. Trilling, *Das wahre Israel: Studien zur Theologie des Matthäusevangeliums*. München: Kösel, ³1964.

C.M. Tuckett, 'The Griesbach Hypothesis in the 19th Century', *JSNT* 3 (1979) 29-60.

The Revival of the Griesbach Hypothesis. Cambridge University Press, 1983.

(ed.), *The Messianic Secret*. London: SPCK, 1983.

(ed.), *Synoptic Studies*. Sheffield: JSOT Press, 1984.

Nag Hammadi and the Gospel Tradition: Synoptic Tradition in the Nag Hammadi Library. Edinburgh: T. & T. Clark, 1986.

M.M.B. Turner, 'The Spirit of Christ and Christology', in H.H. Rowdon (ed.), *Christ the Lord: Studies presented to D. Guthrie* (Leicester: Inter-Varsity Press, 1982) 168-190.

L. Vaganay, *Le Problème synoptique*. Tournai/Paris: Desclée, 1954.

F. Van Segbroeck, 'Les citations d'accomplissement dans l'Evangile selon saint Matthieu', in Didier, *Matthieu*, 107-130.

S. Van Tilborg, *The Jewish Leaders in Matthew*. Leiden: Brill, 1972.

G. Vermes, *Jesus the Jew*. London: Collins, 1973.

D.J. Verseput, 'The Role and Meaning of the"Son of God"Title in Matthew's Gospel' *NTS* 33 (1987) 532-556.

P. Vielhauer, 'Gottesreich und Menschensohn in der Verkündigung Jesu', in W. Schneemelcher (ed.), *Festschrift für G. Dehn* (Neukirchen, 1957) 51-79; reprinted in Vielhauer's *Aufsätze zum Neuen Testament* (München: Kaiser, 1965) 55-91.

'Jewish-Christian Gospels' in E. Hennecke (ed.), *New Testament Apocrypha*, vol. 1 (ET, London: Lutterworth, 1963) 117-165.

B.T. Viviano, 'Where was the Gospel according to St. Matthew Written?' *CBQ* 41 (1979) 533-546.

A. Vögtle, 'Das christologische und ekklesiologische Anliegen von Mt. 28, 18-20", in F.L. Cross (ed.), *Studia Evangelica* II (TU 87. Berlin: Akademie-Verlag, 1964) 266-294.

R. Walker, *Die Heilsgeschichte im ersten Evangelium*. Göttingen: Vandenhoeck & Ruprecht, 1967.

W.O. Walker (ed.), *The Relationships among the Gospels*. San Antonio: Trinity University Press, 1978.

D. Wenham, 'Paul and the Synoptic Apocalypse', in *Gospel Perspectives*, vol. 2 (1981) 345-375.

P. Winter, *On the Trial of Jesus*. Berlin: de Gruyter, ²1974.

H.-T. Wrege, *Die Überlieferungsgeschichte der Bergpredigt*. Tübingen: Mohr, 1968.

A.G. Wright, 'The Literary Genre Midrash' *CBQ* 28 (1966) 105-138, 417-457.

J. Zumstein, *La Condition du Croyant dans l'Evangile selon Matthieu*. Fribourg: Editions Universitaires / Göttingen: Vandenhoeck & Ruprecht, 1977.

Index of Biblical and Other Ancient References

Index of Biblical and Other Ancient References

Index of Modern Authors

Index of Modern Authors